Śilpa in Indian Tradition

Śilpa in Indian Tradition

Concept and Instrumentalities

R.N. Misra

INDIAN INSTITUTE OF ADVANCED STUDY
Shimla

ARYAN BOOKS INTERNATIONAL
New Delhi

ŚILPA IN INDIAN TRADITION

ISBN-10: 81-7305-354-5
ISBN-13: 978-81-7305-354-2

First published in **2009** by

INDIAN INSTITUTE OF ADVANCED STUDY
Rashtrapati Nivas, Shimla-171 005

and

ARYAN BOOKS INTERNATIONAL
Pooja Apartments, 4B, Ansari Road, New Delhi-110 002 (India)
Tel.: 23287589, 23255799; Fax: 91-11-23270385
E-mail: aryanbooks@vsnl.com

Computer Typeset and Printed in India at
ABI Prints & Publishing Co., New Delhi

Preface

This work is a sequel to my earlier work at the IIAS, titled *Ancient Artists and Art Activity* (1975). It attempts to examine three basic and defining elements in traditional Indian sculptures, *viz.*, art (*śilpa*), artists (*śilpī*) and the canon (*Śāstra*), and the conceptualization relevant to them. It makes a brief historical survey of *śilpa* taking up issues concerning its valorization and devaluation, its concordance with form (*rūpa*), its secular domain and, for that reason, its vulnerability. Using both textual and epigraphic sources, its sections on artists and craftsmen of different order – Kokāsa lineage of a millennium-long standing included – deals with the question of their historical antecedents, anonymity, organization, operations and activities, work culture, authority, discipline and dissent, pecuniary gains, and the patronage that made their work possible. In the section on the canon (*Śāstra*), an attempt has been made to underscore their operational and aesthetic bearings in the works of art, within the framework of the formulations in the *Śāstric* texts on traditional Indian poetics and iconography. The book also has an appendix on masons' marks: the marks that serve as the silent assertions of ancient artists' identity and have a presence from second century BCE to seventeenth century. There are many more monuments in central India –temples of Khajuraho, the Sas Bahu temple of Gwalior, monuments in Malwa, even the Mughal works at Fatehpur Sikri, for instance – carrying such marks, but not included in this work, which leaves ample opportunity to those who may like to read these marks further.

It is my pleasant duty to gratefully acknowledge that I owe this work to the encouragement of my *guru* late Professor V.S. Pathak. In fact, the entire scheme of this monograph took shape in my mind, thanks to the regular discussions I used to have with him, long before I started working on it at the IIAS. The entire project would still have remained dormant but for the opportunity that Professor G.C. Pande so graciously offered to me at the IIAS. Not only that, in the discussions that I could have with him at Shimla, he offered sharply focused insights on the academic content of this work in a manner which only he is uniquely capable of. At the conclusion of this work now, I am happy to be able to express my unmitigated gratitude towards both these great scholars, Professor Pande and late Professor Pathak, to whom I dedicate this work.

Pursuing this project at the IIAS was a joy and I should take this opportunity to place on record my sincere gratitude to my friends and well wishers at the IIAS and elsewhere for their support in making this work possible: to the Directors of the IIAS – Professor V.C. Shrivastava and Professor (Ms) Bhuvan Chandel – who were a constant source of inspiration, always willing to help me out in whatever ways required towards completion of this project; to the current Director of the IIAS, Prof. Peter R. deSouza, who expedited the publication of this work which was submitted in the form of a manuscript as early as September 2005; to Professors Bettina Baumer and Karuna Goswamy for reading the manuscript and offering suggestions; to Navajyot Singh for his constant interest and critical comments; to Anu Kapoor and her distinguished students for help in finally re-assembling this monograph together after its completion; to the officers and staff of the IIAS, who left nothing to chance in making my family and me comfortable at the Institute in various ways; to Veena, my wife, who was a constant source of confidence to me specially when I started having doubts about completing the manuscript within the scheduled time as other responsibilities at the IIAS, like: arranging and managing a major seminar and editing a bi-annual journal were heavily impinging on my time. I was even toying with the idea of leaving out certain portions that have finally figured in the monograph, but her encouragement and support made me re-work the materials with profit, and to her satisfaction, which is a matter of great joy to me.

Some words about the form and text of this monograph may also be necessary. For diacritical marks on the terms in it from Indian classical languages (e.g., Sanskrit and Pali), the Harvard-Kyoto convention has been generally adhered to. Barring exceptions, no such marks have been used in describing proper nouns representing names of persons or places. Index is brief because the contents at the beginning describe the issues that have come up for discussions in the work. The realization about the overuse of Sanskrit terms and phrases in the text came to me too late when there was no time to make amends. I am aware that it might make the reading heavy, but then it, in certain ways, does seem to adhere to the spirit and contents of the subject which may perhaps justify their use.

Finally, I express my sincere thanks to Dr. Debarshi Sen, the Publication Officer and Mr. Ashok Sharma, the PRO at the IIAS, and Mr. Vikas Arya of Aryan Books International but for whose active support this work would not have come out the way it finally has.

R.N. Misra

Lucknow
26 June 2008

Contents

Preface *v*
List of Illustrations *xi*

1. *Śilpa* **1**

Prologue; *Śilpa*'s 'Rights' of Passage in Tradition;
Secular Terrains of *Śilpa*; *Rūpa-śilpa* Interface.

2. *Śilpin* (I) **44**

Anonymity Factor; Artists' Outline in History;
The Kokāsa Lineage (*vaṃśa*)

3. *Śilpin* (II): *Śilpī*s' Organisation and Operation **86**

Artists' Organisation: Collectives and Grouping;
*Śilpī*s at Work; The Patron; Operations; Stores and Supplies;
Working Environment; *Sūtradhāra*'s Role;
Work Culture and Discipline; Discipline and Dissent;
Modes of Payment; Discharge; Final Dispensations;
Concluding Remarks.

4. *Śāstra* **141**

Interactive Domain of *Śilpaśāstra* in a kindred Group; Constitutive Elements; Representation-centric Conceptualizations; Creative Process: *Anusandhāna, Anukaraṇa* and *Anyathākaraṇa; Lakṣaṇa;* Compositional Structure.

Appendix 185
Bibliography 207
Index 215

List of Illustrations

Plate 1: Masons' marks on Dhameka *stūpa*, Sarnath.
Plate 2: Masons' marks at Padhavali (District Morena, Madhya Pradesh).
Plate 3: Masons' marks on Ranod monastery and pond (Madhya Pradesh).
Plate 4: Masons' marks on Ranod monastery and pond.
Plate 5: Masons' marks at Suhania (District Morena, Madhya Pradesh).
Plate 6: Masons' marks at Tilori (District Bhind, Madhya Pradesh).
Plate 7: Masons' marks at Mitaoli (District Morena, Madhya Pradesh).
Plate 8: Masons' marks at Mitaoli (District Morena, Madhya Pradesh).
Plate 9: Masons' marks at Jaunpur (Uttar Pradesh).
Plate 10: Masons' marks at Jaunpur.
Plate 11: Masons' marks at the different Mughal sites.
Plate 12: Masons' marks at Taj Mahal, Agra.
Plate 13: Masons' marks on Mughal monuments of Kashmir.
Plate 14: Common masons' marks at Allahabad Fort and the Taj.

1

Śilpa

PROLOGUE

In defining art in Indian tradition, we may perhaps have to necessarily hark back to the concept and instrumentalities that the term *śilpa* envisages in its connotation. For, in pervasively implicating arts, it incorporates and defines creativity and its contingent concordance or instantiated symbolism in respect of the forms and composition that it uniquely creates or crystallises. Indeed, *śilpa,* in its ideological formulations in tradition, contains alternative definitions of art[1] as it seems to have both, what we may call instrumental and transitive roles: instrumental, in mediating between experience and reality in different ways, and transitive in that it is addressed to serve varying requirements of individuals and institutions that seek its mediation for their respective edification. *Śilpa* is occasionally described as a *vidyā,* 'knowledge' as well as *vijñāna,* 'science', or *śāstra,* 'system'. And, in situating it in its various roles and dimensions, we may have to trace the history of the term in some details. This may help in defining the general notions about our understanding of *śilpa* vis-à-vis ancient Indian art, its studies, and whatever they may encompass.

Two views – mutually complementary to each other – seem to be prevailing today about the state of ancient Indian art history. Of these, one holds that a 'proper' history of Indian art has not been yet written and that much of what we have in the current corpus on the subject is largely an appendix to history constituting, in substance, neither history nor art criticism. The other view tends to assail the relevant corpus of art studies as fragmentary and unrepresentative, criticising it for its general inadequacy in foregrounding the social and material milieu that made ancient Indian art possible. In conformity with such perceptions, it is argued that an appropriate history of Indian art would be one that is not only not insular but is also free from rigidities of history, and is appropriately qualified by a concern for artistic forms, systems and theory encompassing also its makers – the artists, patrons and contexts – in concert with the evocative imageries, functions and purpose of the works of art and much more, all securely defined in their respectively interactive domains. In essence, it is thus argued that a true history of art is still a desideratum and that, to be able to come on its own as an independent discipline in India it would indeed require to incorporate the inputs like its social and material underpinnings, its aesthetic and representational framework and ideology, its symbolism and modes of expression – all worked out within a suitable analytical structure in conformity with the discipline of art history but within a general historical mould.

Keeping such contestations in view, we here propose to approach the question of art in conformity with its definition in tradition, and examine *śilpa, śilpī* and *śāstra* as they are integrated in tradition, with an attempt to historicise them in reference to their material, theoretical (or conceptual) and aesthetic underpinnings. All this is proposed with a view to project a wider theoretical framework of ancient Indian art as envisaged and upheld in tradition, considering the fact that Indian arts, in a wider sense, are the inheritors of rich theoretical formulations on aesthetics, especially in literature, music, dance and dramatics, ignoring which would be detrimental to our understanding of Indian arts.

This study is, therefore, premised on textual assertions on powers of *śilpa* ('skill', whether institutionalised or individual) in its being the prime mover and epitome of 'representation'. As we shall see later, *śilpa* in tradition is supposed to legitimise varied phenomenon or entities of experience in a formal structure. It designates all arts and crafts, and implies a technique, an artefact, in fact, anything involving dexterity of hands or mind or both. It is supposed to achieve *rūpa-pratirūpa* convergence (symbol-symbolised identity, in other words), form-to-form (*sa-rūpatāṃ sa-lokatāṃ aśnute, Aitareya Br.*I.6), measure-to-measure, ideally, by inducing rhythm (*chandas*) and self-acculturation (*ātmānam sanskurute*). In the canon of aesthetics a wide range of symbolic imagery is expressed in terms of *lakṣaṇa, vyañjana* (marks), *sādṛśya* (similitude), *vibhāva* (stimulants), *pratibhā*, etc. which, in texts often tend to buttress the convergence of the symbolic meaning into 'representation': with both, in substance, impacting 'cognition'. *Śilpa* as an efficient and potential cause was thus supposed to render into art – whether narrative or iconological – a significance of meaning. *Śilpa* eventually became a generic term for all arts and crafts. In *śāstric* view of art, *śilpa* aesthetically as well as materially had to exist in concord with *rūpa* (form) and together the duo came to constitute *rūpavidyā*, 'the knowledge or science of form', dealing with structures and forms of imaginative composition (*rūpa-nirmāṇa*). The *rūpa-śilpa* duo and co-option of the one into the other thus appears to have become crucial in traditional interpretations of art-experience and its representations.

In visual art, according to the *Viṣṇudharmottara Purāṇa*, the temporal structure (*sākāra*) of form (*rūpa*) has to have a referential anchorage (*sahetuka*) in order to be valid. Therefore, an epistemological stand is sometimes taken to validate *rūpa* through *śilpa* by 'imaginative fiction'. This is particularly true of textual discussions on aesthetics of *pratibhā* and of the entities (*sattā*) of reality whether *pratibhāsika, paramārthika* or *vyavahārika*.[2] It would thus appear that, in concert with *rūpa* (form), *śilpa* stood as a meta-concept in traditional art and iconography as each, namely, *śilpa* and *rūpa*, conformed to or defined the other.[3] These and the kindred enunciations seem to underscore a theoretical temper besides a conceptual framework and aesthetic premises that are perpetually recurrent in the domain of Indian art tradition. Hence the need to historicise these concepts fittingly into the general evolution of early Indian sculptural and pictorial tradition and their institutional network. In brief, the proposed study envisages a look into Indian art for its theory and its conceptual grounding into Indian *śilpa* tradition vis-à-vis its tangible instrumentalities in terms of its regulating mechanism (*śāstra*) and the institutional network of artists and craftsmen (*śilpī*s).

I

Śilpa's 'Rights' of Passage in Tradition

In historical contexts art signifies principles of composition and symbolism, which it uniquely creates.[4] *Śilpa* is the key term that tradition has for art (lit. 'skill'), and its antiquity is Vedic as the term occurs in the *Ṛgveda* twice (*su-śilpa*: IX.5.6; X.70.6) implying aesthetically 'beautiful' or 'effulgent' form. Its meaning kept on expanding subsequently. We may here make an attempt to explain the term *śilpa* and its various connotations or implication in reference to art as it evolved into different nuances in its passage through time.

The task of interpreting the 'rights' of passage of *śilpa* (skill, craft) and *śilpin* (artist, craftsman) is beset with difficulties for their journey in time and history is embedded in contradictions. These contradictions apparently grew out of the 'high' ritual and creative antecedents of the Vedic *śilpa* in its being a divine act of marvel and power or later in *sūtra*s in the 'lowliness' of its being *vṛtti*s (occupations). With one implication intruding upon the other or displacing it altogether, contradictions seem to have been legitimised by practice. The claims and counter-claims of its ascent or descent are encountered time and again in its mobility. So, in historicising *śilpa* (and *śilpin*) and their 'rights' of passage, the modifications in the duo from sublime to commonplace or vice versa tend to reveal both what was 'ascribed' or 'given' to them and what they came to 'acquire' or 'appropriate' in substance. A historical outline of *śilpa* and *śilpin* to define the changing perceptions about these may be relevant here. So, first we take up the meanings of the term *śilpa* and its etymology and define the Vedic *śilpa*. And then we discuss its gradual transformation into *vṛtti*s and what it implied. Later, as we come to the end of this work we will take up its resurgence and resurrection as a *śāstra*, which, read together with these portions, would help in explaining completion of the transformation of *śilpa* from sacred to mundane and the dialectics of such transformations. We would also like to examine the *śilpa-rūpa* conjunctions, which tend to secure *śilpa*'s anchorage in the domain of aesthetics perpetually, away from the religio-ritualistic domain, which continually tended to appropriate it – harnessing it into its service. This tussle between *śilpa*'s appropriation within the space of religion on one hand and its assertion of freedom on the other is constantly in evidence historically. This is in evidence in *śilpa*'s quest for creativity involving experimentations with *rūpa*; and *śilpin*s' quest for an independent realm of experience and action where they stood supreme. *Śilpin*s appear to have been so well-endowed and eminently secure in their independent domain that others from different professional realms seem to have vied to come to terms with them by joining their professional set up, regardless of their own distinctions in other fields: social, political or economic.[5] We may begin with a historical survey of *śilpa* and its ascendance or devaluation with the passage of time.

In its essence, the term *śilpa*, as it developed later, signifies visual arts and formalistic compositions flowing from it. It specially encompasses sculpture, painting, terracotta, etc. representing a 'reconstituted form' (e.g., *silpāt pratimā jāyante, Vāstusūtra Upaniṣad*, I.5), in any medium – wood, stone,[6] metal, colour (e.g., painting), clay or the like[7] – the materials with which an artist could create two- or three-dimensional figural compositions. *Śilpa* in tradition thus designates all kinds of arts and craft and indeed envisages aesthetically crafted forms, in music, dance, figure work and the like, which define the very soul of art in experience or its relish (*rasāsvāda*). The term *śilpa* has a rich history with a semantic multiplicity pervasive in its content. As we said earlier, it encompasses within the ambit of its meaning anything creative, imitative, ideational or skilful which in one sense or the other including analogy, involves dexterity of hand (*hasta*) or mind (*dhī*) or both. *Śilpa* also implies a technique, a ceremonial act, an artefact, indeed anything, which either leads to or is a tangible product of some craft, *kratu* and *māyā* included. It qualifies an experience or exercise, whose product is endowed with *chandas*, 'rhythm', and yet on occasions, it is beyond explanation and thereby a subject of wonder: especially where it creates cosmic elements or even illusions of the contingent reality. To a great extent, in early Indian social history, *śilpas* are symptomatic of changes that mark a progressive transition of Indian society from egalitarian values to the state of differentiation in social status. In this respect, *śilpas* also indicate transformation of an agrarian system into the moulds of urbanisation[8] and, as *vṛttis*, they present a story of their stigmatisation, despite the *Baudhāyana Dharmasūtra*'s dictum about the purity of craftsmen's hand – *nityam śuddhaḥ kāruhastaḥ*.[9]

Śilpa is a *karman* in the *Nighantu* (II.1) and thereby it tends to celebrate 'work', 'action' or 'act' of whatever kind, thus lending it a dignity par excellence. In its literal sense, as it developed later, it relates to 'craft', 'skill' and efficiency in 'realising a form' (*rūpasiddhi*), implicating a concerted learning by training, dedication and hard physical labour (*duṣkaratvenatikleśa-karatvāditi – nipātanād-rūpasiddhiḥ*).[10] Later etymologies derive *śilpa* from the root *śila upadhāraṇe*, 'to learn or to practise' or, it is explained as 'imitative action repeatedly practised or studied' (*śīlayati śīlatīti vā śīlpaṃ*). Devaraja Yajvan explains it as an act which is 'repeatedly practised or studied, such as: potter's act, etc'.[11] Or, as he says, 'that act can be explained as *śilpa*, which makes (its) doer reduced' (i.e., slim). It is so 'because it (*śilpa*) is hard to accomplish and it subjects the doer to great (physical) suffering'.

In that light, Devaraja Yajvan derives *śilpa* from the verb *siñ* 'to make slim', 'to whet'. Alternatively, he derives *śilpa* from *śila upadhāraṇe* (to learn or to retain knowledge), *śīla samādhau* (to concentrate) and *śiñ niśane* (to sharpen or to make slim). The *Amarakośa* (II.10.35) explains it as *śīla samādhau* and *śala gatau* (to move). Etymologically, therefore, *śilpa* implies an act that is hard to accomplish even as it requires great devotion, commitment and energy. Its practice is a tormenting exercise where the sheer effort of doing emaciates the doer but eventually, it does lead to realisation of the intended 'form'. *Śilpa* also implies 'moving', i.e., moving towards the action or exercise of learning.

Though workable, these *post facto* derivations of the term *śilpa* yet seem inadequate in unravelling the totality and depth of implications that the term envisages. So, alternatively, applying the rules of metathesis, V.S. Pathak and Mayrhofer[12] derive *śilpa* from the root *piś* (or *piśr*, to fashion) and its derivatives like *peśas* (*Rk*. II.3.6; VII.42.1), *supeśas* (*Rk*. VII.32.13), *piṃś* (*Rk*. X.184.1), *peśala* (*YV*. IX.8), *āpiṃśat* (*Rk*. X. 110.9), etc. the terms with meanings which are happily encompassed by the term *śilpa*. The derivatives of the Vedic *piś*, signifying 'decoration', 'beautiful', and 'adornment' eminently correspond to *su-śilpa* of the *Ṛgveda* (IX.5.6; X.70.6) and indicate the fit between the two.[13]

These different implications stand confirmed by the usage of the term in the early Vedic texts and also later. In its early occurrences, *śilpa* figures both in the meaning of a Vedic *mantra* that is 'recited' (*śilpāni samśanti, Ait.Br.* VI.27) and, as an act which is 'performed' or 'accomplished' (*śilpāni kriyanta, Kauś.Br.* XXV.12). It also figures in the sense of *pratimā-pratikṛti* or *pratirūpa* (*Sat.Br.* III.2.1.5) or an 'image' (*Yaj.* IV.9) or 'counterpart', sometimes specific in colour, e.g. 'variegated' or 'dappled' (*Yaj.* XXIX.58; XXIV.5). It implies a propensity or skill instrumental in performance of an act (*Taitt.Sam.* II.7.15.4, *Kath.Sam.* XXXVII.8; *Taitt.Aran.* I.17). It signifies 'manifold forms' (*Sat.Br.* I.1.4.3) even as, in certain contexts, it is used as an honorific to designate a *ṛṣi*, e.g., Śilpa Kaśyapa (*Sat.Br.* XIV. 6. 4.33). In the *Saṃhitās* and *Brāhmaṇas*, *śilpa* qualifies divine acts or skill (*Ait.Br.* VI.27; *Taitti.Br.* III.3.2.1) and, in that it is supposed to support the cosmic elements or bring them into being (*Kauś.Br.* XXIX.5; *Tāndya MBr.* XIV.4.1-9). Thus, contextually, the term *śilpa* in its early usage implies primarily an action and secondarily, a mysterious in-dwelling power: a key to generating a wondrous and skilful act. In both the situations it is always creative, sustaining or strengthening.

In its propensities, whether in regard to reciting *mantras*,[14] e.g. *śilpāni samśanti*, in the *Aitareya Brāhmaṇa* (VI.27) or performing ritual acts (*śilpāni kriyanta*), in the *Kauśītakī Brāhmaṇa* (XXV.12), or in supporting the cosmic elements or in other ways, *śilpa*, whether in concept or in instrumentality, seems to possess the basic appurtenances of a *śāstra* in terms of its formal characterisations. A formal validation of *śilpa* as *vidyā*, *vijñāna* and *śāstra* appeared much later when it came to be addressed variously in these terms. We will discuss this point later. But, in the *Svacchandra Tantra* (XI.197), *śilpa* is also conspicuous as a *tattva* (creative element) in primal creation: *śilpaṃ siddhisandohalakṣaṇam*. And, commenting on it, Ksemendra says that characterised by multitudes of power, in the manner of the earth, *śilpa* is a *tattva* inasmuch as it has, among other things, the power or propensity to attract and control.

These implications of the term *śilpa* repeatedly occur in the *Saṃhitās* and *Brāhmaṇas*. Let us examine the point in some details beginning with the Vedic *śilpa*. The *Brāhmaṇas* contain axiomatic statements on *śilpa* like 'whatever is brought forth measure to measure, form to form is *śilpa*' (*yadvai pratirūpaṃ tacchilpaṃ, Śatapatha Brāhmaṇa* (III.1.5.5)) or that *śilpas* are indeed a mode of self culture' (*ātmasamskṛtir vāva śilpāni, Aitareya Brāhmaṇa,* VI.27). We are also told that 'imitation of (*deva*) *śilpa* is accomplished by *anukṛti* (*silpānām anukṛtiḥ śilpam adhigamyate, Ait.Br.*VI.27). The *Aitareya Brāhmaṇa* further says that,

> ... a work of art is accomplished in him who knows thus, as to those works of art the *śilpa*s are a perfection of self; verily by them the sacrificer perfects himself as composed of metres.

It would thus appear that among other things, manifesting the unmanifested is central to the process-product togetherness that constitutes *śilpa*.

Several other passages in the *Brāhmaṇa*s indicate that *śilpa* is, as it were, a source of extraordinary skill, energy or efficiency by which certain cosmic elements take their form, stay firm in their respective places and derive their support. Several of the Vedic luminaries are endowed with its powers and propensities. Kaśyapa (*Tat.Ar.* I.71; *Kath.Sam.* XXXVII.9) creates stability in the Suryas where the skill of endowing that power of stability is implied. Bhatta Bhaskara Misra explains this passage as invoking Kaśyapa in whom *śilpa* is the propensity to create the universe (*jagat sṛṣṭi lakṣaṇam*). Besides Kaśyapa, Prajāpati and Indra also seem to be the repositories of *śilpa*. Prajāpati is so by his own powers and Indra gets it conferred upon him by Prajāpati.

Prajāpati is supposed to be steeped in the skill and power of *śilpa*, for by it he created the cosmic order, and conferred supremacy on to Indra over the *prajā*, 'beings', so that Indra like Prajāpati became endowed with the same *śilpa* (*Tāndya MBr.* XIV.4.3). With *śilpa*, Prajāpati strengthened (*dṛñhat*) the heaven, and made it 'shapely' (*dyām abhipiṃśyat*). With *śilpa* he expanded the speech (*vāc*) thoroughly. By *śilpa* the Adityas were made to shine with an enhanced brilliance so that Sun is seen in numerous rays. By *śilpa* again, speech (*vākam*) is made complete (*ye bhirvākam puṣkalebhikhyayat, Tāndya Br.* II.7.5.3; *Kath.Sam.* XXXVII.9). The commentator emphasises the implications of *śilpa* here in the sense of *yoga* (application), *bala* (capacity) and *sāmarthya* (efficiency) by which the entire world is invested with form, even as from it the cosmic elements derive their origin and strength. Prajāpati is its source and also the one who manipulates it and renders it active. Thus, he figures as the primal as well as the efficient cause of *śilpa*.

Śilpa also composes *prāṇa* (breath) in the *puruṣa* as the latter personifies sacrifice. It has the same efficiency in the *puruṣa* that breath has in a body: it enlivens it and activates it. As *prāṇa* it is the same as *ātman* (body?) for the two are perpetually inseparable and rest in togetherness through *śilpa* (*prāṇāstāni śilpāni puruṣo vai...Kauś.Br.* XXV.12; *Sankh.Br.* XXV.12). The *Kauśitaki Brāhmaṇa* here contemplates an organic unity between *puruṣa* and its counterpart: the sacrifice. *Puruṣa* is perceived both as the abode and the indwelling spirit, which together relate to its *āyatana, prāṇa* and *ātmā.* And *śilpa* is the principle that binds them all.

The centrality of *śilpa* is defined in reference to 'atmosphere' (*antarikṣa*) which too like *śilpa* stays in the middle, but unlike *śilpa* it is bereft of a base or support (*atho antarikṣam vā yeṣa madhyamastrayahaḥ anārambhaṇam idamantarikṣam pratiṣṭhānam. Śilpeṣveva pratitiṣṭhanto yanti'*, *Kauś. Br.* XXIX. 5). So, the efficacy of *śilpa* lies in its being a support or base to the 'atmosphere' (lest it may crumble down and fall). So also, in its being a support to other verses (*Bṛhati* and *Prasthas*), lest they lose their efficacy when recited. It is a potent element in the triplets, namely, song, dance and instrumental music in which it rests inherently even as it establishes them day-by-day (*śilpeṣveva tadaharaḥ pratitiṣṭhanto yanti, Kauś.Br.* XXIX.5). Coming together of any two conformable elements, even if they seem disparate, is also described as *śilpa* as for instance, when *Ṛk* is sung in musical metres of *Sāman*. In other words, when *Ṛk* joins *Sāman*, this coupling is described as *śilpa* (*ṛksāmayoḥ śilpe sthate, T.Sam.I.2.2.1; Maitr.Sam.* I.22) – the coupling constituting the togetherness of the two in the manner of the *sandhi* of black and white colour as seen in an animal skin. This union also uniquely exemplifies the translation of a sound into colour in the manner of a conjunction (*sandhi*) of black and white colours in a skin, which, as it were, replicate and symbolise singing of a *Ṛk mantra* in a *Sāman* tune. And this spectacular replication is explained as *śilpa*. The *Śatapatha Brāhmaṇa* (I.1.4.3) reinforces the idea of such transformation while extolling a sacrifice where *śilpa* (manifold forms) is reposed in the varying colours of an antelope skin. Yet, on its own, in the *Kauśitaki Brāhmaṇa* and *Śankhāyana Brāhmaṇa* (XXV.13), *śilpa* is a potential force that must rest unhindered (*nedacchāvācastha śilpamantaryāmi*). *Śilpa* even lends its grace to the maidens who 'growing like tender creepers go accomplished in the *śilpa* of Viśvedevas (All Gods) to learn speech under the protection of their parents and teachers' (*Yajurveda* XXIV.5).

In sum, conceptually, Vedic *śilpa* signifies an extraordinary potential, a sanctifying principle, a supportive, sustaining and strengthening force, a skill endowed with a sense of wonder for its creative essence, and sometimes a propensity 'divine' in character which remains sanctified even in its emulation. It is also a potential or quality which 'cultures the self'. It is a rhythm that tunes the performer into its harmony. By *śilpa* the divine personages create and strengthen the cosmic forces, and by it a transmutation is brought about in the different and disparate phenomenon. Its centrality in the different phenomena or elements, e.g. sacrifices, *puruṣa, prāṇa, ātman, antarikṣa,* etc. is basic to its conceptual substance. As an ingenuous generative principle it exists amorphous merely in the idea or notion of it, simply by itself. When resorted to, it turns into a boundless energy, which fills the universe with *antarikṣa,* extends the earth, strengthens the Sun and differentiates the *viśvarūpa* (all forms). It is the principle by which the non-manifest is rendered manifest and the manifest derives its corporeality and colours. It manifests the basic forms of arts, e.g. song, dance, music, colour and plastic arts but it is also identified with the quality of 'beauty' and 'effulgence' that may qualify its manifestation. It is an instrument in the hands of Prajāpati, Śilpa Kaśyapa, Indra, Devas and an Acchāvāc priest. All in all, in the early Vedic references, *śilpa* is a product and also a process that sanctifies and enlivens the former and rests there as its very *prāṇa*.

II

But *śilpa* did not remain permanently ensconced in its original Vedic ambience. Its exalted character was diametrically reversed in the *Dharmasūtra*s (c. 500-200 BC) where it is found relegated to the category of 'occupation' (*vṛtti*) generally assigned to *śūdra*s, thus heralding its development in a different trajectory. The vexing and waning of *śilpa* into the highs and lows, between 'knowledge'[15] on one hand and occupations (*vṛtti*) on the other, became the leitmotif of its later development till the Middle Ages. Such a dramatic reversal in the fortune of *śilpa* is apparent in *Āpastamba Smṛti* (V.3), Gautama and later in Manu besides others. Such ascription continued in the *Purāṇa*s as in the *Agni Purāṇa* (151.9), which says that 'service to the twice-borns and all kinds of arts and crafts – these are the means of living of the *śūdra*s' (*śūdrasya dvijasuśrūsā sarvaśilpāni cāpyatha*).

Crafts and their categories had started proliferating during the later Vedic period. The *Vājasneyī Saṃhitā* (XXX.6.21) and the *Taittirīya Brāhmaṇa* (III.4.2.7) mention many of them, e.g. chariot makers, carpenters, potters, smiths, jewellers, herdsmen, etc. Among these, the *rathakāra*s and *takṣa*s were important as they occur in the list of the *ratnin*s who, according to *Maitrāyaṇī Saṃhitā* (II.6.5), annointed a king and thus validated his status. Later, they were relegated to the level of *śūdra*s. For instance, *takṣan*s are *śūdra* and equivalent in status to smith (*ayaskāra*) in the *Mahābhāṣya* on Pāṇini (II.4.10). Ūṣanas enumerates them as of *pratiloma* order, born of a *Brāhmaṇa* female and a Sūcaka male.[16] A total devaluation of *śilpa* had not come about till at least the fourth century BC as *śilpa* still denoted a kind of 'ceremonial act' in the *Āśvalāyana Śrauta Sūtra* (VIII.4.5-8; IX.10.11, 11.2). Such ambivalence about the status of *śilpa* continued even later.

As for *śilpin*, 'artisan', the term came into vogue with Pāṇini[17] (c. 400 BC) in reference to arts and crafts, e.g. dancing, music and the crafts like those of a barber and potter. The *Aṣṭādhyāyī* mentions crafts such as: pottery-making, carpentry, dying, dress-making, along with those concerning work on gems and metals like gold, silver, tin and iron.[18] Pāṇini classifies *śilpin*s into the categories of 'village craftsmen' (*grāma-śilpin*) and the 'accomplished craftsmen' (*rāja-śilpin*).[19] The role of *śilpa* as *vṛtti* is quite apparent in these references. Such craftsmen may have been on the rise economically and some of them even paid taxes to the state.[20] But, their crafts did not command respectability. For instance, Yājñavalkya (III.42) recommends *śilpa* as one of the ten sources of livelihood for the high-borns only in the times of distress. *Śilpa* had indeed turned into *vṛtti*, which are explained in the texts as a source of livelihood (*teṣām tad vartanād vṛttirucyate*).[21] The *śilpins* pursuing many such occupations for living have often been reviled in the *Dharmaśāstras* apparently because those *vṛttis* were considered polluting in character. *Gautama Smṛti* (VII.2) ordains that food offered by a fallen woman (*puṃścali*), artisan (*takṣa*) condemned (*kadarya*), royal servant (*bandhanika*), physician (*cikitsaka*), hunter (*mṛgayu*), *kāru* (*śilpin*), or by one living on left-over food, or one inimical to *Gaṇas* (*gaṇadviṣānāṃ*) must not be eaten.[22] In the same text (VII.1), it is said that a Brāhmaṇa can accept food from a trader who is not a *śilpī*. The *Laghu Hāriti Smṛti* (II.12) prescribes *vṛttis* only to *śūdras*. The *Pārāśara Smṛti* (II.18) prescribes agriculture, trade and *śilpas* exclusively to *vaiśya* and *śūdras*: *vaiśyaḥ śūdrastathā kuryāt kṛṣi vāṇijya śilpakān*. The *Dharmaśāstras* exhibit contempt for *śilpa* and *śilpin* and impart a low status to the different occupational classes in social hierarchy. For instance, *Gautama Smṛti* (X.7) assigns all the occupational crafts (*śilpavṛttis*) to *śūdras*. The *Śankha Smṛti* (I.5) similarly assigns to *śūdras* the service to *dvijas* (twice-born) besides the practice of *śilpas*: *śūdrasya dvijasuśrūṣā sarvaśilpāni cāpyatha*. Manu disallows certain *vṛttis* to the *dvijas* (twice-born) but grudgingly concedes that they may practise these *vṛttis* during the exceptional times of distress. These 'low' occupations consisted of *vidyā, śilpa, bhṛtasevā, vipaṇan* and *kṛṣi*.[23] The reference to *vidyā* here is interesting and it may perhaps refer to non-scriptural (anti-scriptural?) knowledge. We will return to *vidyā* later.

The situation was no different in the Buddhism where in early texts, *sippam* is found split into *hīna* (low), *puthu* (ordinary) and *ukkaṭṭha* (higher) categories of which the first two bear similarity with the *Dharmśāstric* lists. The *Suttavibhanga* describes *nalakāra sippam* (basket making), *kumbhakāra sippam* (potter's craft), *pesakāra sippam* (weaving), *cammakāra sippam* (leather craft), and *nahāpita sippam* (barbers'craft), which are 'disdained' as 'low' crafts. The other crafts like *muddā* (counting on fingers), *gananā* (accounting) and *lekhā* (writing) were not 'disdained' and belonged to the category of 'high' crafts.[24] Even those occupations which once enjoyed a respectable status came to be included, in Buddhist texts, among the vocations of the people of 'low birth' (*hīna jāti*), as early as in the fifth or fourth century BC. For instance, *rathakāra* is sometimes equated with *cammakāra*, both considered 'low', the former by 'birth' and the latter so by 'occupation'.[25]

Incidentally, it indicates a mobility of sorts where people not low took to the occupations which were supposed to be 'low'.

These passages when compared to those on *śilpa* in the *Brāhmaṇa*s and *Saṃhitā*s indicate a colossal change engendered into the earlier glorifying perceptions about *śilpa*.The first hint of *śilpa*s' relegation to a lower status is encountered in the *Chāndogya Upaniṣad* (VII.1.2-4, VII.2.1) where the text lists different *vidyā*s starting with the *Veda*s. It then relegates *devajana vidyā* (consisting of dancing, music and singing) to the bottom impervious of the fact that these accomplishments are designated as *śilpa*s in the *Kauśītaki Brāhmaṇa* (XXIV.5).

The *Maitrī Upaniṣad*[26] (VII.8) contains a discourse to princes on 'hindrances to the sacred knowledge' (*jñānopasarga*s) with an exhortation that 'mingling of heavenly with unheavenly is the root cause of the delusion or false doctrine' where 'fools stick to the clump of grass'. Interestingly, those who 'ceaselessly practised *śilpa* for living' (*nityaśilpopajīvinaḥ*), figure in this category and stand denounced with contempt and disparagement, branded as 'unworthy of heaven' (*asvargyaḥ*) and 'thieves' (*taskara*). It is to be noted that *śilpin*s – denounced here – are also clubbed together with those who were 'ceaselessly hilarious' (*nityapramudita*), those 'ceaselessly peregrinating' (*nityaprasavita*), and 'ceaselessly begging' (*nityayācanaka*). Town-beggars (*purāyācaka*), pupils of *śūdra*s and those *śūdra*s who are proficient in *śāstras*, (*ayajñayājakaḥ śūdraśiṣyaḥ śūdrāśca śāstravidvānsaḥ*) also figure in this 'hate-list'. The enumeration goes on further to include *cāṭa* (mercenaries?), *jaṭa, naṭa* (jugglers), *bhaṭa* (warriors), religious mendicants, stage artists, those engaged in royal service, degraded and outcasts (*cāṭajaṭanaṭapravṛjitarangāvatariṇo rājakarmāṇi patitādayaḥ*).

Also included in the *Maitrī Upaniṣad* list are those who claimed controlling (*śamayām*) demi-gods like *Yakṣa*, etc. Or, those like the *kaṣāyakunḍalin* and *kāpālika*s and those others who 'wish to encounter the Vedicists by (offering) false devices of arguments, (or by) cheating and magic: *vṛthātarkadṛṣṭāntakuhakendrajālairvaidikeṣu paristhatumicchati*. The *Maitrī Upaniṣad* ordains that one should not live with such people for they are 'openly thieves' and 'unfit for heaven' (*prakāśabhūtā te vai taskarā asvargyaḥ*). The contempt for and condemnation of *śilpin*s along with the others of the category expressly stems from the argument of the *Maitrī Upaniṣad* (VII.7-8) that these (heretical) groups were 'no-soul' theorists. The explicit statement about their abilities, e.g. their being 'learned in *śāstra*s', may not be missed in this despise and condemnation. Obviously, these groups of people seem to have earned the encomium of the *Maitrī Upaniṣad* because they did not conform to the Vedic beliefs and temper specially, in their doctrine of *ātman* and, whatever they professed was supposed to be a 'hindrance' to true (Vedic) knowledge. The intensity and tenor of criticism and intolerance here is exceptional. But the criticism of *śilpī* in it is significant in elucidating that they now belonged to a group, which apparently professed a counter-ideology that was not in tune with the Vedic temper.

A fairly strong and learned socio-philosophical tradition encompassing Buddhism, Jainism, Ajivikas, the Cārvākas and Lokāyata besides other minor faiths had crystallized by 500 BC. And, they were all questioning philosophical premises of the erstwhile Vedic beliefs. Those upholding *śilpa* – including the *śilpins* – apparently became a part of this newly emerging tradition to earn condemnation from the orthodoxy in pursuing ideas and beliefs that were heretical to the Vedic tradition. The non-Vedic socio-philosophical systems were, however, offering alternative arguments about the entire question of *ātman* and alternative ways of life and thought. Some of these systems, Buddhism for instance, sometimes exalted *śilpa* and rejected the *Vedas* jettisoning the latter to the level of mere 'training' (*śikṣā*) even as they questioned Vedic learning. Lokāyata, a philosophical order which is clubbed with *śilpa* in the *Udāna*,[27] similarly professed different views in respect of life, heaven, rituals, pain and pleasure. *Śilpa*'s and *śilpins*' proximity with these groups, as indicated in the *Maitrī Upaniṣad* above and in the *Udāna* and other Buddhist texts may have led to their devaluation and relegation to the level of *vṛttis* assigned to *śūdras*, shorn of their Vedic glory.

Since 'no-soul' (*anātma*) belief figures among the reasons for criticising the despised groups in the *Maitrī Upaniṣad*, the condemnation may implicate the heretical systems which upheld it. Buddhism, Lokāyata, Cārvāka, the other minor heterodox systems and the protagonists of *śilpa* would appear to be a part of this category.[28] In any case, *śilpa* and *śilpins* stood denigrated in the later- and post-Vedic society and the situation seems to have continued from *Sūtras* to *Smṛtis* and *Purāṇas* and even in the Buddhist texts with a conspicuous ambivalence till they were resurrected appropriately, later.[29]

III

Like the proverbial phoenix *śilpa* and *śilpins* got resurrected soon enough and ultimately burgeoned forth into prominence. In this resurgence, their earlier moorings especially as *vidyā, vijñāna* and *śāstra* were probably used to their advantage. We had earlier drawn attention to *śilpa*'s connection with *vidyā* and we may now briefly discuss this connection. *Śilpa*'s validity as 'knowledge' – even a kind of knowledge not in tune with theoretical temper of orthodoxy, as evidenced in the *Maitrī Upaniṣad* – may not be doubted. Its exalted pedigree, as we saw earlier, could be traced back to the *Ṛgveda*. Its resurrection was posited in the enunciation in the *Milinda Pañho* (see below), its devaluation as *vṛtti* in Pāṇini, Patanjali and *Dharmaśāstras* notwithstanding.

A quick survey of changing perceptions about the highs and lows of *śilpa* seems to indicate that roots of artists' devaluation or valorisation lay in these formulations. Since the early Vedic times, its association with creativity had received a ritual anchorage *per se* as the very act of its application was supposed to be sustaining and sacred in nature. Later, perhaps in its association with Lokāyata – where the two are found clubbed together – *śilpins* probably fabricated an epistemology upholding 'direct perception' (*pratyakṣa*) as a singular source of knowledge. This epistemological theory was probably grounded in the assertion that 'direct perception (*pratyakṣa*) is the only proof (*pramāṇa*) of the being of things. The *śilpa* texts are in agreement with such a formulation as they, in accordance, valorized *dhyāna, sādhanā* and *bhāvarūpa,*[30] the essential grids of experience, which *śilpins*' skill turned into the directly perceived reality materialised in a corporeal form. Such enunciation tends to establish artist as 'materialists' espousing a traditionally validated materialistic and epistemological doctrine of *pratyakṣa* as the proof of knowledge (*pramāṇa*) for their pragmatic theory in creating artistic representations. An indirect confirmation of this is provided by *śilpa*'s togetherness with Lokāyata in the *Udāna*[31] along with other vocations, and the one identifies the other in juxtaposition. Lokāyata was a *nāstika* philosophical system located in materialism. This epistemological concern with *pratyakṣa* in the Lokāyata philosophy and the *indriya*-based bearings of art, as enunciated later, seem to match happily. And this match may justify the equation of *śilpa* and Lokāyata, as mentioned in the *Udāna.* It may also perhaps explain the devaluation of *śilpa* and of Lokāyata *in tandem*. Both became the objects of disparagement in perceptions of the orthodoxy. But the fact remains that *śilpa* in its own exclusive space continued to elevate its practitioners in that it promised a path to perpetual bliss and even the ultimate liberation – a ubiquitously upheld ancient value – thus internalising an exclusive and alternate spirituality in its core. In that realm it sometimes even sanctified commonplace actions, as in the *Saundaryalaharī*[32] where body movements in a devotional ecstacy are explained in terms of *śilpa*. And, as we shall see below, the *Milinda Pañho* valorises it as a source of *nibbāna* of a different order.

The discussions above may explain reasons for devaluation of *śilpa* to a certain extent even as they underscore the basis of antagonism between the contesting traditions where one upheld the *ātman* and others *śilpa.*[33] In fact, in early Buddhism, in the category of knowledge in the *Milinda Pañho* (150 BC), *śilpa* is supposed to compose the entire knowledge and the *Veda*s are marginalised to the level of mere 'training' (*Veda sikkhāni nāma, avasesāni sippāni sippam*).[34] In the same text, *śilpa* is supposed to lead to liberation (*nibbāna*). The discussions on *sippa* vis-à-vis *nibbāna* here exemplify that the former, in essence, was very much like the latter, almost identical and analogous. It is argued that their *pūrvabhāga* might be mingled with pain and anguish but ultimately, as in *nibbāna* so also in *sippa* bliss was absolute: it not being 'mixed' with anguish.[35] *Śilpa* does have a highly respectable place in these enunciations and assertions.

The texts like the *Milinda Pañho* and *Śilpaprakāśa* acknowledge *śilpa* in terms of a *vidyā*[36] that empowers its practitioner towards absolute bliss (*nirvāṇa*) or 'liberation' (*mukti*). The discourse on what constituted *śikṣā* and what *vidyā* or *śāstra* or whether *śilpa* was within or outside their domain bears out the undercurrents of transformation, which eventually came to have a canonical sanction. This transformation seems reflected often in the claims of the artists. For instance, we have an instance of the fifteenth century in the Ratanpur inscription of Vahara where a *śilpin* proclaims his expertise in different branches of knowledge (*vidyā*) including the *śilpavidyā*.[37] As we shall see later, artists, long before that time, had also assumed the title *vijñānika*[38] where *śilpa* is taken to be a science (*vijñāna*) and *śilpī* – its knower – a *vijñānika*.

IV

Secular Terrains of *Śilpa*

It may also be relevant here to examine the space *śilpa* is conventionally supposed to have encompassed in its quest for creativity, especially the boundaries it transcended or cordoned as it interacted with the domains of religion and rituals on one hand and arts on the other. It might appear from the Vedic contexts (above) that *śilpa* in the early references largely had ritual connotations and propensities. But such a perception may be erroneous, as non-ritualistic meanings independent of religious connotations also seem embedded in the nature and meaning of *śilpa per se* as it qualifies creativity involved in reconstituting the 'form' (*rūpa*).[39] Such connotations of *śilpa,* right from the early stage of its occurrences provide the *rationale* to interrogate the interactive domain of art, religion and ritual and the place of *śilpa* in them. It is indeed significant that whether in the early texts or those later, the independent domain of *śilpa* often seems underscored in terms of its propensities and scope beyond religious, ritualistic domains. Such a binarism of *śilpa* involving religio-ritualistic connotations on one hand and freedom from them on the other, need some explanation, as these seem to occur perpetually.

In historical contexts, art and religion are supposed to belong to separate genealogies of experience; religions' concern being abstract concepts, beliefs and performance-based rituals, and art signifying principles of composition and symbolism which it uniquely creates.[40] But in Indian tradition, this kind of separation may not be universally valid. Art here is sometimes central to religion, sometimes contingent to it and on occasions, totally independent of it.

Śilpa[41] (art, skill, craft) is ambivalently interpreted in terms of its different territories of jurisdiction. It takes on different shades of meaning in the Vedic texts that interpret art and ritual. In the *Ṛgveda* (IX.5.6; X.70.6) prefixed with *su* (e.g., *su-śilpa*) it interprets beauty and the aesthetic connotation involved in its 'effulgence'; or it designates skilful acts of mental and manual dexterity which, by their systematic ordering, create and sustain; or it 'cultures the self'.[42] In the *Śatapatha Brāhmaṇa* (III.2.1.5), the *rūpa-śilpa* relationship seems to originate from the *sandhi* (alliance, conjunction) of colours (in a ritual)[43] which is basically an argument based on visual content and its aesthetic perception. Similarly, in the *Śatapatha Brāhmaṇa* (I.1.4.3) the three-fold science (*trayī-vidyā*) of sacrifice (*yajña*), *śilpa* and the black skin (*kṛṣṇājina*) figure together, with *śilpa* being the discriminating instrument in defining the mystery of their union or coupling. It is supposed to stay in the middle of the two, mediating between them and defining their character. The exclusivity of *śilpa*, independent of the two, is quite apparent here. The mediatory role of *śilpa* as an instrument of action eventually grew in time into different streams but it tends to occur everywhere, explicating or controlling those diverse manifestations. But the connectivity of *śilpa* with rituals first during the Vedic times and then with religions later, remained an ever-recurring phenomenon, as the religions were never found lagging behind in harnessing *śilpa* into their service.

These formulations on *śilpa* and also on *kalā* later, contain alternative definitions for art in early India expressing it in plural categories: as a formalistic construct involved with *rūpa* in general or in reference to sectarian divinities in particular; or as an alternative realm of sheer skill – manual or mental – with its internal laws of governance promising *nirvāṇa*, 'liberation', – the ultimate of the quests in tradition – on its own, unaided by any alternative spirituality and based appropriately on sheer aesthetic experience. In our discussions we may briefly cover the aspects of art-and-religion relationship and also highlight a parallel ideology of art in tradition – an ideology which, despite art's closeness to religion, asserted the former's freedom and autonomy right from the Vedic period. We may also emphasise that, of the different categories of art formulated in the early religious texts in terms of the *deva* and *mānuṣa śilpa*s or later as *indriya rūpā* and *viṣaya rūpā kalā*, only the *deva* category is religion-specific; the rest are essentially secular and suggest separate spaces of action.

There is sufficient evidence to warrant the assertion that the beginnings of Indian art-works were rooted in popular or clan-based communitarian beliefs and ethos, which found favour in Buddhism, Bhagavatism and folk cults. During the early historical phase, as the evidence goes, these cults and religions pioneered the first concretisations of the forms in narratives, memorial stones and icons. Of these, the icons are found exclusively related to folk cults where power and glory were conceptualised in the images of Yakṣas and Yakṣiṇīs, just as the Buddhists enabled the narratives and the Bhagavatas' crafted memorial pillars with *makara, tāla* and *Garuda* capitals. These early objects of art are too well known to need further description. Buddhism, Bhagavatism and folk cults emerge as the pioneers in institutionalising and harnessing art in their different representational modes: narrative in the case of Buddhism, iconic in folk religions and non-iconic[44] in the case of the Bhagavatas. Each of these sects or religions discovered artistic forms if not in a quest for a competitive supremacy then at least in celebration of mundane aspirations: well-being in the case of popular cults; celebration of the memory of heroes in case of the Bhagavatas; and celebration of the folklore in edification of their own faith, in case of Buddhism. Art here seems fulfilling the aspirations of the self-seeking powerhouses of mass appeal. Each of these communities discovered a characteristically exclusive and different form of representation in accord with their respective communitarian concerns. But a look at these early examples of Indian art reveals newly found ecstasies in experimenting with anthropomorphic form along with those non-iconic and non-anthropomorphic, which together defined concretisation of ideas in images from a pre-iconic state to that iconic and their compositional structures. As such the entire question of *śilpa*'s interface with form (*rūpa*) in Indian art and its aesthetic bearings seem to have historical as well as art historical points of reference which, rooted as they were in popular aesthetic sensibilities, were not necessarily tied up with a fundamentally religious experience of art. *Śilpa* tends to be experimenting here both with anthropomorphic and symbolic form.

Arts' internalisation into religion seems to have become intense with the rise of theistic cults later and codification of their canons, e.g. the *Agama*s, *Tantra*s, *Saṃhita*s and *Paddhati*s. Images of gods assumed a crucial hold in the theistic religions for in *arcā* (image), in order to reach out to a worshipper, the anthropomorphic form of god was created as the epitome of *anugraha*[45] (mercy). Through these developments, religion came in to exercise a strong grip on plastic arts. The only exception in this regard is provided in the *Smārta* tradition,[46] which strongly advocated *pūrtta* activities for earning merit. But here too, in building temples, the votaries depended on art and iconography almost endlessly. *Śilpa,* essentially an independent entity in itself, open to wide usage and conformable to different utilities, was thus commandeered to serve sectarian aspirations, among other things, which often compromised its character as an independently identifiable entity essentially secular in its exclusive domain.

This exclusive character of *śilpa* is in evidence, time and again, in early texts right from the very beginning. For instance, the *Aitareya Brāhmaṇa* (VI.27) distinguishes the sacred and secular categories of *śilpa* recognising 'imitation' (*anukṛti*) as the basis of this two-fold division. *Anukṛti* is supposed here to serve as the basis of the privileged as well as the secondary character of arts (*śilpa*). It locates art, by implication, in the sacred space and regards the other manifestations as flowing from that; or conversely legitimates it outside the sacred space and brings the transcendental close to the mundane. In this way, it defines the continuum from divine to commonplace and vice versa in conformity with the traditional view where art is considered a consciously articulated principle or propensity of things approximating the truth (of reality): its power and potential resting in its *abhidheya sattā*,[47] i.e., the power to posit reality by fiction.

Other interpretations of the scope of *śilpa*, especially those based on textual references that emphasise on its secular character in mundane territories, are also possible. Commenting upon the *Aitareya Brāhmaṇa* (VI.27), Sāyana classifies *śilpa* into divine (*deva*) and human (*mānuṣa*, anthropocentric) categories.[48] The division is remarkable for, Sāyana introduces secular (i.e., *mānuṣa*) content into the divine category, while in the original passage, the only human agency to be mentioned is the *yajamāna* (sacrificer), who received the benefit of this exercise. *Sāyana*'s interpolation (?) of a secular terrain (*mānuṣa*) in *śilpa*, specifically distinct from *deva* (divine) category is also significant in that chronologically he locates *mānuṣa* category right into the Vedic tradition, interpreting, in a way, the continuity of the secular terrain of *śilpa* from Vedic times down to the sixteenth century, when he wrote his work. Sāyaṇa explicitly suggests that *anukṛti* (imitation) potentially creates in the mundane world (*manuṣyaloka*) the 'forms in likeness' (*sadṛśya rupāṇi*) of the divine forms whereby art assumes a duality (*dvividha*). The point about the 'duality' must be noted here as it squarely legitimates a core in *śilpa* bereft of religiosity in its manifestations even as it admits of and safeguards the other aspects, i.e., the 'religious'. It is also said there that the practice of *śilpa* imbues the doer with a distinction (*saṃskāra*) which rightly attunes him to the knowledge and rhythmic harmony of aesthetic pleasure (*vedamaya* and *chandamaya*). The secular import of *śilpa* is eminently evident in this passage; and such an import is seen consistently emphasised in Sāyaṇa's commentary on this and other passages from the Vedic texts. It may also be noted that in the original text of the *Aitareya Brāhmaṇa*, the objects enumerated as the products of *śilpa* or as 'works of art' are unexceptionably utilitarian, consisting of an elephant, a goblet, a garment, a gold object, a mule chariot, with little sense of anything spiritual or divine about them.

Sāyaṇa again interprets *śilpa* in the *Śatapatha Brāhmaṇa* (III.1.5.5)[49] as *laukika hi hari turagādi pratirūpa.* The emphasis on *laukika* and *pratirūpa* ought to be noted in defining the contexts of art here for the commentary imparts a non-ritualistic meaning to a sacred ritualistic act mentioned in the original passage. Sāyaṇa's commentary on the *Tāndya Mahābrāhmaṇa*[50] (XVI. 4 B) explains *śilpa* as 'wonder' (*āścarya*), or, a propensity that evokes wonder. The original passage in the text builds up the story of Indra's elevation in the midst of the *prajā*. It describes how Prajāpati bestowed Indra with a garland whereupon people recognised Indra's superiority for, in it, they saw the dexterity (*śilpa*) of the *Pitṛ*. Sāyaṇa's commentary on the text explains *śilpa* here as an act of 'wonder' (*āścarya*) for, by this *śilpa* Indra finds a 'beautiful form' (*svarūpa*). The sense of 'decorative', which is brought about by *śilpa*, is quite apparent in the description. Thus, *śilpa* is more often interpreted by Sāyaṇa in value-neutral, skill-specific terms. It is explained as 'an act of wonder' (*āścaryakaram karma*) in his commentary on the *Aitareya Brāhmaṇa*[51] (VI.27); as 'variegated form' (*citra rūpa*) in the case of the *Śatapatha Brāhmaṇa* (I.1.4.3)[52]; as 'dexterity' (*kauśala*) in the case of the *Taittirīya Brāhmaṇa* (III.3.2.1; II.7.15.3)[53]; and as 'dexterity in action', 'concentration', 'strength', 'capacity' and 'harmonious arrangement' (*karma kauśala, yoga, bala, sāmarthya* and *samyojana*) in the case of the *Taittirīya Brāhmaṇa* (II.7.15.3).[54] Sāyaṇa explains *śilpa* in *Tāṇḍya Brāhmaṇa* (XVI.4.9) as *nānā vastujātam.* The commentary of Bhatta Bhaskara Misra follows the same temper. He explains *śilpa* as 'manual dexterity' (*hastaviṣaya kauśalam*) in his commentary on the *Taittirīya Saṃhitā* (I.2.2.1)[55]; as 'variegated form' (*bahurūpa; citrarūpa*) in the cases of the *Taittirīya Saṃhitā*[56] (V.5.22.1), *Śatapatha Brāhmaṇa* (I.1.4.3) and *Yajurveda* (XXIX.58); and as 'intensely penetrative action' (*sūkṣma karma*), 'a mark of creation of the universe' (*jagat sṛṣṭilakṣaṇa*) in the case of the *Taittirīya Āraṇyaka*[57] (I.7.1). In this last passage, it is said that Kaśyapa's power of action creates the world. Kaśyapa, the eighth Sūrya, 'has a constantly direct perception of the world' (*viśvaṃ sakṣitvena sarvadā paśyatīti kaśyapa*), and he is supposed to be so endowed because of his keen *indriyas* which perceive things. No wonder, his sensuous vision makes him endowed with *śilpa,* which here is apparently a subject of visual perception. There is nothing religious about these interpretations of *śilpa* in terms of the power or propensity of perception or action.

All these passages (above) imply dexterity as the hallmark of *śilpa* and represent the latter as a transitive instrument of power tenable everywhere in the context of accomplishing the act(s), which required skill in whatever contexts, divine or secular. This kind of dexterity was an enabling phenomenon: it was supposed to impart immortality to those who possessed or practised it as is said to have happened in the case of the Vedic Ṛbhus of the Angiras family,[58] who were skilled artisans (*svapasaḥ*) with 'deft hands' (*suhastaḥ*). They accomplished acts by using inventive power (*dhī, dhīti*); performed work with great mental concentration (*manasaḥ paridhyā*) and special knowledge (*vidmān*). They made a unique cow out of the hide of a dead one; fabricated a chariot for the Asvins and a horse for Indra, and made four-fold the one bowl (*camaṣa*) that was supposed to have been originally fashioned by Tvaṣṭṛ. In sum, the mortal Ṛbhus – as the first celebrated craftsmen – conveyed in these acts the essence of the same mental and manual dexterity that is encompassed in the notion of *śilpa*.

Vedic *śilpa* and its cognates essentially denote a power or propensity which was supposed to strengthen the cosmic order. *Śilpa* crucially figures in reference to divinities (e.g., Prajāpati, Indra, Agni, Viśvedevas, Sūrya, Kaśyapa) who exercised it or the archetypal man (*puruṣa*) who is found strengthened by it. It figures also as a generative principle marking the moments of beginning (*ārambhe*)[59]; but its replication by human artisanal activity brings about its secular, anthropocentric differentiation. The entire argument about *śilpa* in the early occurrences is in conformity with the Vedic view of differentiation and convergence where the whole divides into parts and then the parts tend to return to the pristine, protean whole once again. But in the commentaries by Sāyaṇa and Bhatta Bhaskara Misra *śilpa*'s 'secular' (*mānuṣa*), anthropocentric character is more than rehabilitated. In these details, *śilpa* is seen to acquire different dimensions of action and it encompasses a vast realm from transcendental to mundane.

V

Rūpa-Śilpa Interface

The same mundane, anthropocentric (*mānuṣa*, as against *daiva*) terrain of *śilpa*, independent of the sacred, is seen in its interface with *rūpa* with which it is inalienably and interminably connected. Both are coterminous in the texts – Vedic, as well as the later ones – it being assumed that *śilpa* recreates, formulates or extends forms (*rūpa*s), through their likeness. Some instances of their juxtaposition are adduced here to substantiate the closeness of their interface. The *Taittirīya Brāhmaṇa* (III.1.5.5) speaks of *vāc* (speech) of 'varied forms' (*viśvarūpa*) being extended all over by *śilpa*: *Prajāpatiḥ yebhirvacim viśvarūpaṃ samavyayat*. The commentary of Sāyana on the *Aitareya Brāhmaṇa* (VI.27) describes replicated forms as 'forms in likeness' (*sadṛśya rupāṇi*) obtained by *śilpa*. Hence, the *Śatapatha Brāhmaṇa* (III.1.5.5) dictum: *yadvai pratirūpam tat śilpam*, i.e., 'whatever is brought forth measure to measure, form to form, is *śilpa*.' In the later texts, *rūpa* is regarded as essential for achieving a meditative comprehension (*dhyāna*) of a deity, *na ca rūpam vinā* *devo dhyātum kenāpi śakyate (Viṣṇu Purāṇa* XXIX.5.5). It would thus appear that the *rūpa-śilpa* correspondence eventually led to reproduction of many forms that were not only sacred and ritualistic but also utilitarian, decorative, mechanical, anthropomorphic and theriomorphic; the most significant of these in arts being the anthropomorphic form. The last is particularly relevant in the *laukika* context. We borrow the term *laukika* from Sāyaṇa's commentary on the *Śatapatha* (III.1.5.5).

Both *Śatapatha Brāhmaṇa* (III.1.5.5) and the commentary of Sāyaṇa on the *Aitareya Brāhmaṇa* (VI.27) describe replicated forms (*pratirūpa*) and therein they tend to convey the interdependence of the duo, namely, *rūpa* and *śilpa,* leaving little doubt that forms (including images, later) are 'produced' by *śilpa*. In the later texts, *rūpa* is regarded as being essential for *dhyāna* (meditation) of a deity, *na ca rūpaṃ vinā devo dhyātuṃ kenāpi śakyate* (*Visṇu Purāṇa* XXIX.5.5). In the *Nighanṭu* (III.7) *rūpa, varpaḥ* and *śilpa* synonymously occur along with other terms (like *apsuḥ, psuḥ, piṣṭaṃ, peśaḥ, aruṣaṃ,* etc.) under the sixteen terms for *śilpa*. Of these, the two terms *apnaḥ* and *śilpam* occur in the *Nighanṭu* (II.1) as synonyms of *karman* (action). This is significant in that the sense of artificing often lies inherent in such connections.

As *rūpa-śilpa* interface is quite recurrent in tradition it may be useful to examine *rūpa* and its concept in some details here, in order to look for the non-sacred contexts where the duo figure often. In art and aesthetics *rūpa* has a centrality as it addresses idea and image, experience as well as representation whether manifested or conceptual. It is relevant to arts especially as it often signifies 'colour' or 'image' and such specialised connotations of *rūpa* are of interest both conceptually and in terms of figural representations as in paintings and images. The varying shades of meaning that the term *rūpa* encompasses may help in historicising the hierarchies of perception about 'form' in both religious and secular contexts, and underscore their validity in reference to *śilpa*.

Rūpa, in Indian tradition, both religious and secular, encapsulates a highly wide spectrum of meanings on the materialised, gross phenomena and has both aesthetic and philosophical import. But it eminently meets the essentially relevant fabrication-centric premise in regard to the constituted 'form' in Indian art, its aesthetics and philosophy specially, as it reinvents and transcribes experience into a visual structure or a representation. Its major implication rests in the validity of 'form' through the argument of immanence in it of the essence that lies invariably behind it and of which it is the formal 'reflection'. In Vedic contexts it legitimates content in 'speech' or in 'colour' and is paired with *nāman* and *pratirūpa* as the principles of differentiation. *Rūpa* also defines the formal particularities in visual and performing art. Its close links with *śilpa* are addressed time and again. The details follow.

Śilpa is supposed to produce *rūpa* skilfully: *saṭśilpānga prayogena prajanayanti rūpāṇi,* i.e., 'art forms are produced by means of six disciplines' (*Vāstusūtra Upaniṣad* I.2.). Or, *śilpāt pratimā jāyante,* 'by *śilpa* images are created' (*Vāstusūtra Upaniṣad* I.5). This happens on the basis of *pramāṇa,* which constitutes both a system of measurement (*tālamāna*) and the *lakṣaṇas,* which infer identities so that even the incomprehensible could be brought within the ken of visual experience. The point has been made in the *Viṣṇudharmottara Purāṇa* (*etaddhi tasyapratimasyarūpaṃ taveritam sarvajaganmayasya*).[60] And the idea recurs elsewhere too as in the *Nāgāvaloka* where it is said: *apratyakṣe'pi eva nāmarūpaṃ likhyate,* or even in the *Vāstusūtra Upaniṣad* in a *sūtra* that reads – *arūpādrūpam tasya phalam. Hṛdaya* is supposed to be the element of action in comprehending *rūpa* while it is still in the form of an incorporeal *bhāva,* not yet materialised (*rūpasya bhāvo mukhyah, Vāstusūtra Upaniṣad,* III.1; or, *tad bhāvādrūpaṃ rūpam pratirūpaṃ jāyate, Vāstusūtra Upaniṣad).*

In several instances since the Vedic times, an ingenuous felicity of action – felicity of *śilpa* – implying 'fashioning' with great creative élan is meant when *rūpa* occurs in conjunction with the root *piś-,* 'to fashion', as in the *Ṛgveda* (X.184.1): *Tvaṣṭā rūpāṇi piṃśatu,* 'May Tvaṣṭṛ duly shape the forms' (Tr. Griffith). The cognates of the root *piś-* convey the same ingenuity. This is so again when, for instance, the term *rūpa* occurs in conjunction with the cognates of the root *piś* such as the root *kṛ-,* or *vi-+ kṛ-,* 'to make', 'to modify', as in the *Taittirīya Saṃhitā* (I.5.9.1-2): *yāvaccho vai retasaḥ siktasya Tvaṣṭā rūpāṇi vikaroti tāvaccho vai tatprajāyate,* 'as many modifications of seed when poured as Tvaṣṭṛ makes, in so many shape does it become fruitful, (Tr. A.B. Keith). Creativity is latent in such formulations.

Sometimes in such a creative act, instrumentality of a mechanical device is also involved. Thus, in the *Atharvaveda* (XII.3.33) Tvaṣṭā, the divine artificer, creates form with a chisel (*svadhiti*): *taṣṭeva rūpam sukṛtaṃ svadhityaina.* Or, a 'wise one (*kaviḥ*) puts on all forms' (*viśvā rūpāṇi prati muñcate kaviḥ, RV* V.81.2). In the *Ṛgveda* (V.42.13), a 'mould' is suggested where *rūpa* occurs in collocation with the root *han-,* 'to mould'. Indra is here praised for 'laying' or 'moulding' a 'form' in the wombs (*vakṣaṇā*) of the daughters: *āhanā duhitur vakṣaṇāsu rūpā mināno.* In the *Ṛgveda* (I.188.9) Tvaṣṭā is the 'maker of all forms': *tvaṣṭā rūpāṇi hi prabhuḥ.* The act of creating a 'noble form' involves not only the skill of hands but also the skill of intellect – *dhī* (wisdom), the mental capacity, as in the *Ṛgveda* (I.95.8), *tveṣaṃ rūpaṃ kṛṇuta...kavirbudhnaṃ pari marmṛjyate dhīḥ,* which according to Pathak[61] 'refers to the shining form ... of a big-bellied pot ... where burnishing of the pot may be intended'.

Artificing and skill are implicit in the instances above for, *rūpa* in those citations is coincident with the roots *piś-,* 'to fashion', and its cognates like *han-*, 'to mould', *kṛ-*, 'to make', *vi-kṛ-*, 'to modify', *rup-*, 'to break', etc. signifying the processes which eventually 'produced' different forms. It must be remembered that the term *śilpa* itself is supposed to have derived from metathesis of *piś* or *piśra* and the implication of 'fashioning' and artificing (which is conveyed in the other cognates of the term) is implicit in it etymologically. The usages of the roots above including that of *piś-* reinforces the secular validity of the *rūpa-śilpa* interface in creativity and their reciprocity, in spite of the instrumentality, sometimes, of the divine beings involved in such cases. This interface also tends to define *śilpa*'s territory as essentially autonomous. No wonders, those who have skilful hands have also the power and control over form, as was the case with Tvaṣṭā, who is *rūpavikartā*, 'modifier of form' (*Bṛhaddevatā* III.25) – 'deft-worker, skilful, helpful, holy' (*sukṛt supāṇiḥ svavān ṛtāvā*, *Ṛgveda* III.54.12) or one who goes about making the beauty perfect (*Ṛgveda* X.70.6)). Possessed of all the *rūpa*s and in that singularity, as the lord and the essence of all *rūpa*s he merrily goes about adorning the heaven and earth with forms of all kind and thereby making 'the beauty perfect' (*deva Tvaṣṭar yat ha cārutvamānāt, Ṛgveda* X.70.6). He created the Heaven and Earth and the mankind and so on: *rūpairapiṃsadbhuvanāni viśvā*, *Ṛgveda* (X.110.9). Or, deft of hands, holy and helpful, he (*Ṛgveda* III.54.15) creates all forms (*RV* I.188.9).[62] As the fashioner of 'perfect beauty' he adorns the universe with forms rendering them beautiful by his power and skill. The implication of adornment (*tvaṣṭā rūpāṇipipiṃśatu, Ṛgveda* X.184.1) is contextual for, as explaind by Yāska (*Nirukta* VIII.11), the word *peśas* implies 'beauty'; it being derived from the root *piś-*, 'to adorn'. In the *Śatapatha Brāhmaṇa* (III.8.3.37, *T. Sam* VI.3.11.2) he shapes the form (*rūpa*) endowing it with a uniformity of the signifier (*salakṣma*). *Rūpa* is immanently located in him but he shapes out corporealities by his artificing skill and thereby adorns the universe with multiple, pleasing forms (*rūpa*).

The association of *rūpa* with the roots like *kṛ-*, *vikṛ-*, *han-*, *bhu-*, *siñc-*, 'to cast', *piś-*, 'to fashion' or 'to adorn', denoting manual or mental action distinctly exemplifies the early, pre-industrial craft technology and the processes of artificing in which the contexts may be divine or sacred but implications are often mundane in terms of the crafts. Significantly, in arts, *rūpa* tends to constitute a temporality, which defeats the philosophical definition of the universe as a category of falsehood. As such, it seeks to create and communicate a universe replete with sensuous pleasure or aesthetic delight.

Etymological and semantic considerations relate the term *rūpa* to the root *rup-*, 'to pierce', a variant of the Indo-European *lup*, 'to break'.[63] Pathak regarded the root *rup-*, 'to pierce', as distinct from root *rup-*, 'to charm', that 'indicated breaking, piercing, and scratching' and thereby, in his opinion, it implied 'an object imprinted with a design'. Craft and artificing and also the forms so produced are thus latent in the root *lup-* and its variant *rup-* from which the term *rūpa* may have derived. In that derivation, it had a substantive Indo-European heritage as it came into the Vedic Sanskrit, as in the *Ṛgveda* (I.95.8) where, used in collocation with the root *mi-*, 'to kill', (e.g., *budhnaṃ parimarmṛjyater dhīḥ*) it implies devising 'a most noble form of splendour' (*tveṣaṃ rūpaṃ kṛṇuta*). The sense of 'breaking' in *rup-* is retained when it is explained as *rūpanat rūpaṃ iti (Abhidharmakośa Bhāṣya* I.13), i.e., 'because of being broken, it is called *rūpa'*. The same implication of the term is found in Pali *rūppati*, 'to break', to destroy', as in *rūppanto rūpam* in the *Visuddhamaggo* (588) or in the *Samyutta Nikāya* (III.86): *ruppatī ti tasmā rūpam ti vuccati.*[64] The meaning will have a legitimacy in the process of carving a figure from stone or wood: by breaking, chiselling, etc. And, the aesthetic bearings of the term *rūpa* seem to come out best in its derivation from the root *rūp-*, 'to charm'.[65] In any case, the term has multiple meanings in different spheres. But in the early occurrences of the term, its association with artificing – and therefore, with *śilpa* – is unmistakably apparent.

Although *rūpa* and its implications carry us through a wide spectrum of meaning in different areas of enquiry including religion, philosophy, poetics, drama, yoga, medicine, astronomy, polity and economy yet, literally, it (*rūpa*) implies 'form', 'design', 'figure'; or, as explained by Monier-Williams,[66] 'any outward appearance or phenomenon or colour' or 'shape'. Yāska (III.13) derives it from the root *ruc-*, 'to shine', but the derivation is uncertain. Quoting Pāṇini (*Dhatupatha* XXV.79), Monier-Williams regards *rūpa* as a nominative from *rūpa-* as in *rūpayati*, 'to form, figure, represent', 'exhibit by gesture, act, feign .... .' Following perhaps Yāska (*Nirukta* III.13), he connects *rūpa* with the Vedic *varpa* or *varpas*, which implies 'a pretended or assumed form, phantom' or 'any form or shape, figure, image, aspect'. For instance, see the *Ṛgveda* (VI.44.14) where Indra is characterised as 'knowing' or 'skilled in many forms' (*puru varpāṃsi vidvānindro*). There is also the instance where 'Indra moves multiform by his *māyā*': *indro māyābhiḥ pururūpa īyate* (*Ṛgveda* IV.47.18). The connotation of *varpas* as *rūpa*, 'form', is quite apparent in the above citations.

In the Vedic texts, very much like *śilpa*, the term *rūpa* occurs often in conjunction with the roots or words denoting creative action, which brings about different manifestations, or supports and sustains them. Thus, *rūpa* is sometimes the product of *māyā* (*Ṛgveda* IV.47.18), *māyā* being a 'marvellous act'; not guile or 'illusion' (as in the *Devi Bhāgavat Purāṇa* X.12.31 where the demon assumes various forms by his magic power) but an act of someone endowed with *prajñā*, as in the case of Indra in the *Ṛgveda* (III.38.7b): *ni māyino mamire rūpamasmin*, where *māyinaḥ* is explained by Sāyaṇa as *prajñāvantaḥ*, i.e., 'endowed with intellect'. Those capable of producing 'varied forms' are supposed to be *vidvān*, 'knowing', e.g. Indra, who is in the 'habit of becoming form in every form'[67] for he is endowed with *māyā*: *rūpam rūpam Maghavā bobhavīti māyāh- kṛṇvānastanvaṃ pari svāṃ* (*Ṛgveda* III.53.8ab), i.e., 'Maghavan weareth every shape at pleasure, effecting magic changes in his body' (Tr. Griffith). Here, *māyā* is a faculty that endows 'a special ability to create form', an inexplicable power of a High Being to assume an outward appearance, 'to appear in or as phenomenal worlds'.[68] Neither illusion nor guile is intended here in the creative act of 'being the corresponding form in every form'.

In examining the meanings of *rūpa* it is seen that right from the early occurrences in the Vedic texts it implicates varied imageries and connotations – cosmogonic, verbal (as in a speech) symbolic, anthropomorphic and terrestrial – including those faunal and even those relating to time and space. But, apart from its supra-sensual, symbolic, notional character, 'forms' there are essentially located in three major categories of embodied materiality. These three categories of the embodied materiality of *rūpa* respectively refer to *rūpa* as: (i) colour, (ii) words or sounds as uttered in a recited speech or in verses that would constitute the contingent ritual, and (iii) creatures or things populating the universe and sensually perceived or experienced. Let us examine some of these contexts of *rūpa* for, apparently, its implications eventually tied up with figural art (*śilpa*).

Rūpa meaning 'colour' has Vedic antiquity.[69] In the *Ṛgveda* (IX.71.8; IX.74.7), either 'white' or a 'radiant hue' is a *rūpa* which Soma is supposed to 'assume' or 'wear'. Assuming the *rūpa* (colour) of a particular kind also means becoming endowed with the quality and function of the entity so represented. So, in the *Śatapatha Brāhmaṇa* (XII.1.4.1, 3). *Puruṣa* as *samvatsara* (year) has both day and night latent in him as white and dark *rūpa*. The *Chāndogya Upaniṣad* (III.3.3; 8.3; 9.3; VI.2.3) conceives of different deities like Vāyu, Agni, Sūrya, Rudra, Āditya, Maruts and Soma in different *rūpa*s (forms, colours). The same text (VI.4.1-7) interprets *rūpa* primarily as colour and its diversification implies its distinctions from *rūpa*, i.e., colour – the primary truth – and its derived counterparts denoted by speech, which is supposed to represent its designated (*nāmadheya*) modification.

Of these imports of the Vedic *rūpa*, we are told that words or speech (*vāk*) when articulated or verbalised turns into *rūpa*. So, a speech is the uttered form of the words: *svam-rūpaṃ śabdasyāśabdasamjñā* (Pāṇini I.I.68). The point is significant for in craft tradition, especially in weaving and in *paṭa* (scroll) painting, respectively in Kashmir and Murshidabad, even today, the graffiti-based coded notations (*talima*) that a master craftsman sings in musical renderings are simultaneously converted into intricate motifs by the weavers at work. *Rūpa* (form) here is thus constructed through speech (*vāk*). Once manifested, *rūpa* turns into a phenomenal entity and, in order to go back to the original manifestor, the illusion of the manifested form has to be necessarily transcended. As the eyes make a vision of 'form' possible through *dṛṣṭi*, the perception has to be visual. In the traditional formulations, such a perception regarding 'form' rests fundamentally on its being a counterform or 'reflection' of the primal source from which it emanated and which it phenomenally signifies, provided the intervening illusion is crossed over. For instance, the divine lords of the season themselves are not always visually perceived even though they supposedly are there. Of the three such divinities, namely, Agni, Sūrya and Vāyu, the last one is ever elusive for his *rūpa* is unseen (*dadṛṣe na rūpam*, *Ṛgveda* I.164.44).

The early Vedic *rūpa* is mostly expressed in terms of differentiation of identities whether in shape or colour, pliable in essence and generally controlled by the skill or power of divine personages, some of whom, e.g. Tvaṣṭā, Indra, Earth are adorned with it while these same along with others like Agni, Sūrya bring it forth or multiply it. But for any form created, there always has to be a creator. In the *Ṛgveda*, for any manifestation of form that may come into being there always has to be a power or an instrument of action behind it. Thus, the seasons, guided by their divine lords, modify such *rūpa*s (*vikṛtāni rūpaśaḥ*). In the later Vedic phase, the pre-eminence of Tvaṣṭā as the fashioner of form (*rūpa*) or as its repository is taken over by other deities, especially Brahman (*SBr.* XI.2.3, 3 and 5) and Prajāpati (*T.Br.* II.2.7.1), Puruṣa (*MN. Up.* 24; *Jaim. Up.* I. 27), the Great Soul (*Bṛ.Up.* I.4.6), and *Sat* (*Ch.Up.* VI.2.1-4, VI.3.1-3). In the *Taittirīya Br.* (II.2.7.1), the beings when created were indeterminate till Prajāpati 'entered' *rūpa* unto them. So, Prajāpati is said to be the 'form' (*rūpa*). In the *Chāndogya Upaniṣad* (VI.2.1; VI.3.1-3; see also VI.3.2-3; VI.4.2-4) *nāma-rūpa* differentiation is attributed to *Sat* who Himself is known through the instrumentality of *nama-rūpa*. Here, *nāma* is only a manner of speech that formalises the truth; or it is the sign that signifies the particularity of each *rūpa*, apparently in its specificity or nature. The *nāma-rūpa* compound therefore interprets the particularity of a thing and also its determinate character. The duo is supposed to be the basis of all empirical knowledge for, *indriyas*, 'sense organs', as well as *manas* have to function within the realm of the two, namely, *nāma-rūpa*. Cognition of *rūpa* is considered possible only when it is brought into the realm of the visual; till then an experience is bound to remain latent in the *manas*. Hence the dictum in the *Kauś Up.* (I.3), that 'visual' is actually the counterpart of the 'mental'.

Citta is supposed to be the locus of *rūpa*.[70] Its consciousness is aroused in *citta* for, according to the *Abhidharmakośa Bhāṣya* (VIII.3), *arūpya*s have no *rūpa* as the latter is supposed to arise only from the mind (*citta*). In the philosophical systems like the Nyāya-Vaiśeṣika[71] and Mīmāṃsā[72] *rūpa* is the special quality that is cognised by eye alone or, its cognition is dependent on *sannikarṣa*. It is fundamentally *anitya* though it is an essential component of the universe and its perception depends on a medium without which a form may remain elusive.[73] In the *Kāvyālankara* (V.10) of Bhamaha *rūpa* is supposed to be produced only from an object (of cognition). The *Purāṇas* reckon *rūpa* in many ways, either in its significant togetherness with *liṅga, guṇa, nāma rūpa, māyā, sūkṣma, sthūla* phenomenon or as a secondary manifestation open to cognition through senses, including *manas, buddhi, cakṣu.*

But appreciation of *rūpa* in the sense of beautiful lies in the field of aesthetics. Literature on the subject is vast and there are schools and schools in poetics as in performing and visual arts relating to its interpretation. Each of them has its uniqueness in propounding theories either on delight, relish (*āsvāda*), taste (*rasa*), experience (*anubhava,* or *pratīti*), gratification (*bhoga*), absorption (*nirvesa*), mood (*bhāva*) and bliss (*ānanda*). These tend to figure eminently in ancient literature. In poetics, appreciation sometimes is posited in terms of *alamkāra, rasa, guṇa, rīti, dhvani* and *vakrokti* within a general framework of *rasa* that may be realised through the *bhāvas*.

In general terms, aesthetic pleasure and sensuous delight ultimately seems to fuse with arts such that they tend to identify each other. Literature on the subject is vast and conceptualisations immaculately constructed. So, it may be said that in Indian tradition both 'aesthetics' and the 'aesthete' have a prominent perch and no theory of art may do without going into these points. After all, appreciation depends on a connoisseurs' taste, which, on its turn, depends on *āsvāda,* a term derived from the root *ad-,* 'to eat'. In figural representations, *āsvāda* or relish derives from a cognition of simulated reality by bringing about a congeniality between the object and its representation through *lakṣaṇa, vyañjana*, etc. This phenomenon is different from the one that factors other variables like *abhidheya sattā, āhārya jñāna, vikalpa* and *viparyaya* as in poetry.

So, traditional formulations in regard to aesthetic pleasure are quite unique and seem to have an independent history in terms of antiquity, content and categorisation. Aesthetic experience targets both 'beauty' and 'relish' where beauty (*saundarya*) may be explained, among other things, in terms of *rūpa*, even as *rasa* may implicate *rasika* and *rasāsvāda.* In their pervasiveness, these categories tend to appropriate and encompass the domain of religion also where even the beauty of the 'holy' becomes a subject of sensuous delight and converts it to an aesthetic category of significance. For instance, see the *Bhāgavat* (I.1.3), which invokes *rasika* into the pleasure of the holy, saying 'Drink O you, Rasika on earth who have a taste for the beautiful (*bhāvuka*); drink again and again, this nectar of mood (*rasa*).' There is a typical instance of Lalitā Tripurasundari of thousand names with one of the names invoking her as *rasyā,* the 'one who is to be tasted aesthetically' or, 'one who is the essence of all things that we enjoy'.[74] The necessary condition here for an aesthetic delight is the 'congeniality' between the object and its viewer. This state is made possible and valid by the *sādhāraṇīkaraṇa* theory in poetics where the appreciation of even the 'holy' would come to the level of visually delighting sensuous experience. In the situation, the latent essentialities (*adhikāras*) implicit in their divine status would stand deferred and suspended (*adhikāra-bheda*) for the period of that momentary experience.[75]

For instance, in the *Rāmāyaṇa*, Sita describes herself as a youthful (*taruṇa*) damsel (*śyāmā*), large-eyed (*viśālākṣī*) (*R*. II.61.4-5), delicate (*sukumārī*) and effulgent like the rays of moon (*candrāmśusadṛśī-prabhā, R*. II.60.16). She says that her *rūpa* is praised even by those who are well versed in prognosticating the *lakṣaṇas* (*R*., Yuddhakanda, 48. 8-13). She says that her hair is light, uniform and blue (*keśaḥ sukṣma samā nīlāḥ*), eyebrows well-parted (*bhruvau ca' sange mayā*); and she is blue-throated (*nilakanṭhī*) with red lips (*bimbosṭhī*); and that, she has a well-formed row of teeth (*dantaśca'viralā*), conch-like eyes, hands, toes and finger-webs (*śankham netre karau pādau gulphāvuru me cita*). Her nails, she says, are round and shining (*anuvṛttanakhā snigdhā*) on well-proportioned fingers (*samāścangulayo mama*) and her soles with ten fingers fall on ground evenly; and also that she is well formed, shining like a diamond (*pīnastana taṭamadhye vajravedisamaprabha; ... amitamadhyasi ... sahatastanī; stanau ca viralau pīnau mamemau magnacūcakauḥ*). She further describes her face being like a full moon (*pūrṇacandra nibhānanā*) and that she is auspicious (*śubhā*), lotus-eyed (*padmapalāśākṣī*) and stands on legs that are like the trunk of a tusker (*viśāla jaghanam pīnam uru karikaropamau*) with a thin waist which had a deep navel and high *kukṣi* (*magnācotsanginī nābhiḥ pārsvoraskaśca me citāḥ*) and that she, well-formed, attracted attention. She also says that she is endowed with auspicious *lakṣaṇas* (*śubhalakṣaṇam*), (*Rāmāyaṇa* III.34.15-20). No wonder, Sita in the *Rāmāyaṇa* as elsewhere, is also described as unique in her beauty like of which was not seen on earth: *naivarūpā mayā nārī dṛṣṭapūrvā mahītale* (*Rāmāyaṇa* III.34.15-20). Laksmana tells her that she was unsurpassed in beauty: *vākyamapratirūpam tu na citram strīṣu Maithilī* (*Rāmāyaṇa* III.45.29). She was modest (*suśīlā*), with a beautiful body and the very incarnation of *rūpa* on earth (*sa suśīlā vapuḥ ślāghyā rūpeṇapratimā bhuvi, Rāmāyaṇa* III.34.19). Well balanced in her limbs, she was the crest jewel among women, decked with ornaments: *sumadhyamā samavibhaktāngī strīratnam ratnabhūṣitā*, (*Rāmāyaṇa* III.31.29). Such graphic details of a divine personage brought to the level of aesthetic appreciation of the 'holy' would be an imager's delight as the *lakṣaṇas* are specifically rendered in a language fit for *śilpīs* to emulate.

We have other perceptions too about *rūpa* in other sources. In the Buddhist tradition, *rūpa* signifies 'matter' or 'corporeality'[76] amongst the five aggregates (*skandhas*) and it is 'transitory', 'un-substantial', 'un-individual' and 'injurious',[77] like the other *skandhas*. It includes 'ten elements of matter' (*daśarūpa dhātu*), the 'ten spheres of matter' (*daśarūpa āyatana*) and 'matter' in the sphere of 'mental objects' (*dharma dhātu*)[78] and derives from four elements: earth, water, fire and air. But *rūpa* qualifies 'beauty' in other contexts. Dalhana in his commentary on *Suśruta Saṃhitā* (V.27) interprets *rūpa* as *saundarya* (beauty): *rūpamiha lāvaṇyam vivikṣitam, tatparyāyaḥ saundaryam.* In the Śāradātanaya's *Bhāvaprakāśana* (III.94), *rūpa* is beauty or a 'natural shapeliness'. The text says that if a person is devoid of adornments like *āvedhya* (a special type of ear ornaments), *āropya* (necklace, etc.), *nikṣepya* (wristlet or anklet) and *bandhanīya* (*śroṇīsūtra, angada,* etc.) and yet he appears adorned, then that adornment indeed qualifies his *rūpa,* 'beauty'. The most eloquent representation of *rūpa* in the sense of beauty is found in the *kāvya* texts which illuminatingly articulate its delicate charm. Kalidasa's narratives are typical in this regard. He aggregates the different kinds of *rūpa* in terms of beauty in his inimitable poetic imageries. He professes, with an ecstatic flourish as it were, a hierarchy in *rūpa* describing the delectable charm of divine, semi-divine and human *rūpa* and finally making a categorical statement that 'beauty of form does not lead to sin': *na rūpam pāpavṛttaye.* Pārvatī, Urvaśī, a Yakṣī, Mālavikā and Śakuntalā are the archetypal models of beauty. Urvasi is described as 'of enticing form' (*manoharamidamrūpam*), born of that 'aged anchorite' (the sage Narayana) who had 'grown dull through the study of the *Vedas*'.[79] She surpassed even Śrī in beauty: *pratyādeśo rūpagarvitāyāḥ śriyaḥ (Vikramorvaśī* I, prose under 3). Menaka's *rūpa* had 'intoxicating charm' (*unmādayitṛ rūpa, Śākuntalam,* under V.22). Sakuntala, her daughter, had 'unearthly form' (*Śākuntalam* I.23). Malavika's 'flawless form' (*rūpa*) was similarly much celebrated (*Mālavikāgnimitram* II.3). The Yakṣī of the *Meghdūta* (II.22), is the Creator's prototype of an ideal maiden (*yā tatra syādyuvativiṣaye sṛṣṭirādyeva dhātuḥ*): slender, youthful, with (proper line of) teeth, and red lips like a *bimba* fruit, a thin waist and a glance like that of a startled doe; she was one with a deep navel and a measured gait owing to the weight of the hips; and she stooped slightly from the weight of her bosom'.

VI

Such details of *rūpa* as 'beauty' came to be celebrated in arts as *śilpa* re-invented female form in all their delectable varieties. *Śilpa* texts' concern for a beautiful female form is narrated in the *Viṣṇudharmottara Purāṇa*[80] in Markandeya's account to the prince Vajra describing how Urvasi, the very epitome of beauty, was brought skilfully into being (*Urvaśī ca katham jātā*) by a well-accomplished *muni* of perfect ascetic grace, steeped in rigorous austerities. We are told that just to shame the *devastrīs*, the sage Narayana, who had the power of *tapas*, quite nonchalantly enlivened a womanly figure into an unsurpassingly beautiful Urvasi from the figure he drew out with juice (of a mango fruit). The story is laid in the midst of a quiet hermitage in Badari forest where Nara and Narayana, the two celebrated sages, were engaged in penance. The *devastrīs* (*Apsaras*) had descended there in a joyful mood, intending to disturb their *tapas*. But then, the sage Narayana, steeped as he was in *dharma* and endowed with the capacity to transcend anger and passion, brought Urvasi into being in an impulse of creativity for the 'welfare of the people' (*lokānām hitakāmyayā*): *sahakāra rasaṃ gṛhya urvyām cakre varastriyam/citreṇa sa tato jātā rūpayuktā varāpsarā.* The secret of this entire marvel of creativity lying in an impulse, as suggested in this text, is categorically explicit in a later work which speaks of *hṛdaya* as the locus where *rūpa* is perceived by the *kāmācārins*, i.e., 'those who are moved by impulse'.[81]

Beauty, in tradition, is taken as auspicious and pure, devoid of even a tinge of sin. Kamadeva, the very epitome of 'beauty', for instance, is *ananga*, 'formless' and seems to rest only in the idea of it. Parvati's divine beauty, tempered with the discipline of *tapas* (austerities), was the essence of purity:

> *yaducyate Pārvati pāpavṛttaye na rūpamityavyabhicāritadvacaḥ-/*
> *tathā hi te śīlamudāradarśane tapasvināmyapyupadeśatāṃ gataṃ,*

i.e., '... that beauty of form does not lead to sin, is infallibly true; for thy character, O lady, large eyed, is an exemplar even to the sages' (Tr. Devadhar).[82] Obviously, the concepts about beauty of the body have kept on changing even as they continually impacted art tradition in India. They emphasise varyingly on spiritual, physical or mental charms of the (female) form. As for Parvati, she was the epitome of beauty, as described in the *Kumarasambhava* (I.49): 'She was created by the Creator, with great effort, from all materials of comparision moulding each limb as if the world's creator would behold all beauty centred in a single mould'.[83] To be able to understand the perceptions about the reconstituted *rūpa* we may here examine its manifestation in *śilpa* texts.

Rūpa is posited as the essence resting in the transcendental, un-verbalised, un-manifested primary cause that goes into difference in many ways. Yet, in such distinctions, it invokes the primary source from which it derives, thus mediating between the source and its materialised manifestation. In early references, Indra, the 'wearer of every shape at pleasure' (*Ṛgveda* VI.47.18) is one in many: *rūpam rūpam prati rūpo babhūva tadasya rūpam praticakṣaṇāya/Indro mayābhiḥ pururūpa īyate*, i.e., 'In every figure he hath been the model: this is his only form for us to look on. Indra moves every form with his illusion ...' (Tr. Griffith). The phenomenon of transcendence in form-counterform is categorically an act of great skill (cf., *S. Br.* III.2.1.5: *yadvai pratirūpam tat śilpam*). It is central to the vision of the archetypal model even as that model may tend to divide and diversify itself in the act of creation. The reconstituted material phenomenon thus brought about may be epistemologically perceived or understood as the reflection of the un-manifested in its multiplicity. Essentially, *rūpa* is of two kinds in the *Br.Up.* II.3.1: the formed (*mūrta*) and unformed (*amūrta*); the mortal and the immortal.

Often its manifestation is conveyed in terms of merely a reflection (*chāyā*). There will be more about *chāyā*, later in this work. But the imagery of reflection in a mirror or in water is fairly pervasive right from the Vedic times.[84] In the *Chāndogya Up.* (VIII.8.1), we have Prajāpati directing the representatives of gods and demons to look at their shadow in water to enable them to realise the *ātman*. The person, whose reflection in water identifies him, is supposed to rest in *rūpa* (*rūpānyeva yasyāyatanam*), which is his abode, and the *rūpa-pratirūpa* combination is quite evident here. Such a *rūpa-pratirūpa* correspondence is explicit in describing Indra's multiplicity in the *Br. Up.* II.5.19 and it is also expressed often in terms of *pratibimba, anurūpa, tulyarūpa,* and *sādṛśya.*[85]

The *Śilparatnakośa* (p. 174) refers to *rūpa* as conceptual as well as representational (*vyakta* or *avyakta*), and it figures centrally in arts in terms of the *rūpavidyā* (Comm. on *Vāstusūtra Up*). The term connotes an 'image' or 'sculpture' (*Vāstusūtra Up.* I.2; III.7; *Mayamatam* XV.28, etc.) as well as its characteristic. The explicit compositional structure and the *bhāva* (mood, implication, nature) in a *rūpa* constitute *rūpavidyā*, which interprets both the principles and concept of composition. In that sense, whatever is crafted morphologically is also validated aesthetically, in concurrence. The re-constitution of *rūpa* in an image is canonically described as *rūpa-nirmāna* for instance, in the *Viṣṇudharmottara*[86] in which compositional features have to be 'purposive' (*sahetuka*) in import. While a divine entity in a state of its consciousness may bring about forms merely by its will (*icchā*),[87] an artist renders the experience of his creative consciousness into representational reality in accordance with the principles of composition. Identities are thereby inferred in plastic art with the help of *lakṣaṇa* and *pramāṇa.*[88]

Rūpa implies both material form and its property according to the *Viṣṇu Purāṇa* (I.2.1: *sadaika rūparūpāyaviṣṇave sarvajiṣṇave).* Even the 'formless', if it comes into the ambit of *nāma-rūpa* (form), is realised in arts, regardless of its being invisible. As is said in the *Nagavaloka* (p. 58*) apratyakṣe' pi evam nāma rūpa likhyate,* 'though invisible her form is nicely painted'. In the

Viṣṇudharmottara Purāṇa (III.48.20) the 'all-pervading' un-manifested *rūpa* is described in terms of its *lakṣaṇa*s as: *etaddhi tasyāpratimasya rūpam taveritam sarvajaganmayasya*. All this falls within the range of *śilpa* which by definition is given to creating identities of form by manual skill. So we have in the *Viṣṇudharmottara Purāṇa* (III.2.1) the emphasis on the manner of inventing the forms (*devatā rūpanirmāṇam*) so that the image made according to rules may always manifest the desired figure. In a similar fashion, the *Vāstusūtra Upaniṣad* (V.21: *arūpādrūpam*) goes into conceptual as well as compositional details of diverse forms, even as it lays stress on conformoity of a re-constituted image with its archetypal model. It visualises both the primary and secondary forms, positing that 'from formless arises the form'. The commentary explains that '... due to diversity of conceptions arises the form of the divinity, and through the form arises diversity. That becomes the image (*pratirūpa*, or secondary form)'. Reconstitution of *rūpa* therefore has to be understood as *bhāva rūpa* only: *tad bhāvādrūpam rūpam pratirūpam jāyate*, i.e., 'The image corresponding to every (original) form arises on the basis of that *bhāva*'[89] (Tr. A. Boner).

A reconstitution of form in arts, as we have said earlier, is appropriately dependent on *śilpa*: *ṣaṭ śilpānga prayogena prajanayanti rūpāṇi* (*Vāstusūtra Upaniṣad* I.2): 'Art forms are produced by means of six disciplines'; or, *śilpāt pratimā jāyante*, 'By *śilpa* images are produced'. According to the Commentary on the *Vāstusūtra Upaniṣad* (I.8), this 'production' requires the 'knowledge of stones' (*śailam*), 'compositional diagrams' (*khilapañjara*), 'carving of stones' (*śailabhedana*), 'arrangement of limbs or parts' (*angaprayoga*), 'the emotional disposition evoked by the composition' (*nyāsabhāvanā*), and 'the understanding of the integration of the composition' (*sambandha prabodhana*).

Sometimes, in texts, the discourse on 'form' often posits that it is implicitly notional in character instrumentally brought into the range of comprehensible. The non-visual modes like recitation of songs and myths are supposed to be the instruments of mediation in making its comprehension possible. The point is made in the the *Vāstusūtra Upaniṣad* (I.7) which says: 'From the archetype gradually arises the knowledge of principle of images, from the knowledge of principle comes clear conception, from clear perception sacred songs and myths arise among people. From sacred songs (*gāthā*) the *sthāpaka*s derive images. This experiential series in *śilpa* is designated in the *Vāstusūtra Upaniṣad*, comm. (I. 8) as *rūpavāstu saḍangam*, 'six branches of the art of image imaking'. *Rūpa* thus has an absolute primacy in sculpture or in visual arts. Its reconstitution by *sthāpaka* is possible when its *tattva*s (principles), *dhāraṇā* (conception) and *gāthā* (mythical content) have been expropriated in an image. Reconstituting *rūpa*, in the situation, requires series of action in translating one mode into another whereby the concepts and principles turn into myths which then help in composing the image (*rūpa*). The images have to necessarily conform to their conceptual content: *yathā prakṛtistathā rūpalakṣaṇam*, 'the features of image are conform to nature'.

Artisanal modes are prescribed in the canons of art to materialise *rūpa*, 'image' or 'sculpture', with the aid of practical artificing devices. In such application, according to the *Śilpaprakāśa* (II. 192 a, b.), *rūpa* (image) conforms to its conceptual and material format: *yantrānusāri yad rūpam dhyanānusāritam tathā*, i.e., '... his form should be in accordance with the *yantra* and with the *dhyāna*'. The second chapter of the *Vāstusūtra Upaniṣad* on *khilapañjara-jñānam* prescribes the use of compositional diagrams for image making. It recommends drawing circles and lines on a stone piece and suggests that once a diagrammatic format has been systematically laid out, the *rūpakarma* 'image making', should proceed from the centre (*Vs.U.* II.10). 'Infusion of feelings' (*bhāva*) and *rūpa* in an image may vary depending upon the *rasa*s to which it may relate. In all these details *rūpa* in arts, especially in sculpture, seem to encompass the creative process which brings out the conceptual into the range of sensual perception and aesthetic appreciation. Despite the fact that *rūpa* in spiritual domain is considered *anitya* (transient) or 'impermanent', its significance in arts and aesthetics is appropriately established as something pleasing to senses and valid both in secular and religious domain.

VII

The secular credentials of art are seen in the post Vedic times also even as they occur in the contexts which are religious or philosophical. We may refer to the relevant enunciations about arts (*kalā*) as they occur in the *Sarvadarsanasangraha* in reference to the Pāśupata Śaivism. In the Pāśupata philosophy,[90] art, as dependent on Īśvara, is split into *kāryākhyā* and *kāraṇākhyā* categories or in other words into the *indriyarūpā kalā* (art of sensual perception) and *viṣaya rūpākalā* (art of the consciousness).[91] The terminology is considerably modified here as the conceptual bearings of art are now located in the domain of empirical categories explained in terms of cognitory senses and those relating to consciousness, though the transcendental nature of the arts is concurrently postulated on the basis of the immanence of Īśvara in them. Īśvara is supposed to be the principle of immanence as well as of differentiation in the *indriyarūpā kalā* (art of sensual perception) and *viṣayarūpā kalā* (art of consciousness). These categories are significant as they bring into the discourse on art considerations about sensual experience and perception and thus locate art in the intuitive and cognitive realm.

These categories in essence are devoid of spiritual or religious dimensions except for their ultimate validation, which comes through the positing of Īśvara's immanence in them. Here, the creation of a transcendental dimension of art out of the entities of experience is intended to cast God in the image of a creative artist, a theme often emphasised in Śaivite ideology of creation. The creation myths in the *Śaivagama*s describe Śiva as the great artist who creates the world of experience by his sheer will, out of himself, without recourse to any other stuff. The *Śaivagama*s as well as *Parimala* reiterate this.[92]

An *indriyarūpā kalā* is defined as one in which perceptions of the senses[93] lead to cognition,[94] every form of cognition, in turn relates to one of the five *mahābhūta*s,[95] i.e., the elements which are supposed to make the *jagat*. Art figures here as a cognitive principle of perceiving the universe with the aid of the senses. The appreciation and pleasure of the arts is dependent upon the senses, which affect the *sādhāraṇīkaraṇa* (universalisation) of experience from mundane to transcendental level and *vice versa*. The *indriyarūpā kalā*, in that manner, connects the series of sensual-perceptual continuities unto the level of the *pañca-mahābhūta*s, which, in essence, are the differentiation of the Īśvara *tattva*. One can see them in their ascending as well as descending order, but their cognition, in the first place, is dependent on the senses (*indriya*s). The *viṣayarūpā kalā* relates to knowledge and perception (*jñāna* and *darśana*); *antaḥkaraṇa* is its locus. *Antaḥkaraṇa* or *citta* is also the crucible in which *rūpa* (form) is born or is intuitively created, for, like *citta*, it removes the *pravṛttis* and *āvaraṇa* which lead to cognition and realisation of form. *Viṣaya* is characterised as being contingent (*anubandha*) to *kalā*.

The two-fold arts postulated in Pāśupata Śaivism bring into reckoning the psychological categories of perception and experience and mark a modification on those (e.g., *deva-* and *mānuṣa-śilpa*) as posited in a Vedic text and its commentary, mentioned earlier. Apparently, they reveal psychological categories of experience. The classification suggests different levels of art-experience with its beginnings in *citta* or *antaḥkaraṇa* and perception as well as identity by the *indriya*s. It explains the experience-to-reality phenomenon more cogently in a terminology, which is comparatively free from restrictive bindings of a religious dogma. Secular content in this classification is contextually established; for arts here seem to belong to the realm of experience, and transcendence is posited only by the intrusive logic of the immanence of Īśvara in the work of art. In these formulations, art seems to be holding on tenuously to a secular, this worldly, non-spiritual terrain.

This terrain is better defined in the textual discussion on *rūpa* in conjunction with *śilpa*. As we have seen above, *rūpa*[96] (form) is basic to the arts, and to the visul arts in particular. It has significance both in reference to the ideal and its counterpart, a combination, which is expressed in terms of *rūpa-pratirūpa, tathārūpa, sādṛṣya, pratibimba*, etc.[97] The conjunction implies that every (subsequent) manifestation or reconstitution of the ideal *rūpa* must have in it the inherent plausibility of the 'being' so represented. It therefore tends to convey the correspondence of the formal and representational elements by the rhetoric of implied suggestion.[98] It must be underscored here that *rūpa* does not always convey beauty, although it may sometimes imply it. Its primary meaning relates it to categories which are specific to particular formal structure and which are open to comprehension and cognition through sense perception (*indriyas*) and *darśana*.[99] But everywhere, the *lakṣaṇa* (mark) or *vyañjana* (suggestion) are the necessary indicators of a differentiated identity conforming to the ideal identity, but distinguished by a particular *nāma* in each case. The *rūpa-pratirūpa* continuum underscores the ideal at two levels: in the ideal beyond a direct perception (*atīndriya*) as in the case of the *tattvas*, and then again in the (imagined) counterpart of the ideal as represented in a visual (or verbal) structure. The idea-image continuity explains the formal and representational aspects of the *rūpa-pratirūpa* in the early historical tradition. *Śilpa* is the element of action that brings about such continuity. And, the idea of such conjoining (*sandhi*) is fairly old going back to the Vedic times.

The anthropomorphic form eventually pervaded the entire range of Indian art. The human figure occurs there in rapturous ecstasy. Considering *śilpa*'s conjunction in *puruṣa* and also the anthropocentric (*mānuṣa*) category of *śilpa* mentioned above, the pervasive depiction of human figure in art appears more than fortuitous. According to the *Parama Saṃhitā*[100] and the *Viṣṇudharmottara Purāṇa*[101] even God is supposed to have opted for the anthropomorphic form by his own initiative and preference. Puruṣa received his form from Tvaṣṭṛ, the divine artificer,[102] though Puruṣa himself, according to the *Ṛgveda* (X.90.6), was the basis of all the different forms, including that of man on the earth. The association between *śilpa* and Puruṣa is seen in the Vedic contexts in the *Kauśītaki Brāhmaṇa* (XXV.12) and the *Śāṅkhāyana Brāhmaṇa* (XXV.12) where *śilpa* is supposed to bind Puruṣa into its physicality (*āyatana*) by strengthening its breath and *ātman*. In the Vedic context, both Puruṣa and *śilpa* have sacrificial import but other floating traditions eventually helped in devising an ideal male (and female) form in figural art by the early historical phase, for which contemporary sources offer sufficient evidence.[103]

In plastic art, the commonplace anthropomorphic form is first seen in the Yakṣa images. But *kāvya* and the Buddhist texts contain details encompassing contemporary sensibilities about the ideal human form.

Expressed in terms of *lakṣaṇa, vyañjana* and *cinha*,[104] the details of what constituted an ideal *mahāpuruṣa* appear significant for many reasons. For one, they precede *śilpa* texts by a few centuries; secondly, they do not present *lakṣaṇas* in terms of attributes consisting of *vāhanas*, etc. or objects held in hand or depicted on the figure. On the contrary, they define human figure in terms of its plausible as well as extraordinary morphological structure, qualitatively signifying man as *mahāpuruṣa.* The contention that these formulations relate to secular realm becomes plausible on the basis of the *sādhāraṇīkaraṇa* theory of *kāvyas* where, through the *adhikāra bheda*, the divine is brought into the realm of an aesthetic category of experience. In that conceptualisation, for instance, the details relate to Rama, Sita and others in the *Rāmāyaṇa*, which was composed as a *kāvya*, and to the Buddha, who was not *lokātīta* initially.

The formulations relating to the Buddha are well known; those in the *Rāmāyaṇa* may be mentioned here in brief. In the case of the Buddha, the standardised list enumerates thirty-six *lakṣaṇas*.[105] In the case of Rama, his figure (*gātra, vigraha*) is described in reference to thirty-seven marks. But if the internal division of these marks into threes, fours, fives and sixes, etc. is taken into the reckoning, the total number of such marks (*lakṣaṇas, cinhas*) goes up to one hundred and seven.[106] In the case of Sita, these marks collectively make a sum of thirty-seven in numbers.[107] These *lakṣaṇas* define the ideal human figure and are bereft of any notion of spirituality. To some extent their significance lies in locating the notions of ideal (male or female) human figure in Indian art, outside the realm of religion. Later on, other types, e.g., *haṃsa, bhadra, śaśa, mālava, rucaka*, etc. each with their distinct personality traits, came into reckoning. They are mentioned in the *Bṛhat Saṃhitā* of Varahamihira,[108] a text on astronomy. The relevance of such a categorisation, whether ideal or typological, in arts is confirmed by their occurrence, with some modifications, in the *Citralakṣaṇa* of Nagnajit.[109]

These selections from tradition indicate the possibility of an alternative ideology concerning art, especially plastic arts, which lies outside the religious space, an ideology that was much advocated but not universally recognised. *Śilpa* was honourably situated in the Vedic texts; so were those who practised it, namely, Prajāpati, Kaśyapa, the *yajamān* and also the Ṛbhus. Outside the religious contexts, i.e., in the social categories, artisans formed a part of the *viś* (the Vedic community), with no stigma attached to them.[110] But the situation got modified in the post-Vedic phase when both *śilpa* and *śilpin* were devalued and the latter was relegated to the lowest status in the four-fold *varṇa* hierarchy. By the time of the *Dharmasūtras*, *śilpa* had come to imply occupations (*vṛttis*) till further modifications were introduced later.[111]

NOTES AND REFERENCES

1. Misra (1994): 1:60.
2. Cf., Misra (1994): 2: 97-106.
3. *yadvai pratirūpam tat śilpam, Śatapatha Brāhmaṇa*, III.1.5.5.
4. About the varying concerns of art (and ritual), cf., Ian Hodder (1982), *The Present Past*, pp. 159-72; 173-93.
5. Misra (n.d./1984): 68-69.
6. Baumer (2002): 28-37.
7. *Śilpaprakāśa I.5, 6a: śilpavidyā tu mahatī tanmadhye pañcadhottamā, dārupāṣānalauhañca svarṇa lekhya tathaiva ca.* The skills that constitute *śilpa* figure in the *Śukranītisāra* (IV.3.84-90) in its list of sixty-four *kalās*. The text (IV.3.84) also says that 'making of the pots of clay, wood, stone and metal are four different arts; painting too is an art'.
8. Misra (1988): 145. For different implications of the term *śilpa*, see *Ibid.*, pp. 145-167.
9. *Baudhayāna Dharmaśāstra*, Umesh Chandra Pandey, ed. (1972), Varanasi: Chowkhambha Sanskrit Series, p. 59.
10. Misra (1988): 145, according to the comm. by Devaraja Yajvan.
11. See his comm. on *Nighantu* II.1.
12. Mayrhofer (1976), Vol. III, pp. 343-344, sv. *Silpaḥ*. Mayrhofer explains it as: 'many-coloured'; 'handwork'.
13. Mayrhofer also draws attention to the Indo-Iranian and Indo-European connections of the root *piś* (Vedic), *paes* (Avesta), *pingo* and *peik* (Latin), *pikros* (Greek), *peig* (German) and *feh* (Gothic). Everywhere, the derivatives mean 'embroidering', 'colouring', sketching', and 'adornment', which sense is conveyed by *śilpa* inasmuch as it implies these and qualifies 'beautiful'. Cf., Mayrhofer (1976), pp. 267, 288-9, 312, 342ff.
14. This seems to mark the beginnings of *śilpa* as *śāstra.* It may be pointed out that the word *śilpa* is used to denote '*śilpa* verses' as a particular kind of *śāstra* or a hymn of a highly artificial character recited on the sixth day of the *Pṛṣṭhya Sadaha* at the Visvajit sacrifices. In this ritual context, *śāstra* means recitation of some Vedic *mantras* by the *hotā* and his assistants. And, singing, as an accompaniment to the *grahas* at the *Soma* libation, is not involved in its ritual context. Imitation of the Vedic *mantras* is to be noticed in this *śāstra* and for that reason (of *anukaraṇa*) it is called *śilpa. Śilpa* thus is the imitation of chanting the Vedic *mantras* or hymns, and it becomes *śāstra* in the context of the *Ṛgvedic* Brāhmaṇas while in the context of the *Sāmavedic* Brāhmaṇas it becomes *stotra.*
15. *Vidyā, vijñāna* and *śāstra* constitute categories of knowledge independent of *śilpa*. Sometimes they identify with *śilpa* and merge into it or, on occasions, the one graduates into the other or even reverts to its moorings regardless of occasional claims of their reciprocity or conjunction. So, to understand the quality of such conjunction and disjunction it may be necessary to analyze these different terms in their independent domains. Like *śilpa*, these terms, e.g., *vidyā, vijñāna* and *śāstra* have an operative value in conformity with their independent and autonomous domains. In qualifying *śilpa* they

respectively valorised each other in that convergence. This was so because *śilpa* in the Brāhmaṇas and Saṃhitās stood as a sanctified, sacrosanct entity, highly edified for its inherent powers and potential, which more or less canonised it. This edification was rendered more efficacious as a result of investiture of the qualities of *vidyā*, *vijñāna* and *śāstra* into it. Those terms of value may not represent immutable categories of 'knowledge' or action (*karma*) but the fact that they figure in discourse on *dharma*, *dhyāna*, *darśana*, *sakṣātakaraṇa*, etc. lends credence to them. For further discussions, see below.

16. Cf., Kane (1941), Vol. II (1): 82-83.
17. *Aṣṭādhyāyī*, VI.2.62 and also Patanjali IV.4.55.
18. Cf., Agrawal (1955 First ed.): 229-35.
19. *Aṣṭādhyāyī*, vii.
20. Cf., Manu, VII.138; Gautama X.31; Viṣṇu 32. According to *Vaśiṣṭha Dhs.* (XIX.28), in lieu of taxes they could work for one day in a month for the king. The *Arthaśāstra* of Kautilya refers to *kāruśāsistṛ* and *savittakāru*, the former running workshop and the latter working for the market. Cf., Misra (2002).
21. *Baudhāyana Dharmaśāstra*, IX.6.1. The *Sarvadarśana Sangraha* defines *vṛtti* as *annārjanopāyām vṛttayaḥ*, Cf., Bohtlingk and Roth (Rep.1966) sv. *vṛtti* for such and other meanings of the term.
22. Mihir Chand, n.d.: 600.
23. Chattopadhyaya (1977): 220. In the *Nīlamata Purāṇa* (V.522) *karmajīvins* and *śilpins* are assigned to śūdra *varṇa*; the latter included weaver, carpenter, goldsmith, silversmith, blacksmith who commanded respect and exchanged gifts with the higher *varṇas* during the *Mahīmāna* celebrations. They worshipped their tools in the temple of Durga. Dharmaśāstra allowed them to ply the trade of *vaiśyas*. Cf., Vedkumari (1968): 86, 87.
24. Cf., Horner (1942-63), Vol. II, p. 176. The *Dīgha Nikāya* distinguishes between the kinds of low birth and low occupations. Cf., Horner, *op. cit.*, p. 173, fn. 7.
25. Cf., Horner (1942-63), Vol. II (London), p. 173, fn. 7.
26. Limaye and Vadekar (1958): 355.
27. P. Steinthal, ed. *Udāna* (PTS, London), pp. 31-32. It lists the higher *śilpas* (*sipanam agam*) where Lokāyata besides *kāvya* and writing, figures among the 'foremost *śilpas*'. *Udāna* (III.9) says: *asippa jīvī laghu aṭṭhakāmo yatindriyo sabbadhivippamutto/ anokasārī amamo nirāso hatvā maram eka carosa bhikkhu, ti.*
28. The inclusion of *śilpins* in the group marks a phenomenal transformation of *śilpa* from its earlier exalted ambience. Certain reservations may still be there in such modification. Even though *śilpa* and Lokāyata are clubbed together in the Udāna, *śilpa*'s conjunction with *ātman* has a different orientation in earlier texts. For instance, the duo have a togetherness in the *Kauśitakī Brāhmaṇa* (XXV.12: *ātmā vai pṛsthyāni praṇāh śilpāni*) which says that the *Pṛsthas* are *ātman*, the *śilpas* are the breaths; assuredly the two are not separable. But, condemnation of *śilpin* in the *Maitrī Upaniṣad* would indicate changes that must have happened as *śilpa* covered new ground and acquired other connotations.
29. Cf., Misra (n.d./1984): 65-72.

30. *Vāstusūtra Upaniṣad*, V.1 *bhāvasyāropaṇam rūpakarmāṇi;* III.1 *rūpasya bhāvo mukhyaḥ;* V.12 *tiryag rekhāyām rūpāngabhāvaḥ prakaṭo bhavati;* III.4 *rūpasaubhagyād dhyāna bhāvo jāyate;* III.14 *dhyānaprayoge rūpa sauṣṭhavam spaṣṭam bhavati; śilpa rūpasya sādhanam.* For *bhāvarūpa, Ibid.*, pp. 23, 25, 82, 111, 125, 128, 140, 150.
31. Cf., P. Steinthal, ed. (Rep. 1982), (PTS, London), pp. 31-32, where the list consists of *hasti-, asva-, ratha-, dhanu-, tharu-, muddā-, gananā-, lekhā-, kāvya-, Lokāyata-* and *khettavidyā-śilpas.*
32. *Saundaryalaharī*, 27; Norman Brown translates the passage as follows: 'Let my idle chatter be the muttering of the prayer, my every manual movement, the execution of ritual gesture, my walking, a ceremonial circumambulation, my eating and other acts, the rites of sacrifice.'
33. In the Buddhism, the *sippa* besides *kula* and *kamma*, rather than *varṇa* and *jāti* were the fundamental markers of status. Cf., Chakravarty (1987).
34. Misra (1988): 155.
35. In the *Milinda Pañho* the discussion starts with a statement: *acāriyānām sippavantanam sippasukham namati.* Is there bliss in a craft for those teachers? The answer is given in affirmative. But again there is a query whether this bliss in a craft is not mixed with anguish? Because, pursuing a *śilpa* means mortifying one's body by rising up in *abhivādana* to *ācārya*, fetching water, sweeping house, providing tooth sticks and water for rinsing, etc. accepting left over food for eating, messaging and bathing the *ācārya*, total surrender to him, taking hard bed to sleep, and bad food to eat, which all try the endurance of the body. This, we are told, is certainly not bliss! In answer, it is said that this is only the *pubba bhāga* of *sippa pariyeṣaṇā* and that after the teachers have sought a craft with anguish ... they experience the bliss of craft. And this bliss is 'unmixed with anguish' (*sippasukham dukkhena amissam*). We are told that 'this bliss in a craft is one thing, anguish another' (*annaṃ taṃ sippa sukham annaṃ dukkhaṃ ti*), just as *nibbāna* is entirely blissful and is not mixed with anguish – *ekanta sukham nibbānaṃ na dukkhena missam, annaṃ dukkhaṃ annaṃ nibbānanti.* Cf., Trenckner, ed. and tr., *Milinda Pañho*, p. 315.
36. Cf., J.E. Carpentier, ed. and tr. (1976), *Dīgha Nikāya* (PTS), London, Vol. III, p. 158, where we are told as to how in craft the Buddha may learn to know with ease: *sippesu vajja caranesu kammesu – kathamvijaneyya lahuti*? Parents are similarly advised to minister their child to *sikṣā* of *śilpa* and teachers are supposed to teach *śilpa* to their pupils. *Ibid.*, Vol. III, p. 189. In the *Majjhima Nikāya*, ed. Trenckner, 1979 (PTS). London, Vol. II, p. 94, an apprentice is supposed to learn *sippa* only if he is without any disability of body and mind.
37. Mirashi (1955), Vol. IV, Part 2: 556-557 where Chītaku, a master craftsman, is described as *pañcavidyā mahodadhi* and expert in *yantravidyā* which is described as *mahavidyā*. Chītaku is *vidyāpati-gambhira* and his brother Mandana is a *śāstrajapī* as well as an expert in *Jyotiṣa śāstra.*
38. Cf., Misra (1975): 40, 67, 53, 54, 71, 72. A Khajuraho Stone Inscription describes Chicchā, a master artist, who built a temple at Khajuraho as *vijñāna*

viśvakartā, Cf., *Epigraphia Indica*, Vol. I, p. 146, verse 60. Other expert craftsmen in arts, i.e., the *vijñānika*s are also mentioned for instance, Jalhana and Uheno who were *vijñānika*s of the Chandellas in Central India, Cf., *Epigraphia Indica*, Vol. XXI, *JASB*, XLVII part I, p. 73, *Indian Antiquary*, Vol. 16, pp. 202-207. *Vijñāna* is defined as *niravaśeṣaśāstraviṣayam granthato'rthataśca siddhijñānam*, Bohtlingk and Roth (Rep. 1966), sv vijñāna.

39. In this connection as pointed out by Baumer, the kind of dexterity that is envisaged in the connotations of *śilpa* is very much like what is said of yoga. '... in Pāṇini's *sūtra* 4.4.55; *śilpam* has been explained by the *Kāśika* as *abhyāsapūrvakam kriyāsu kauśalam silpam*, art is dexterity in action preceded by practice. And yoga according to the *Bhagvadgītā*, is *karmasu kauśalam* (2.50). *Kauśalam* is certainly more than dexterity or skilfulness; it is an action which is proper, right, harmonious and beneficial. Both in yoga and art, there is a creativity involved which requires a state of harmony or balance between the inner attitude, the action itself, the material it uses, and the result of the action. Thus, both yoga and *śilpa* are perfect action, art in complete sense.' Baumer (2000): 78-79.
40. About the varying concerns and contexts of art and ritual, cf., Ian Hodder, *The Present Past*, 1982, pp. 159-72, 173-93.
41. For a detailed discussion on *śilpa*, see Misra, 1988: 145-69.
42. Misra, 1988: 150.
43. J. Eggeling, the relevant passage is as follows, 'He then squats down behind the two skins and while touching them thus at a place where the white and black (hair) join, he mutters, "... ye are the images of the Rik and Saman, an image doubtless is what is conformable". "Ye re conformable to the Rik and Saman", he thereby means to say'. See, Misra, 1988: 154.
44. Besides Yakṣa images and narrative art, the latter connected chiefly with early Budddhism, the only other early works of art in stone (second century BC) are the *dhvajastambhas* of the Bhagavat heroes, Vasudeva-Kṛṣṇa, Sankarsana and Pradyumna who are respectively represented in the *garuda-dhvaja, tala-dhvaja* and *makara-dhvaja*. Their symbolic representation in that manner may be regarded as noniconic or even totemic, related to the heroes and heroic culture-myths of the Yadus (a tribe constituted by seven clans – the *Sattvatas*). Contemporary anthropomorphic representations of these heroes also came up at Bhita, Kausambi and at Mathura. Pillars figure significantly in Mauryan art and their symbolism have been variously explained.
45. Cf., *Parama Saṃhitā*, III.5.6: 'In His mercy to men, He (i.e., God) assumes human shape so that they may recognise Him and turn to Him.' Smith (1969): 2-3.
46. Cf., Pathak (1987): 37-66.
47. Mukherji (1972):19.
48. Keith translates the passage in the *Aitareya Brāhmaṇa* (VI.27), as follows: 'These are the works of art of the gods, in imitation of these works of art here is a work of art accomplished an elephant, a goblet, a garment, a gold object, a mule chariot are works of art ... a work of art is accomplished in

him, who knows thus, as to those works of art (*śāstras*) the *śilpas* are the perfection of the self; verily by them the sacrificer perfects himself as composed of meters.'

49. The text has it as follows: 'He then squats down behind the two skins with his face towards east, with bent (right) knee, while touching them at a place where the white and black (hair) joins, he mutters "... ye are the images (*śilpa*) of Ṛik and Sāman: an image is doubtless what is conformable (*pratirūpa*). Ye are conformable to the Rik and Saman", he thereby means to say' (Tr. Eggeleing). Cf., also, *Vājasneyī Samhitā* IV. 9.
50. The passage in the *Tāṇḍya Mahābrāhmaṇa* is translated as follows: 'That Prajāpati desired that my Indra should become supreme amongst the people. He bestowed garland on Indra. Then people began to recognise Indra as supreme, seeing the same *Śilpa* in him, which they saw in Prajāpati.' I owe this translation to Professor R.V. Tripathi.
51. For the translation of this passage, see above, note 48.
52. Eggeling translated the original passage as follows: 'Now the same threefold science is sacrifice; that manifold form, that varying colour of this [science] is what is [represented by] this black antelope skin.'
53. The original passage in the *Taittirīya Brāhmaṇa* refers to *divasśilpam*.
54. The original passage in the *Taittirīya Brāhmaṇa* (II.7.15.3) is translated as follows: 'with these *Śilpa*-s the Prajāpati stabilised the heaven shapely. With these, he expanded the speech thoroughly. O Agni, you make the king imbued with those splendours by which the Sun is seen with numerous rays, by which the speech is made complete and capable of denoting all meanings. O Agni, you make the king imbued with those splendours." I owe this translation to Prof. R.V. Tripathi. The translation is based on the commentary by Bhatta Bhaskara Misra.
55. This passage of the *Taittirīya Saṃhitā* (I.2.2.1) also occurs in the Madhyandin *Sukla Yajurveda* (IV.9). Devi Chanda translates it as follows: 'After the study of the *Ṛgveda* and the *Yajurveda*, I commence using their scientific aspects, i.e., theoretical and practical. They protect me in this *yajña* in which texts are recited. O Yajña, thou are happiness; give me happiness. Here are those oblations of corn for thee; forbear to harm me."
56. This passage occurs in the *Kāṭhaka Saṃhitā* (II.3; XLVIII.1). Satavalekar translates it as follows: Rik-Saman combined, this you are *Śilpa*. I begin those (*Śilpa*). May they protect me in this *yajña* in which texts are recited. O Yajña, thou are happiness; give me happiness. Here are those oblations. May you be a benefactor and grant me benefaction. Obeisance to you; save me from violence.
57. The original passage reads: *yatte śilpam Kaśyapa rocanāvat indriyāvat puṣkalam citrabhānu; yasminathā Sūryārpita- saptasākam*. *Śilpa* is here the force that brings about strengthening.
58. Dervane (1989-91): 36.
59. *Śukla Yajurveda*, IV.9; see note 16 above for a translation of the passage.
60. Bhattacharya (1991): 19.
61. Pathak (1981): 11.

62. For the details of Tvaṣṭā, see: Misra (2002)/2: 79-81.
63. Pathak (1981).
64. Davids and Stede (1997), sv.
65. Pathak (1981): 2.
66. Monier Williams (1996), sv. *Rūpa.*
67. Gonda (1959).
68. *Ibid.*, (1959): 128.
69. Even in this, the complementarity of *rūpa* with *śilpa* is quite apparent for *śilpa* also signified colour. See, *Śatapatha Brāhmaṇa* I.1.4.3, for instance.
70. Cf., *Vāstusūtra Up.* III.15. The commentary on the *sūtra* (III.15) explains the point further by introducing *hṛdaya* as the element of action in comprehending *rūpa: rūpasya svabhāvānukrameṇa rūpāṇi bhavanti/ teṣāṃ-tattad guṇāh- prabhavanti kāmācāriṇam- hṛdaye iti*, i.e., 'The forms of images are according to their own nature. They manifest their qualities corresponding to each form as they arise in the heart of those who are moved by creative impulse. Desire is the most permanent impulse of human beings'. (Tr. Boner *et al.*, 2004).
71. *Tarkasaṃgraha,* 19.
72. *Mimāmsānyāyaprakāśa* of Apodeva, p. 6.
73. *Nyāyasūtra Bhāṣya,* IV.2.33.
74. Wilke (2002): 108.
75. Tracing out aesthetic formulations in the domain of the 'holy' is a recently emerging phenomenon. But its possibilities are tremendous for often in describing the gods and goddesses in tradition, the details are not found wanting in graphic description of their 'beauty'. In fact, such descriptions become the stimulants and assist in the *bhakti.* A significant example in this regard is the description in the *Rāmayaṇa* about Sita who was as endowed in spiritual grace as she was in body. Sita's un-paralleled *rūpa* is described time and again in the text. It also describesAnjana, Sachi and Mandodari, etc. in similar terms in respect of their physical charm but Sita was a class apart (*Rāmayaṇa* III.34.15-20) and womanly features of unequalled charm distinguished her eminently.
76. *Aṭṭhasālinī* on Dhammasanganī, II. 42, 55.
77. Johnston, tr., *Saun.* XVIII. 15
78. *Abhidharma Samuccaya,* 16
79. Tr. Devadhara (1984-99).
80. Mukherji (2001): 3-9.
81. *Vāstusūtra Up.* III.15.
82. The construction of the dictum that 'beauty of form does not lead to sin' is apparently based on the premise that *rūpa* is something ideal and sin arises from confusing it with the body which may be so endowed with it. In substance, beauty is here regarded as an accidental property – *a daihika upādhi* – accidentally superimposed on a person, and sin arises from confusing beauty with body. In the *Kumārasambhava* (V.1), Parvati herself deprecates that kind of *rūpa,* which rests in its beauty alone for it is ephemeral and destructible, as was the case with the mind-born Kama whose fate lay

in his immolation. Parvati therefore decided to invest her beauty with the rigour and discipline of penance (*Kumārasambhava* V.2): *iyeṣa sā kartumvandhya rūpatām- samādhimāsthāya tapobhirātmanah.*

83. Devadhar (1984-1991).
84. Misra (1980): 179ff.
85. Misra (2002): 2: 116.
86. Bhattacharya (1991): 41.
87. Bhattachrya (1991): 16, verse 5-6.
88. Misra (1994): 2: 105-10. Also, *infra*, Ch. 4.
89. This commentary on the *Vāstusūtra Up*. (IV.2: *rūpāngāni sañjāyate-*) offers a different interpretation of *bhāvarūpa* in arts than that in philosophy leading to misapprehension. For *bhāvarūpa* in philosophical notices, cf., M. Hiriyanna (1964): 354. In arts it seems to signify the latent in the manifested form which makes a comprehension possible by suggestion, much in the manner of 'moon reflected in water' (Misra 1989). Therefore the dictum – *rūpasya bhāvo mukhyah* – (*Vs Up*. III.1), 'the character of the form is essential', in the act of carving. (Hereafter, *Vāstusūtra Up*. is also abbreviated as *Vs.Up*, and all translations of its passages are by Alice Boner.)
90. Sharma (1984): 263.
91. *Ibid.*
92. Cf., Misra (1989). Also Baumer (1985): 79-86, quoting from the *Mahārtha Mañjarī*, 48, as follows, 'Having traced the picture of the world with the brush of his own Self and contemplating it with his own Self, Parameśvara rejoices.'
93. The five senses are: *pāni, cakṣu, rasanā, ghrāṇa* and *stotra*.
94. i.e., *sparśa, rūpa, rasa, gandha* and *śabda*.
95. e.g., *Akāśa, Vāyu, Agni, Jala and Pṛthvī.*
96. In the early contexts in the Vedic literature, *rūpa* has three different implications. It is a design or a form including 'shining form'. It literally signifies scratching, carving or beating into shape, tearing or breaking, derived from the root *rūp* (to pierce). Cf., Pathak and Misra (1986): 282-83. Its etymological meaning derived from the root *rūp* (to charm), is relevant to the arts. For discussion of *rūpa* and arts, see also: Misra (1989).

    Early historical literature indicates different shades of meaning in *rūpa*. It sometimes represents a totality and if subtracted it turns into *virūpa* (*Rāmāyaṇa* I.3.20). This state is mentioned as *rūpa-viparyaya* (*R*. I.22.12) or *rūpa-hāni* (*R*. I.22.12). *Rūpa* is also the opposite of *virūpa* (*R*. III.17.28; 18. 20; 19.1; 23.25; 26). Sometimes *rūpa* and *tanu* are interchangeable (*R*. I.29.8); the same is the case with *veṣa* (*R*. I.48.18). *Rūpa* is sometimes transcended by guile, and in that situation, it is mentioned as *adṛśyarūpa*, a power giver to supernatural beings. It is paired with youth (*R*. I.32.45). It is also the splendour qualifying men (*R*. I.6.16). When paired with youth it is endowed with grace. In these contexts, *rūpa* primarily implies beauty, as in the case of Sita or the *apsaras* Ghritaci or Menaka (*R*. I.32.44; 63.5; III. 34.19). Sometimes *rūpa* is merely a characteristic feature of the specific things but it may turn comely if endowed with proper *lakṣaṇas* (*R*., I.4.11).

97. The notion of the ideal and its counterpart is expressed in these terms as well as by others like *anurūpa, tulyarūpa*, etc. For the *rūpa-pratirūpa* combination, see *Rāmāyaṇa*, I.4.11; III.48.24; VII.94.13.
98. In the Dhvani School of Indian Poetics the quality of poetry lies in the *vyañgya* (suggestion), thereby *sphoṭa* (essence of sound) is supposed to burst out through the process of suggestive and non-eternal series of sounds. Cf., *Kāvyaprakāśa*, p. 2.
99. *Rāmāyaṇa*, I.1.55.
100. See above note 45.
101. III.46.5.
102. Cf., Baumer (1988): 31. Also, Baumer (1982): 27-34. Tvaṣṭṛ fashions all forms in the *Ṛgveda*, X.110.9.
103. *Ṛgveda*, X.90.1, *sahasraśirṣā puruṣaḥ sahasrākṣaḥ sahasrapāt/ sabhūmim viśvato vṛttva, tyattiṣṭhad daśāngulam*. See also *Ṛgveda*, X.90.2-4. The *śilpa* and *puruṣa* association is explicitly established in the *Kauśitaki Brāhmaṇa*, XXV.12.
104. For the *lakṣaṇa, vyañjana* and *pramāṇa* in connection with *rūpa*, see *Rāmayaṇa*, III.17.7-9; 19.6; V.34.33; 35.15-20, 22. In these references, the different *lakṣaṇa*s, *vyañjana*s and *pramāṇa*s of Rama's *rūpa* or identity (*cinha*) are described by Hanuman. These occur in reference to Laksmana also. See also, Ch. 4.
105. Cf., *Dīgha Nikāya*, III.7. They are mentioned in the *Lakṣaṇa Sūtra* of the *Dīgha Nikāya* and in the *Majjhima Nikāya, Sutta Nipāta, Lailtavistara* and *Milinda Pañho*. Cf., Pandey (1990): 127.
106. *Rāmāyaṇa*, Sundarakanda, 35.15-20 describes Rama as follows:

vipulāṃso mahābāhuḥ kambugrīva mahāhanuḥ
gūdhajatruḥ sutāmrākṣo Ramo devajanaiḥ śrutaḥ
dundubhihsvan nirghoṣah snigdhavaṛnaḥ pratāpavān
samaḥ samavibhaktāngo varṇaśyāmamsamāśṛtaḥ
tritāmras triṣu ca snigdho gambhīrastriṣunityaśaḥ
trivalivaṃs trayavanataśca caturvyanggas triśīrṣavan
catuṣkalas caturlekhas catuṣkiṣkus catussamaḥ
caturdaśa samadvandas caturdaṃṣṭraś caturgatiḥ
mahoṣṭha hanu nāsasca pañcasnigdhoṣṭha vaṃśavān
daśapadmo daśabṛhat tribhirvyāpto dviśuklavān
ṣadunnato navatanus tribhirvyāpnoti Rāghavaḥ

Rama, besides Balin and Manuputras is supposed to have had ideal proportions in Nagnajit's *Citralakṣaṇa* (III.149). For the *lakṣaṇa*s in terms of *dīrgha, hṛsva, sūkṣma*, etc. see *Aparājitapṛcchā* 238.5-7.
107. *Rāmāyaṇa*, 'Yuddha Kanda' 48.8-13; II.61.45; III.31.29; 34.15-20; 46.11-23; VII.27.7.
108. Pandey (1990), quoting *Bṛhat Sāṃhitā*, 69.7.
109. *Ibid.*: 143.
110. Misra (1975).
111. Misra (1988): 165.

2

Śilpin (I)

Indian art studies, till recently, have conspicuously evaded issues pertaining to ancient Indian artist and taken Indian art as anonymous.[1] The notions about anonymity have perpetually thrived, aided by western scholarship till early twentieth century that judged Indian art in the light of oriental or classical archaeology and by brāhmaṇical texts that consistently devalued crafts and craftsmen relegating them to the rank of *śūdra*.[2] Even Coomaraswamy, whose contribution to Indian art studies is substantial, held that traditional artist was not given to self-expression.[3] In a marked contrast to such notions, recent researches have afforded useful information on artists, their role in different departments of art activity and the social realities that governed their status and function.[4] The relevant information, so brought forth, helps in eroding assertions about anonymity of ancient Indian art tradition adding at the same time significant epigraphic data on artists and their specific work.

Information thus accumulated, comes from different parts of India, including Karnataka,[5] Madhya Pradesh,[6] Himachal Pradesh[7] and Rajasthan.[8] A document from Orissa,[9] besides some field data from Madhya Pradesh in the form of masons' marks, afford valuable evidence on artists and their work.[10] These materials also help in exemplifying their organisational and institutional network and add significantly to whatever little had been written on the subject by Kramrisch,[11] Sivaramamurti[12] and others.

These materials tend to indicate a vibrant scene of art activity in ancient India where artists emerge as masters diligently performing their designated tasks despite pressures, pulls and ambivalences of the prevailing social, economic and political order in which they found themselves engulfed. If patronage lasted, these institutionalised and debilitating pulls seem to have been neutralised, as their liberty in professional domain generally remained secure and unchallenged. The works accomplished by artists in their time stand today as a living testimony of their skills and dedication. The quality of their work seems to have stemmed essentially from their professional competence rather than from coercion.[13] In the work situations they figure close to their patrons, strengthened by an endearing bond, which – as inscriptions testify – brought them both recognition and status.[14] The masterworks that have survived today indeed testify their primacy in figure work, masonry practices, supervision and performance, in conceptualising the different works, and in managing their layout or construction.

Yet, general impressions of the anomie of ancient Indian artists still exist even as the textual and archaeological materials, now available, wait to be profitably used for insights into individual identities and into the nature and function of artists and their community. We intend to deal with some of these issues in this and the following chapter, starting at the outset with the question of individual identities, including anonymity and follow them up with a brief historical survey of artists' fluctuating fortunes in time up to the Middle Ages. In the last section of this chapter, we propose to highlight a distinguished lineage of a highly acclaimed artist, which lasted for a millennium in the recorded history.

I

Anonymity Factor

The roots of ancient Indian artist's anonymity may be traced back to the peculiar dialectics of textual sources where one comes across contrary assertions about their identity, with priestly class prescribing disabilities on them, and artists appropriating both symbolic and substantive privileges in their exclusive domain of *śilpa.* In that domain, they generally seem to have exercised unmitigated authority and skill – with power to make (or even unmake) the divinities. One may also read into anonymity-identity phenomenon a systematic valorisation, as a result of the priestly temper, of mental pursuits to the detriment of the manual vocations, which, among other things, led to relegation of artist into obscurity. The *Maitrī Upaniṣad* (quoted above) very explicitly offers a glimpse of such prejudices. Several forces were at work in the status formation of artists and craftsmen and their organisation, and the contrary pulls – in which the orthodoxy gained an upper hand – eventually, succeeded in relegating them to a 'low' status, consigned to anonymity. The reasons for this may lie also in the rigidity of an orthodox social system in which the orthodoxy came to deprecate the dissenting systems (e.g., the materialist philosophers) as well as the manual vocations (e.g., *śilpa* and *śilpins*, including architects, masons, sculptors, metal workers and so on) regardless of their merit and worth.

This was despite the fact that manual work, in the beginning, did not have any stigma attached to it,[15] including the stigma of pollution versus purity. *Karma* and *śilpa* occur synonymously in the *Nighaṇṭu* (II.1). In the *Nighaṇṭu* (III.7) again, 'action' as *karman* occurs coincidental to *varpa, apsu, psu, piṣṭa, peśa, aruṣa* besides *śilpa* and *rūpa* – the terms laden with meanings relating to creativity. The juxtaposition of *karman* with *śilpa* and other kindred terms in tow is significant in that 'action' *per se*, including the physical and mental skills involved in it, in the beginning of history stood valorised in the act of 'fashioning' an object. And, in that, it culturally and socially celebrated its dignity and also the powers that it was embedded with. The modes of performance lay essentially in *karman* (from the root *kṛṇ*, 'to perform', with the affix *aṇa* added), a generic term implying 'action', or deeds of any sort –mental, manual, sacrificial, ritual, etc. Its usage tends to underscore a socially accepted norm where 'action' was held high with no pejoratives attached to it. And yet, in time, *śilpa* as well as *śilpī* who were highly regarded in performance of 'action' were eventually relegated to lowly categories with disabilities attached to them in *śāstric* prescriptions. This eventually seems to have had its obvious impact on artists, leading to their anonymity.

A probe into the question of anonymity of ancient Indian artist may, in the situation of such changing perceptions, involve examining individual as well as group identity. Independent of field studies, our source material concerning *śilpins* – both artist and craftsmen[16] – consists primarily of epigraphs and literary texts. In case of the latter, the sources are both secular and religious. Identities whether of individual artists or of their collectively designated groups have to be largely inferred because generally, in texts, references are neither identity-specific nor direct. Inscriptions however refer to distinct personal identities both in terms of their names and designations like *rūpakāra, sūtradhāra, śilpins, vijñānika* or others, which make inferences possible.[17] But the texts including the *Dharmaśāstras* in particular, fail to distinguish artists, i.e., those exclusively involved in creating the works of art, from the general category of artisans and craftsmen pursuing different manual occupations as they are found clubbed together in an all-encompassing basket of the term *śilpin*. This perhaps was because they perceived social reality mainly in terms of the *varṇa-jāti* differentiations and *śilpins* of different orders and skills were all clubbed together in a consolidated occupational group dependent on *vṛttis*, 'occupations', and consigned to the status of *śūdra*. In the situation, a comparison of the literary text with epigraphs turns out to be quite revealing in that while the texts underscored *śāstric* prejudices against artisans and craftsmen, the epigraphs succinctly instantiate their particular categories and their specific (artistic) work, without any hint of disparagement.

Historically, the early Vedic texts tend to exalt craftsmen and consider them as a significant constituent of the *viś*, 'Vedic community'. As we saw earlier, a counter-ideology devaluing both *śilpa* and *śilpins* is seen only later: in the *Maitrī Upaniṣad*, and in some other texts (c. 500 BC to 200 BC).[18] Such a bias of ancient Indian sacerdotal tradition seems to reflect assertions – overt and covert – of competitive rivalry between occupational and ritual-oriented groups for *śilpa* is sometimes explained as a ritual act: *śilpam śruve kriyādike-iti viśvaḥ.*[19] The prejudice against *śilpas*, as they surfaced eventually, proved detrimental to crafts and their practitioners in terms of the latters' social and economic status. In the circumstances, it may not be difficult to infer that the stigmatisation of *śilpa* and *śilpin* and imposition of disabilities on the latter by sacred texts accelerated a process that blurred their identity, relegated them to anonymity, and resulted in their going down under.

While the hostile attitude of brāhmaṇical orthodoxy towards *śilpins* in the post-Vedic age might have aided in obscuring the latter's individual identity, it obviously could not obliterate their pre-eminence as a professional group engaged in artistic pursuits. Assertions of intolerance towards them seem to have never ceased and it may perhaps also explain why craft technology in India, through the ages, did not develop in the manner it did in other climes[20]! Or, why community of artists and craftsmen in ancient India came to be generally dispossessed of a higher status in society despite the dynamics of mobility in ancient Indian society. As for the texts, they continued harping on the lowly status of art-and-craft-related acts including figural work, uncompromisingly. Such attitudes were so pervasive that the *Amarakośa* (II.10.35-37), a lexical compendium, clubs *śilpa*, its collateral terms, e.g. *sthūṇa, pratimā, kalā*, etc. and even the other kindred terms such as *pratimāna, pratibimba, pratimā, pratiyātanā, praticchāyā, pratikṛti, arcā* and *pratinidhi*, under the *śūdra* category.

As against such a rigid devaluation of crafts and craftsmen in the brāhmaṇical sources, the Buddhist texts seem to have accorded greater recognition to them, mentioning the crafts hierarchically in terms of *puthu* or *ukkaṭṭha* occupations. *Śilpa* (vocation) besides *kula* (lineage) and *karma* (action) were primarily the distinguishing markers of social prestige in the Buddhist community. It may be noted that *śilpa* finds a prominent perch here as a denominator of social status.[21] In fact, the ascendancy of Buddhism from around the sixth century BC onwards, seems to have brought about an improvement in artists' status facilitating their greater recognition and identity. Their prescribed status as *śūdra*s must have altered when occupations grew in number[22] and their practitioners came to acquire, among other things, mobility, affluence and group-solidarity in alliance with the Buddhist *Saṅghas*.[23] A settled agrarian economy along with a developing trade and commerce in the wake of second urbanisation also seems to have aided in creating a sympathetic social climate for artists.

In early historical times, departments of activity seem to have multiplied remarkably in the realm of art. And these encompassed *śailālaka, rūpakāra, rūpadakṣa, karmika, navakarmika, āveśanin, śaila-vardhakin,* etc.[24] Diversifications within the different skills of the same craft and their specialisations created new categories along with the pre-existing ones including altogether the categories like *citrakāra,* 'painter', *vardhakī-rūpakāra,* 'carpenter', *kārupatrika,* 'carvers', *pustakāraka,* 'the modelers of clay', *pustakarmakāraka,* 'plasterer', *lepaka,* 'decorator', and *sthapati-sūtrakāra,*'architect'.[25] The *Manusaṃhitā* (VI.47-48) seems to fix a hierarchy of artists consisting of *sthapati,* 'master architect', *sūtragrāhin,* 'surveyor-designer', *takṣaka,* 'sculptor', and *vardhakin,* 'carpenter', in the descending order. The *Arthaśāstra* indicates state patronage and control that came to encompass artists even as it prescribed a system of payment in cash as wages to them.[26] The text also refers to artists like *savitta-kāravaḥ* and *kāru-śāṣitāraḥ* who either had their own capital and workshop and worked for the market.[27]

These developments point to the rising status of artists along with a diversification of their skills in the changing times. Income, occupation, acculturation and prestige are specific alterable factors, and artists and craftsmen must have benefited in these areas, thanks to the rising trade and commerce in the wake of urbanisation, which apparently empowered artists and promoted their individual identities. Epigraphic evidence, coupled with burgeoning art activity under the Buddhist *Saṅgha*s, proves the point.[28]

There are references to special craftsmen attached to royal houses or to wealthy *śreṣṭhin* families and these artists apparently did not work for the market. Patanjali states that a carpenter engaged to work for a ruler did not entertain private work.[29] Acceptance of Buddhism by artists and craftsmen and their ordination into the Buddhist *Saṅgha* without imposing limitations also helped in dispensing with the erstwhile stigma of ritual impurity on them within the Buddhist system.[30] Increment of prestige in the process must have induced greater mobility in the ranks of artists.

The changing social equations as a result of ascendancy of the Buddhism, with *śilpa* besides *kula* and *karma* defining the social status, and socio-economic fallout of the second urbanisation, seem to have rendered the erstwhile purity-pollution model based on *varṇa-jāti* less severe. These developments must have helped in negating the constraints on artists and craftsmen, as they rose up in the wake of new dispensation especially in the process of urbanisation. The anonymity-identity valuation on the grounds of *varṇa-jāti* therefore becomes grossly inadequate in the changing perspective. Firstly, the Brāhmaṇic equivalence of particular *jāti*s with specific occupations automatically collapsed in the cases where artists and craftsmen espoused Buddhism.[31] Secondly, in the new order, the stigmas of ritual impurity also got eroded in respect of *śilpin*s for such converts to Buddhism, regardless of whether they represented individuals or were members of a collective community of artists, ultimately became a part of the *Saṅgha*. The *Dharmaśāstric* injunctions must have lost their force in the emerging situations. The ensuing confidence and the newly found freedom of those pursuing *śilpa*s (crafts) may be read in the *Milinda Pañho* where, in respect of attainments, even *nirvāṇa* was promised to those who practised *śilpa* (see, Chapter I). To artists and craftsmen it signified the privilege of a passage to spiritual fulfilments, a privilege that had remained denied to them in the brāhmaṇical *Dharmaśāstric* tradition.

Yet another aspect of the identity-anonymity problem and status valuation of artists in Buddhism relates to artists' own set-up and their interaction with patrons of art activity. Epigraphs from the Buddhist monuments in central and western India and the Deccan refer to different kinds of artists, their specialisation and functions. Some of them figure as *bhadanta* or *thera* signifying their respectable status in the *Saṅgha*.[32] These categories are art-specific and indicate a diversification, as we saw earlier, in the growing network of functionaries in the professional domain of art activity. In this situation, professionalism, marked by skill, must have become the hallmark and individual artists got opportunity to excel themselves in different departments of art activity, which proliferated with the ever increasing patronage. Buddhism with its wide-ranging monuments and works seems to have espoused them strongly. A Kanheri inscription, for instance, gives a long list of *navakarmika*s, 'overseers', namely, Acala, Gṛhala, Vijayamitra, Bodhika and Dharmapāla, describing them as monks and elders (*bhadanta* and *thera*), along with a *navakarmika*-merchant named Aparenuka. The inscription adds that the work of excavating the relevant cave was 'executed' by *bhadanta* Bodhika, the pupil of *bhadanta* Seumla who was the overseer of the works.[33]

At least five different and parallel sub-systems seem to be operating within the professional structure of *śilpin*s in the early historical times comprising of, besides the (1) artists of eminence who apparently formed an independent category, those working under: (2)-the Brahmaṇical *varṇa-jāti* model, (3)-the Buddhist *Saṅgha* and its various sects, (4)-the autonomous system of *śreṇis*, 'guilds', and (5)-royal patronage or that of elites or the community.[34] Artists' anonymity seems to have continued in respect of the

Brāhmaṇical *varṇa-jāti* category. In case of the third, i.e., the Buddhist *Saṅgha*, art activity having been institutionalised within its framework, artists' identities generally seems to figure within the pre-eminence of the *Saṅgha*. Such a primacy of *Saṅgha* is evident in the inscriptions, which ascribe patronage and control of art activity to the Sthaviravadins, the Haimavatas, the Vibhajyavadins, the Sarvastivadins, the Vatsiputriyas and the Mahasanghikas at Sanchi or to the Apara Mahavanaseliyas, the Bahusrutiyas, the Arya Saṅgha and the Mahisakhas at Nagarjunakonda.[35] In such a scenario, artists often turned into monks imbibing the occupational and temporal roles together, within the framework of the Buddhist *Saṅgha*. The task of staggering the twin roles in one and the same individual in such circumstances is rendered difficult unless they are found pointedly and specifically recorded. The monk-cum-artist status of artists may have offered them security within the orders of the *Saṅgha* but it often thwarted recognition of their professional singularity, individuality and identity. Inscriptions sometimes unravel artists' individual identity even within the *Saṅgha*. But this happened when the community dedicated works to Buddhist creed and in recording the gifts of the community, the relevant inscriptions made a mention of both the donors and artists, even if the latter were monks.

Such a conclusion is indeed possible for we have inscriptions referring to *thera*s, *bhatudesaka*s, *bhānaka*s and *bhadanta*s performing the role of *navakarmika*, 'foreman' in the Buddhist works of art and architecture.[36] Some ambivalence is often observed regarding the artists' mixed identity within the *Saṅgha*, for while the Buddhist texts tend to ignore the relevant monk-artist distinction in the twin roles, the inscriptions often pointedly record it. This ambivalence might be attributed to the contrary pulls on the system in which one, representing the primacy of the *Saṅgha*, blissfully led to individual artists' anonymity while the other, dependent upon task-performance, unhesitatingly underscored them. In any case, it may reasonably be argued that identity and prominence of artists was relatively more secure in the Buddhist system than they were in the other systems.

In the third scenario, namely, that of the guilds, the anonymity of artists seems to have remained eroded in them as the organisation (and its leaders) in that set-up would be more important than its individual members. But information on artists' guild is scarce. This might be due either to the itinerant character of artists or due to stiff competition among them, which often did not allow their coming together under a unified banner.[37] Their identity under the distinguished patrons – rulers and elites – and in their own eminence could never be extinguished and it kept being recorded selectively all through both in early historical times and later, especially in the Middle Ages.

Instances during the post-Gupta period seem to indicate a strong presence of artists with their identities marked explicitly in their names, designations and functions. But, the extent of their freedom in work-situations remains debatable. They still seem to have generally remained servile to their patrons but they skilfully tried to negotiate canonical prescriptions of *śilpaśāstra*s. So, while their personal identity in name and skill remained generally safeguarded, its assertion remained ambivalent as other dictates weighed on him.[38] A text from Orissa, however, reveals a different story in respect of *śāstric* interventions and artist's freedom in such works. The text refers to the brāhmaṇas of Atreya lineage who were settled at Vedapura near the work site when the Sun temple at Konarak was under construction. The specific instances of their function[39] in the camp indicate that while they decided the auspicious moments related to different works or rituals, their actual participation in art and architecture of the temple was of little consequence. On the contrary, the community of artists lodged in the camp took most of the decisions regarding constructional aspects of the work. The artists of ranks lesser than that of a *sūtradhāra* are found instrumental in resolving the controversial points relating to iconography. This may indicate artists' unquestioned professional expertise in professional work.[40] It might also reflect the waning priestly authority on artists and their work, though it will be conceded that ritual status and authority of priests remained unaltered.

Patronage was by far the most significant variable in bringing about mobility in the ranks of artist and in eroding their anonymity. Artists' patrons consisted of princes, commoners, co-religionists, priest[41] and sometimes even those who followed ritually impure professions like that of a cobbler.[42] The instances of artists serving royal patrons turn out to be most numerous in the epigraphs of medieval India.[43] Such patronage generally seems to have ensured artists' identity

The rigours of artists' anonymity were dented further during the Middle Ages, as subordinate ranks of state's bureaucracy, namely, *kāyastha* and *karaṇika* graduated into performing the tasks related to art and architecture. In these cases, their names and functions along with their designations are found accurately recorded in inscriptions. That *kāyastha*s formed a part of state bureaucracy needs no elaboration, but their act as builder of works is worth noticing. Thus, *kāyastha* Devagana is mentioned as *rūpakāra śiromaṇi*, 'the crest jewel among sculptors', who built the temple of Śiva-Bilvapaṇi at Samba (District Bilaspur? Chhattisgarh).[44] Similarly, the *vāstavya*s Vidyadhara and Purusottama designed and built a temple of Rama and excavated a tank somewhere near Rewa.[45] Likewise, a 'writer' of records claims 'adeptness in *śilpa*'.[46] Several *karaṇika*s, some of them *kāyastha*s, are mentioned in the Gahadavala records though their connections with *śilpa* tradition are not specifically mentioned.[47] It is quite probable that engravers of the records were *śilpī*s in the first place, taking up on sideline the job of engraving the records on stones or copper-plates as they were no narrow specialists. We have the Rajim Stone Inscription mentioning Jalahastin, a *śilpaśālin* whose son, the 'pious' (*sādhu*) Durgahastin engraved the record.[48] Such instances represent a role-shift and seem laden with hints of competition. Artists like Devagana a *kāyastha-rūpakāra* may indicate artists filling the ranks of state's lower bureaucracy rendering those offices fit enough to undertake artistic works. Such instances may also indicate competition for the same space between artists of distinction on one end and the state's subordinate bureaucracy on the other, with their incursion into each other's respective domains even as the incumbents merrily proclaimed their competence in art-related vocations. Such a telescoping of two roles into the same office must have allowed the incumbent to switch over to other works even as his original occupational station remained secure.[49] It thus turns out that *śilpī*s, especially architects and sculptors, had perhaps managed to secure the ranks of *vāstavya*s, *karaṇāka*s and *kāyastha*s, which originally were (non-caste specific) bureaucratic positions in the state. Similarly, the *vāstavya*s, *karaṇika*s, etc. had also made inroads into the exclusive art-related territory of *śilpī*s. In the cases quoted above, it is seen that none of those *kāyastha*s and *karaṇika*s really relinquished his other original role or title while performing the works that fell normally into the exclusive domain of artists. What needs being underscored is that merger of different roles into the same office allowed the incumbents in bureaucracy or *śilpa* to switch over to other functions even as their traditional functions, whether in arts or in bureaucracy, continued. The emergent situation may also indicate an increasing involvement and patronage of rulers and state in art related enterprises. Artists' identity is writ large in these instances.

It is likely that such transformations took place in the Middle Ages due to the affluence, honour and authority that *śilpī*s and *sūtradhāra*s might have come to command. No wonders, at the exalted level of *sūtradhāras*, instances of the elites competing with artists for that rank are fairly recurrent. For instance, an inscription from South India refers to Mallavijaya, son of a Daṇḍanāyaka, as the *sūtradhāra* responsible for enlarging a town.[50] The cases of Nagapala, the son of Paṇḍita Uhila, and Jayatasimha, the son of a Bhogika,[51] mark similar transformations.[52] Recognition of artists by rulers and chieftains brought prestige to their ranks even as it acquired for them some political power. The use of certain feudal titles, like *ṭhakkura, rāṇaka* and *sāmanta*, for *śilpī*s seem to support this conclusion. Artists' status seems to have been eventually sanctified even in orthodox tradition. The *Brahmavaivartta Purāṇa* (I.10) attempts to impart a brāhmaṇical origin to them. It states that as a result of a blessing from Brahmā, Viśvakarmā was reborn in a Brāhmaṇa family and the progeny of his union in marriage with Ghṛtācī, an *Apsara* re-born as a milkmaid due to a curse, made up the *jātis* adept in the *tantravidyā.* This story seems to invent a divine-cum-brāhmaṇical lineage of artisans with the semi-divine elements thrown into it through Ghṛtācī.

Strangely enough, while all these developments were apace, artists' professional structure continued to remain asymmetrical marked by a hierarchy of professional stations with diversified categories within,[53] with little evidence about their internal solidarity. Their guilds are conspicuous by their absence, failing to emerge for want, perhaps, of suitable internal alliances. As a result, individual identities in the lower rungs of the structure tended to remain shrouded though they may be ascertained anonymously in the codes of Masons' Marks. These marks have a long history and widespread presence as evinced in their occurrence on different architectural parts of temples and other monuments, especially in North India (see, Appendix).

Thus, in historicising *śilpa* and *śilpin* and their rights of passage, the modifications in their status from sublime to commonplace or the opposite tend to reveal both what was ascribed to them and what they came to 'acquire' or 'appropriate' in substance, with the passage of time. Such elisions and additions altered artists' individual or group identity especially after the relegation of *śilpa* to the category of *vṛtti.* But additions and elision also reorganised *śilpa* as constituting a *śāstra* in its enunciation as *vidyā* or *vijñāna.* There is reason to believe that in elevating *śilpa*s those interventions and modifications also crafted ideological premises for their ascendancy, guaranteeing an alternative future – a future devised, wrought and assured by artists exclusively for themselves. And this future and its logical consequences assured them both release and liberation through an alternative spirituality regardless of social, ritual and spiritual constraints imposed upon them in the brāhmaṇical texts. This progression also imbibes into itself the ascribed status, which *śilpin*s contested, and the appropriated status, which they were able to carve out for themselves. The fact that both the *Milinda Pañho* and *Śilpa Prakāśa* refer to practise of *śilpa* as a means of *nirvāṇa, mukti, siddhi* (liberation from worldly bondage), speaks for an alternative spirituality devised by artists for themselves to the exclusion and banishment of all others from this privilege. The *Milinda Pañho* promised them *nirvāṇa* through *śilpa*[54] while the *Śilpa Prakāśa*[55] assured them the ultimate liberation through the practice of *śilpa,* thus ensuring absolute freedom to them from the cycle of birth and rebirth. They also made a claim to be adept in *vidyā* which was universally supposed to liberate. This *vidyā,* 'knowledge', as we have said earlier, was a practical science,[56] non-scriptural in its content and laid on materialistic bearings with an epistemology espousing *pratyakṣa* alone as the 'proof of knowledge' (*pramāṇa*) and *lakṣaṇa* as the basis of representations or reconstitution of forms.

II

Artists' Outline in History: Vedic Times to the Middle Ages

There seems little in the Vedic texts to distinguish an artist from craftsman though, as we saw earlier, works of art besides techniques and skill are often mentioned in them and have significance in their original context as well as in the ideational perspectives drawn from them that developed in literature subsequently.[57] Early texts have little information in respect of figural representations. But, as we said earlier, *rūpa,* 'form', in reference to material reconstruction or concretisation[58] of the things or objects phenomenal in nature, is often a subject of speculation interspersed with metaphysical overtones. *Rūpa* in the *Ṛgveda* is a 'universal principle'; its primal source and secondary manifestations standing *in tandem.*[59] It is 'fashioned' in a variety of ways and artifice is often implicit in such descriptions. A work of art and beauty is defined by the term *śilpa.*[60] Many Vedic terms explain techniques that have a direct bearing on the processes involved in artificing but artists or craftsmen *per se* do not categorically figure in such contexts. Similarly, 'skill' (*śilpa, śilpatva, daṃśa, kratu*),[61] the essential action or attribute that defines something as a work of art or someone as an artist, is sometimes explained as flowing from the 'intellect' (*dhī*).[62] This adds a different dimension to the Vedic perceptions on a work of art in so far as it may ideally be regarded as a product of the intellect, something incorporeal or evanescent, and yet qualified as a work of art.

Artist also, at this stage, hardly seems to be represented as a distinguished individual constituting a class engaged exclusively in fashioning the works of art. In the *Ṛgveda* (IX. 112), a carpenter or a physician, or a girl grinding corns are all included in the category of poets whose forte lay indeed in composing hymns. Early Vedic texts refer to *vardhakin* (*Ṛgveda* V.35.6; 36.6; VI.32.1), *takṣan* (IX.112.1), *hiraṇyakāra* (I.122.3), *carman*[63] besides *rathakāra* and *kāru,* who are credited with producing works that may fall in the category of works of art in being the products of specific skills. See for instance, the skill of a *takṣan* who embellishes his work with pleasing carvings: *priyā vyaktā taṣṭāni* (*Ṛgveda* X.86.2). Or, see the instance of a carpenter having a disposition to mend broken things, in which, as the passage makes explicitly clear, he might bring his talent or skill to a satisfactory use.[64] The *Aitareya Brāhmaṇa* (III.10) alludes to the dexterity of a weaver mixing patterns at intervals in his work in the fashion of a litanist reciting *nivid*s interlaced with the *uktha* at intervals. Thus, the phenomenon of creativity in the early Vedic framework of ideas is tied up with thoughts and action, ideas and performance, of different orders.

Whether as a divine being or merely as a mortal craftsman, a Vedic artificer seems to stand exalted in his act of creating beauty. A work of art is indeed a *rūpa* 'fashioned' into a phenomenal object. This implication is clear in the texts where the roots *pimś-* and *sic-* occur in the sense of 'carving', 'moulding' or 'fashioning' of an object.[65] Vedic roots like *piś-, han-kṛṣ-, tvaks-* and *ma-*, relate to the technique and artifice involved in the process of the relevant performances and the consummate product of such acts is supposed to manifest itself in *citra, rūpa* and *śilpa*.[66] Ṛbhus, who were mortals turned into divine beings, possessed 'good hands' (*Ṛbhuvaḥ suhastaḥ, Ṛgveda* 1.35.3) and carved the limbs with pointed implements.[67] The action is conveyed here by the root *piś-*.[68] Similarly, as we mentioned earlier, a carpenter (*takṣan)* embellishes his woodwork with pleasing carvings.[69] Or, a 'form' is 'measured' to beings.[70] The process of cutting and shaping is explained by the root *takṣ-* which also implies chiselling and polishing in the *Ṛgveda* (V.2.11: *ratham na dhīram svapā atakṣam*; or *Ṛgveda* III.38.1: *adhitaṣṭeva dīdhayā manīṣān*), implying 'brightening up a song in the manner a carpenter makes a piece of wood shine'. Viśvakarmā, the divine artificer, creates things out of *dhātu* and the act is known as *sanghamana*.[71] Creation is not necessarily a manual activity in the *Ṛgveda*. It is often achieved by sheer mental excellence or by mysterious powers out of nothing tangible, as it were, for we have in the *Ṛgveda* (I.51.10) Uṣanas who fashions (*takṣad*) 'power with power'.[72] Or, we have Sarasvatī in the *Taittirīya Brāhmaṇa* who creates internal beauty.[73] Skill is essentially an attribute that defines someone as an artist and the terms *daṃśana, śaci, kratu, māyā* and *dhīra* imply skills or propensities in producing or fabricating forms, whether material or non-material.[74] Of these different terms, *dhīra*[75] is especially relevant to artisans' skill.

Brief though the details reproduced here are, they yet seem to clarify skills of early artists and craftsmen, divine or human, and their relevance in concretising forms. The act required mental or manual dexterity or both and elevated the doer in that creative act of doing. The idea of art lies embedded in skills, manual or mental, which help in such fabrications. The enunciations contain explicit hints of idealisation of crafts and craftsmen and underscore their exalted status in Vedic society for they were supposed to be endowed with mysterious power.[76] Thus, a *kāru,* as a dear *vipra* to warriors accompanies them to battlefield,[77] or invokes gods' help for peaceful possession of property.[78] In a society that was graduating from pastoral to sedentary life, growing with different kinds of settlements,[79] artisans, craftsmen and artists enjoyed respect of the community. Social relationships then seem to have been based on interdependence within the community and craftsmen fulfilled an important role in producing utility goods for the communuiy even as a *kāru*, a *vardhakī* or a *takṣan* occasionally produced a work of art in wood and justly qualified to the rank of artists in doing so. In any case, the passages quoted above help in identifying the presence as well as function of artists and craftsmen in early Vedic society. Vedic conceptualisations about *śilpa* (Chapter 1) presuppose an exalted status of its practitioners: artists and craftsmen.

Eventually, artists seem to have lost their pre-eminent status as a result of growing occupational divisions in society. The class of warriors and priests eventually rose up while powers and privileges of the community declined.[80] The priestly bias against *śilpins* is indicated by the disabilities, which the sacred texts imposed on the *śilpīs*. The texts from the middle of the first millennium BC contain hints of tension between different sections of society and show that practice of crafts was no longer in tune with priestly temper.[81]

The rise of towns in the wake of second urbanisation from the sixth century BC onwards seems to have produced mobility in the ranks of artisans. Isolation of artisans working within the village communities apparently ended with the strengthening of the process of urbanisation. Works of art found a market and artists found patronage as demands for their work increased. Pāṇini (500 BC) for instance, in a *sūtra* (*ive pratikṛtau*) makes a distinction between the images made for earning livelihood and those made for (sale in) market.[82] The *vardhakīs* and *takṣans* among the *śilpīs* seem to have taken advantage of the emerging situation when stone came into use for monuments.[83] They started working on stone and swelled the ranks of artists exclusively engaged in artwork. The coming into being of craft organisations (*śreṇi*) from the sixth century BC through the Mauryan times onwards[84] and proliferation of Buddhist monuments besides the rock-cut caves of the Ājīvikas on the Barabar and Nagarjuni hills of Gaya under the patronage of the Mauryas, must have contributed to this development.[85] There are specific mentions of art-related works in the contemporary texts. A *Jātaka* refers to a goldsmith who was invited by a prince to make a female figure out of a quantity of gold.[86] The carpenters collecting wood from a forest and constructing dwellings to the satisfaction of their clients, figure in the *Alinachitta Jataka*.[87] The *Milinda Pañho* mentions an architect who plans out and raises a city, and when 'the city was fully developed he might go away to another district'.[88] A *Jātaka* (IV.207) refers to a brāhmaṇa who plied the trade of a carpenter (*vardhakī*). This indicates that the *śāstric* rules about practice of crafts by *śūdras* alone were not always adhered to. *Śilpīs* had now been able to elevate their economic status through crafts. The *Anguttara Nikāya* (III.363) refers to practise of crafts (*sippādiṭṭhāna*), which earned prosperity, elevating the practitioner into the rank of a *gahapati*.[89]

Reference in the *Arthaśāstra* to *kārus*, namely, the *kāruśāsitāraḥ* (master craftsman) and to *savittakārus* who had sufficient capital (*vitta*) to run their own workshops, seems to suggest that different kinds of artisans and craftsmen had come up during the Mauryan times. Some among them had become affluent and resourceful enough to be able to establish their own manufactories and employ others for work. There were still others among them who plied their skills independently, relying on their own resources.[90] The *kāruśāsitāraḥ* and *savittakāravaḥ* were prosperous enough to employ artisans and work with their own capital. Of the two, the *kāruśāsitāraḥ* belonged to the 'class of the rich', and were perhaps 'some sort of master-artisans with assistants working under them'. Employing the artisans for work, they were like 'middlemen who received materials from customers and then entrusted the work to artisans'. The *kāruśāsitāraḥ* describe the artisans who had their own workshop and worked on their own, dealing directly with their customers.[91] Yet other artists operated under the direction and control of institutionalised religions like Buddhism and Bhagavatism.

Thus, a hierarchy seems to have developed among artists distinguishing ordinary workers from those who occupied a position of authority. Such an authority also came from the patronage of rulers or institutionalised religions. Specialisation in particular departments of work also grew among the class of artists now. Their skills seem to have been appropriately utilised by the Mauryas as Patanjali categorically states that 'they introduced images to augment revenue': *mauryaiḥ arthabhiḥ arccā prakalpitā*. The *Arthaśāstra* of Kauṭilya refers to *śilpī, kāru* and other artisans who performed work and received wages. A *vardhakī* is recommended two hundred *paṇa*s as wages while a *kāruśilpī* received only one hundred and fifty *paṇa*s. It is difficult to decide whether rules of forced labour (*viṣṭi*) applied on the artists who were engaged exclusively in works of art and architecture.[92] The Junagarh inscription of Rudradaman of the first century proclaims that in renovating the lake Sudarśana he desisted from resorting to *viṣṭi*.[93] This may have been an exception rather than the rule. But those artists who worked for rulers might have enjoyed better status and economic benefits than others as a result of such proximity. Patanjali, as we have already indicated, says that a carpenter engaged to work for a king did not entertain private work.

The rise of Mauryas appears to have given a great fillip to art activity, promoting both artists and their work. Megasthenes assigns artisans to the fourth caste, but speaks of 'their privileges, like: exceptions from state tax and entitlement of maintenance grant from royal exchequer'.[94] The Chinese travellers to India in the fifth and seventh century – Fa-hien and Yuan Chwang – have remembered the Mauryas, especially Aśoka, for such patronage.[95] Tārānātha, a Tibetan Buddhist historian, mixing legends in the making of Mauryan works, speaks of semi-divine artists performing the tasks under the command of the Mauryas.[96] The vast resources of the

Mauryan Empire facilitated the state to harness artists from different regions into their service, including those of other ethnic groups from the frontier regions of the empire. As we will see below, the recent finds eminently bear it out.

While the *Arthaśāstra* of Kauṭilya refers to the state control and organisation of artisans, the short Kharosthi inscriptions on cylindrical stone-blocks, recently brought to light from Baragaon,[97] (near Chunar, in the Mirzapur District, UP) point to the Kharosthi-knowing stone workers – quarriers, carvers and transporters – at the site. They obviously came from the northwestern region of the empire, and were engaged in quarrying huge cylindrical blocks of the sandstone, the stone that made up the Mauryan pillars. These able and proficient stone workers from the northwest and their supervisors apparently came to occupy a temporary settlement in the heart of Ganga valley while the quarrying and stone carving lasted during the Mauryan rule at what today is Baragaon. The Mauryan date of the extant stone blocks (that remained un-utilised and were discovered only recently), is suggested by Pant and Jayaswal who regard them to be similar 'in length and thickness to the Aśokan Lion capital at Sarnath'. Inscriptions on these blocks refer to two stone workers Śamadama and Hakṣa, the latter being a disciple of Śaḍajaḍa. Eṭhaka, yet another worker, is curiously mentioned in a label inscription as 'one who slept carelessly'. That the work continued at the site in an atmosphere of gaiety, frolic and fun seems indicated by the scribbles on shafts of which one refers to a shaft's capacity to bear 'excessive carving', another to 'road pleasure' which the shaft deserved while in transit, and the third refers to the transportation charge of twenty-one (*da*, i.e., *drammas*?) to be paid as labour charges on the particular shaft.[98] These northwestern artists seem to be of Iranian origin who went into circulation after the fall of the Achaemenids and came to India leaving their marks at Mansehra and Shahbazgarhi in the Peshawar region, Baragaon in the Ganga valley and Brahmagiri in the Tungabhadra region. The evidence of their presence in Brahmagiri is provided by reference to Capada, a Kharosthi *lipikāra* who engraved some letters in Kharosthi in the Brahmi edict of Brahmagiri (and Siddapur), explicitly announcing his act: *capaḍena likhite li(pi)kareṇa*,[99] which seems exceptional in that Mauryan epigraphs do not contain the names of engravers or writers. The liberty taken by Capada might perhaps indicate his eminence or his special recognition in the region where he worked.

Apart from the Mauryas' patronage to artists of Iranian descent, their interest in Greek artistic practices is also in evidence in some of the Mauryan images, such as: the Lohanipur torso, Didarganj Yakṣi and the Rajendranagar *śālabhañjikā* of the Patna Museum. The proportions in human anatomy in these images come out palpably close to the Greek standards of such representations. A comparison of anatomical proportions in the images, mentioned here, indicates only a small degree of deviation from Greek standards with the variations in their Indian counterparts ranging between 1.5 per cent to 5 per cent: 1.5 per cent in the case of the Lohanipur torso; 2 per cent in the case of the Didarganj Yakṣi, and 5 per cent in the case of the Rajendranagar *śālabhañjikā*.[100] Mauryan artists did not always adhere to such Greek proportions and we have other images, the Parkham Yakṣa image for instance, with 'an exaggerated chest proportion', which has a difference variable to the extent of 15 per cent in comparison to Greek standards.[101] The label inscription on the Parkham Yakṣa image tells that Gomitaka, an apprentice (*antevāsī*) of Kunika, made the image. The figure of Lāyāva Yakṣī from Jhing ka Nagla, a close companion to the Parkham image, was carved by Nāka (Nāga?), another *antevāsī* of Kunika and seems quite out of reckoning in such a comparison.[102]

The term *antevāsī* occurring on these images is of some significance. As a designation, it qualifies an apprentice, or an artist in making. The term defines a preparatory stage in an artist's training as he came to join a master-artist to receive lessons in a craft. The term remained in currency for more than a millennium. First occurring in the third century BC inscriptions of the Parkham Yakṣa and Jhing ka Nagla Yakṣī images from the vicinity of Mathura, as mentioned above, the term is found again on a ninth century image of Sūrya from Bengal, now deposited in the British Museum, London. In the Parkham and Jhing ka Nagla images the term *antevāsī* is used to define the teacher-disciple relationship between Kunika and his two disciples, Gomitaka and Naka; and in the Sūrya image it refers to the similar relationship between Ācārya Indranilamani and his apprentice (*antevāsī*) Amrita.[103]

The term *antevāsī* occurs elsewhere also. For instance, Narada refers to five different kinds of *karmakaras* consisting of *śiṣya, antevāsī, bhṛtaka* (who was engaged on wages), superintendent of *bhṛtaka*, and *dāsa*.[104] In this categorisation *antevāsī* is defined as one who may come from a different place and lodge with an *ācārya*, 'master-artist'. The *ācārya* in the situation was supposed to provide to an *antevāsī* residence and food in his home, as he would do to his son.[105] According to Bṛhaspati,[106] the *antevāsī* was required to offer domestic help while in residence. But Katyayana enjoins that the *ācārya* was liable to punishment if he did not train him or if he engaged him in works other than those for which he sought training.[107] The trainee also had his duties spelled out. According to Katyayana, an *antevāsī*, on his part, was required to defray, as *guru-dakṣiṇā* to his teacher, a part of the gains that would accrue to him from works while he resided as a trainee or apprentice with his teacher. The apprentice was allowed to leave his teacher's home only after the latter's consent. If an *antevāsī* was found to be a derelict, uninterested in his work, he was liable to punishment by his teacher. In such a situation, the master-artist could chastise the *antevāsī* or imprison him in his house. On the other hand, if the *antevāsī* found his teacher uninterested in imparting training, he was free to leave him.[108] The apprentices apparently worked for their masters (*ācāryas*) and in accomplishing the prescribed work they had to acknowledge the *antevāsī-ācārya* relationship either for legitimacy or in order to assert their competence that such a reference would certify. Such an acknowledgement might have been necessitated by competition in seeking work or in recruitment.

In the domain of *śilpa,* late during the Mauryan period, the emergence of workshops of master-artists and of apprentices working under them give reason to suggest the beginnings of the *gharānā* system amongst artists and their *gharānā*-related skills. The *gharānā*s may have operated through the direct descendants of master-artists and through apprentices (*antevāsī*s) or disciples who were accepted in the fold as they came from distant places and returned after completion of their training. One may also note the reference in the late Mauryan times, to a guild called Nibhada (Chapter 3), where Gomitaka made the image of a Yakṣa.

In effect, the end of the third century BC chronologically represents the starting point of epigraphic references to artists, especially those connected with art activity though, as we saw earlier, antiquity of this class goes back to the Vedic times. Soon enough, with the rise of Buddhism and other religions, especially Bhāgavatism, the demand for artists and craftsmen rose up phenomenally through Mauryan to Śunga-Sātavāhana-Kuṣāna times. Inscriptions indicate a flurry in art activity, thanks to the patronage of community even as evidence points to individual donors too, vying to construct or install religious works like a *stūpa,* a *caityagṛha,* an image or the like and in doing so, zealously seeking, sometimes even monopolizing, the spiritual merit that might accrue through such 'meritorious' act.[109]

Work now seems to have been available in plenty and artists of diversified skills emerged with titles that denoted their specialties to suit different kinds of contingencies. Evidence on this comes from a large number of sites, including Mathura, Bharhut, Sanchi, Amaravati, Deccan and western India. Bharhut inscription refers to *rūpakāra* named Budharaksita who might have had something to do with construction of the *stūpa* and 'creation of a gateway and stone work (*silākammanta*) by Dhanabhuti' in it.[110] Sanchi refers to two such artists, namely, Artha and Abhaya mentioned as *karmika.*[111] Sanchi also refers to Ananda, the *āveśanin* under the Satavahanas, who built the southern gateway of the main *stūpa.* An Amaravati inscription speaks of an artist (name missing), son of Dharmadeva and a resident of Virapura.[112] Inscriptions from Jagayyapetta in Andhra Pradesh mention Siddhartha, an *āveśanin* of affluence, making a substantial gift to the Mahacetiya at Velagiri. Siddhartha is mentioned as a resident of Mahakandurura while his father, also an *āveśanin*, resided in Nadatura in the district of Kammaka.[113] We also know of *varḍhakī*, 'carpenter', Svamin of Dhenukataka who made the *gharamugha*, 'door', of the cave at Karle,[114] and of Baluka who worked at Kondane. Many of these artists were in the category of carpenters, transformed into *śailavardhakins*, 'carpenters in stone', with their expertise redefined in handling work on stone in place of wood.[115] Inscriptions refer to individuals like Dharmagupta, a *navakarmika*, supervisor of works, who was a pupil of Arya Prasannaka.[116] Mathura comes up with several artists like, Rama, Dharma, Jotisa, Dasa, and Śivarakṣita.[117] A statue of a Bodhisattva (only the pedestal of it survives now) that was consecrated at Sravasti by the Kṣatriya brothers from Vilista and sons of Dharmananda of Mathura, was made (*kṛtā*) by Sivamitra of Mathura, who is styled as *śailarūpakāra*. The pedestal of the image carrying this inscription is now in the Lucknow State Museum.[118] From these citations about individual artists and their titles it may be concluded that in different parts of India, especially in Mathura, Central India, Deccan and in western India, artists of different ranks and skills had emerged to take care of works that came up, thanks to the patronage of the community and elites.

The titles and designations of artists mentioned in epigraphs bring out distinctions and differentiations within their rank. The titles like *āveśanin*[119] (Sanchi) and *navakarmika* seem to indicate authority, signifying a supervisory role of those who had such a designation. Other designations like *rūpakāra* (sculptor), *rūpadakṣa* (painter-sculptor), *śailālaka* (worker on stone), *miṭhika* (stone polisher), *kaḍhichaka* (brick-layer, taking on stone work), *śaila-varḍhakī* (carpenter-turned stone-worker) and *daṃtakāra* or *mahakaṭaka* (ivory-carver)[120] point to respective artists' specialised domains of work. The *Mahāvastu*[121] mentions many other specialists like *citrakāra* (painter), *varḍhakī-rūpakāra* (maker of images in wood), *kārupatrika* (carvers), *pustakāraka* (clay-modellers), *pustakarmakāraka* (plasterer), *lepaka* (decorater), *sthapati* (architect), and *sūtrakāra* (expert of measurements by thread). Such titles and designations appear to be significant denominators of the artists functional categories. This they do covertly or overtly: overtly, as in the case of *rūpakāra* (a sculptor, who fashions forms), *mithika* (a stone worker who polishes stones), *kaḍhicaka* (a worker who lays bricks), *śaila-varḍhakī*, etc. which are work-specific terms signifying the particularity of expertise of the person so designated, and covertly, as in the cases later, in the Middle Ages, of *kāyastha, karaṇika* and *vāstavya,* who were not necessarily in the domain of art but who selectively graduated into the rank of artists with the passage of time.[122]

Little is known about artists of the Gupta times. A notable exception, however, is the instance of Yaśa Dinna of Mathura who carved the Buddha images that have come down from Mathura and Kushinagara.[123] But the Gupta works stands as a testimony to Gupta artists' skill and aplomb. While the contemporary epigraphs contain little information about them, their presence is firmly indicated in the masons' marks that occur in plenty on the Dhameka *stūpa* at Sarnath (see, Appendix), affording some evidence on their muted identity in the instance. These marks together with the Brahmi alphabets seem to represent the particular insignia or symbols (*cinha*) of artists' organisation, prescribed as essential in the later texts.[124]

Coming to the post-Gupta times, between sixth and ninth-tenth century, our information about artists starts growing but relevant details about their specific works of art are generally missing in the sources. There are instances of artists designated as *mahattara, vijñānika* or *sūtradhāra* who often figure merely as engravers of official records. But some of them were skilled artists indeed is indicated in a reference to Jalahastin, a *śilpaśālin* mentioned in the Rajivalocana stone inscription.[125] Others who figure in similar non-specific art work include the *mahattaras* Videsasvamin (sixth century), *mahattara* Suryadeva (seventh century),[126] Sridatta, the *suvarṇakāra* Acalasimha, Dronasimha and the *akṣaśālin* Golasimha, all belonging to the sixth century.[127] The copper-plate inscriptions of the Panduvamsis of Mekala and of south Kosala in the seventh century refer to *akṣaśālin, suvarṇakāras* and a *sūtradhāra*[128] but there is little hint in these sources to their works of art other than engraving the royal charters.[129] Certain categories of artists designated as *sūtradhāra, vijñānika, śilpī* and *rūpakāra* also figure in inscriptions. We will return to them later.

The early Middle Ages, marked by a phenomenal growth in art activity, seem to have witnessed substantive changes in the life and works of artists.[130] Temple building now became a broad-based socio-religious movement in which donors representing a cross-section of contemporary society seem to have participated with great fervour. Apart from the patronage to artists from rulers, even the monasteries offered them work and settled them within the monastic establishment. The Malkapuram inscription (Andhra Pradesh) refers to sculptors, goldsmiths, coppersmiths, carpenters, stone masons and architects employed by the Viśveśvara golakī, the local Śaiva Siddhānta monastery.[131] Rulers across the country drafted artists for work, sometimes even promoting their settlement in the vicinity of temples that they had built.[132] The Teli inscription of Korai Ravi mentions about administration and management of a temple in which painters and sculptors also figure with their assigned roles.[133] The *Samarāngaṇa-Sūtradhāra* (III.30) refers to the *śilpakalāpaṇyopajīvinaḥ* indicating that a professionally endowed community of artists living exclusively by practice of arts had become established in society, serving its different requirements related to art work.

As regards the professional set-up of artists in the Middle Ages, changes are evident in their functional categories. A comparison of the contemporary data with that of the earlier phase indicates – (i) disappearance of some of their erstwhile categories like: *rūpadakṣa, śailālaka, śaila-vardhakī, kammantika, āveśanin, navakarmika, sūtrakāra* and *sūtragrāhin,* (ii) continuation of the earlier categories of *sthapati, takṣaka, varḍhakī, śilpī,* and *rūpakāra*, and (iii) emergence of new categories like *sūtradhāra, akṣaśālin,* and *vijñānika.* There will be more about these last three categories, later. But it may be noted here that different chronological phases indicate different sets of titles and designations pertaining to artists. While some terms, especially *karmika, bhṛtya* and *antevāsī* occur throughout the span of early history down to the Middle Ages, the rest may be dated fittingly into the pre-Gupta and post-Gupta phases.[134]

Sūtradhāras came to occupy the highest position in artists' professional set-up. They planned their work as 'Pṛithu planned the earth'.[135] They recruited workers and other experts for carrying out the work. It seems that the status and role of the *sūtradhāras* had become so crucial, prestigious and lucrative that people of different *varṇas* and ranks competed to usurp not only that role but also that title or designation. An inscription from Rajasthan (AD 966) refers to a *kṣatriya* who took up the occupation of a *sūtradhāra.*[136] Instances of incursion of persons of other ranks and status into the functional set-up of artists are available in records, especially in the cases of *vāstavya, kāyastha* and *karaṇika* to which a mention has been made earlier.[137] The emergent situation, in any case, represents social mobility in the ranks of artists, indicating at the same time opening up of the opportunities at the level of certain offices of the state where their entry allowed them to intermix and interchange their functions and skills with other functionaries who traditionally performed other roles.

Yet, the exclusion of artists such as, *sūtradhāra, śilpī, rūpakāra, vijñānika,* etc. from royal charters in the list of addressees on one hand and on the other, an exclusive presence of those categories of artists outside the state's bureaucratic apparatus, as evinced in the epigraphs, apparently betrays mutual exclusivity of the two domains. It appears that artists' organisational set-up was more or less exclusive, though coexistent in relation to bureaucracy. In seeking work they seem to have been constantly on the move, which would forestall their stay at the same place for longer times. The itinerant character of artists vis-à-vis the state's officers can be gauged from the instance of a Kalacuri scribe named Kumarapāla who continued in his job of 'writing' the royal charters from the time of second Pṛthvideva to that of third Ratnadeva for a period of 14-15 years (AD 1167-68 to AD 1181-82) while artists, drafted one after the other during his tenure, kept on changing. Thus, Kumarapāla came to team with six artists on different occasions including Sampula, a *sūtradhāra* as well as a *rūpakāra* (on two occasions), Devagana, a *rūpakāra-śiromaṇi*, Dhanapati, Jatu and Isvara, the *śilpins*, and Chhitaku, a *sūtradhāra*.[138] This would indicate a comparatively short term of engagement of artists with rulers' work: they tended to leave as soon as the work for which they were drafted came to a conclusion. Itinerant *sūtradhāras* and artists are known from many other sources too. The Baijnatha Śiva temple inscription (year 1126) of the time of Jayaccandra speaks of Nayaka, 'the high-minded son of Asika, who occupies foremost position among *sūtradhāras*, and who came for work (to Baijnath) from Susarmapura as did Thodhuka, the son of Sammana.[139] Similarly, the Girivada stone inscription of AD 1287 refers to restoration of a temple and to the engraver Gangadeva, son of Mumadeva, a *vāstavya* who came for work to that place from Roheda in the Sirohi district, Rajasthan.[140] Master-artists never seem to have remained confined to their native places as demand for their work kept growing. Such itinerant artists figure in inscriptions from early Christian Era down to the Hoysala times.[141] For instance, Someśvara, a skilled *śilpī* from Magadha, worked for the Chandra rulers of Assam.[142] An inscription from Baijnath, east of Kangra district refers to *sūtradhāra* Nayaka who hailed from Nagarkot but combining with another artist of the same place he 'fashioned with chisel' a Śiva temple at Baijnath. They both are said to have accomplished this work 'in accordance with the teachings of the *śāstras*'.[143]

Some of these master-artists came to achieve higher positions in the contemporary feudal set-up, rising up to the status of a *rāṇaka, ṭhakkura* or a *sāmanta*. We have already mentioned a *rāṇaka*, Sulapani of Varendra. Pannaka/Panaka figures as an engraver in one record but in the Nibinna Plates of Mahasivagupta Yayati (tenth century) he figures as *ṭhakkura*.[144] Obviously, the title *ṭhakkura*, which did not belong to him originally, came to him in course of time. Similarly, we find the *akṣaśālin* Khandimalla sometimes mentioned as *sāmanta*.[145] Such titles seem to have feudal overtones. But the rise of some of the artists to such ranks with the privilege of a feudal title (and whatever went with it, which is not indicated) signifies their substantively growing status during the medieval times. This brought to them material privileges and economic well being (see below), and perhaps some ritual freedom too. For instance, we have an inscription referring to a *śilpī* who indeed was a *śāstra-japī*, 'one who could recite *śāstra*'.[146] If we assume that artists were typed into the role of *śūdra*, denied of ritual freedom in respect of reading and reciting *śāstra*, this reference may cancel out the rigours of priestly injunctions or restrictions.

An important development of the Middle Ages in respect of artists relates to their women sometimes joining this profession. In such cases, the skills in a family did not remain limited only to the male members. Family and the homestead had ever remained the hub of artists' training, with home serving as a school as well as the workshop where father and other elders of the family would assume the role of a *guru* for younger members of the family. Women might have learnt the skills in their stride and they, in some rare cases, are found participating in the work, sometimes with distinction. We know of Citrakāra Śrī Sātana whose *vadhū* (daughter-in-law) made the famous statue of Tara, discovered from Mahoba in Uttar Pradesh.[147] Similarly, an inscription of the Chahamānas of Nadol in Rajasthan, refers to Jasadevi along with Pāhini in reference to construction of the *maṇḍapa, akṣasāma* and *damā* of a Śiva temple for three hundred and thirty *drammas*, using stone and bricks for construction.[148] When not engaged in temple-building, the artists settled in villages served the community by performing various tasks.[149] Some served in army; others worked as tool-makers or depended on agriculture or hunting. Kariya Madivoja-Candoja, a Hoysala sculptor who was proficient with a chisel (*uli*) claims to be like Rama in battle. We have the instance of Nemoja who died fighting in a cattle raid and his brother set up a memorial stone to celebrate his memory. There are several such instances indicating artists involved in battles or skirmishes where they ended with sacrificing their lives.[150]

The developments traced out above seem to indicate a gradual rise in the status of artists, which ended up in their remarkably improved positions in the Middle Ages. They came to a close proximity of the upper sections of society, especially the ruling class, which had immense resources, and the priests and pontiffs who controlled large and resourceful monasteries. They also seem to have gained ritual freedom in reciting *śāstra*. As their work diversified, their women also selectively entered the profession. They moved from place to place seeking work and getting it as temples were built in profusion during the times. All this must have ensured their comparative well being and a socio-economically secure place in the contemporary society where they could enjoy the fruits of their labour with dignity. The instances of the compensations they sometimes received in lieu of work indicate substantial dispensations in their favour in terms of grants.[151] Sometimes they received land as reward; sometimes payment to them was made in cash. Work used to be done by them on contract also.[152] The details in the Malkapuram inscription of Rudra indicate that officials and others, including the artists employed by the *Viśveśvara golakī maṭha*, were assigned land, the emoluments of which they seem to have enjoyed with the rights of ownership.[153] In any case, the size of land that was in the hands of the monastery could not have been handled without sharing, and the artists, like sculptors, smiths, etc. attached to the monastery came to acquire some rights on the *maṭha*'s landed property. Ownership of land being the most concrete marker of social and economic status, its possession by them seems to leave no doubt that they gained a respectable status in the relevant instances. Land grants to them come out substantially in the *Baya Cakaḍa* and the details may be quoted here to illustrate the point.

The *sūtradhāra* Sadasiva who planned and executed the Konarak temple was turned into a landed magnate with liberal land grants comparable to those ordinarily received by Brāhmaṇas, or the *agrahāras*! Thus, on the day when the image of *mahābhāskara* was taken up for *pratiṣṭhā maṇḍapa* and installed on a *siṃhāsana*, the *sūtradhāra* Sadasiva *Sāmantarāya* Mahāpātra was given land, etc. to be named *sāmantapura* after his *sāmantarāya* title. Along with the land grant he also received 27 lotus-marked gold *māḍhas*.[154] The *sūtradhāra* also received three *krośa* of land extending from east to west in Lankapada *viṣaya* as a 'life endowment' with a *dakṣiṇā* of 20 *māḍhas*.[155] In addition, he also received a final gift of 100 gold coins.[156] In comparison, the *rājaguru* had received a village and 100 *tola* gold.[157]

The system of granting land or dispensing salary or wages in cash, or making payment according to contractual work in cash and kind – as happened in constructing the Sun temple at Konarak – might have been followed in regard to works elsewhere too. An inscription from Karnataka of the time of the Cālukyas of Kalyāṇī suggests a land grant to a *chittārī* (painter-sculptor) named Jakka.[158] There are several epigraphic references to cash transactions with artists, in connection with their work on monuments. In respect of a Śiva temple in medieval Rajasthan, the cost of building some of its parts has been computed in the related epigraph to a total of three hundred and thirty *dramma*s. This amount perhaps accrued to Pāhini who had constructed the temple with the help of some other artists.[159] The Markula (Himachala Pradesh) image inscription similarly refers to making of an image (*ghaṭita*) by Jinaka at the cost of 'two thousand' (coins?). There is a mention of yet another amount of 4645 (?) in the inscription.[160] But, the figures remain uncertain in terms of their monetary value because of the fragmentary nature of the reference. The Lui Fountain inscription of AD 1105-06 in Himachala Pradesh refers to a fountain made by carpenter Kaṃloṇe, (under the direction of) a *sūtradhāra*. The inscription quotes the cost (contract money?) as 20 (30?) *drammas*.[161] Monetary transactions in respect of payments to artists seem to have become common in the Middle Ages and these references attest to it.

III

The Kokāsa Lineage (*Vaṃśa*)

This narrative is about reconstructing the lineage of an ancient Indian artist named Kokāsa who finds mention in numerous literary texts. Interestingly, the name of Kokāsa does not figure in inscriptions till AD 1159 after which his scion keep appearing in firm historical records till the fifteenth century. As we go back and forth in antiquity in this narrative of lineage reconstruction, Kokāsa turns out to be a historical figure recast into a legendary personage. There is reason to believe that Kokāsa and his descendants continued to make their mark through centuries as they accomplished tasks in different parts of India and beyond.

Recurrent references to his lineage also indicate hereditary character of artists' vocation where skill was perfected within the exclusive domain of a family, which came to provide a firm basis apparently for artistic modes and style. Going backwards in history from the fifteenth century, we propose here to describe the works by Kokāsa and his descendants. We may begin with a fifteenth century inscription from Ratanpur (Dist. Bilaspur, Chhattisgarh). This inscription, dated in Vikram Samvat 1552/AD 1495-96, is engraved on a wall of the sanctum of the contemporary Mahamaya temple. Composed in an indifferently constructed Sanskrit, the inscription begins with a salutation to Viśvakarmā, the patron deity of artisans and reads like a eulogy of the descendants of Kokāsa in eight verses, which follow:

> Among *sūtradhāras*, Chhitaku, the light of Kokāsa family [*vaṃśadīpaka*], is well-known for his proficiency in *śilpaśāstras* and has the virtue of compassion in his heart (*hṛdayam dayādharmaḥ*). By the favour of gods and preceptors, he is the ocean of five sciences (*pañcavidyā mahodadhih*), a veritable Narayana in respect of draftsmanship (*rekhā Narāyaṇovā'pi*), meritorious and truthful.The *sūtradhāra* Chhitaku can work on wood and stone and also on gold, with ease (*kāṣṭha pāṣāṇake caiva kanake 'pi ca līlayā*). He possesses knowledge of the great science, the science of machinery (*yantravidyā mahāvidyā*). The *sūtradhāra* Chhitaku knows how to play on *vanka* and *trivanka* (*vankatrivanka vādanam*) and to carve (?) creepers and leaves (*vallīpatrādikaiḥ*). He knows also the *tritāla* and *saptatāla* (*tritāla saptatālam ca*). The *sūtradhāra* Chhitaku, the able son of Manmatha, is a perfect master of sciences (*vidyāpatiśca gambhīraḥ*) and has fixed his heart on Kesava. His younger brother is Mandana, devoted to three deities (?) and a reader of scriptures ... (*upānga rūpavādi ca kāmasāra grahe sadā, śāstrajapī tribhaktaśca Maṇḍanam laghubāndhavaḥ*). He is devoted to Brāhmaṇas (*brāhmabhaktaḥ*). All merits (*sarvaguṇaḥ*) together with the knowledge of astronomy (*jyotiḥ śāstra*) will be found in Mandana by the favour of Viśvakarmā. The writer is Dityana, the sculptor (*rūpakarmaśca*), (who is) well conducted (*vidyā sarvaguṇeśu ca*) and devoted to his brother, and is praised for his knowledge of sciences and all merits. May there be always bliss![162]

* * * * *

One can here see a reference to four artists of the Kokāsa lineage, namely, Manmatha and his three sons Chhitaku, Mandana and Dityana who are all represented as well-accomplished artists. Chhitaku, a 'master architect' as his title *sūtradhāra* implies, was the eldest among the brothers and most eminent in his profession by virtue of his expertise in draftsmanship, his knowledge of standard measurements in carving sculptures and in architecture, and his skill in carving creepers and floral designs. He was equally proficient in playing on musical instruments, which combined well with his knowledge of the canons of *śilpa*, 'arts'. The record claims his complete mastery over art-related *vidyā*s, 'streams of knowledge', relating to sculpture, architecture, music, measurements and proportions and draftsmanship. He was also blessed with a brother who was proficient in *śāstra*s, 'canons of art', which he expertly recited. In addition, he was well-versed in the science of astronomy, a discipline essential for architectural layout, measurements and proportions, which were extremely important to artists in their work. The youngest brother Dityana is mentioned in the inscription as a sculptor (*rūpakāra*) and he is said to have been a 'writer' also who engraved the inscriptions in question. If we were to accept the claims made in the inscription as literally true it can safely be claimed that together these artists made a complete team endowed with sufficient capacity to undertake and conclude the work commissioned unto them. In fact, the inscription reads like a manifesto advertising their skills with all humility, quite devoid of the brazen manner in which certain master-artists of the Karnataka region in peninsular India proclaimed their merits.

Going back in time we find reference to two other artists of Kokāsa lineage in a copper-plate record of AD 1167 from Central India.[163] This copper-plate inscription from Jabalpur mentions two artists, namely, Talhaṇa, a sculptor (*rūpakāra*) and his father Palhaṇa. Both these artists are stated to have descended from *Śrī* Kokāsa. The honorific *śrī* prefixed to the name of Kokāsa indicates that he had already become eminent and respected as a progenitor of the lineage by the time this inscription was engraved. The reference to lineage is categorical in the inscription in the term *vaṃśa*, which is used while mentioning Palhana, and his son Talhana. The name of Palhana is found in many other inscriptions also, which will be clear from the details below. But in the inscription under review, these two artists are specifically mentioned as belonging to the lineage (*vaṃśa*) of Kokāsa. Talhana is mentioned as a 'sculptor' but he is credited with having engraved the copper-plate after the letters of the document were 'written' by Vatsaraja, an officer of the state.[164] The fact that Vatsaraja, a state functionary, collaborated in the job with Talhana may indicate that like Vatsaraja, Talhana too was perhaps employed by the state and the two together performed their respective roles before the land grant was finally proclaimed. The official character of the copper-plate grant is incontrovertibly authenticated by the fact that it is about a royal endowment of a village to a donee involving the latter's rights of ownership of property. We hear about Palhana again, first along with his teammates and then independently in certain other records which refer to his father Rājapāla also. It shows a growing diaspora of the Kokāsa lineage.

For that, we may come down to a decade earlier, to AD 1159 when we find a Kokāsa as a member of a collective group of artisans who possibly constructed a temple of the goddess Ambika and a *ghat* which is designated in the inscription as *ṣaṭaṣaḍikā*.[165] The Ambika temple was constructed near the road leading to that *ghat*. The inscription itself was found near a cave of Alhaghat (District Satna, Madhya Pradesh), which serves as 'one of the natural passes of the Vindhya hills by which the Tons River finds its way from the table-land of Rewa to the plain of the Ganges'.[166] The inscription is important for our purpose because it is the first ever of the records to mention Kokāsa. But this Kokāsa has none of the aura of a legendary figure, the originator of a line of distinguished artists; he just happens to be a member of a confederation of five artisans including, beside himself, four others, e.g. Soma, Palhana, Dalhana and Kamalasimha; the last being the foreman. All these artists possibly belonged to Kokāsa lineage along with an eponymous member adopting a name after the progenitor of the lineage. For the progenitor, we may have to look elsewhere. The inscription, however, is significant in mentioning Palhana whose accomplishments are reported later from the territory of the Candella rulers of Central India.[167] This would indicate that after completing the work at Alhaghat in the Kalacuri domain he moved over to the realm of the Candellas unsullied by the constraints of immigration from Kalacuri territory to that of their adversaries, looking forward to the new promises and possibilities.

Thus, Rājapāla's son Palhana of Kokāsa lineage, mentioned above, had a reasonably hectic career under the Candellas in whose records, as we noted earlier, he figures in different capacities for fourteen years from AD 1165 to AD 1178. After completing the work at Alhaghat in AD 1159, Palhana came under the Candellas who ruled co-terminous to the Kalacuris in the neighbouring Jejakabhukti region. He is mentioned in a Candella record of AD 1165 as a brazier *(pītalakāra)* who engraved an inscription. Five years later, in 1170, he came to be designated as an artist (*śilpī*) and two years hence, he came to receive the title *vijñānika*, 'knower of the science (of architecture and allied work)'. These developments seem to mark a rise in his professional status. The upward mobility of Palhana in artisans' hierarchical ranks from *pītalakāra* to *śilpī* and then on to *vijñānika* continued even further and, in two inscriptions respectively of AD 1175 and AD 1178, he is mentioned as an 'expert in the discipline of Viśvakarmā' (*vaidagdhī Viśvakarmā*).[168] These different designations applied to Palhana indicate his active career of nearly three decades (1159-1178) in the employment first of the Kalacuris and then of the Candellas with ever rising professional status as indicated by his changing designations, which represented hierarchical positions in an ascending order. Applied to Palhana these designations and titles help in linking up the different ranks and in concluding that professionally artists rose up in hierarchy with accretion of experience and expertise.[169] Above all, the references to Palhana indicate a diaspora of the Kokāsa lineage between AD 1159 and 1178 in neighbouring territories regardless of their different political antecedents of war and peace.

There is more about Kokāsa lineage in literary texts from the Gupta times onwards. Kokāsa story is told in the *Vāsudevahiṇḍī*,[170] a text of the fifth century and is further developed in the commentary of Haribhadra to *Avaśyaka*[171] and in the *Bṛhatkathā* of Hariṣeṇa with mythical overtones.[172] According to the *Avaśyaka Cūrṇi*[173] there used to be a carpenter named Kokāsa who lived in Surparaka (Sopara, Maharashtra). Using his knowledge of crafts (*śilpavidyā)*, he made mechanical pigeons that would fly into the royal palace and collect the royal crop of rice in their beaks. Later, the ruler commissioned him to make a mechanical *Garuda* (a large bird), which could fly in the sky. Kokāsa is said to have successfully crafted this contraption and the prince took great pleasure in flying through the skies in company of his queen. Still later, on being commissioned by the ruler of Kalinga, he built a seven-storied large and beautiful palace for him. In the *Bṛhatkathā śloka saṅgraha* of Buddhasvamin Kokāsa seems to be mentioned as Pukvasa who according to Manu (10.18) represented the offspring of a Nisada man and a *śūdra* woman. The story of Pukvasa (same as Kokāsa), an artisan of King Mahasena of Ujjeni, is given in the *Bṛhatkathā śloka saṅgraha* (5.200-279). The variants of Kokāsa as found in the Jaina texts include Kokkasa, Kukkasa, Kukkāsa, Kokasa, Kakkosa, Kokkāsa and Pukvasa. The Jaina texts like *Avaśyaka Niryukti* (924) and *Viśeṣāvaśyaka Bhāṣya* (3608) also refer to him.[174] In all these texts, he figures prominently as a master-craftsman. In the *Vāsudevahiṇḍī*, the earliest of these texts, he is said to have belonged to Tamralipti and went to Yavanadesa (Greece or Bactria?) with a traders' caravan. Once there, he learnt woodcraft from a carpenter of that land. Coming back to Tamralipti, he established himself as an artist of repute and made a mechanical horse that could fly! The *Bṛhatkathā kośa*, a text of tenth century, refers to Kokāsa as a carpenter who was expert in elegantly crafting female figures in wood. We are told that these female figures were unrivalled in beauty and grace and they put to shame the work of best of the sculptors in comparison.

Kokāsa thus turns out to be a great sculptor who is varyingly associated with the different cities like Ujjeni, Alhaghat, Jabalpur, and Jejakabhukti in Central India, Ratanpur in Chhattisgarh, Tamralipti in Bengal and

Yavanadesa beyond the frontiers of India. But the saga of Kokāsa seems to have been picked up further in the Marathi literature from the thirteenth century. The *Līlācaritra,* a Mahanubhava text of that date refers to Cakradharaswamy who went to Elapura (Ellora, in Maharashtra) and stayed there for ten months. It is said in one of the *līlā*s of the text that when Baisa asked of Sri Cakradhara about the makers of Ellora caves she was told that they were excavated by Kokāsa, the carpenter.[175] The *Kathākalpataru* of Kṛṣṇa Yajnavalki (c. AD 1470-1535) assigns Kokāsa to Paithan and regards him as the master craftsman who excavated the Manakesvara cave (Cave X) of Ellora to alleviate the misery of Yelurai and his wife Manikavati. The text describes the event in some detail and we are told that Kokāsa *vadhai* (*vardhakin,* 'carpenter') of Paithan lived a pious life. He would not take his food without taking a dip in the Godavari River everyday. He was like a veritable Viśvakarmā and was destined to build Śiva's shrine at Ellora. He worked with a contingent of seven thousand artisans and the king's minister was commissioned to bring Kokāsa from Paithan. We are told that on being commissioned by the king to excavate a temple,

> ... Kokas proceeded to carve the mountain and before the sun rose on the morning of the seventh day (he) showed the rock cut tower of the shrine to the queen Manikavati. (When she) saw the tower (she) ... took her food. Kokas thus carved out in a topsy turvy style, the shrine which was named Manakeśvara. He carved many other caves. Thus, a beautiful settlement was raised by Yelurai. It came to be named Yelura.[176]

Kokāsa surfaces again in the *Śrīkṛṣṇa Caritra,* a Mahanubhava text from Maharashtra. But his character is largely mythical in this text. He is identified in the text with the demon Margajasura who is killed by Kṛṣṇa. But he is said to have had a friend named Drumil who is 'credited to have excavated an underground settlement in Ellora caves'.[177]

The foregoing account presents Kokāsa both as a skilled master-craftsman and a mythical figure. He is associated with many a place within the Indian subcontinent, the places like Sopara, Paithan and Ellora in western India, Ujjain, Alhaghat, Jabalpur and Jejakabhukti in Central India, Orissa on the eastern coast, Tamralipti in Bengal and Yavanadesa beyond the frontiers of India. Kokāsa legends may be traced back to fifth century in the Jaina texts. But his accounts are not limited to texts alone. References to him in the copper-plate grants are authentic and their historicity may not be in doubt. These inscriptions are significant in historicising Kokāsa lineage firmly. The repertory of such heritage could be vast and fairly expansive for Kokāsa lineage is credited with having built temples, *ghat*s and rock-cut caves and crafted sculptures at many sites between fifth and fifteenth century.

In tradition, there apparently exist two distinct streams in regard to *śilpins*. One stream identifies them with occupations and consigns them to the occupational groups practising crafts considered low in the hierarchy of social stratification. The other stream relates them to the acts of creativity in terms of figural and structural compositions where they find mention mainly in reference to the specific works that they accomplished. This latter stream exhibits their highly elevated professional status as against the former where they are found subjected to all kinds of debilitating restrictions in status and value.

NOTES AND REFERENCES

1. Cf. Misra (n.d.), 'Anonymity of Ancient Artist', *Kalakshetra* (Madras), Vol. V, no. 4, pp. 3-9.
2. *Supra*, Chapter I.
3. Such views are no longer tenable and have been considered ahistorical in content. Cf., Desai (1984): 61.
4. Misra (1975).
5. Cf., Settar (1992); (1973): 419-435; Padigar (1986): 74-88; Padigar (1988): 398-405; Misra (1985): 185-190. Also see, *Ibid.*, pp. 191-193.
6. Singh (1993): 222-237; Misra (n.d./1984): 65-72, Fig. 1.
7. Cf., Thakur (1986): 303-312.
8. Vashistha (1995).
9. Boner, Sharma and Das (1972): 45-178. It contains the edited and translated version of a text, called *Baya Cakaḍa* which affords a biography of the Konark temple as it grew from scratch to completion and consecration. It is a unique treasury record, important especially for its materials regarding different operations in constructing the temple. It was maintained as a ledger of expenses by an accountant who, for a period of more than twelve years, meticulously documented receipts and expenditure incurred in building the temple and in sustaining at least three camps of artists, namely, Rupasa, Pateli and Duai (Boner *et al.*, 1972: 62, 71, 76, etc.) in Konark, as the work progressed there. These exclusive camps accommodated construction workers and their helpers.
10. These marks are found in different shapes and size, often crudely etched on stones of the particular works, and represent undefined signatures in symbolic, geometrical drawings. The graphemes perhaps represented workers' guilds – mobile and itinerant in character – that seem to have remained in operation, sometimes for centuries.
11. Kramrisch (1958): 224-230.
12. Sivaramamurti (1934): 31-54; 158-199.
13. Evidence of coercive pressures on artists, whether as individuals or as part of the manual workers' community, is generally absent except for the fact that Dharmaśāstric codes assigned to them a socially lower status as *śūdras*.

The available information points to their uninterrupted involvement with and commitment to work. Even wars and change of ruling dynasty failed to hinder them. Cf., Misra (1994)/3: 211-215 quoting a Chandella inscription of VS 1298 and a Kalachuri inscription of the time of Vijayasimha (AD 1188-1220) which refer to Dage (an *ayaskāra*) and his son Kukem (a *vijñānika*) and grandson Kikaka of Kakredi, a flourishing town in the Rewa region. The occurrence of the name of these artists in the inscriptions of both the Candellas and the Kalachuris – who were at war – indicates that battles between and changes in the ruling dynasties did not affect the artists or their work. The artists, mentioned above, plied their trade unhindered: receiving both patronage and work, regardless of whoever came to power. No wonder that Kakredi became renowned for its 'sky-high mansions of gods' and a temple of Rama.

14. Padma, a Chandella artist, is described as 'able' one, superior to all other artists. He was as eminent as was his father. In addition, he was a favourite of the Candella ruler Paramarddi. When the latter composed a eulogy for Śiva, Padma, his favourite, engraved it. Misra (1994): 211-212. A Kalachuri artist (name missing) similarly proclaims having made an image of a goddesss, as he was 'absorbed in the glory (springing from) the ocean of liberality, prowess and justice of ... Karna', the Kalachuri ruler. Cf., Mirashi (1955): 252.

15. Mark the rigour underlying mental or manual work, identically extolled and considered *at par*, in early references, e.g.: 'Indra composes a song like a carpenter makes a chariot: *aham taṣṭeva vadhuram paryacāmi hṛdā matim*', *Ṛgveda* X.119.5; or, 'with wisdom (*dhīra*), a poet composes a poem like a carpenter fashions a chariot': *ratham na dhīram su'apā atakṣiṣu*, in the *Ṛgveda* X.130.6; or, the *Ṛgveda* I.67.10 where the sages 'make him as if building a seat'; see also, the *Ṛgveda* V.2.11; V.29.15 where the chariot-maker, e.g., a carpenter, is supposed to be *dhīra* (wise). The Commentary explains *dhīra* as *dhīmān*, 'full of wisdom', and *svapā* is there is explained as *śobhana karma*. Identity in mental and manual dexterity is expressed again in the case of Ghoṣā, the Vedic poetess who 'composes' a hymn like the Bhṛgus fashioned a chariot, in the *Ṛgveda* X.39.14. See also the *Ṛgveda* V.2.11; V.73.10; IV.16.20; or in respect of *vidmanāpaśaḥ*, *Ibid.*, I.111.1; I.31.1 or in the case of the *kārus* in *Ibid.*, II.39.8; VIII.62.4. The root *takṣ* signifies *śobhana karma* that involves fingers of the 'wise' (*Ṛgveda* I.130.6) for a *dhīra* is supposed to be intellectually endowed even as he may be equipped with beautiful fingers (*śobhanānguli yuktaḥ*, Comm. on the *Ṛgveda* I.64.1), if he happened to be a manual worker too. These references bear out the parity between mental and manual work in the beginning with no pejoratives attached to the work by hand, a point that was made later in Baudhayana who says *nityam śuddaḥ kāruhastaḥ*. For the Bhṛgus, the celebrated Vedic craftsmen with deft hands (*suhastaḥ*) and skilful, and who could even grant dexterity, cf., *Ṛgveda* X.33.1, 8; III.60.1, 3, 4; IV.35.8; V.35.3; I.110.4; V.35.3; I.110.4; I.20.1, 8; I.21.6, 7; I.111.2. Also, the *Bṛhaddevatā*, III. 83-88.

16. It may be stated at the very outset, that, in tradition, artist, artisan and craftsman seem to be interchangeably clubbed together within the conventional term *śilpin*. All crafts figured as *śilpa* (*sippa* in Buddhist texts) and their practitioners as *śilpin*. In texts and inscriptions, the works of art e.g., an image, a painting, an architectural work and so on, are often recorded as works of special skills (*śilpa*) edifying the doers who invariably had a specific title or a designation that marked their status in the hierarchy of artists' community. Such edifications through titles and designations represent a tacit recognition of an artist's specialised skill, suggesting that ordinary workers (*karmakara, bhṛtya*) were catapulted into hierarchically higher ranks commensurate with their specialised vocational skills. Such designation(s) are, in a way, the tangible markers of the stations in an ordinary worker's elevation from ranks to the higher cadres (e.g., *rūpakāra, śilpin, vijñānika, sūtradhāra*, etc.) of the artists of recognised standing. It may be therefore, suggested that designations and titles represented an ordinary craftsman's elevation and rehabilitation to the level of an artist. Yet, it must be underscored that such elevations never precluded the possibility of an exalted artist performing craft-related sundry works in addition to those concerning his specialised domain, which had initially earned him a specific title or designation. The ordinary work and the specialised skilled work seem to have coexisted in the work ethic of artists in ancient India.
17. Misra (1975): 34-56.
18. Such attitudes are quite in contradiction with *Jaiminīya Brāhmaṇa* (III.1 where *śilpa* (art work) is involved in the gold of two orders, 'pure' (*avikṛtāni* and 'impure' (*vikṛtāni*). It is said that Prajāpati made this world out of a mass of unwrought gold. In the *Jaiminīya Brāhmaṇa* (I.26) again *śilpa* is classified into *varṇa* categories in that it occurs in reference to three caste (*trivarṇika*) metres with their respective art objects like, elephant, *niṣka*, mule chariot, horse chariot, *rukma, kaṃsa*, cow, horse, golden elephant, goats and sheep, etc. which are differently classified in *varṇa* categories.
19. Cf., Panasikara (2002): 349, sv. *Śiti*. Similarly, in the *Śāṅkhāyana Śrauta Sūtra* (VIII.2.2) *śilpākhyaśāstra* is a technical term in which the *Ṛk* verses are recited in imitation. The idea of imitation occurs also in the *Gopatha Brāhmaṇa* (II.6.2 where *śilpa* is indeed the lauding of divine world: *yadeva śilpāni śaṃsati, ta svargasya lokasya rūpam.*
20. Needham (1965): *Science and Civilization*, Vol. II, Cambridge; Burnell, 1969 *Science in History*, Vols. I-IV, Penguin; Farrington, ed., 1963: *Greek Science* Penguin; 1947: *Head and Hand in Greece*, London; 1946: *Science and Politics in Ancient World*, London.
21. Chakravarti (1987): 111.
22. The *Jatakas* refer to eighteen crafts (perhaps, a stock number), the *Majjhima Nikāya* refers to twelve, the *Dīgha Nikāya* to twenty, the *Milinda Pañho* to seventy-five and the *Mahāvastu* refers to forty-five *śilpāyatanas* (crafts). For different *śilpas* in practice and their practitioners, as mentioned in different texts and inscriptions, cf., Misra (1975): 4-11.

23. Sometimes artisans received a share in the grants made to the *Saṅgha*. There is a specific instance of five per cent share of the land grant made to *Saṅgha* going to artisans. Cf., Misra (2002)/1: 1276.
24. Cf., Misra (1975): 8-12; 15-18.
25. *Mahāvastu* (tr), J.J. Jones, III.112, 414.
26. The *Arthaśāstra*, V.3.12, 16, in connection with the salaries of artisans employed by the state, prescribes two thousand *paṇa*s for a *vardhakin* but only one hundred and twenty *paṇa*s for a *kāruśilpī*. The *Arthaśāstra* (IV.1.2-4, 65) also lays down rules for protecting artisans and for guarding troubles from them.
27. Kauṭilya's *Arthaśāstra* IV.1.2. Pāṇini's *Aṣṭādhyāyī*, preceding Kauṭilya, also refers to different kinds of craftsmen, e.g., *grāmaśilpin* (VI.2.62), *grāmatakṣa* (V.4.95), and also, as mentioned by Agrawala, to *kauṭatakṣa*. Of these craftsmen, a *grāmatakṣa* worked for the entire village while a *kauṭatakṣa* worked independently in his own workshop. Cf., Agrawala (1963): 230.
28. Misra (1975): 9ff; Also, Misra (2002)/1: 1273-1277 indicating, among other things, supremacy of the community rather than *varṇa-jāti*, and the role of community in building activity in which the artisans played a major role with the support of the Buddhist *Saṅgha*. This also brought benefits to the artisans.
29. Desai (1976).
30. Misra (1975):19.
31. Cf., Misra (1975): 19.
32. Buddharakṣita, a *thera*, styled as *bhadanta* and acting as *navakarmika* is mentioned in an Amaravati inscription, Misra (1975):18.
33. Cf., Bühler, ASWI, IV, p. 76. The cases of Nandibala, a *śailālaka* of Mathura, of Siddhartha, an *aveśanin* from Jaggayyapetta, and Ananda from Vidarbha who went to Sanchi to work, prove that professionally competent artists – both sedentary and local, and those itinerant and willing to move out – were in circulation, making their mark. They were apparently in demand in recognition of their skill and expertise. Misra (1975): 15-16.
34. For patronage of the community, cf., Misra (1975): 26-30; also, Thapar (1992): 19-34; Dehejia (1992); 35-45 in Miller (1992).
35. Misra (1978): 87, 117.
36. Misra (1975):18, 21-22; Mehta and Choudhury (1976): 121,179.
37. For a description of some individual artists, see: Sivaramamurti (1961): 1-14.
38. It may have been incumbent upon them to function under the dictates of *śāstra*s as formally interpreted by a brāhmaṇa priest. For instance, we have a tenth century metal image from Hatkoti containing an inscription about its being conceived (*kalpitam*) by Bhattasri (a brāhmaṇa, as the name would suggest), and made (*ghāṭitam*) by Padmanatha, son of Ḍahila, a *kāyastha*. Cf., Chauhan (2002): 57-61. Our translation varies from that of Chauhan.
39. *Baya Cakaḍa*: 52, 69, 91, 101,125,130.
40. In one of such cases, as described in the *Baya Cakaḍa*, a sculptor named Viśī Mahapatra, supplied three *kanyā* figures on contract, to be set up on the

pīdhā of the Konark temple. Narayana Mahapatra objected to one of these figures saying that it was a portrait of Viśī's wife. The image objected to, was consequently rejected and only the other two images were accepted for installation and payment. So, Viśī received a payment of only four *māḍhas* (one *māḍha* was worth two grains of gold) for the two figures. But that was not the end of the episode. Ganga Mahapatra (who carried the title of *pāthuriya paryanga kulanāyaka)* soon intervened, declaring that the discarded image had indeed been carved on a lotus pedestal, as required for a divine image and therefore, its rejection was not in order. As for its likeness with Viśī's wife, it was explained as accidental and of no consequence. So, the third image too was accepted which brought to Viśī two more *māḍhas*. Cf., Boner, Sarma and Das (1972): 157.

41. The Jhalarpatan Varāha image inscription refers to a Lakulīśa saint Isānajamu with Sīhaṭa as a *karmakāra-bhṛtya,* serving him. Cf., D.R. Bhandarakar, *JBBRS*, Vol. XII, pp. 151ff. A Khajuraho image of four-legged Sadāśiva with an inscription similarly describing the Śaivite *ācārya* named Ūrddhvaśiva who must have commissioned it but the name of artist is not mentioned in this case. Cf., Deva (1990): 378. In early historical times, specially during the Suṅga-Satavahana phase, the community emerged strongly in offering patronage collectively with contributions from *śreṣṭhins*, scribes, ploughmen, perfumers, carpenters, corn-dealers, *gaṇikā*, etc. besides the ministers, princes and chieftains. Cf., Misra (1975): 25-29. But instances are known where state functionaries also executed royal works. The instances of Ananda, a Satavahana master-artist (*āveśanin*, cf., J. Marshall *et al.* (1939) Vol. I, insc. no. 398), Skandasvati, cf., Lüders (1909-10): insc. no. 1186) and Suvisakha (*Ibid.*, insc. no. 965) support these conclusions. Skandasvati was a minister as well as a *kammantika.*
42. Cf., Misra (1985): 188, quoting an inscription of the Kalacuris of Raipur in Chhattisgarh which reads as follows: 'There shines Devapala, the son of a repository of merits named Sivadasa and grandson of ... Jasau, a shoe-maker ..., who is clear in performance of his work (e.g., shoe-making) ... (who) is fond of various pious deeds. He has caused to be constructed a temple of Narayana together with a *maṇḍapa.*' The work was done by *sūtradhāra* Ratnadeva. The, *Praśna Saṃhitā,* a Pancaratra text, permits a *śūdra* or even an *anuloma*-born to build a temple. Cf., *Śrī Praśna Saṃhitā* IV.16-18.
43. Misra (1975): 31-75; Agrawal (1957): 321-334.
44. Mirashi (1955), insc. no. 93.
45. *Ibid.*, pp. 357-358. For a *vāstavya taṭṭhakāra* named Harivardhana, under the Bhauma-Karas of Orissa, cf., Tripathy (2002): 108. Panaheda stone inscription of Mandalika of AD 1059, under the Paramaras of Vagada was engraved by Asaraja, the son of Sridhara of the *kāyastha* family of Valabhi. Trivedi, n.d., *CII*, Vol. VII (ii), p. 285. It seems that the family had shifted from Valabhi but their roots continued to be recalled. The inscription refers to building of a Śiva temple. The father and son find mention again (*Ibid.*, p. 289), but they figure as 'writer'(s).
46. Mirashi (1955): 470.

47. Cf., *Epigraphia Indica*, IV, pp. 101-124. Inscriptions also refer to *karmakaras*, which is explained as 'chief artisan'. Cf., Sircar (1965): 373, 374.
48. Tripathy (1997): 166.
49. In these instances none of those persons whether artists or the *kāyasthas*, *karaṇika*, etc. relinquished his original role or title while performing his work one way or the other. Which may indicate that due to incursion of artists into the state service or those of the services into the mould of artists, different roles got telescoped into the one and the same office so that persons in such position could conveniently switch over their roles to the contingent requirements even as their traditional functions in their original station might have continued unabated.
50. *Epigraphia Carnatica*, V (i), no. 194, p. 433; transl. p. 187. The *Rājavallabha Maṇḍanam* of Mandana is the only text which reserves the title of *sūtradhāra* only for a *brāhmaṇa*. No such proclivity is seen in the other *śilpa* texts like the *Aparājitapṛcchā* (ch. 49.1-18; ch. 50.1-14) or the *Samarāngaṇa Sūtradhāra* (ch. 44) when they discuss the qualifications of the *sthapati*.
51. For a *bhogika* (precisely, a *dharabhogika*) engraver of an eighth century record, cf., Tripathy (1997): 148.
52. Cf., *Epigraphia Indica*, XXX, 248; XXXII, 304. Bhandarkar's List: insc. no. 2048. There are many *simha* ending names of engravers and *sūtradhāras*, e.g. Kelisimha, Karmasimha, etc. Cf., Bhandarkar's List, nos. 578, 610. In the former, a record of vs 1330, Kelisimha is said to have engraved the record 'with further help of *śilpī* Delhana. In the second record of vs 1342 he finds mention as a *sūtradhāra*. Among the *simha*-ending names we have Dronasimha also. *Epigraphia Indica*, XXXI, 106, 316. There are other instances where the first generation names consisted of artists like Nahada and Vahada while their following generation assumed the names like Punasimha and Kumarasimha. Cf., Bhandarkar's List, nos. 611, 491.
53. Boner, Sarma, Das (1972): 259 refer to 52 such categories; some artists, covered under those categories, are identified in the text.
54. *Milinda Pañho* (ed. Trenckner), p. 315.
55. *Śilpa Prakāśa*, II.809: Of All the *Śāstras*, the Śilpa taught by Viśvakarmā is the highest. Constructing an excellent temple gives liberation (*muktidām*) and bestows all *siddhis* (*sarvasiddhipradāyam*), Also, *Ibid.*, II.710.
56. *Śilpa Prakāśa*, I. 557-569 refers to different terms derived of *śilpa*, e.g., *śilpaśāstra*, *śilpanirnaya*, *śilpavidyā*, *śilpānga*, and finally comes to describe its composer as an 'excellent *śilpī*' (*śilpipravara*). The *Śilpa Prakāśa*, I.558, also says that canonical prescriptions differ according to regions and times in the canons of Śukrācārya and Viśvakarmā.
57. Cf., Misra (1989): 178-181.
58. For instance, Tvaṣṭṛ adorned all beings with 'form': *Ṛgveda* X.110.9; or see the *Ṛgveda* X.184.1: *Tvaṣṭā rūpāni piṃśatu* "he created all 'form' (*rūpa*)"; whether in humans or in beasts, *Ibid.*, I.88.9.
59. As for instance, in the *Ṛgveda* (VI.47.18) where 'form' and its 'counter form' seem to stand ever in corelation: *rūpam rūpam pratirūpo babhūva tadasya rūpam pratichaksaṇāya*.

60. Cf., Misra (1988): 145-169.
61. For *śilpatva*, see, *Tāṇḍya Mahābrāhmaṇa* (XVI.6.3), *uṣṇiṣam bibharti śilpatvayā*: 'He wears a turban for the sake of its being an object of art'. See also, Monier Williams (1996) sv. *Silpatva*, as quoted in the *Pañcaviṃśa Brāhmaṇa.*
62. Cf., Chattopadhyaya (1978): 260ff.
63. Macdonell, Vedic *Index*, Vol. I, pp. 234, 257.
64. *Ṛgveda* IX.112.1.
65. Pathak (1981): 12-13. Thus Tvaṣṭṛ 'carves' (*piṁśatu*) the 'forms' (*Tvaṣṭā rūpāṇi piṃśatu, Ṛgveda* 10.184.1) or the beauty of Uṣas is described as *suśilpa* (*Ṛgveda*, IX.5.6; X.70.6) or, the works of art and craft like an elephant, a goblet, a garment, an object of gold or a mule chariot are made in 'imitation' (*anukṛti*) of 'divine crafts' (*deva śilpa*). In the *Aitareya Brāhmaṇa* (VI.27), 'harmony' (*chandas*) characterises such works, which in performance are supposed to 'culture the self' (*ātmānam samskurute*).
66. Cf., Pathak and Misra (1986): 280-290.
67. The *Ṛgveda* VIII.76.12 refers to a chisel which is designed to move on.
68. *māmsamekaḥ pimśati Śūnayabhṛitaṁ, Ṛgveda,*1.161.10.
69. *priyā vyaktā taṣṭāni, Ṛgveda*, X.66.5
70. *ni māyino māmire rūpam asmin, Ṛgveda,* III.87.7; III.87.9. In these references or even elsewhere the word *māyā* from the root *mi* implies acts relating to an object or things; for instance, *Cyavanaḥ sudair abhinīti vedī,* in the *Ṛgveda* X.61.2; or the *Śatapatha Brāhmaṇa* 6.5.3.3 where brick work is intended. In the *Atharvaveda* III.12.5 or IX.3.6 the term *māna* from the root *mi* is used for building. The term *nir-mā* similarly implies 'fashioning', 'making', 'producing', etc. by craftsmen. Cf., Gonda (1959): 67.
71. Misra (1975): 5, quoting Agrawala (1965): 40.
72. *takṣad yat Uṣanā sahasaḥ sahaḥ, Ṛgveda*, I.51.10.
73. *Sarasvatī vayati peśo antaraḥ, Taittirīya Brāhmaṇa*, II.6.4.1. It appears that the root *piś-* and its derivatives occur in the sense of artistic creations connoting adornment, ornamentation, painting, designing, moulding, etc. There might be different agents, mythical, divine or human, for such artistic creations, e.g., Uṣas, Saraswatī, sacrifice, and even an *adhvaryu*. Cf., *Ṛgveda* I.92.5; *Taittirīya Brāhmaṇa* II.6.4.1; *Ṛgveda* II.3.6; VII.42.1. Prem Sagar Chaturvedi,'The term *śilpin* and its meaning', an unpublished paper.
74. Cf., *Ṛgveda* I.119.7; 7.69 7 for *damśana; Ibid.*, I.117.13; I.112.8 for *śaci; Ibid.*, I.39.1 for *kratu*. For *māyā*, cf., Gonda (1959): 119-193.
75. Cf., *Ṛgveda*, I.64.1, *apaḥ na dhīra manasā suhastyaḥ*. According to *Sāyana dhīra* implies someone endowed with intellect (*dhīmān*), and *suhastya* qualifies one having 'good fingers' (*śobhanāguli)*. Attention may be drawn to the *Ṛgveda* V.2.11; V.29.15 and to I.67.5 (*sadmeva dhīraḥ samayā cakruh*), in this reference. In these references *dhīra* seems to denote an expert or an artisan.
76. Cf., Gonda (1959): 187ff.
77. *Ṛgveda*, 10.61.23.
78. *Ibid.*, VII.82.4. Artisans also make a thunderbolt (*vajra*) for Indra, *Ibid*. X.92.7. They figure in the coronation ceremony of a king. By certain special acts, they accord recognition to royalty. For chariot maker (*rathakāra*), blacksmith

(*karmāra*) and woodcarver (*takṣan*), Cf., Sharma (1983). About *rathakāra*, cf., Jha (1974): 39-47.

79. Misra (1985): 73-78, 24-26, 56-60 and 24ff., for discussion on different settlements like *vraja, chhardi, pastya* and *grāma*.
80. Sharma (1983): 74ff.
81. See, chapter I, also, Chattopadhyaya (1977).
82. Cf., Misra (1978): 35. In the *Sūtra* V.4.95, Pāṇini distinguishes between a village artisan (*grāma takṣan*) and a *takṣan* who worked in his own workshop.
83. The term *śaila-karma* and *śaila rūpa-karma* in the inscriptions of early Christian Era apparently distinguish stone work from wood work and thus indicate changes in techniques and medium employed by artisans. A new class of *śaila vardhakī*s seems to have emerged now with carpenters (*vardhakī*s) turning into workers on stone (*śaila vardhakī*s). Svāmin, one such worker on stone, made the facade (*gharamugha*) of the rock-cut cave at Karla. Balaka, another such artist, did similar stone work at Kondane. Inscriptions from Karla and Kondane provide the relevant information. Cf., Misra (1975): 27, 24, 22.
84. Thaplyal (1996): 24-36. As we shall see later, a corporate *pūga* finds mention in the Parkham image inscription of the Mathura Museum.
85. *Ibid.*, pp. 9-10. The *Arthaśāstra* of Kauṭilya directs the state to protect *śilpī*s. The state also exercised control over manufactories (*śilpīśālā*s) and regulated the salaries of artisans.
86. Cf., Misra (1975): 8.
87. Cf., E.B. Cowell, ed. & tr., *The Jātakas*, Vol. II, p. 18. Another *Jātaka* (no. 461) refers to a chief of *vardhakī*s.
88. Cf., Misra (1975): 9.
89. For a detailed discussion on the status and function of *gahapati*, cf., Chakravarti (1987): 65-93.
90. Cf., *Arthaśāstra* in its chapter on *kārukara rakṣaṇam*: IV.1.1-65 refers to these and other categories. Among them, a reference to the artisans called *kāruśāsitāraḥ* and *savittakāravaḥ* is also made. They were protected by their guilds and supposed to be men of means (*arthyapratīkārāḥ*), possibly considered fit enough to make 'good of anything connected with the object entrusted'. Cf., Kangle (2000): Vol. II, p. 254, fn. 2 for the interpretations by Meyer and others.
91. Cf., Kangle (2000): Vol. II, p. 254, fn. 2 for different views on these two terms and their implications.
92. Manu imposes 'forced labour' (*viṣṭi*) on *śilpin*s. Cf., Shukla (1984): 151-152.
93. Cf., Sircar (1965)/1: No.67: 179-80.
94. Settar 2003: 15.
95. Cf., Davids and Bruschell (1904-05): 334.
96. Cf., Chattopadhyaya (1970). Tārānātha refers to the 'Caityas of the eight sacred places and the inner boundary walls of Vajrasana built by Yakṣa artists during the time of Aśoka ...' He further says, 'The images thus made by the Devas, Nagas and Yakṣas created the illusion of real objects for many years. In later period, under the influence of time such creations were no

more and there remained practically none with the knowledge of the techniques concerned'.

97. Pant and Jayaswal (1990-91): 49-52. Also, Mukherji (1990-91): 53-57. Mukherji assigns a Kuṣāna date to these finds but T.P. Varma takes them to be Mauryan in date.
98. Recently, Settar has re-examined these label inscriptions, which he regards as 'the first representative voices of the working class recorded in the south Asian history' and his conclusions are that, the Kharosthi knowing artisans 'formed a compact community' and 'neither lived nor worked in isolation'. They received wages in cash, were not in the category of slaves, could record their grievances against the intermediaries, as the case of Eṭhaka testifies, and as he says, 'the hidden tone of these records reveals that they were not only literate but also accomplished artists: they were able to judge the quality of stone, provide guidance for its safe transport and even recommend wages for transporters, Cf., Settar (2003): 12-15.
99. Eggermont and Hoftijzer (1962): 33, 34. In the Siddapur edict the name Ca (*pada*) is incomplete.
100. Cf., Valley (2000): 9-10. The proportions here have a reference to distances between breasts; from breast line to navel and from navel to bottom of torso.
101. Valley (2000): 12.
102. Sharma offers the reading of the Parkham image (Mathura Museum no. C 1) inscription as: '*nibhada puga rāna ... atha ... pi kuṇikānte vāsinā gomitakena katā*, i.e., in the guild of Nibhada (in the reign of) the king ... made by Gomitaka, the pupil of Kuṇika'. Similarly, he reads the three-line inscription of the Jhing ka Nagla Yakṣi image (Mathura Museum no. 72; 5) as (Line 1) '*sa putehi kārito* (Line 2) *yakhilā yava kuṇikāte* (Line 3) *(vāsina nāke) na katā*', i.e., '(This image of) Yakṣī Lāyāva has been caused to be made by the sons of Sā, and made by Nāka, pupil of Kuṇika'. R.C. Sharma (2002) (unpublished paper).
103. For the Parkham inscription, cf., Sharma (1976): 29. The *antevāsī* Amṛta is mentioned in an inscription of Sūrya image in the British Museum. Cf., Chanda (1936): 66, Plate XX. Yet another inscription mentioning an *antevāsī* has been published by Rakesh Tiwari and K.K. Thaplyal in the *Pragdhara,* the Journal of UP Archaeological Organisation, Lucknow. I owe the information about the *Pragdhara* publication to Dr. Rakesh Tiwari.
104. Cf., Narada, V.2.8 (Jolly's translation, p. 131).
105. Yājñavalkya, II.14.8; Narada, V.16.17 (Jolly's translation).
106. XVI.6 (Jolly's translation).
107. Kātyāyana, 713 (Kane's translation).
108. Yājñavalkya (2.14.8), Nārada (5.16-17), Bṛhaspati (16.6) and Kātyāyana (713) ordain that an *antevāsī* could leave the house of his *ācārya* only with the permission of the latter. He was liable to punishment for dereliction from duty. But an *ācārya* was liable to punishment if he showed indifference to apprentice's work. Epigraphic reference to *antevāsī* in relation to master-craftsmen, gives us sufficient ground to suggest existence of ateliers and

workshops in the homesteads of master-artists from where particular traditions, styles, and expertise disseminated. And, to that extent, the *antevāsī* title, besides others, offer us an opportunity to look into the processes which were part and parcel of ancient Indian art activity.

109. Misra (2002)/1: 1273-1277. People of even non-Indian ethnic stocks followed such practice of donating works for spiritual merit. A Buddha image inscription from Anyor records that the image was a gift of Susa Hārusa to the '*vihāra* of Susa Hārusa'. Susa Hārusa himself is mentioned in the inscription as a Śākya lay brother. The gift was collectively offered with his parents: all of them desiring the 'welfare and happiness of all sentient beings'. Janert (1961): 135; An epigraph of the times of Śakas in Mathura refers to a brāhmaṇa treasurer of *mahākṣatrapa* Soḍaṣa who made a gift of a *puṣkaraṇī* (tank), an *udapāna* (well), an *ārāma* (garden), a *stambha* (pillar) and a *śilā-paṭa* (stone slab). Similarly, an epigraph from Mora, refers to Svāmi, a son of the *mahākṣatrapa* Rajuvula, setting up the images of the *pañcavīra*s (five Vṛṣṇi heroes, Sankarṣaṇa, Vāsudeva, Pradyumna, Aniruddha and Sāmba) in a *śaila deva-gṛha* (temple of gods made of stone). An inscription from Ganeshra records the gift of a *prāsāda* (stone palace), *sabhā* (assembly hall) and *śilāpaṭa*s (stone slabs) apparently at Mora. Cf., Janert (1961): 64, 113, 178. The practice of such donations continued in the Kuṣāna times.
110. Waldschmidt and Mehandale, *Bharhut Inscriptions*, C.I.I., Vol. II (ii), p. 36, 11ff.
111. Marshall *et al.* (1939): insc. nos., 199, 448.
112. Lüders List, no. 124.
113. *Ibid.*, no. 1002; 1203-4.
114. *Ibid.*, no. 1092. Cf., also *selavaḍhakī* in *Epigraphia Indica*, inscription F, line 4, p. 22; *iṭṭhikā vaḍḍhakī*, 'brick mason', *Mahāvaṃsa* XXIX, 5, 30.
115. Lüders List, nos. 987 (*śailavardhakī*), 350 (*śailakarma*), 345 (*rūpakarma*), 687 (*silākammamta*), 1087 (*selaghara*).
116. *Ibid.*, insc. no. 157: from Sonari. A Bharhut inscription refers to a *navakarmika* named Arya Ṛsipālita who is also styled as *bhadanta* and *bhānaka*.
117. Janert (1961): 133, 239. Other names of artists have also been read by R.C. Sharma who refers to: Simga figuring on a rail post (no. Mathura Museum, 56: 4239) from Sarai Azampur that carries a figure of a male under a tree with a conical headgear and a bunch of lotus flowers; to Deyahu (No. J. 15), to Nayasa (on no.16; 1252), to Viṣṇu and Jayakula – all belonging to the Kuṣāṇa period. R.C. Sharma (2002) 'The Artists of Mathura' (an unpublished paper).
118. *Ibid.*, Sharma quotes Dayaram Sahni who assigned it a pre-Kuṣāṇa date.
119. Lüders (1909-10): nos. 346, 1202-04, 1298. The term *āveśanin* (chief of artists' workshop) occurs seven times in epigraphs: once at Sanchi in case of Ānanda, a Sātavāhana artist who carved the South Gate of the main *stūpa*, and six times in the cases of artists in ancient Vengī region in Andhra Pradesh. The lexicons explain *āveśan* as *śilpiśālā* (manufactory or workshop). On the analogy of *akṣaśālā* mentioned in the *Arthaśātra* (II.13.1), and its commentary the word may be explained as a manufactory. As such, *āveśanin*

should be taken as the foreman or in-charge of the manufactory. The *silpalaya* and *śilpagṛha* find mention in the *Bṛhatsaṃhitā* and *Brāhmavaivartta Purāṇa*. Cf., Monier Williams (1996), sv. The workshop of artists had come into being already in the times of Pāṇini (4th century BC), and particularly during the Mauryan rule. Some of these workshops or manufactories perhaps served as places where an *antevāsī* came to learn the craft(s).

120. Misra (1982): 35-38.
121. Jones (1956): Vol. III: 112, 443.
122. The titles and designations of artists appear to have been function-specific (e.g., *sūtradhāra*), honorific (e.g., *vaidagdhī Viśvakarmā*), or indicator of authority or skill. They often are indicative of different kinds of emphases in regard to the jobs performed by artists in various ways. Thus, the term *miṭhika*, 'stone polisher', implied a specialised function or techniques pertaining to specific work; the term *rūpakara* had aesthetic connotation involved with the understanding of *rūpa*, 'form'; the term *bhṛtya* and *karmakāra* indicate a social bias; the term *kāyastha* points to a petty bureaucratic status while the terms *rāṇaka*, *ṭhakkura* and *sāmanta* relate to authority. All these terms separately tend to define the status and authority that artists occupied or were capable of acquiring in substance. Some such terms (e.g., *rūpadakṣa*) identify the quality of an artist while others (e.g., *śilpī*) indicate his vocation as well as his collective identity. There are titles, which denote relative superiority, while certain other titles identify the departments of artists' activity (e.g., *citrakāra*, *rūpakāra*) or relative aggradations in status (e.g., from *rītikāra* to *śilpī* to *vijñānika*, etc.
123. Cf., Subrahmanyam (1991): 125-128.
124. The *Śukranīti* (II.128ff) describes different types of workers and it prescribes (II.148) that each one of them should work, regulated and identified with their respective marks: *ukta sanjñāna sva sva cinhair lañchchitānśca niyojayet*. The banners and insignia of the guilds of washermen, merchant-cum-bankers, caravan-merchants and artisans are mentioned also in the *Arthaśāstra* of Kautilya (IV.1).
125. Tripathy (1997): 166.
126. Tripathy (1997): 183; 198.
127. Cf., Shastri (1995): 9, 15, 18, 22, 26, 30, 33, 37, 41, 44, 48, 54, 57.
128. A seventh century record of the Panduvamsis of South Kosala refers to Vasuguna, son of *sūtradhara* Ṛsigana as the engraver of the copper-plates. Shastri (1995): 159.
129. For such *suvarṇakāra* engravers (seventh century), under the Panduvamsis of Mekala, see Ajai Mitra Shastri (1995): 76, 83, 91 (Mihiraka, and Dronaka, the sons of Isvara). Similarly, the records of the Paduvamsis of South Kosala (seventh century) refer to Nagadeva, son of Gollarkka, Shastri (1995): 164; to *akṣasālin* Yotranaga's son Boppanaga, *Ibid.*, p. 106, fn. 115 and to an engraver named Prabhakar, *Ibid.*, p. 149.
130. The emergence of artists' guilds distinguishes this period from the earlier ones. There will be more to guild of artists, later.
131. Cf., Misra (n.d./1984): 68.

132. Such indeed was the case with the Sun temple of Konark. After the completion of the temple, the ruler is said to have established two hundred and twenty-four *pāthuriyās* (stone masons) nearby, granting fifteen *mānas* of land to each of them. Vāsudeva Mahāpātra, a master-artist was similarly settled in a village. Cf., Alice Boner (1972): 257-272.
133. *Epigraphia Indica,* Vol. XXVII, pp. 210ff.
134. We must hasten to add here that both in their import and significance these titles and designations indicate changing patterns of work in art activity and that their occurrence or the lack of it over the centuries reflects a gradual replacement of the earlier designations and titles by new ones later. Thus, the terms like *śailālaka, āveśanin, miṭhika* and *kaḍhicaka* were set aside as *vardhakī*s took to working on stone. With this emerged the rank of *śailavardhakī*, which eventually grew into many other hierarchical categories.
135. Cf., Misra (n.d./1984): 68
136. *Epigraphia Indica,* Vol. XXXVI, pp. 47-48. An inscription from Kusuma (Rajasthan) similarly refers to a *kṣatriya* named Sthavira as the engraver of the record. *Ibid.*, Vol. XXXIV, pp. 47-49.
137. Etymological derivatives of the terms *kāyastha* and *vāstavya* have distinct association with *sthapati;* and *karaṇika*, in that context, may tentatively be explained as those who derived their title from their expertise to work on the *karṇa* part of a temple.
138. Mirashi (1955): insc. nos. 93, 96, 98, 100; pp. 488, 507, 524, 539.
139. Nayaka and Thodhuka together fashioned a lofty temple of Śiva at Baijnath together with its porch, 'where the statues of a host of *gaṇa*s, constructed by following the views (expounded in) the codes of architecture, are shining forth'. The inscription refers to the temple of Śiva constructed by Manyuka and Ahuk. Agrawal (2001): 317.
140. Trivedi (nd.): 276.
141. The evidence about itinerant artists may suggest their freedom of passage, a freedom from controls of residence, which allowed them the liberty to move at will in search of a suitable work. As against this category there was perhaps also a category of artisans who, like imprested or contract labour, were forced to live at the site of work till the work was wound up. For highly mobile, itinerant artists under the Hoysalas cf., Settar (1992): 97-143. As an instance of such itinerant artists in the late third century we have a master craftsman (*āveśanin*) Siddhartha of Amaravati and his father, the residents of Nadatura in the district of Kammaka (Andhra Pradesh). Siddhartha is known to have moved from his native place to work at Jaggayyapeta. Lüders (1909-10): nos. 1002; also, 1203-1204. Similarly, an inscription from Amaravati refers to an artist who was a resident of Vīrapura but he came to work in Amaravati. Cf., Lüders (1909-10): inscription no. 85.
142. Bhandarkar's List, no. 1727.
143. *Epigraphia Indica*, Vol. I, p. 107, Vol. XI, p. 463. Also Thakur (1986): 307.
144. Cf., Shastri (1995): 245, 245, fn. 63.

145. Cf., Bhandarkar's List 2048; *Epigraphia Indica*, XXX, 26.
146. Cf., Mirashi (1955): inscription no. 104.
147. Cf., Sivaramamurti (1961): 5-6.
148. Cf., *Epigraphia Indica*, Vol. IX, (1911-12), pp. 47ff: The Nadlai Stone Inscription of vs 1228.
149. Artist also rendered community service of which instances are known from the Hoysala inscriptions. Cf., Settar (1992): 92.
150. *Ibid.*, 90.
151. The *Bayacakaḍa* refers to huge land grants made by the Ganga king to artists and artisans after the completion of the Sun temple at Konark. A *sāmanta* who had recruited labourers for work received land in Tirupatana (Boner *et al.* 1972:168); blacksmiths received land in Sanalapura to build their own houses (Boner *et al.*, 1972: 166); 108 *pāthuriā*s who had supervised the entire work of stone construction received land in Sanapura (Boner *et al.*, 1972: 166); *mahanta* Banudasa who had supplied coconuts received land for a *matha* (Boner *et al.*, 1972:166); 224 *pāthuriā*s who had worked from beginning to end with loyalty and devotion received 15 *māna* (one *māna* was equal to one acre or 4820 square yards) of land by the side of the Konakana temple to establish a centre for the *pāthuriā* community. They also received, in addition, a pair of cloth and 2 *māḍha*s each. Towards the building cost, Niranjana *pāthuriā* received 130 *māḍha*s. Boner *et al.* (1972):167.
152. In case of the artists employed at the Rūpāsa camp at Konark when the Sun temple was under construction, the payment on account of contracts, salaries and wages were handed out to them both in cash and in kind. The text records that artists and other workmen received gifts when the camp was dispersed following completion of the temple.
153. Cf., Misra (n.d./1984): 68.
154. Boner *et al.* (1972): 61.
155. *Ibid.*, 171.
156. *Ibid.*, 67.
157. *Ibid.*, 163. There were still others who received land grants for different purpose in compensation of their work for which the Ganga king Narasimhadeva I was beholden to them. Thus, Kurudha Malla who had supplied *pan* received land in the village Bahania (Boner *et al.* 1972:168); Sadananda Pattanayaka who, on king's orders, had looked after the workers at the site received a gift of land in village Sạdanandapura. *Ibid.*, p. 169. Sweepers received land. *Ibid.*, p. 169. Twelve people who were appointed to guard the two portals of the newly constructed temple at Konark every day, received gift of land in Sripurapatana for building houses. *Ibid.*, p. 170. For similar landgrants and other monetary privileges to artists, cf., Sattar (1992): 91.
158. Cf., Settar and Sontheimer (1982): 323. Also Settar (1992): 91-92.
159. Nadlai stone inscription of Kelhana (Vikrama) Samvat 1228, in *Epigraphia Indica*, Vol. XI (1911-12), pp. 47ff.
160. Agrawal (2001): 258.

161. *Ibid.*, p. 225. Sometimes the contributions of the donors in making a work are also mentioned with the share of each of the donor in case it was a corporate gift. The Bhadund stone inscription of the time of Purnapala (c. AD 1040-1060), of the Paramara dynasty of Candravati refers to twenty-two Brahmanas, members of a *goṣṭhikā*, who constructed a well possibly with the help of four artisans, namely, Dharesvara, Deūā, Devaū and Lahaṃpa. The inscription records the share of donation, both in words and figures, of each of those twenty-two contributors. Trivedi (n.d.): 235-237.
162. Mirashi (1955): 556-557.
163. Mirashi (1955): 330-31.
164. Mirashi (1955): 331, verse 29. The inscription records at the end that it was 'engraved by the sculptor Talhana, the son of Palhana of the illustrious Kokāsa family'.
165. Mirashi (1955): 323-324.
166. *Ibid.*, 322.
167. Misra (1975): 53.
168. Bhandarkar's List, insc. nos. 359, 371, 1931. Also, *Epigraphia Indica*, Vol. XX, p. 131; Vol. VI, p. 170; Vol. X, p. 49; *Indian Antiquary*, XXV, p. 208.
169. Misra (n.d./1984): 68.
170. P. 61, line 24-64, 1.
171. Pp. 409a-410.
172. 55.174.
173. Jagdish Chandra Jain (1965):148.
174. Misra (1987): 137-8.
175. *Ibid.*, 109.
176. *Ibid.*, 116-117.
177. *Ibid.*, 118.

3

Śilpin (II): *Śilpīs'* Organisation and Operation

The last chapter examined the problem of ancient artists' anonymity-identity, besides attempting a historical survey of *śilpīs* and reconstruction of the lineage of Kokāsa, a distinguished ancient artist. The details so far have still not accounted for certain significant aspects of the community and its function and role, like: how they were professionally organised, or how they operated individually or collectively in the given situations; what constituted their work culture, discipline and honour and how all these translated into economic and political gains and rewards. This chapter intends to examine these aspects, as they obtained during the middle ages, especially in respect of their organisation and operation, their work ethic and culture, including their interface with authority in terms of conformity, dissent or protest.

We, in our discussions will depend, among other sources, on the inputs from an Orissan palm-leaf manuscript entitled *Bayacakaḍa*,[1] (*Vyayacakra*, lit. 'Expense cycle'), a ledger recording transactions in money,[2] goods and services in the instance of construction of the Sun temple at Konarak in the thirteenth century. This text refers to ordinary workers, men and women, and many a distinguished architect and *śilpī* with high-sounding designations like *nāyaka, mahārāṇā* or *mahāpātra, kulapata sāmanta*, etc. who were recruited and engaged by the Ganga ruler Narasimhadeva I (AD 1238-1258) to materialise his vision of a monumental enterprise.[3] Before passing on to that text and its material on artists and their work, we may first deal with the evidence concerning artists' organisation in terms of their collectives and groupings.

ARTISTS' ORGANISATION: COLLECTIVES AND GROUPINGS

The materials about artists' organisation tend to categorise them separately in different groupings. Guild formation among them is conspicuous for its rarity. One notices a divided and dismembered artists' community – with some in it competitively asserting their individual supremacy over others due to the sustained patronage they could acquire and hold on to[4]; others appear organised under the banner of a clan or family or in rare cases even under a *gaṇa* or a *goṣṭhī;* and yet others, largely the ordinary workmen, surviving on the periphery, beholden to the more endowed masters in higher cadres who as leaders would have to fall back on to the community of workmen to carry out specific ventures. Inscriptions in their cryptic details identify and name them and their particular cadres in reference to their specific works.

Such a disorganised state of the community could not be conducive to creating a strong corporate organisation among the artists. In the situation, the master-artists, i.e., the *sūtradhāra*s, highly individualistic in their work culture, apparently stood in a commanding position acting as providers to the community and perhaps also beholden to it especially as they needed contingents, large or small, of different skills to complete the work that came to them. There will be more about *sūtradhāra*, later. But the nature of artists' professional work which required of them to be on move from one territory to another or from one patron to another, apparently impeded their bonding in a guild-like formation.[5] Their itinerant character often precluded their settling down permanently at a fixed location even as intense competition for patronage promoted rivalries, exclusivity and strong individualism in them, thwarting corporatisation of the masters in a guild-like organisation. In the inscriptions all over the subcontinent one comes across highly individualistic master-artists who extolled their own merit[6] while running down their rivals.[7] The self-exaltation expressed in terms of elitism and one-upmanship seems to signal their exclusivity rather than comraderie. As early as eighth century, we have an early Cālukyan artist Narasobba claiming that 'There has not been and there shall not be in the Jambudvipa, any wise man proficient in (building) houses and temples, equal to myself'.[8] Such claims occur perpetually in records and mark both competition and rivalry among the master-artists, but it will be conceded that all the master-artists were not so aggressively brazen and impolite. We have the instance of a self-effacing *śilpin* named Karnabhadra who calls himself *nālpabuddhi*, 'not lacking in intelligence', and yet *bhadra*, 'courteous', and *vinaya-namra*, 'polite'.[9]

Apart from a cluster of such independent and suitably acclaimed master-artists, excellent individually, other groupings of artists are also in evidence. In some rare cases, we do come across expressions like: *gaṇa, goṣṭhī, prakṛti* signifying an artists' guild. One of the earliest occurrences of such a grouping relates to the Mauryan times when the fragmentary inscription on the Yakṣa image from Parkham refers to its being established in the '*puga* of the Nibhada .... ' The fragmentary inscription leaves it unclear as to who – whether artists, or merchants or others – constituted the 'Nibhada *pūga*'? Artists' guilds, discussed below, were possibly not as common as were those of weavers, potters and other such occupational classes, which figure noticeably in their typically corporate character and function.[10]

Yet another grouping identifying certain professional cadres (if not the collectives) of artists, also surfaced with the passage of time in the post-Gupta phase. These cadres consisted of *sthapati,*[11] *sūtradhāra,*[12] *śilpī,*[13] *vijñānika*[14] and *rūpakāra,*[15] etc. which seem to have been the categories of substance in artists' hierarchy. Such cadres seem to have received a wider sanction including the state's recognition, which may be inferred from their pointed references inscribed in official records. Their actually being in place is confirmed by *śilpa* texts, like the *Mayamatam* and the *Mānasāra.*[16]

The three groupings, mentioned above, consisting of individual master-artists, guilds and cadres do not account for the vast masses of artisans who constituted the community. Some of them may have remained centred around their family, clan or *gharānā* – with the last of these being based on *guru-śiṣysa-paramparā* (teacher-disciple-continuum) – with the patriarchs of the family, clan or *gharānā* pursuing their particular demand-oriented worth and work in competitive situations. The family, clan and *gharānā* thus seem to constitute yet another grouping of artists. The Kokāsa lineage (*vaṃśa*), *rāṇaka* Śūlapāṇi of Vārendra, and the master-artist of Mauryan times (i.e., Kuṇika with his disciples Gomitaka and Naka (Nāga), mentioned earlier) would be the typical examples respectively of family (*vaṃśa*), clan and *gharānā*. Other instances of family and clan may be seen in the cases of the master-artists at Koṅarak, namely, Gangā, the *pāthuriyā paryanga kula nāyaka,* and Gadādhara, the *kulapata sāmanta* where the first refers to the chief of a *kula* (family) and the second implies a larger confederation of families under a clan with its patriarch designated as *sāmanta.*[17] The clan or family perhaps represented an independent category constituted of ordinary craftsmen as well as the distinguished, privileged and successful master-artists, the latter being much sought after. In holding on to their distinct identity such families or clans perhaps tended to distance themselves from ordinary craftsmen due to their exclusivism even as the mass, unorganized, remained socially and economically weak in their ability to negotiate or bargain and therefore beholden to the masters-artists' patronage for livelihood, recruitment and work. Sometimes, as the *Bayacakaḍa* has it, even in recruitments the distinguished patrons and their officers made their own selections leaving little to *sūtradhāra* who remained content only with distribution of work to those who joined the work force and served under his general direction.[18]

Thus, the distinctions and fragmentation among artists and their groupings, as indicated above, betrays a disorganized community with fractured loyalties. Guild formation among artists at least held the possibility of ensuring their security and welfare to certain extent but information on artists' guilds is scarce. Some details, however, about it follow.

Early instances of stonemasons' guilds are few in number and are found only from Bandhogarh[19] (AD 159) in Central India where they made the *āsanapaṭṭas*, 'stone-benches'; from Siyadoni[20] (eighth century) in Uttar Pradesh where the *śilākūṭas* together with betel sellers and oil-millers made a gift to a local temple; and in the Lakṣmeśvara inscription[21] (eighth century) they are mentioned among the eighteen *prakṛtis*, 'artisans' (who constituted guilds of different kinds). The last two instances would point to the stonemasons' rising economic status in the early Middle Ages. This seems specially so in the instance of Siyadoni where, endowed as they were with resources to make a corporate gift to a local temple, they are found bracketed with merchants and local traders. One may read into the instance of their gift an example of a corporate decision in respect of community financing. But the decision-making procedure in collection and distribution of such funds is not seen forthcoming in the instance. In the second instance, *śilpī*s figure as a corporate body (*prakṛti*) in a wider federation of such corporate groups, which is symptomatic of an organised craft economy in the instance.

Some evidence on artists organising themselves into *gaṇa*s, or *goṣṭhī* 'guilds', comes from eastern, central and Peninsular India.[22] Thus, a *goṣṭhī* of the *śilpīs* of Vārendra (North Bengal) is mentioned in the Deopada stone inscription of Vijayasena (c. 1096-1159 AD). The inscription refers to *rāṇaka* Śūlapāni, 'the crest jewel of the guild of artisans of Varendra' (*Vārendraka śilpigoṣṭhī cūdāmaṇi).* The inscription also mentions his father Bṛhaspati, grandfather Manodāsa and great grandfather Dharma.[23] The title *rāṇaka* – a title probably having clan-related connotations which may signify the position of such titled person as the patriarch of his clan – is used for him indicating his high rank and authority. This is besides the fact that *rāṇaka* is a title ordinarily used for persons of authority in the feudal set-up of state or it may even connote the status of an artist as the master of artists' guild. In another instance, a Cālukyan inscription refers to *sarva siddha ācārya*s who were well versed in the 'secrets of *śrī śile muḍḍe*'.[24] The term points to a confederation of artists in the instance and the inscription seemingly points to the modalities of expulsion or banishment of artists from their fold and their re-admission back into it, perhaps after they had complied with the dictates of the arbitration. The inscription thus seems to indicate that artists belonging to particular guilds were bound to observe a code of discipline, failing which corrective steps became necessary.

The label inscriptions on the temples of Khajuraho in Madhya Pradesh might support the existence of artists' guilds if the Brahmi alphabet *ga* suffixed to some proper names in these inscriptions is read as an abbreviated expression for *gaṇa*, 'guild'. Seven such *gaṇa*s comprising Anurā, Bhaita, Mata, Savara, Sidha, Ṭemaṇa and Ṭhavaṇa, among others, have been identified in Khajuraho.[25] These names seem essentially provincial in character, and a collective formation in the regular sense of an artisans' group, in their cases, may not be certain. But, inscriptions from Karnataka clearly refer to the artists of Sarasvatī *gaṇa*.[26] Scattered references to Dasojja, an artist of Balligame (Shimoga District of Karnataka) who belonged to Saraswatī *gaṇa* affords details of particular works performed by him in different temples in Karnataka. Similarly, the titles like *pāthuriyā-paryanga nāyaka*, *śilpī-nāyaka* and *kulapata sāmanta* designating *śilpī*s and *sūtradhāra* in eastern India,[27] indicate existence of artists' confederation whose chiefs carried those titles. It is also likely that some provincial guilds of artists came into existence, as a result of their concentrated localisation in particular villages in strength. The records from Karnataka indicate such a concentration of artists in the Shimoga district.[28] In a similar vein, eastern Indian inscriptions refer to Pośali, a village in Bengal that produced many famed artists. Among them occur the names of several artists like: Mahendra, son of Vikramaditya; Śaśidhara; Pushyāditya, son of Chandrāditya; and Śaśideva, son of Hṛiddeva.[29] They all belonged to Pośali and some of them belonged to the same family. The Nagari Plates of the third Anagabhima refer to a flourishing village of artisans with *śilpī*s too living there along with merchants, perfumers, workers in conch shells, goldsmith, brazier, sellers of betel, florists, weavers, etc.[30] It was not unusual for the rulers to establish artisans on the lands close to the temples.

The most prominent grouping of the artists that emerges from inscriptions in the post-Gupta phase consisted, as we said earlier, of a hierarchy with *sūtradhāra*, 'master-artists', at the apex and *vijñānika* (or, *vijñānin*), *śilpī* and *rūpakāra* below him in a descending order, with all these categories coexisting together in varying combinations, in actual practice.[31] These cadres find mention in inscriptions, which seem to prove their formal recognition. Our argument in interlacing these categories in a hierarchy follows from the case of Palhana, a Candella artist, mentioned earlier (Chapter 2), who graduated to each of these positions excepting that of *sūtradhāra* in thirteen years during the rule of the Candellas in Central India. As an engraver of the Simra Plates of Vikram Samvat 1223 he is first designated as a *pītalakāra* (a brazier), a position parallel to that of *rūpakāra*, a sculptor; the only difference being that he would be an expert in metalwork unlike *rūpakāra* who handled stone. Five years later, when he engraved the Icchavar Plates he had become a *śilpin* and an expert in carving letters' – *varṇaghaṭanā vaidagdhī*. After a further experience of two more years when he engraved the Mahoba Plates (VS 1230) he was a *vijñānin*. His eminence seems to have continued even after this, for in the Pachhar Plates of VS 1233 and the Charkhari Plates of VS 1236, the same Palhana is mentioned as an 'expert in the craft of Viśvakarmā' – *vaidagdhī Viśvakarmaṇā*. It is apparent from these references that escalation in the rank came to Palhana with accretion of experience, and the grades that he gradually came to, would logically represent the particular hierarchical positions in artists' functional set-up. Palhana proves again that the categories representing *sūtradhāra*, *vijñāika*, *śilpin* and (*rūpakāra-*) *pītalakāra* respectively were not merely ephemeral expressions of epithets, pure and simple. They seem to have indeed been substantive in nature and real: denoting artists' gradually mounting positions of power and status in their professional domain, socially acknowledged by the community and politically reckoned in the official records of the rulers. They were cadres of substance, outside the state bureaucracy and they figure universally all over the country, even as particular regions are seen introducing other provincially popular or acceptable designations for their master-artists.[32]

Starting with *vijñānins*, we may very briefly refer to these cadres mainly in their positions of eminence. The Rayapur (Dharwad taluk, Karnataka) Plates of Kalacuri Āhavamalla and Kadamba Permāḍideva (AD 1182) refer to Paṃdaya as *rājavijñānin*: *utkīrṇṇaṃ rāja-vijñāninā Paṃdayena*.[33] The prefix *rāja* to the title indicates his elevated position acquired apparently through his proximity to the royal patron. The *vijñānins* were experts in *śilpaśāstra*, which was considered a science unlike the *Veda*s, etc. which constituted higher knowledge that liberated: *mokṣe dhīrjñānam vijñānam śilpaśātrayoḥ*. Jalhana and Uhena were the *vijñānika*s in the Candella territory while Kuke bore that designation in the contiguous region under the Kalacuris. *Vijñānika*s such as Madhava, Madhumanthana, Sankhuka, Vaheru and Mangaka, etc. figure in the records of the Soma and Ganga kings of Orissa, the Ranakas (of Bihar and Orissa) and the rulers of the former Baudh state in Orissa.[34] The *vijñānika* category, however, is less frequent in its mention in epigraphs compared to the other categories of our foursome classification. Its comparative rarity may indicate its relative importance, so borne out by its selective acceptance. *Śilpins*, next in hierarchy in the descending order, figure prominently in epigraphs in different situations, building edifices, carving sculptures, engraving records and doing other kinds of work.[35]

The terms *śilpa* and *śilpin* are generically applied to any skilled work or worker and by definition they tend to include all kinds of crafts and craftsmen. In a special sense, the term *śilpin* denoted a 'sculptor'. *Śilpins* figure prominently in reference to the works of art, generally proficient even in respect of their knowledge of its theory. The Methi inscription of the Yadavas[36] refers to an image of a god fashioned in accordance with the principles of iconometry. The inscription was engraved by *śilpin* Hemadeva who perhaps made the image, while Siddha Saraswat of Kasyapa family prepared the stone slab bearing the record. The nature of work as divided between the two indicates the *śilpin* in a superior role. *Śilpins* seem to have been well endowed with requisite skills of their craft. Amrit, a *śilpin* who carved a Sūrya image in Bengal in 8th-9th century, proudly declared himself to be 'wise' and 'proficient'.[37] Another acclaimed *śilpin*, proud of his 'Magadhan' origin (*śilpāvin Māgadhaḥ*), but active in Kamrūpa figures in the inscription of the Chandra rulers of Assam.[38] The inscriptions of the Kalacuris of Ratanpur refer to many a *śilpins*, e.g. Dhanapati, Isvara and Jatu: the first two being mentioned as 'skilful' and 'best' and the last described as a 'knower of *śilpa vijñāna*'. Similarly, Hasala, another *śilpin*, is acclaimed as 'intelligent and a repository of the *śilpa vidyā*'.[39]

Rūpakāras, the last in this foursome group, generally appear to have been sculptors. Skill and its eventual recognition assisted them in their rise to superior positions. The Dhar *praśasti* speaks of *rūpakāra* Sihaka whose son Ramadeva turned out to be a *śilpin*.[40] The Ratanpur inscription of Vahara, which, as its contents suggest, was aware of the different cadres of artists, namely, *sūtradhāra* and *rūpakāra*, refers to *rūpakāra* Dityan as an acclaimed artist 'praised for his knowledge of sciences (*śilpavijñāna*) and all other merits'.[41] Sometimes, a *rūpakāra*, is not restricted merely to sculpting, and is credited with building a temple, as happened in the instance of Devagana in ancient Chhattisgarh. He is described as a *rūpakāra śiromaṇi* who built a temple dedicated to Śiva-Bilvapāṇi. The inscription refers to Sampula, a *sūtradhāra*, merely as the engraver of the record. Here, a *rūpakāra-śiromaṇi* stands superior to a *sūtradhāra* but situation seems to have changed soon for, in another inscription Sampula, described as 'one who has seen farther shores of the ocean of various crafts', figures not as a *sūtradhāra* but simply as a *rūpakāra*.[42] Obviously, he appears not to have been able to hold on to his higher position and had to revert to his substantive position of a *rūpakāra*.

The cadre of *sūtradhāra* seems to have been highest in the hierarchy of master-artists.[43] Yugadhara of Ajanta (Cave XV) with his name painted there, seems to be among the earliest of artists carrying the title *sūtradhāra*.[44] Sometimes references to *sthapati*[45] also occur, as in the Tapar inscription of AD 1158 which speaks of *sthapati* Laksmana who built a monument in

Kashmir.[46] But the scarce mention of this rank in inscriptions, compared to a profusion of *sūtradhāras* would reflect gradual displacement of *sthapatis* by *sūtradhāras*,[47] leading to relegation of the former into obscurity. *Sūtradhāra*, as a 'holder of the *sūtra*' signifies a pre-eminence which is further re-enforced when God[48] or *Kāla*[49] (time) are described as *sūtradhāras* who regulate the three worlds.

The different usages of the term *sūtradhāra* tend to indicate that this office was common to the spheres of drama and architecture.[50] This identity is best illustrated in the *Harṣacarita* (Kane's ed. I.15), which brings out the similarities in the functional status of *sūtradhāras* in the two realms even as it describes the plays of Bhasa comparing their constitutive elements with those of temples. The comparison in the *Harṣacarita* is made by punning on the terms like *bhūmikā* ('role' in drama; 'storeys' in temple) and *patākā* ('sub-plot' in drama and 'fluttering flag' on a temple). Thus, with the help of three paronomastic clauses the relevant verse says that Bhasa gained as much splendour by his plays with their introduction spoken by the *sūtradhāras* and by furnishing them with several characters and roles in a manner a temple is erected, adorned with several storeys and decorated with fluttering banners. One may further add that the role of a *sūtradhāra* in art and architecture may be more ancient than that in the realm of drama and it may go back in antiquity architecturally to the later Vedic period when *vedīs* (sacrificial alters) were made with the help of a *sūtra* (thread or cord) by the *sūtas*. The context from the *Mahābhārata* (I.47. 14-15) seems to support the suggestion as *sūta, purāṇika, sthapati* and *sūtradhāra* are all mentioned as separate designations qualifying the same personage, viz., a *sūta*.[51]

In the field of art and architecture the participants in the building activity seem to have been accorded different designations in accordance with their roles. Inscriptions indicate that artists were divided into different schools like those of Kaśyapa, Māya, Viśvakarmā, Śukrācārya, etc.[52] and were also variously designated at different points of time as *rūpakāra, rūpadakṣa, sthapati, vardhakin, takṣaka, āveśanin* and *sūtradhāra*, etc.[53] according to their specialisation and skill. Ancient texts and inscriptions contain useful material on these categories of artists and craftsmen and the pre-eminent status and position of *sūtradhāra* stands vindicated in these different categories on the grounds of his role, theoretical and practical knowledge of the craft and the privileges in the work that devolved upon him.[54] It must have taken some time for the office of *sūtradhāra* to evolve into a cadre, or a standard category of master-artists, for if the *śilpa* texts are taken into account, they continued to enumerate artisans and craftsmen other than *sūtradhāra* even after the latter had made a strong presence. The *Mayamatam* (V.13-25) thus refers to four types of *śilpins*, namely, *sthapati, sūtragrāhin, vardhakin* and *takṣaka*. *Sūtradhāra* is missing in this list, but the epigraphs from seventh century AD onwards repeatedly refer to them in connection with building activity.[55]

As a designation, *sūtradhāra* is not mentioned prior to the inscriptions of the sixth century though the *Manu saṃhitā* (IV.47-48) does refer to *sūtragrāhin* and *sūtrakāra*. It seems likely that these designations derived from the function of measuring the proportions, preparation of layout and *hastalekha*, etc. in which the use of *sūtra* (thread) was essential, requiring an expert handling. *Sūtra* was an essential part in the exercise related to building activity at every stage.[56] And whoever was in-charge of such an operation was designated as *sūtradhāra* owing to his specific function of measuring out the proportions and executing the works accordingly. *Sūtragrāhin* in later texts is sometimes defined as the son or disciple of the *sthapati*. The *Mahāvastu*,[57] a Buddhist text of the second-third century AD refers to *sūtrakāra* also within a kindred group of artisans and craftsmen like *citrakāra, vardhakin, kārupatrika, pustakāra, lekhaka* and others. But, in essence, these terms, e.g. *sūtragrāhin, sūtrakāra*, and *sūtradhāra* relate them essentially to *sūtra*, which thereby defines their function, and thus designates them accordingly. Eventually, these different categories seem to have been merged into the office of *sūtradhāra* who gained supremacy in building activity by appropriating the roles of other similar functionaries. Texts and epigraphs from different parts of India seem to prove the point.[58]

In inscriptions known almost all over India, *sūtradhāra*s occur as a universal category of ancient artists who performed different roles and functions related to building activity. They figure as engravers of letters of inscriptions or they are mentioned as planners and executors of buildings; specially, the temples, monasteries and other sundry works[59] that came to be raised whether singly at one site or severally in a larger complex. They are mentioned as serving the monarchs or their family as they commissioned building works. Private individuals including pontiffs and priests employed them. References indicate their supremacy and their skills and even their relative superiority to other artisans in the same craft. In the *śilpa* texts as well as in the inscriptions, the qualities that *sūtradhāra*s were supposed to possess are often described in details. Examples to illustrate these different aspects of *sūtradhāra* may be quoted here from inscriptions, which as a source appear to be more authentic and securely dated.

Thus, we know of a *sūtradhāra* from Karnataka region whose name was Gorakṣasvāmī and who is mentioned as endowed with great creative élan: *sakala bhuvana nirmāṇaika sūtradhāra*.[60] Others are similarly eulogised. Vasuguṇa, a *sūtradhāra* who functioned under Panduvamsi rulers of Chhattisgarh has been described as *sakala karma kīrti guṇa gaṇonnatimāna*.[61] He was particularly adept in the task of building a temple. Inscriptions of the time of *Rāṇā* Kumbha of Chittorgarh refer to *sūtradhāra* Jaita and his five sons: Nāpā, Puñjā, Bhūmi, Chuthi and Pomā who built the Samādhīśvara temple of Chittor besides the *raṇapolī, kīrtti stambha* and *mahāpratolī*. That Jaita became celebrated early in his career is proved by his image installed along with his two sons whose inscribed figures facilitate their identity. These figures occur on the outer wall of the Kumbhalasvami temple of Chittor.[62]

The expertise of *sūtradhāras* in temple building or in expertly carrying out other architectural works is proved by the texts that they composed on the subject. Mandana, a *sūtradhāra,* wrote such works, e.g. the *Vāsturāja Vallabha,* the *Devatāmūrti prakaraṇa* and the *Rūpamanḍana.*[63] In the same manner, the *Bhuvana Pradīpa,* an Orissan text on architecture, refers to *sūtradhāra* Ahidhara.[64] In details, these texts clearly indicate distilled wisdom of these architects and sculptors who packed an entire tradition in those texts. The verses in these texts are impregnated with practical insights on architectural enterprises, image making and iconography, among other things.

Although the patronage of the ruling class was plentifully available to *sūtradhāras*, it is strange that they failed to make the grade in the state's bureaucracy. This is suggested by their absence in land grants from the list of the addresses who invariably find mention as witnesses to the donation of the designated land. We are not aware of any grant so far, in which *sūtradhāra* might have figured either as an addressee or witness. This may perhaps indicate their high mobility whereby they moved out to a better pasture as soon as the task in hand at one place was complete. In the instances from Chhattisgarh, at least six *sūtradhāras* are known to have changed in a single regime of a state-appointed *lekhaka* who remained anchored unchanged in his position for a period of sixteen years.[65] This clearly brings out the short duration of *sūtradhāras*' tenure of work as well as their mobility as they moved from task to task in different territories. There might have been exceptions to it also, particularly in the cases where monastic establishments or their priests were their patrons. A Jhalarapatan inscription of 9th-10th century AD refers to an *ācārya* of Lakulīśa-Pāśupata sect of Śaivism whose name was Iśānajamu and who had the *sūtradhāra* Sīhaṭa as his *bhṛtya.*[66] This kind of proximity of a pontiff with a *sūtradhāra* may indicate a longer duration of patron-artisan relationship though the fact is not specifically stated in the case. But, in the case of some Śaivite monasteries, e.g, the Viśveśvara *golakī* of the Malkapuram stone inscription, we are expressly told that *sūtradhāras* were among the ten different categories of artisans who were employed permanently by the monastery, living on the land grant whose benefits they, besides other artisans, enjoyed perpetually.[67] That the practice of *śilpa* was hereditary in the family of *sūtradhāra* seems indicated by several instances, one of these being that of Manthala, the son of *sūtradhāra* Sahira who carved his name on the image of Vāgdevī from Dhara (now in the British Museum, London). The image carries an inscription on its pedestal reading *sūtradhāra Sahirasuta Manthalena ghaṭitam*.[68]

The expertise of *sūtradhāra*s in different areas of their realm of activity is indicated in case of *sūtradhāra* Chiccha who was an 'expert in the *śāstra* of Viśvakarmā';[69] or in the cases of Madhava, Mahidhara and Namadeva who were known as 'crest jewel among the *sūtradhāras*' – *sūtradhāra śiromaṇi*.[70] *Sūtradhāra* Pīṭhe is mentioned in an inscription from Bheraghat near Jabalpur where he is credited with planning and constructing temples and other works in the manner in which 'Pṛthu had planned the earth'.[71]

*Sūtradhāra*s find mention in the different regions of the country, which indicates a wide acceptance of this category all around. The inscriptions of the Guhilas of Mendapata refer to the *sūtradhāra*s Mandana, his son Isamde and also to Govinda. Similarly, the inscriptions of the Vaghelas (Cālukyas) of Gujarat mention the *sūtradhāra*s Alada, Kalada, Nahada and others. The inscriptions of the Guhila rulers of Rajasthan refer to the *sūtradhāra*s Kesarin, Karmasimha, Bhaila, etc. The records of the Chahmanas of Naddula, Sakambhari and Ranthambhor refer to the *sūtradhāra*s Mahadua, Indaraka, Jasodhara, etc. Palhana finds mention in an inscription of the Paramaras of Candravati.[72] There are references to a Palhana in the Candella inscriptions also.[73]

Professionally, *sūtradhāra*s were indispensable in the domain of art when a work of substance was contemplated. It is therefore natural to assume that a high level of skill and expertise was expected of them. The *Nāṭyaśāstra* of Bharata described the qualities that a *sūtradhāra* was supposed to possess. According to these details, a *sūtradhāra* was expected to be an expert in the technique of (*nāṭya*) *śāstra*, music, science of rhetoric, *rasa* and *bhāva*, astrology, knowledge of religious sects (*pāṣaṇḍa*s), poetics, genealogy of kings, etc. besides being wise, pleasant, pious, truthful and accommodative of the points of view of others.[74] These details compare well with the qualifications of a *sthapati* as described in the *Samarāṅgaṇa Sūtradhāra*,[75] the *Matsya Purāṇa*[76] and the *Aparājitapṛcchā*.[77] It follows from these details that merely the skill in the theory and its application was not enough for a *sthapati*; a ready wit, modest behaviour and honesty were equally important for him in his practice of crafts.

Above all, the institution of *sūtradhāra* affords an example of upward mobility of the artisans in ancient India. That they could rise up to the status of a *sūtradhāra* and thus achieve dominance, which assured them a close proximity with the upper crust of society, especially the ruling class, is amply borne out by specific instances. The instance of *śilpin*s and *sūtradhāra*s who were dear to the rulers indicate such proximity and there are cases where such artisans even managed to secure the titles like *rāṇaka* and *ṭhakkura*.[78] Such instances are rare yet they are significant in indicating the capacity of this class of artisans to defy the rigours, which the *varṇa* system had unequivocally imposed on them.

ŚILPĪS AT WORK

From the preceding discussions, artists' cadres, e.g., *sūtradhāra, vijñānika, śilpī* and *rūpakāra*, rather than their guilds, clans, family or *gharānā*, seem to emerge out prominently in their organisational set-up and in professional activity. These and other regionally accepted categories of artists seem to have been active and consequently, they engage attention.[79] In exemplifying their roles and status in works that advanced, it may be relevant to explore as to how a project was planned; who planned, supervised, conducted and accomplished the works; how the work force of different specialities was recruited, maintained and involved in different operations? How the entire exercise was regulated as large groups of people of different callings were assembled together? What moved them to work and how did they graduate from task to task as the work on a monument progressed, amidst what pressures, contingencies, work ethic and rewards? While an answer to all these queries may not be forthcoming, one may still attempt to reconstruct the atmosphere of the workplace with operations on move and artists at work to bring up a monument that would redound the glory of the patron whose munificence made it possible. We propose to make an attempt here to reconstruct this scene keeping the materials from the *Bayacakaḍa* in focus.

The *Bayacakaḍa*, a thirteenth century text (copied in nineteenth century from the surviving ancient manuscripts) from Orissa, pertains to construction of the Sun temple at Konarak. Its singularity lies, among other things, in its almost day-to-day account of the dynamic ambience that lay imbued in a creative enterprise for more than a decade. While accounting for the expenses,[80] the *Bayacakaḍa* records in its stride cryptic, fragmentary details of the role and performance of the patron, artists, and others as the temple burgeoned through an extensively collaborative exercise performed on a tremendous scale at great expense.[81] This text merits attention in facilitating generalisations on the dynamics of a building operation in its diverse nuances and in answering, to a large extent, the questions that we raised above.[82]

THE PATRON

Patron's control over the entire operation seems writ large through the entire course of the project of the Konarak temple. Aided by his representatives, feudatories and officials, Narasimhadeva I seems exercising a firm control both covertly and overtly over the operations, providing infrastructure and finance, recruiting master-artists, artisans, craftsmen and workers of different orders, providing them lodgings in special camps, setting a time-schedule in completing the work, enforcing discipline through his officers in the camp of the artisans, doling out awards, defraying payments on wages, contracts and salary through a treasury established in the camp with its officer and clerks in place, and in various other ways. He intervenes in disputes and disagreements, demands regular reports of the progress of work with men dispatched to make inspections (*Bch.* Leaf XII, 12) and messengers detailed to report to him (*Bch.* Leaf XII, 11). He appoints spies to know what was being talked about in *śilpin*'s camps.[83] He periodically visits the site to watch the work and reward the workers;[84] demands building plans of the *sūtradhāra,* with little inhibition in suggesting incorporation of the works of his fancy, and such amendments or incorporations are generally carried out unflinchingly. He wishes to have his image made 'in the attitude of a triumphantly returning warrior', and that is arranged immediately (*Bch.* Leaf XXXVI, 6). But sometimes he yields to the counsel of his *śilpin*s disregarding the wishes of his queen.[85] He even seems setting the pace of work, rushing the *sūtradhāra* and the workers on with deadlines to complete the works as he reprimands them for delays.[86]

He seems liberal with awards especially when some important work was involved,[87] and when the work on temple came to an end he received the *śilpin*s who had survived retrenchment and presented to each of them two pairs of clothes and one lotus-marked gold coin 'with his own hands' (*Bch.* Leaf LXIII, 8). The awards could sometimes be substantial for, in an instance, the beneficiary had a village granted to him, and a title in addition, in recognition of his role in supplying materials useful in construction of the temple.[88] Sometimes, presents from the king came in celebration of an event of his personal fulfilment, like birth of the crown prince (*Bch.* Leaf XLVII, 4). The members of his family or his officers generally chipped in to award people on successful completion of particular works,[89] and the father-in-law of the king or his queens or feudatories also sent presents to *śilpī*s or replenished the stores in the *śilpin*s' camps (*Bch.* Leaf IX, 24). Despite all this, *śilpī*s sometimes were disappointed when the expected presents did not materialise (*Bch.* XXII, 9).

OPERATIONS

Work on a temple or other monuments generally began with recruitments to execute design of a proposed edifice and many texts, besides the *Bayacakaḍa*, offer the relevant information on these issues.[90] It seems that artists generally worked on contracts, which find mention in the *Bayacakaḍa* and elsewhere. For instance, the *Vāstupalaprabandha* indicates that artists negotiated a contract on fair terms and were prone to resist force.[91] In addition to a contract, other modes of compensation, like salary, wages, awards, retaining allowance, facilities of residence and victuals also seem to have been in practice. One finds a huge work force in the instance of Konarak with predominance in it of the *sūtradhāra*, *śilpin*s, *pāthuriā*s (a local term for stonemasons), *citrakāra* (painters), *cūnurā* (plasterers), *ojhā*s and *kamarakanṭa* (iron smith), carpenters, stone cutters, quarriers and specialists of different skills, etc. who had their tasks clearly laid out.

The highly charged atmosphere at work site comes out clearly as the *sūtradhāra* plans and executes the work with great foresight, with tasks carefully distributed and earmarked. The master-artists receive contracts in quick succession, and deliver them *sans* fault. The supply of materials, e.g., those for scaffoldings, stones, iron clamps, timber, plastering material, tools and implements, etc. and of men remained unhindered. Before a work began, the dressed stones were numbered and laid at the work site.[92] As one layer of dressed stones was set the next layer, already laid, waited for use. The artists were constantly re-deployed as particular works at the site got completed, so that no one would remain idle. Families of artists too remained appropriately set to work.[93] The construction moved with little interruptions. Holidays were rare and the work was rarely stopped.

Artists and craftsmen are found performing their designated tasks and invariably receiving payments according to their specific work contracts. Numbers of different kinds of artisans and craftsmen and their tasks seem to have been decided with discrimination but if exigencies so required even an expert would perform routine errands alone or in groups. We have, for instance, the expert *śilpī*s simply cutting laterite stone (*Bch.* Leaf VI, 29); seventy-four *śilpin*s building the *pīṭha* of the temple (*Bch.* Leaf IV, 14), two hundred and three (other) *śilpin*s working on the walls of *jagamohana* up to the prescribed heights (*Bch.* Leaf XIII, 7) besides performing many other tasks in various ways. Sometimes, in fun and frolic, they even organised a feast employing cooks and making payments to them from their own community funds (*Bch.* Leaf XLVII, 5). We have groups of expert *śilpin*s meticulously doing the chisel work (*sūcī-kama*), with drinking water and *pān* served to them in consideration. Dama *mahārāṇā*, an expert in fine works (*Bch.* Leaf IV, 25) sometimes led others into doing such works. We have *śilpin*s handling the work on *garbha* 'according to the design' (*Bch.* Leaf IX, 19) and on other parts of the proposed temple as they came up; preparing lion figures on ground before they were to be set on *pinḍī* (*Bch.* Leaf XVI, 25, XVII, 3); carving the wall with decorative work, above the *pīḍhā* and for making the *kanyā* figures to be set up on *pīḍhā* (*Bch.* Leaf XVI, 3, 2) and so on. The *pāthuriyā*s (sixteen such under the supervision of Lakhana Mahāpātra) made images (*Bch.* Leaf XXX, 5), set up a stone wall to support the weight of *pīḍhā*s (*Bch.* Leaf XVI, 9), made a big lion figure in stone (*Bch.* Leaf XV, 4), made stairs (*Bch.* Leaf VII, 2), worked on basement (*Bch.* Leaf VIII, 15), and under the supervision of Lakhana Mahāpātra, completed the upper part of *mukhaśālā* setting up the *āmalaka* on it (*Bch.* Leaf XXIII, 1), arranging stones for the *garbha ganḍi* (*Bch.* Leaf XXII, 21), etc. We have *ojhā*s: smelting iron and copper pipes and huge copper channels (*Bch.* Leaf 25, 23); preparing iron cramps with points in opposite direction or with parallel points when *ganḍi* was under construction (*Bch.* Leaf XXII, 22); filling the foundation with gravel, a work done elsewhere by *swānsya* (*Bch.* Leaf IV, 9). This instance of an unskilled work being carried out by a skilled artist is similar to another such work where a *jālī* cutter is employed to bring stone for construction of the *pīṭha* (*Bch.* Leaf VI, 32). We have *swānsya* (stone cutters) setting rough stones into foundations (*Bch.* Leaf IV, 8); cutting huge numbers of stones (3732 stones) for the *garbha* (*Bch.* Leaf XVII, 27); or carrying stones with labourers for setting up the corner part of the temple (*koṇaka*s) (*Bch.* Leaf XXII, 1). Sometimes even the physically disabled, lame person, Chota Śiva Mahāpātra for instance, could be drafted to render a highly artistic work. The *sūtradhāra* is said to have assigned him the work to carve and deliver two images of the king's 'fiend-destroying' battle horses which he did with aplomb and received one hundred lotus-marked *māḍha*s for completing the work (*Bch.* XLVII.11).[94]

Nature of work varied according to the requirements and, from the *Bayacakaḍa*, we get to know of different operations, which endlessly kept cropping up from time to time. When the construction was launched, setting the camps became necessary as artists joined work (*Bch.* Leaf II, 18). The preliminaries started as the ground was levelled for raising the temple and its adjuncts (*Bch.* Leaf II, 2, 3); water tanks had to be dug up and readied to facilitate water supply to the camp (*Bch.* Leaf II, 14). Even a deep canal of 1702 *hasta* was dug out, extending from a river to a pool on the western side of the temple site, to deliver stones. Building the canal cost 8340 *māḍha*s in which 835 persons participated. Even elephants were deployed in the work (*Bch.* Leaf III, 6; IV, 1). Many stone quarries were identified and selected (*Bch.* Leaf III, 5), even as quarrying at other sites was in progress (*Bch.* Leaf II, 5). Large consignments of stones had to be delivered in boatloads at great cost of 3077 *māḍha*s (*Bch.* Leaf XVII, 30), and boats had to be conveyed from one place to another (*Bch.* Leaf III, 10); the stones when received were unloaded, squared and arranged (*Bch.* Leaf II, 11, 12); timber was delivered on elephant-driven carts (*Bch.* Leaf II, 13), and so on and so forth. These operations are mentioned in the text throwing light on the massive scale on which the work was distributed to different groups of artisans, craftsmen and ordinary workers, requiring different skills and varied modes to accomplish them. But these operations do not include artistic work, which were assigned to master-artists all the while the building operations lasted. Small contracts continued to be given to the less skilled workmen. For instance, we are told of twenty-seven workmen carving steps for 2 *bharaṇas*, 14 *gaunīs* and one *māḍha* (*Bch.* Leaf IX, 8); or of nine stone workers who received two *bharaṇa*s and 22 *gaunī*s for making the round steps for an inner door (*Bch.* Leaf IX, 9). But, more specialised work went to the masters.[95]

Artwork was regulated in terms of both its volume and time schedule.[96] For instance, on the fifth day of *śrāvaṇa* month (early August), a contract to supply two hundred dancing female (*kanyā*) figures in three months was granted to some artists (*Bch.* Leaf LVI, 2). Time schedules required strict adherence. We learn from the *Bayacakaḍa* that construction of the *pīḍhā* tiers started in November after assembling the scaffolding up to the roof of the *mukhasala*. In three months time, by the end of January next year, six tiers of the *pīḍhā* had already been set. More stones were brought in February for further work to set up dancing (*kanyā*) figures on *pīḍhā*s, a job completed only in the second-half of March. In the meantime, preparations started to construct the roof of *pīḍhā*. The hauling over and setting the *kanyā* figures on *pīḍhā*s must have been complete by the beginning of April as final payments for setting those images at their appointed location were then made to the artists, etc. The entire job of installing the *kanyā* figures on *pīḍhā* thus took six months from November to April.[97] Constructional operations on other parts of the temple continued simultaneously while this work was in progress (*Bch*. Leaf LXV, 5; XVI, 16).

There could be no let up in works and *śilpin*s were moved from one job to another as need to do so arose. Thus, when work was stopped on *garbha*, *śilpins* were set to do other sculpture work (*Bch*. Leaf XXXVII, 3). Once a work started, care was taken to carry it on carefully to the finish. Nothing except a calamity, a royal visit (*Bch*. Leaf XVIII, 3) or a celebration of festival (*Bch*. Leaf XXIII, 5) would suspend or stop the work. The rainy season was an exception. But when the work was stopped for the four months of *cāturmāsya* (rainy season), workmen's accounts were settled before they left and they were given parting fees too in *māḍha*s (*Bch*. Leaf IV, 30). Those who were retained received the retaining charges (*Bch*. Leaf XI, 13). Recruitment ceased during the rains and if a *pāthuriā* came looking for work he was paid for his journey and dispatched (*Bch*. Leaf XII, 8).

There are glimpses in the *Bayacakaḍa* of working methods concerning particular works as operations proceeded. The details indicate that the general layout plan was prepared by the *sūtradhāra*. Measuring the proportions and marking the layout was particularly his responsibility. He carried it out either by himself or with the assistance of fellow workers who held the thread as he did the job.[98] Measurements were important and required a keen expertise in geometrical proportions in order to ensure stability of the monument and standard proportions (*tālamāna*) in figure work. The work started along the prescribed lines only after the *sūtradhāra* had measured the ground with his thread and marked out positions of different parts of the temple. These marks lie hidden under the monument but one can even today observe the cut marks on stones of the Konarak temple at lower levels on the *bhitta* or other portions where piles of dressed stones were required to be set up as the monument grew up in elevation.

There were different methods in practice for different works. Before starting a work the experts and workmen arranged dressed and chiselled stones (*Bch.* Leaf XXI, 13). As constant handling disturbed the piles of stones they were re-arranged on the ground and secured, on the orders of the *sūtradhāra* (*Bch.* Leaf XXXVII, 2). Sometimes, the stones were numbered for particular work and sent for setting in a numbered order. This we see when Gadadhara fixed the pedestal of the Aruna Pillar (*Bch.* Leaf XXXVII, 9). Hauling up of Aruna Pillar was an elaborate affair requiring six heavy cables with support underneath, and ropes to lift it. It took forty-seven workers to conduct the operations with elephants and labourers for three days (*Bch.* Leaf XXXVII, 9-15). Sometimes two separate artists made a single image. This happened in the case of a lion figure made in two parts (*Bch.* Leaf XXI, 15). Similarly, after setting up of the *āmalaka* made of sixteen pieces, three *pāthuriās*, two workmen and one water carrier filled the joints with *karāla* and rubbed the joints until it became 'as if made of one single stone' (*Bch.* Leaf XLIV, 11); works in pieces by separate artists would have required much coordination. But that was not found wanting.[99] A trial sometimes became necessary to test whether or not a particular job, when concluded, would serve the purpose. So, after the *garbhagṛha* was completed, it was flooded to test the outflow of water (*Bch.* Leaf XXXIII, 5). The help of ordinary labourers was taken in non-specialist works. We find labourers engaged in eighteen teams under their chiefs removing the sand for digging foundations of the temple (*Bch.* Leaf IV, 7). Sometimes, work could be an exacting exercise. In an instance, pairs of labourers carried 60,362 pieces of stone sent by a Nayaka, delivered them and received 203 *māḍhas* as labour charges (*Bch.* Leaf VI, 4). The time taken in completing this task is not specified. Labourers were appointed to assist *pāthuriās*. When twelve *pāthuriās* set stones on three sides of the *mukhaśālā*, forty-three carriers were deployed to assist them (*Bch.* Leaf VIII, 21). The *pāthuriās* also quarried the stone and the boatmen delivered them to the designated places (*Bch.* Leaf XII, 9).

STORES AND SUPPLIES

To build a huge temple complex like the one of Konarak required huge expenses and a substantial infrastructure. The *Bayacakaḍa* seems to provide carefully recorded details about it in terms of deployment of work force, materials and services. That the expenses were phenomenal, is borne out by treasury records indicating payments, which flowed, in gold and silver coins in *māḍhas*, *aśrapī*, *Badshah tanka*s and *sikka*, and in *gaunī* and *bharaṇa*, the latter representing the measures for cereals.[100] The king had established a treasury and a well-provided store[101] at the work site to meet the required dispensations for different purpose. He had appointed Haricandana as the officer in-charge of accounts with the duty to maintain stores and treasury (*Bch.* Leaf 1). The king also appointed the Dalabehera of Rupasagada as the officer in-charge of camp administration (*Bch.* Leaf 1).

These officers in the camp had several facilities at their bidding to run the affairs of the work site, ensuring a regular supply of men and materials. They had two tax collectors, namely, Ramacandra and Narayana Simha, who collected tax from shopkeepers of the Rupasa and Pateli camps and deposited the collection in the local treasury (*Bch.* Leaf XXVI, 12). They had accounting clerks (*Bch.* Leaf XXVI, 11), watchmen (*Bch.* Leaf IV, 30), guards (*Bch.* Leaf VII, 1), scribes and messengers.[102] They had a well paid contingent of overseers and superintendents to supervise temple construction (*Bch.* Leaf V, 5, 6, Leaf IX, 23; Leaf XV, 6; Leaf XVII, 18). The *Bayacakaḍa* has an entry about the overseers receiving 'numerous presents from all over the state', apart from 4503 *asrapī*s, 3472 gold coins and an annual accrual of 3408 *bharaṇa*s (of grains) from the treasury (*Bch.* Leaf XXIX).

The camp also maintained horses, elephants, and their attendants (*Bch.* Leafs I, 6; III, 1-2; XV, 6; XXIII, 10), bullock carts (*Bch.* Leaf I, 5), bullock carter (*Bch.* Leaf IX, 22) and elephant carts (*hātīsagaḍa*, *Bch.* Leaf III, 13). These were constantly used for transport and travel. Boats (*Bch.* Leaf III, 7) were employd for river transport and they helped in transporting huge supplies of stones (*Bch.* Leaf III, 10; XVII, 30) by river. The work required all kinds of supplies, which makes an almost inexhaustible list.[103] It was a challenging job for the store to handle a constant supply of these materials and their finished products, a job they were able to handle carefully. From the details it follows that carpenters and iron-casters manufactured most of the tools at the site from the raw materials supplied through the stores. Every time a supply was made or a job was finished on those supplies, payments invariably followed in *māḍha*s or in *gaunī*s and *bharaṇa*s depending upon the nature of work.

While the king's munificence took care of payments for supply and works, materials in the store were augmented with presents pouring in from different sources, including family of the king, his feudatories, besides from bureaucrats and administrators, land-owners, military chiefs and temples or their priests. These presents included currency, cereals, clothes, iron lumps, stones, timber, and host of other materials; and sometimes even *śilpīs* to work on the temple. Every time the presents came, the courtiers were chivalrously offered a parting gift before they left.[104] When the king won a war and plundered the treasury of his rival, the booty was sent to the stores for being spent in building the temple.[105] Despite such dispensations in meeting the expenses, the recurring cost of construction went on mounting relentlessly. And, perhaps as a measure to control the exhausting outflow of revenue, the king had to devalue the state currency in the midst of temple construction. Thus, in place of the earlier sun-marked *māḍha* coins of four to a *tola* of gold the king ordered the issue of new *Padma*-marked coin of five to a *tola* of gold.[106]

WORKING ENVIRONMENT

A ruler had commissioned the Konarak temple, and state functionaries took care of material requirements and welfare of *śilpins*, ordinary workers (*kārīgars*), stone-cutters (*pāitālas*), overseers and water carriers.[107] They were lodged in three camps, namely, Rupasa, Pateli and Duai in the vicinity of the work-site, receiving wages[108] (*vartanā*) and victuals and other facilities from time to time. As artists and craftsmen worked in temporary sheds at the site,[109] engrossed in their respective tasks, the water-carriers moved around satiating their thirst and betel-carriers offering betels to the more distinguished among them.[110] Apart from enjoying the facilities of a common mess (or even cooking their meals in the camp),[111] the workers had shopping facilities nearby where traders and shopkeepers opened shops and paid taxes to the treasury for this facility.[112] *Vaidyas*, 'doctors in traditional medicine', with their royally funded dispensary were employed for workers' benefit to dispense medicine to the sick or wounded and they too received a salary for the same.

Cowherds supplied milk to the camp and besides receiving payments for the supply they sometimes got rewarded too.[113] Festivities punctuated the hectic life in camp amidst relentless work, and festivals like *Ḍolā* (the festival of colours), *Vijaya daśamī,* and worship of tools on the *astrapūjā* day and the New Year Day were celebrated with feast and a holiday.

There is little evidence in the *Bayacakaḍa* or elsewhere of coercive innuendoes against artists or workers even as discipline was meticulously enforced. For instance, when a pilot failed to conduct a boat that was to carry a large chlorite stone of thirty-two *hasta*, he was fined three *māḍhas*. A guard (*pāik*) Chanda Simha collected the fine from him some five months later, and perhaps for this delay he had to deposit seven instead of six *māḍhas* in the treasury. Or, Ganga Mahāpātra imposed a fine of two *māḍhas* on Yogi, the *jālī* cutter. The fine was collected by a guard (*pāik*) and deposited in the treasury.[114] These small incidents of dereliction apart, the small details from the instance of the Konarak temple tend to indicate a just and sympathetic working environment where different components of its working organism functioned in concert with each other with the participants performing their specific roles in that vast collaborative enterprise. Evidently, artists and workmen depended on the regular flow of resources to ensure timely payment to them in cash or kind. Completion of a work was contingent upon such payments for there is evidence elsewhere of even ambitiously planned monuments being abandoned by artists if the resources of the patron dried up.[115]

All this is not to say that the work on the Konarak went on without accidents, casualties or dissent. Mishap happened and conflict-situations sometimes did arise. But they were rare in occurrence and as they surfaced they seem to have been humanely resolved.[116] Accidents were generally caused by the faults in scaffoldings, especially when heavy sculptures or architectural pieces were hauled up on or through them. Scaffolding with sloping ramps was put in place all around the temple (*Bch.* Leaf XVII, 7). These were essential in providing working platforms to artists as the monument gathered height gradually.[117] There were different kinds of scaffoldings: straight, ramp-like, ladder-like and others. Sometimes they contained 'wooden platforms (fitted on to the) palmwood posts, and secured to the wall up to the required height.[118] It follows from the *Bayacakaḍa* that it required both smiths (*ojhās*) and stonemasons (*swānsya*) to construct scaffoldings. The store supplied materials like ordinary as well as oiled and powder-coated ropes, iron pulleys fixed on cranes (*kalagayala*), etc. for the purpose of maintaining and securing them. Artisans once made a huge and sloping scaffolding (ramp?) for fifty *māḍhas*, which is a respectable amount in the scales of payment in Konarak operations. Smaller ramp-like scaffolding was also built at lesser cost. Scaffolding also contained planks of two *hasta* to allow artists to sit while working (*Bch.* Leaf XVII, 13); Rajiva Mahārāṇā was an expert of scaffoldings and so important was this task that he was appointed by the *sūtradhāra* for the job right after his own appointments. Efforts were made, apparently under his supervision, to assemble the scaffoldings carefully, taking precautions to appropriately secure them for safety. Thus, as a scaffolding became loose on an occasion while the construction work was on, twelve people laboured for twenty days to tie, fasten and secure it and received payment on completing the job.[119]

Despite such precautions, mishap still remained unavoidable. The *Bayacakaḍa* records that when ornamental work on the third *pīḍhā* of the

Konarak temple started, Madhu Mahārāṇā, a master-artist, fell down from heights; *sūtradhāra* became sick and Ganga Mahāpātra, another celebrated artist of the Konarak temple, aware that the scaffolding was insecure, refused to work despite the *sūtradhāra*'s request. In these circumstances, the work had to be stopped under the *sūtradhāra*'s orders and the unsafe scaffolding was dismantled. In the instance, caution saved loss and injury.

But there were occasions when tragedy did strike. In such events, steps were taken to mitigate the pain and suffering of the aggrieved with a compensatory grant from the treasury in addition to the liberalities of the local artists' community which operated its own community fund deposited in the treasury.[120] In an instance of accidental death of a worker, a land grant made to the family of the victim ensured more than a lifetime's guarantee of well being to the kins. In this instance, when a Sūrya image was being lifted on the scaffolding, a workman – Damejena – fell down and died. His son Raghua was given a 'life-sustaining sum' (*ghaṭapoṣaka*) of thirty *māḍhas* and ten *gunṭhas* of land (in a village), as compensation. The work was stopped immediately only to be resumed after a break. In another accident, when workers fell down from scaffolding, Pathani fractured his arms but Agadhu, another worker, succumbed to his injuries. A message was sent to the *rājā* of Mayurbhanja (who was instrumental in recruiting some of these *śilpins*) informing him of the mishap. Simultaneously, Dandi, the brother of the deceased, working on the site with another team, was promptly informed and granted forty *māḍha* to perform the last rites of the departed kin. He further received three *māḍhas* and six *gaunīs* as compensation. Sometimes the entire community of artists at the site contributed to support the victim of an accident. So, when Yogi Mahāpātra fell from the scaffolding and died, Balasri, the officer in-charge of the camp of artisans came forward to personally meet the expenses for his cremation without waiting for a grant from the treasury. *Śilpins*' support to the victim's kins, in that instance, came later when they received their wages and offered succour. Thus, they gave one hundred *māḍhas* from their 'charity fund' to the family of Yogi. Balasri further added a sum of seven *māḍhas* to it as his personal contribution.

Casualties spared none: neither the ordinary workers nor the master artists. Accidents could always happen, even in the presence of the king as he watched the work. Thus, when a figure of a lion was being hauled up with the king watching the operations, the scaffolding shook, felling twelve people including Narayana Mahāpātra, a master-artist. Relief work was soon launched and thirty guards were detailed to lift the wounded and carry them to a *Vaidya*. Humane considerations are not found wanting in other cases too when the king was absent from the scene. So, when Nidhi Mahāpātra, a master-artist, fell ill he was sent back to his village on a bullock cart. The carter received payment from treasury for his labour. Or, when Visu Mahārāṇā was immobilised by sickness, his dues were cleared with a payment of ten *māḍhas* along with a gratuity and he was sent back to his village on a bullock cart. Sometimes, human frailties also precipitated ugly situations as for instance, in case of a *śilpin* committing theft in the storeroom. The theft was soon noticed and a guard (*pāik*) was sent to apprehend him and, as a punishment to him, the stock of cereals in his house was confiscated. We also have in the text an incident of an elephant dying; his body was carried away for burial with payment made for his carriage. There are enough hints in these details to indicate that work at the site went on despite minor irritants, accidents, calamities and even death. The humane attitude is not found wanting especially in tragic and unfortunate episodes nor was the victim or his family left in lurch, uncared. Sometimes the entire community including the resident officers of the state rose up to support the family of the departed.[121]

SŪTRADHĀRA'S ROLE

The *Bayacakaḍa* provides many interesting details on the role of *sūtradhāra* and others in constructing the temple at Konarak. It was a celebrated event when, after performing the religious rituals, Narasimhadeva I (AD 1238-1258), drafted Sadasiva *sāmantarāya* Mahāpātra as *sūtradhāra* of his work and presented to him a piece of linen (possibly, a turban cloth) as a token of his appointment. This he did in an assembly attended by the *rājaguru*, officials and feudal chiefs and a large contingent of seven hundred *śilpins* and seven *ojhās* (iron-casters). It would appear from these details that recruitment of the work force was already complete when the *sūtradhāra* was appointed but the experts in different skills still remained to be formally designated, a task that was to be performed by the *sūtradhāra*. So, as the *sūtradhāra* took charge, he formally appointed Gadadhara Mahāpātra as *karmakāra* (executive architect) and *parīchā* (superintendent of works), Vidyadhara Mahāpātra as *mūrtikāra* (chief of image makers), Aintha Mahārāṇā as *swānsya* (head of the stonemasons), Rajiva Mahārāṇā for making scaffoldings, Bindu Mahārāṇā as *cūnurā* (plasterer) and Puria Mahāpātra as *kamarakanṭa* (iron caster).[122] The titles of these appointees suggest their elevated status among the fellow workers. The speed with which these major appointments were made would suggest that a consensus had already been reached about them earlier, and contracts perhaps effected; and the assembly of *śilpins*, *ojhās* and dignitaries had gathered only to receive a formal announcement of those dispensations.

As the construction work moved, the *sūtradhāra* is seen taking control of the proceedings: planning and supervising the works routinely or in emergencies, personally carving major sculptures[123] and directing others to perform particular tasks with specific instructions.[124] His decisions were generally taken as final. When there was a dithering about what kind of stone should be used for the main icon of Sūrya in the *garbhagṛha*, the *sūtradhāra*'s view prevailed (*Bch*. Leaf LIII, 2). In case of serious disagreement, the matter was referred to the king for his final word. Such an occasion arose when Narayana Mahāpātra, in-charge of setting up the horses on the *pīṭha* disagreed with *sūtradhāra* in putting three and four horses on either side of the *jagatī*. Instead, he wanted one horse on the front and a set of three others on each side. So, the *sūtradhāra* referred the matter to the king (*Bch*. Leaf XXXVII, 16), and Narayana was overruled. But such differences were rare and we find the *sūtradhāra* directing the work all over, apart from doing many jobs himself. He supervises levelling of the ground at the site and measuring different levels as the work proceeded. He lays out the plan of the temple with the thread (*Bch*. Leaf I, 3); determines the position of an entrance to the sanctum with the help of a *śanku* (plumb bob) (*Bch*. Leaf IX, 10). Amidst *Homa* sacrifice he measures out the figure of Mahabhaskara, the main cult image, on a stone (*Bch*. Leaf XXIV, 11); he traces the design of the door jambs with the assistance of Angai Nayaka (*Bch*. Leaf IX, 15) and so on and so forth.

The *sūtradhāra* owed his position to the patron-king and his occasional interactions with the patron, Narasimhadeva I, underscore both his loyalty and his qualified subservience to the patron. It seems to have been a sensitive relationship without the ruler being overbearing or the *sūtradhāra* being intransigent. There was an occasion when the ruler himself called on the *sūtradhāra* to satisfy himself about his work on the *pūjā* image of the *mahābhāskara*-Sūrya.[125] On his part, the *sūtradhāra* remained in touch with the patron: reporting him directly,[126] taking instructions of him in the matters of plan and design of the temple and its adjuncts.[127] If need arose Sadasiva *sūtradhāra* wrote to the king to apprise him of the situation (*Bch*. Leaf XXI, 9). While the treasury at the site ensured regular payment to him on salary,[128] and on account of his sundry jobs, he took decisions about the order of constructions and their timings. For instance, he prescribes the time schedule for finishing the work on a ceiling and twenty-four stonemasons (*pāthuriyā*s) are given a contract of one hundred and ten *māḍha*s to complete the job within the allotted time (*Bch*. Leaf XXI, 5). Examples of such work-allotments by the *sūtradhāra* can be multiplied at will.

He even distributed awards to master-artists on successful completion of a significant work. Thus, when the *navagraha* stone panel was hoisted on the iron girders above the portal, he presented cash awards in *Ganga māḍha* to Nidhi Mahāpātra (who had distinguished himself in this work) and himself received a *Ganga māḍha* as a present in his honour (*Bch*. Leaf XIV, 6).

On yet another occasion, when presents were distributed and the king failed to turn up for this ceremony, the *sūtradhāra* received the cash for the purpose and deposited it into the treasury (*Bch.* Leaf XVII, 5). He enjoyed respect and in conformity with his dignity he sometimes moved on a *palki* or on the back of an elephant if work required it: on a *palki* when, with Ganga Mahāpātra and Gadadhara Mahāpātra, he went to mark (the plan of) a temple by thread and, after completing the work, they all stayed in the camp on treasury expenses (*Bch.* Leaf III, 8); and on an elephant's back when he went to attend the New Year festival (*Bch.* VIII, 20). His presence and directions were so crucial that if he had to go out for an urgent work even temporarily, he did so only after handing over the charge to an expert of his choosing.[129]

Apart from his professional responsibilities in the camp, he had to attend the distinguished visitors and honour them befittingly. Visitors kept coming in to see the work. In the instance of the Konarak temple, these included *mūrtikāra*, *citrakāra*, brass worker, etc. from different parts of Orissa, Andhra, Karnataka, Bengal, Gaya-*kṣetra*, Kalinjara, etc. These visitors were not only taken around but received gift from the treasury (*Bch.* Leaf XXXIV, 9). There were standing orders of the king to the temple guardian to show the temple under construction to any person 'well-versed in *śilpa*' (*Bch.* Leaf XXXIV, 10). Sometimes the visitors also rewarded the *śilpin*s. When one of the queens of the ruler came to visit the temple along with the *rājaguru*, she gave awards to *śilpins* through the *sūtradhāra* who distributed four hundred and one of these *māḍha*s to *śilpin*s as reward and deposited the remaining two hundred and ninety-nine *māḍha*s in the treasury. The queen also desired that *pāthuriā*s be sent to build another temple elsewhere (*Bch.* Leaf XXXV, 3). When, on the invitation of a king, the chief of a religious *maṭha* made a state visit to the work site for eight days, the *sūtradhāra* performed his *pādapūjā* with a coin provided by the treasury. The Svami, impressed with the *sūtradhāra*, requested him to make a Sūrya image in the *siddha yoga* pose for his use and the *sūtradhāra* received stone to work on and some gratuity (*piṭhakiā*) for carrying out this job.[130] It thus appears that some visitors, inspired with the quality of work and skill of the workers, offered a casual or substantive work to the *sūtradhāra* and others. This meant additional money to the *sūtradhāra* and promise of employment to others even as they had an assignment in hand.

The *sūtradhāra* assigned work to all and sundry including the master-artists and ordinary workers. There are clear instances of his writ being followed both by artists and the paymasters. Thus, when he ordered an image of a warrior Suasamalla to be made in the act of fighting on horseback it was carved and delivered, and set by workmen (*Bch.* Leaf XLVII, 20). Sometimes, he even ordered special work on special wages. When the king desired to include in the temple statuary 'two large fiend-destroying horses in the likeness of the (king's) two horses, one white and the other black, in their battle harnesses and ... riders', the *sūtradhāra* assigned this work to Dharama and Śiva Mahāpātras who 'received in all' one hundred *māḍhas* for the work which was a respectable amount by Konarak standards (*Bch.* Leaf XLVII, 11). The *sūtradhāra* also had the authority to receive the completed work for scrutiny before a payment could be made for it. Thus, *kansāri* Nayak received payment of five *māḍhas* only after he delivered a portable victory image, cast in metal, to the *sūtradhāra* (*Bch.* Leaf XXXVI, 3). Similarly, Dama Mahāpātra delivered to the *sūtradhāra* the Viranchi-Sūrya image, a composite icon with the features of Brahmā and Sūrya combined in a single image (*Bch.* Leaf XXXVI, 12). Many other instances of such procedure occur in the text of the *Bayacakaḍa*, indicating the authority of the *sūtradhāra* in such matters.

WORK CULTURE AND DISCIPLINE

There is enough in the *Bayacakaḍa* to indicate a humane, just, collaborative and cooperative working culture at the workplace while operations lasted. There are though a few instances of rivalries, dissent or conflict among *śilpins*, they seem being resolved quickly. *Śilpīs* in the camps seem to have lived a life of honour and dignity where their skills stood recognised, their well being safeguarded,[131] and compensations assured in case of mishaps, as they worked honourably in the tasks assigned to them. They led a simple life with facilities far less than those at the bidding of the officers in the camp. This difference comes out clearly by comparison.[132] Even the *sūtradhāra,* his commanding position notwithstanding, lived a simple, Spartan life in the camp with few things of comfort at his disposal.[133] Perhaps the convergence of interests of a patron and his contingents of artists and artisans ensured a favourable working atmosphere conducive to an efficient work-performance. A patron would seek realisation of his vision in a building project and artists and their contingents recruited and assembled together for a designated work, would look up to him for professional and pecuniary gains. This was despite rivalries within the artists' community with leaders, independent of each other, competing for gains that would accrue to them (and perhaps to their contingents of workers) through assignments.

An instance of such a rivalry at Konarak is seen in respect of the *śilpins* from Madurai and, in their spat with the *sūtradhāra* they emerge mollified, thanks to the king's intervention. The *Bayacakaḍa* records that ten *śilpins* (the terms *kārigara* and *śilpin* are interchangeably used) from Madurai were sent 'as presents' by the Pandya ruler, the father-in-law of Narasimhadeva, to work on the Konarak temple. On arrival, they were provided a temporary lodging, which labourers had quickly assembled for them. They also received twenty-one *māḍha*s per month as salary (which works out to be more than that of the *sūtradhāra* who on an occasion is said to have received seven *māḍha*s as three month's salary!) and fine rice to eat. But when they delivered their work to the *sūtradhāra* he rejected it. Offended by the rejection, they, in protest, abstained from taking food. A horse rider was sent to report the matter to the king, and a letter came from him with instructions for the *sūtradhāra* to allot to the Madurai *śilpin*s the task of carving creepers and other decorations. This was a compromise, which resolved the differences: the Madurai *silpī*s got a reprieve and remained in employment and the *sūtradhāra*'s decision and honour was upheld. That they were assigned the work of carving creepers is clear from the instance of an award of two *māḍha*s to each one of the ten Madurai sculptors for doing the creeper work. But the tension perhaps continued haunting the Madurai *śilpins* as well as the *sūtradhāra*, for we find the Madurai *śilpin*s uprooted and moved to the western side from their originally allotted camp on the eastern side, regardless of the additional expenses involved in this shifting. Eventually, however, these artists seem to have been accommodated in the team, doing jobs that came by. The *Bayacakaḍa* mentions that four of the Madurai *śilpin*s were engaged in a team with other *śilpin*-Mahāpātras to set the first tier of six *pīḍhā*s, fix them and carve elephants and *rājabandha*, 'royal scenes', on their faces. For this work the team received a payment of forty *māḍha*s, one *bharaṇa* and twenty-four *gaunī*s. On other occasions, the Madurai *śilpin*s received two *māḍha*s for ten images and again seven of them received forty *māḍha*s for some unspecified work. Their participation continued unabated as it is said that the *sūtradhāra*, on the instruction of the king, called all the ten Madurai *śilpin*s along with four hundred and eighteen other stonemasons (*pāthuriā*s) to an important meeting, which led to the drawing and distribution of a new work schedule. The plans and measurements of the upcoming edifices were also discussed in the meeting and sent to the king. Eventually, when the Madurai *śilpin*s left for their home after the conclusion of work at Konarak, they received eighty-two *māḍha*s as a parting gift. But their special status is not missed in the small details that one sees in the text as, in an instance, one finds them sent on a *palki*, on treasury expenses, to witness the anniversary of the first Narasimhadeva's investiture celebrations.[134]

Certain norms prevailed in the *śilpin*s' work, which seem to have been conventionally followed in work. Adherence to time schedule was generally the part of contracts and it influenced the scale of payments also. Both these find mention in the *Bayacakaḍa*. Thus, four sedant lions (*varasimha*s) and four *cīrasimha*s were hauled up on scaffoldings around *mukhaśālā* in three days. The workers – two hundred and forty of them divided into eight bands of thirty workers each – received one *bharaṇa* and twenty-four *gaunīs* for the job (*Bch.* Leaf XXVI, 6). Similarly, to set the lion figures on pedestals below the *alaśrī* figures, fifteen *pāthuriās* worked for eight days under Dama Mahārāṇa and received one *bharaṇa* and thirty *gaunīs* in all to compensate for their work.[135] The treasury made payment to the designated workers only when *sūtradhāra* had authorized them to perform specific tasks.[136] The finished work, including the images, etc. came up for his scrutiny and he could accept or reject such a work. As we have seen above, his rejection came in the instance of the Madurai *śilpins*.

Work was mostly a cooperative venture generally assigned to teams with their leaders designated for the purpose. The leadership norms had come into action right from the start of the work as the king in an assembly of workers and others divided the work force of seven hundred *śilpins* and seven *ojhās* (blacksmiths) into three groups with a master-artist placed to lead each of these groups. On their turn, they all were placed under the command of the *sūtradhāra* Sadasiva. As a token of their appointment, each of these three team leaders and the *sūtradhāra* received a turban cloth from the king. As the work began we find it being parcelled out on contract to individuals independently or in pairs or to teams; and all these modes turned into a standard practice whenever particular jobs were contemplated.[137]

As regards contract to individuals, we find the skilled master-artists receiving them in large numbers. Ganga Mahārāṇā was one such of the celebrities, much acclaimed for his work on the *jagatī* wheels of the Konarak temple. He received the *sūtradhāra*'s orders and a contract of thirty *māḍhas* to make Dikpala images of 'one *hasta* and nine *yavas*', 'with his own hands'. Similarly, without any assistance from others, he made an image of Brahmā-Gāyatrī for *garbhagṛha* and the Sūrya image for southern niche for thirty-four *māḍhas* (with a silken cloth received, in addition). He also made the Biranchi Narayana image (a six-armed Sūrya image holding two *padmas*, two *Vedas*, a *kamanḍalu* and an *akṣamālā*) for seventeen *māḍhas*.[138] The works of Dama Mahāpātra (*Bch.* Leaf XXXVI, 12) and others, like Visvanatha, Narayana, Narasimha), etc. are similarly mentioned.

Others figuring in individual contracts include: a carpenter Basu getting seven *māḍhas* plus a contract for making a wooden palanquin inlayed with ivory-work meant to carry a victory image in a procession (*Bch.* Leaf LVII, 11); carpenter Govinda for consolidating the scaffolding with twenty wooden props (*Bch.* Leaf VIII, 11); Narasimha Mahāpātra 'and others' receiving an eleven *māḍha* contract for providing Beki Bhairava and Alasakanya figures (*Bch.* Leaf XIV, 8). Similarly, on contract, Lakhana Mahārāṇā worked on wheels (*Bch.* Leaf XXXII, 10) and Dharani Mahāpātra 'and eight others' made *kautuka bandha* (lion with human head) and *virāla* images (*Bch.* Leaf XXXIX, 10). There is no dearth of such individual contracts in the text of the *Bayacakaḍa*.

It seems that in addition to cash payment to artists on contract, materials like wood or stone required for the work were also provided to them; the cash payment compensated primarily for their manual, artistic work. This seems indicated in the case of Bhagavan Nayak whose contract for casting two portable bronze images included materials provided by the store and the facility of a foundry where the images were to be cast. The materials included gold, silver, iron, lead, copper and bell metal. A wax model of the images was made and shown to the king before making the image (*Bch.* Leaf XXXII, 3-4).

Among such accomplished master-artists, Visvanatha Mahāpātra seems to stand out for reasons other than merely professional.[139] Although he was equally adept in carving iconographically intricate and artistic divine images, like Mahiṣamardinī,[140] Nārāyaṇa (a form of Viṣṇu) and others, or secular motifs, like crocodile/gorgoyle heads, he is seen assiduously promoting himself by presenting some of his independent works to the patron-king and priests, obviously to make an impression. Thus, he sends a royal image (portrait?) to the king and receives a gold ring in return. Once he presents a portrait sculpture and, in return, receives 20 *māḍha*s on expenses (*Bch.* Leaf V, 8). For yet another image representing a royal procession, similarly presented, he receives one *māḍha.* When he sends an image to a temple, he receives a New Year present, some gratuity (*piṭhakiā*) and two *māḍha*s in return. Visvanatha seems to have been a highly energetic and active *śilpin* to find time amidst other assigned works to make those images and present them to influential people. There is no mention of contracts for such images but he gets paid alright, without perhaps the *sūtradhāra* intervening![141] But, as we shall see below, Visvanatha ran into trouble when, on an occasion, he supplied the *kanyā* figures on contract.

The construction work required teams, and these, apart from individuals, were generally engaged on contract to accomplish such works. For instance, Narayana Mahāpātra and fourteen other people get a contract of 'arranging on ground sixteen large sections of an *āmalakī*' before it was hauled and set up (*Bch.* Leaf XXXI, 4); Rama, Nila, Gopi and Ganga Mahāpātras have a joint contract of five *māḍha*s per image to make six erotic (*bandha*) images,[142] and they received an advance of thirteen *māḍha*s for the work (*Bch.* Leaf XXXVII, 8); Mukunda and five other Pathurias got a ten *māḍha* advance on a thirty *māḍha* contract to make a big lion figure (*Bch.* Leaf XV, 4). Vidyadhara, Yogi and Vira got a contract of thirty *māḍha*s to carve fretwork on a *padmapīṭha* and received four *māḍha*s as advance and another payment of twelve *māḍha*s soon after (*Bch.* Leaf VIII, 12). Collaboration remained in practice all through the construction work.[143]

Even in collaboration, helpers were appointed to assist the master artists, which meant additional expenses.[144] Thus, the *sūtradhāra* had three helpers with him when he was assigned work on the images of the western side of the temple for ten *māḍhas* and forty *gaunī* (*Bch.* Leaf X, 15); Gadadhara Mahāpātra, head of his community (*kulapata sāmanta*), likewise was entrusted with similar work on the northern side on the same dispensations (*Bch.* Leaf X, 15-16). Four master artists, including Visvanatha Mahāpātra, as leaders (with others to support them) similarly got three workmen to assist them in carving the *dvārabandha* (doorway) within six months for 212 *māḍhas*. They also received an advance of 120 *māḍhas* for the work (*Bch.* Leaf IX, 16). Narayana, Mukunda and Dharma – all of them Mahāpātras – and fourteen others were given a contract of two hundred and thirty *māḍhas* for making two *navagraha* stones without any advance being offered to them (*Bch.* Leaf XIII, 6). Later, when another team took over to perform further work on that errand, only Dharma continued from the previous team and teaming with others he hoisted and placed the *navagraha* stone at its designated location (*Bch.* Leaf XIII, 12).[145]

Nobody refused an assignment whether or not it was commensurate with his specific skills and nobody was an exception to the culture of teamwork. A narrow specialisation was not the practice either. Gadadhara, a master-artist himself, assisted the *sūtradhāra* in arranging stones in front of the sanctum entrance, with the help of a mason's thread (*Bch.* Leaf IX, 13). Gadadhara Mahāpātra directed thirteen people including Nidhi and Rama Mahārāṇā to complete the work on the *anuratha śikhara* of *mukhaśālā* (*Bch.* Leaf IX, XVII, 19). Fourteen *pāthuriās* with Gadadhara marked the rampant lions on the west and south side of the *gandi* and received 'one instalment of 30 *māḍhas*' (*Bch.* Leaf IX, 25). Gadei (Gadadhara) and Ganga with a team of thirteen workers made six *kanyā* figures of six *hastas* for twenty *māḍhas*; and, on another contract of three hundred and three *māḍhas* to carve *kanyā* figures of eight *hastas* for *garbha*, they received another payment of two hundred and thirty *māḍhas* 'in clearance' (*Bch.* Leaf XXII, 6). Gadadhara worked with Ganga for making the Dikpala images (*Bch.* Leaf XXII, 7) and again with Narayana Mahāpātras he got a contract for smaller *kanyā* figures for the second *pīḍhā*, thus receiving (an advance? of) forty *māḍhas* straightaway (*Bch.* Leaf, XXIII, 3). Four master-artists including Visvanatha Mahāpātra, got a contract of 212 *māḍhas* to complete the work on sanctum doorway within six months. For this they received a down-payment of 120 *māḍhas* (*Bch.* Leaf IX, 16).

Often the work assigned might not have been commensurate with the expertise of the receiver but it was carried out nonetheless, without demur. Vidyadhara Mahāpātra, a *jālī*-cutter and a *mūrtikāra* (*Bch.* Leaf VIII, 7; Leaf I) supervised levelling of ground with the help of a large contingent for twenty-one days (*Bch.* Leaf II, 2). Or, when Gadadhara Mahārāṇā, a *karmakāra* and *parīchā* appointed by the *sūtradhāra*, was required to fill up the *pīṭha* he did the job assisted by experts like Madhu and Nidhi, the *mahārāṇās*, along with others (*Bch.* Leaf VIII, 4).

Caste and community discriminations were absent in the camp as well as at the work site. But women always seem on the losing side. We will come to this point later. The *Bayacakaḍa* refers to twenty-one different kinds of workers performing different tasks in temple building and interestingly they included people of different communities and sex. Apart from references to the brāhmaṇas settled in the Vedapura camp to officiate in rituals of temple-building, caste is only once mentioned in the entire text of the *Bayacakaḍa* when 'twelve attendants' of 'good caste' are said to have been appointed for offering service to the king when he visited the camp (*Bch.* Leaf XXXIX, 5). Otherwise, the work plied untainted with caste-prejudices, and artists and craftsmen were mentioned invariably in terms of their different professional cadres or titles like *mahāpātra, mahārāṇā, swānsya, pāthuriā, śilpin, ojhā, pāik, pāitāla*, etc. The workplace thus had a specific non-casteist, professional ambience with tasks for everyone according to their ability and skill. The camp's atmosphere was strictly professional with works assigned, taken and completed in quick succession for which payments quickly followed. A corporate life marked with common celebrations, common living and common motivations was the order in the camp of artisans with little to occasion caste rivalries or privileging. Merit and skill alone counted in works, which comes out clearly in the contracts that were offered and taken. Master craftsmen sometimes combined for work on a single image; but teamwork predominated.

The same professionalism seems to be in place in respect of the religious communities. Suja Mohammed of Bhadrak (Bhadresvari *manḍala*) figures in the text as a highly rated iron-caster. He smelts iron and receives forty *māḍhas* for his work (*Bch.* Leaf VI, 17). He pairs with Basu *Ojhā* in making iron (copper?) channels of different size (*Bch.* Leaf VI, 25). He collaborates with others too in casting iron girders for which he was rewarded with pieces of cloth: a *dupaṭṭā* and two strips of *phuṭṭā* (a cloth) for a *jāmā* (*Bch.* Leaf XI, 7). He also received two *māḍhas* as an award from the funds that the chief queen had set for the purpose (*Bch.* Leaf XXIII, 14; XXIV, 1). Surkhan Mohammed was another Muslim figuring as a trader helping with the materials required for the temple. He supplied two hundred and fifty *palas* of lead on payment of two hundred and ten *Badshah sikkās*. The lead was required for mixing in iron to strengthen the ironworks (*Bch.* Leaf VI, 16).

Women figure among the workers doing small jobs on petty payments in *bharaṇas* and *gaunīs*, but their status seems low in terms of the monetary advantages that accrued to them. In an instance, thirty-five women are said to have worked for twelve days to lay the laterite stones on the floor of *mukhaśālā* for which a payment of only four *bharaṇa* and twenty-seven *gaunīs* was made to them. Their recruitment was mainly for menial jobs, which, as instances indicate, required from one to thirty-seven women workers, with payments never going beyond seven *bharaṇas* in one case, thirty-seven *gaunīs* in another and two *bharaṇas* of rice in yet another instance. When the compound of the Konarak temple was filled up with powdered limestone by thirty women and seven other persons (men?) the entire contingent received only a *bharaṇa* for the work they had rendered. On another occasion, thirty-seven women levelled a floor for three days with a mixture of limewater, *kendu* juice and jaggery, and received one *bharaṇa* and thirty-seven *gaunīs*. Women were employed for pounding stone and filling the cavities of the floor; for oiling the bellows that served the furnace in casting iron girders; for making bamboo pegs in large numbers, a hundred in an instance; preparing mixture of pulverized *sal* resin with oil; preparing a mixture of lime, *til* oil, molasses and pulse for use in filling the joints between the stones of the ceiling; fixing iron cramps on joints of the *āmalakas* made of sixteen pieces; and in one case, polishing a *simhāsana* made by Visi Mahāpātra and others.[146] These instances indicate little participation of women in works of superior skills. They did sometimes participate in working on an *āmalaka* or in polishing an image, the instances when they were indeed close to handling an art work. But only minor jobs of fixing and polishing came to them and works of more challenging and artistic nature mostly went to men. There is, however, an exceptional instance of Suna *pāthuriānī* (woman sculptor), a highly distinguished artist, who is seen standing equal to men in the profession: both in terms of her skill and in the scale of payments which that skill brought to her. The details, though sketchy, follow.

Suna *pāthuriānī* seems to have been employed since the beginning of work as she is found receiving a payment of two *māḍhas* sometime in the 8th *anka* (year) of temple-building work, between July and September, when other artists, including the chief of sculptors, also received their wages. (*Bch.* Leaf V, 9). Five years later, in the 13th *anka* (year) of work, she is mentioned again in a different context, which records her pregnancy due to a (clandestine) relationship with Samanath, a worker in the camp. The pregnancy made her abscond from the camp with her lover. As the two lovers ran away from the camp without notice, their act was taken as a breach of discipline in the camp. Therefore, a guard was sent to apprehend them. He 'got hold of them' and they were brought back. But, as Samanath gave an undertaking to maintain Suna *pāthuriānī* for life, the entire affair ended on a happy note with both 'becoming eligible (once again) for work on the site' (*Bch.* Leaf XXIV, 6). Suna is mentioned again, in the 17th year of work, receiving 'one instalment' of ten *māḍhas* for 'working on the doorjamb', a work which Narayana and Ganga Mahāpātras, the highly illustrious artists and three others, had shared with her (*Bch.* Leaf XLIV, 6).[147]

DISCIPLINE AND DISSENT

Discipline was an essential part of the professional work culture. This is seen in the uninterrupted course of work, both in its planning and execution. That is how the entire temple complex consisting of the main temple, the *Nāṭya maṇḍapa,* the Thakurani and the Nisa temple and Aruna pillar, etc. came up in quick succession. The coordination between different elements involved in supply of materials and execution of works remained impeccably systematic. Shortages are not in evidence; failures are rarely seen. In case of a boatman, mentioned above, failing to deliver the required stone in time, a fine was imposed on him and the matter closed. There is an exceptional case of Ganga Mahāpātra not returning from his village in time for work. As a result of this, a lion figure could not be placed on *rāhā,* as scheduled. Ganga surprisingly is neither reprimanded nor fined. Instead, a bullock cart is sent, on treasury expenses, to fetch him and the carters receive payment for bringing him back to the camp (*Bch.* Leaf XLVII, 10). What prompted overlooking Ganga's indiscretion is not mentioned in the text, but his highly distinguished work in building the *Nāṭya maṇḍapa,* the Thakurani temple and the Aruna Pillar are all well documented in the *Bayacakaḍa.* He carved some of the most significant sculptural works like the Sūrya on horseback for the Nisa temple, *mithuna* and Bhairava figures for *mukhaśālā,* musicians on the *pīḍhā* and large *kanyā* figures of eight *hasta* for the *vimāna,* etc. A regard for his eminence might have helped in condoning his lapse.

Some instances of resistence, dissent, protest seem to surface out in the administrative interventions in specific incidents of disputes and conflict, and in the instances where an 'offender' absconded from the camp. Small indiscretions were allowed to pass. The incidents involving Suna *pāthuriānī* or the Madurai *śilpins* were resolved amicably; the former within the camp with the consent of the artists' community and the latter with the intervention of the king who safeguarded both the honour of the Madurai *śilpins* and the authority of the *sūtradhāra.* The only instance of a dismissal relates to the 'tell-tale' Balaji *pāthuriā.* He was dismissed from his job and a fine was imposed on him, in addition. The offense of the *pāthuriā* is not recorded but we are told that a 'wage' of seven *gaunī*s was given to the guard who went to collect the fine (*Bch.* Leaf X, 10). Yet, there was at least one episode, serious enough to bring the entire work to halt, something unusual in the entire duration of the building operation of the Konarak temple. Although details of what provoked the episode are missing, it definitely created a stir, and we find some highly regarded craftsmen abandoning the work as a result and absconding from the camp. The details of the incident, as available, follow.

This happened when the work was in the 12th *anka* (year) of the king's rule. The *Bayacakaḍa* laconically records that on the 10th of the *caitra* month, a quarrel broke out among the forty *pāthuriās* who were working on the main temple. The quarrel must have been serious as the 'orders were sent to stop work'. Overseers had a consultation and they reported the matter (not specified in the text) to the king. Two guards took the message to him. (*Bch*. Leaf XXIV, 2-5). Immediately after this entry, the text mentions a payment to Vaidyas, which, if consecutive recordings in the text have some connections, may indicate that some workers might have been hurt in a quarrel, and they probably received some treatment. Immediately after this entry the *Bayacakaḍa* speaks of three artisans – Suja Mohammed, Sukhi Mahārāṇā and Bhima Mahārāṇā – leaving without notice. The first of them 'left the work site' with his tools, 'without saying a word'; and the other two left for another place (to the Puruṣottama temple in Puri) similarly 'without saying anything and without asking for leave'. So, the guard Bandhu Singh went on a horse to apprehend them. Suja was found in an orchard and he was brought back. But obviously, the tensions had not subsided. So, 'to prevent further trouble and quarrel', Balasri sent four guards who arrested the other two and 'took them to a jail' (*Bch*. Leaf XXIV, 5). This episode indicates a harsh resolution of conflict but one does not know what happened to the *pāthuriās* who really had started the quarrel in the first place. All these three craftsmen were iron casters, with nothing to do with stone masonry which the *pāthuriās*, obviously the victims in this quarrel, handled. The text is silent about the juridical procedures and powers and also about who exercised them in the camp. But reference to two craftsmen being put into a jail indicates that officers in the camp exercised the powers to incarcerate the defaulters! We have no information about how the matter was finally resolved and therefore the entire incident remains shrouded in mystery. We also find Suja Mohamed brought back and left free, unlike Bhima and Sukhi who were jailed. Perhaps this may indicate their respective innocence and guilt?

The *Bayacakaḍa* refers to a five-member Discipline Committee in the camp which consisted of the chief supervisor of the camp, the camp supervisor and three others, namely, Damodara Pattanayaka, Ghana Pattanayaka and Maharatha. The Committee was set up to settle disputes that might arise in the camp. The last three received 14 *māḍhas* each when the camp was closed after the temple's construction ended. As for the first two, they 'declined to accept (any) payment' (*Bch.* Leaf LXV, 11). We, however, have no reference to the Committee's role in disputes, or even in the situations of conflict and their resolution. There is an instance of a contractual work being faulted when it was delivered. But others, not the Committee, are seen intervening in the instance. Thus, when the much-celebrated Visi (Visvanatha) Mahāpātra, mentioned earlier, supplied three *kanyā* figures, Narayana Mahāpātra objected to one of them saying that it was a portrait of Visi's wife and therefore it could not be placed on the temple. The image was rejected on his objection and only two images were accepted for which Visi received four *māḍhas* as his dues. But Ganga Mahāpātra intervened and said that the (rejected) image had indeed been carved like that of a goddess on a lotus pedestal and so it merited acceptance (on points of iconography). As a result of this intervention, Visi's third *kanyā* image too was accepted and he received a payment of two *māḍhas* for it. These images were eventually set up on a *manḍapa* (*Bch.* Leaf LX, 12).

Discipline was endemic in the camp and it covered financial discipline too. The *Bayacakaḍa* seems meticulous in its entries about receipts, services and expenditure. So were the king's officers who checked the stores and made an inventory of things in its possession. Similar financial discipline is in evidence in the leaders of a team of 342 people who went to collect stone from different places. When they returned they are found scrupulously rendering the account of expenses incurred on clothing, quarrying, loading the stone on boat besides the amount spent in buying paddy for victuals (*Bch.* Leaf XXV, 6-12). We also have an instance of Nidhi Mahāpātra returning the extra sum of money as the payment he recieved was in excess of the required amount (*Bch.* Leaf XXXVI, 8).

MODES OF PAYMENT

Some explicit instances of work assignments indicate its distribution by the *sūtradhāra* who, as other instances show, also received the finished work for rejection or approval. Rejections were rare. Assignment by the *sūtradhāra* was perhaps essential in entitling the assignee to receive payments or advances from the treasury. If a particular job was handled by more than one person, the leader of the group received, after the conclusion of the work, a consolidated payment for distribution in the group plus his own share separately. No clue is found in such cases to work out the proportionate sharing of the amount within the group. But the share of the leader seems to have remained ensured.[148]

The *Mayamatam* (IX. 130; X.94) recommends payment from a prince to the *śilpins* in terms of land and cows. The *Bayacakaḍa* indicates that every work was paid in cash or kind and sometimes such a dispensation was extended even to a visiting *śilpin* not engaged at the site. Even the works not routinely assigned, e.g., Visvanatha Mahāpātra presenting an image to the king, were honoured with presents or payment. A fairly efficient system of payments seems to have been in place involving contracts, one-time payment, part payments, advances on contracts, instalments of payment, settlement of the account, etc. Yet, there is a reference to a master artist and his team receiving a delayed 12-*māḍhas* payment as the 'balance of wages' (*Bch.* Leaf X, 12). Gratuities were also awarded occasionally (*Bch.* Leaf XXIII, 11).

The payments covered varying kinds of contingencies and disbursements were handled with flexibility, depending upon the terms of contract. So some artists and craftsmen got wages,[149] others a salary,[150] still others a one-time payment. Work on contract was most common and sometimes artists also received a retaining fee[151] when they were dispersed in the rainy season. The 'one-time payment', among these modes perhaps covered those contracts which would not permit either an advance or instalments. Such 'one-time payment' came even to highly accomplished master-artists like Ganga Mahāpātra. He is said to have received a 'one-time' contract of 43 *māḍhas* to carve royal figures on *taralabandha* (lower part of the temple wall). We also come across expressions like the 'clearance of accounts', which would perhaps indicate the final payment in a contract, in full settlement of dues. Gadadhara Mahāpātra, Ganga and thirteen other workers received such a contract to make six *kanyā* figures of eight *hasta* each. When the job was completed the sculptors received 230 *māḍhas* in 'clearance of account' (*Bch.* Leaf XXII, 6).[152] But, such a clearance came only after making a proper verification as we are told that the accounts of seven *śilpīs* were 'checked' before making a 'final settlement' (*Bch.* Leaf XXXVIII, 8). The checking would obviously imply verification of advances made or instalments paid to the assignee of the contract.[153] Payments for specific jobs were settled after its completion. So, when the work on a basement concluded the *pāthuriās* received 102 *māḍhas* (*Bch.* Leaf VIII, 15). Similarly, for setting stones on three sides of the *mukhaśālā*, 12 *pāthuriās* and 43 carriers received thirty *māḍhas* (*Bch.* Leaf VIII, 21) and twelve workers who lifted and installed heavier Sūrya images at the designated place with the help of scaffolding, received seven *māḍhas* and 24 *gaunī* (*Bch.* Leaf X, 14).[154] Gadadhara and Narayana likewise received a 'clearance of their dues' after 'finishing the task of supplying sixteen smaller *kanyā* figures' (*Bch.* Leaf, XXIII, 3). Little discrimination is seen in contracts offered to *śilpins* regardles of their status. It seems that work, not status, decided the quantum of payment. For instance, the job of making images for the northern and western sides of the temple were entrusted respectively to Gadadhara and to the *sūtradhāra* for ten *māḍhas* and forty *gaunīs*, with each having three workers to assist them (*Bch.* Leaf VIII, 16). Again, after the images were set up in the niches by the *sūtradhāra* and Gadadhara, both received the same amount in payment, irrespective of their status (*Bch.* Leaf, XIII, 11).

DISCHARGE

The details, as above, indicate the pace of work as it went on, negotiating the contingencies as they came by. In the entire operation one sees both coordination and team spirit. It appears from the *Bayacakaḍa* that the work in the beginning was more relaxed but as it progressed the pressures increased which often meant offering more work on contract to resident artists than allowing its completion in its stride through the centrally provided resources in the camp. Pace of work tended to quicken up with the passage of time, and, in the text, the pressures to deliver are seen articulated time and again in setting deadlines, e.g., six months to complete the doorway by four artists with the assistance of three more helpers (*Bch.* Leaf IX, 16); nine month's time to complete the entire work, and so on. Tension mounted for instance, when large works like a *navagraha* stones was hoisted and fixed or when huge iron girders were cast.

Curtain eventually came on the entire operation when work on the temple came to a close with its consecration. Artists were dispersed with presents, which were substantial. Sometimes, even before the final discharge (*nikāsī*) there were occasions when artists and craftsmen were let off on their own request or for other reasons. Even early during the construction, such decisions had to be taken. On such occasions, care was taken to clear the dues of those who would decide to leave. There were no dismissals in the entire thirteen-year plus operations except when a 'tell-tale' artisan who 'spoke too much', had to be turned out. But the discharge of artisans, voluntary or otherwise, did take place once in a while. Thus, we hear of the discharge (*nikāsī*) of suppliers (*Bch.* Leaf LXV, 3); of other artisans (*Bch.* Leaf LXI, 6, LVII, 6); of 40 *pāthuriās* who left after receiving their dues while others continued with their work (*Bch.* Leaf VI, 30). Fourteen iron workers (*karadis* and *ojhās*) were given leave and paid off (*Bch.* Leaf XII, 1); 103 *śilpins* went to their villages and before leaving they received, in clearance of accounts, 70 *māḍhas*, three *bharaṇa*, 14 *gaunī* of rice and 24 pairs of cloth (*Bch.* Leaf XVII, 23). While 40 *pāitālas* and 170 men who had worked through the rainy season carrying stones from boats received clearance (from work) after receiving a payment of 2811 *māḍhas*, others who were still retained included 48 stone carriers, eleven accounts clerk (*karji*), eight blacksmiths and ordinary iron workers (*Bch.* LeafXXVI, 11). That the *sūtradhāra* had a role in such discharge may be deduced from the instance of the *pāthuriās* who, as they were discharged, went (in a delegation?) to meet him in his camp. One does not know whether this was a visit in protest or in gratitude. It could have been both as, after this visit, we find some of them going to work on *rathas*, 'chariot', elsewhere and then returning to work. On thus rejoining the work at Konarak, they once again received a payment (*Bch.* Leaf XLVII, 21-22, XLVIII, 1). The record states that all of them, including those who later returned, had received payment from treasury in settlement of their dues, before leaving. In this case, some of the discharged persons did not return while others did and those who returned received payment again even after they were discharged.

There is an interesting case of the discharge of 'strong young men' (*bheṇḍā*) who were initially recruited at fourteen different places for the construction work. Of these, 530 joined the king in his battle against the 'Kakatiyas of Vijaywada'. The rest were lodged in the Rupasa camp (*Bch.* Leaf III, 9). Of these 'strong young men', 340 young *pāthuriās* who had served for twelve years, joining the king in fighting the war and constructing the temple when not on war, made a request to be released. One does not know whether these 340 soldiers-cum-artists were the survivors from their original contingent of 530 young men. But the record says that the king acceded to their request and sent for each of them a small farewell gift wrapped in cloth from his personal treasury. From the temple treasury they received in clearance of accounts and for their journey 1034 small *māḍhas*, three *bharaṇas* and one *bharaṇa* of *mung*. The accountant writes that 'what was contained in parcels, I do not know' (*Bch.* Leaf XLVI, 2). This instance would indicate that wars and temple building went hand in hand in the patronage system of the royal order and those who so served were like the standing army of the state fighting battles in war times and building temple in the times of peace.

FINAL DISPENSATIONS

The final discharge and dispersal eventually came as the magnificent temple at Konarak stood constructed in its full glory. Compensations and rewards were now distributed liberally, but care was taken, even in this dispersal, to settle enough artists and workers in the vicinity of the temple in order to ensure a regular maintenance of the recently constructed temple. The final dispensations thus took care of settling down all kinds of people whose services might have been essential to run the temple in its full glory. So, Madhava Misra Bhatta and 40 other people received the land on the western side of the temple as gift plus 70 *māḍhas* to carve out a small village to accommodate temple servants (*Bch.* Leaf LIX, 9). *Paṇḍa*s with the job of supplying water to temple were settled in a village called Madhipur (*Bch.* Leaf LXI, 3). Others who were liberally rewarded included Gadadhara Mahāpātra who received the title of *śilpī nāyaka* with the *rājaguru* tying a turban on his head as a mark of special honour to him (*Bch.* Leaf LXII, 4). Gadadhara also received 54 gold coins and Ganga, the chief of *pathuriā* community, received 134 gold coins.[155] The agents who had moved around recruiting *śilpin*s were given a village called Paikrayapura (*Bch.* Leaf LXII, 5); Maharathi, the *nāyaka* of Vingurugada who too had recruited *śilpin*s was given the title of *mahānāyaka* (*Bch.* Leaf LXII, 7); Vasudeva Mahāpātra was made the administrator of food offerings and settled in a village Gadavinguda, near Rupasa, on an annual stipend of 13 *māḍha*s (*Bch.* Leaf LXVII, 11). But obviously the best of these grants came to *Sāmantarāya* Sadasiva Mahāpātra, the *sūtradhāra*.[156] On the day when image of *mahābhāskara* was taken up for *pratiṣṭhā maṇḍapa* and installed on a *siṃhāsana*, he was given land, etc. in a village christened as *sāmantapura* after his title: *sāmantarāya*. Along with the land grant he also received 27 lotus-marked gold *māḍha*s (*Bch.* Leaf LXI, 7). He further received three *krośa* of land extending from east to west in Lankapada *viṣaya* as a 'life endowment' with a *dakṣiṇā* of 20 *māḍha*s (*Bch.* Leaf LXVIII, 7) besides a final gift of 100 gold coins (*Bch.* Leaf LXV, 9). The *rājaguru* received a village and 100 *tola* gold (Bch. Leaf LXII, 9).

CONCLUDING REMARKS

The account above tries to recapture the harmony in the processes of work and spirit of the artist, artisans and others as evinced in building the Sun temple at Konarak. In the entire course of its construction extending through a period of thirteen years plus, there were only two incidents of misconduct on the part of the *śilpī*s: once when two craftsmen were jailed and then in the incidents involving Suna *pathuriāni* and three other expert artisans who fled away from the camp without notice. This almost flawless record of work, bereft of dereliction or caprices of the participants in carrying out their designated tasks time and again ceaselessly, speaks for their discipline and commitment as they individually or collectively collaborated to accomplish the entire project with remarkable dignity and honour. We have little evidence of administrative interference in the professional domain of artists even as the state officers in the camp kept the channel of supplies and payments active throughout the spells of construction work. As the *sūtradhāra* executed his plan of work, the camp administration continued uninterruptedly discharging its duties: managing receipts and payments, keeping an eye over the progress of work, reporting to the king, receiving visitors and in case of accidents, offering help to the victim and succour to their family. Building operations, all the while remained in the hands of the *sūtradhāra*. In the accounts of the *Bayacakaḍa,* the administrative and professional segments of the camp are seen acting in concert with each other and they are seen acquitting themselves well with efficiency and without dithering. The *sūtradhāra* relentlessly executes the work, distributes the tasks and receives the finished work for his scrutiny, fulfils the deadlines, deploys the craftsmen all around to meet the work requirements, which all became possible with the support of his bands of *śilpin*s and other craftsmen including the ordinary workers. Together, they were always ready even to manage a crisis if it ever arose.[157] The readings from the text give an impression as if the honour of the community was at stake and it had to redeem itself by delivering the work entrusted to them. The text helps the conclusion that the honour of *śilpin*s and other categories of artisans remained ever unsullied as they worked on the monument. There is little hint in it of any covert or overt innuendos to compromise that honour. Perhaps this concern for dignity and honour of the artists and workmen actuated the harmony and pace in conducting the entire building operation up to its conclusion. This may also explain a total absence in the artists' camp, of any agency or instruments of coercion, throughout the entire course of work at Konarak. Dignity and honour may not be quantifiable but they explain the commitment and efficiency with which the work was completed. They also explains why the king specifically convenes an assembly of *śilpins* to announce the temple and make necessary appointments for the different tasks; or why the *sūtradhāra* convenes an assembly of *śilpin*s, including the Madurai *śilpin*s, for consultation before he would submit the revised plans of the temple to the king; or why the treasury officials fudge the records in favour of the *sūtradhāra* when, instead of him, his son finally sets the *kalaśa* on the temple, marking its completion; or, why the work flows at the site flawlessly with the *sūtradhāra* finding little fault – except in a single instance – in the works delivered; or, why when Madurai *śilpī*s protest, the king upholds their pride even as the *sūtradhāra*'s authority is not compromised, and so on and so forth. The work on the Konarak temple, or any other monument anywhere else, was, for the artists and artisans, an act of honour, which spelled a dignified renewal of confidence and pride of *śilpī*s in their skills. While pecuniary gains were not missed in such projects – in fact they seem to have flowed in regularly and *śilpī*s needed them for their livelihood – their honour too and perhaps that of the community was at the stake in such a work which they accomplished with pride.

NOTES AND REFERENCES

1. Boner, Sarma and Das (1972): 47-194. This work contains cryptic entries of payments, such as salaries and wages, contracts, including advances on those contracts, grants, presents, gratuities, rewards, etc. made to particular artists, workers or their groups to complete the specific tasks. These payments came to different persons, e.g., master architect and sculptors, supervisors, suppliers, administrative staff and others, both men and women, in cash or kind in lieu of the tasks they performed in temple-building and other sundry works. These artists and workers included a large contingent of experts, e.g., *sūtradhāra*, architects (*sthāpaka, sthapati*), executive architect (*karmakāra*), sculptors (*śilpī*), the chief of sculptors' community (*śilpī nāyaka*), instructors in *śilpaśāstra* (*śilpa-śāstra-vakhāniyā*), painters (*citrakāra*), stonemasons (*swānsya pāthuriyā*), plasterers (*cūnurā*), carvers of fret-work (*jālikara*), stone worker (*kārigara*), stone cutters (*pāthuriā*), stone specialists (*pathara cinharā*), stone providers (*pathara risālyā*), goldsmith (*cinhurā*), iron caster (*kamarakanṭha*), brass and bronze casters (*kansārī*), head of stone quarriers (*kaṭalī nāyaka*), chariot builders (*rathakāra*), etc. Cf., also, Boner (1970): 259-272.
2. E.g., gold or silver coins or measures of grains consisting of *māḍha, aśrapī, Badshah kālā tankā, sikkā, Bankalekha, kauḍī*; or measures like *gaunī, pala, bharaṇa*. Cf., Boner *et al.* (1972): 270-271.
3. Boner *et al.* (1972): 259. Thus were recruited different kinds of skilled artists and craftsmen besides other workmen from different trades and communities – mostly Hindus but some Muslims too – and also the officers of the state, guards, priests, physicians (*vaidya*), messengers, transporters, boatmen, diggers, rope-makers, experts in making scaffoldings, etc. The work contains a precise record of their respective work and the payments or rewards they received in lieu.
4. After the decline in the erstwhile community-patronage of the Śunga-Sātavāhana-Kuṣāna times, artists' activity in the Middle Ages inexorably came to be regulated under the patronage of the ruling class, nobles and elites or priestly heads of religious institutions. Their ever-recurring interface and proximity with influential patrons apparently profited them, and ensured their enhanced socio-economic status. But it also rendered them or their organisations largely dependent on and subservient to those prime movers – especially the ruling class and priests – for any significant work. In the situation, uncertainties were bound to persist in an artist's functional status till recruitment landed him into a specific assignment of some substance.
5. For the peregrinating artists, cf., Settar (1992): 97-118.
6. Sangama, Madhava and Sreshthin, the master-artists under the Kalacuris of Central India, are refered to as 'excellent *sūtradhāra*', Madhava, in addition, claimed to be 'an expert in the science of Viśvakarmā'. Mahidhara is described as '*sūtradhāra śiromaṇi*' and his father was known as '*sūtradhāra agraṇī*', 'foremost among the *sūtradhāras*'. Cf., Misra (1985):186.

7. Inscriptions from Karnataka (Belur, Somanthpuram, etc.) record many instances where artists are found strongly deprecating their rivals. Thus, Dasoja claims to be 'a smiter of the crowd of titled sculptors'; his son being like what 'Śiva was to cupid' or like what a '*bherunḍa* would be to a *śarabha*' (i.e., a killer). Cikka Hampa bore the title of 'a champion over rival sculptors'; Malliyana calls himself 'a tiger amongst sculptors' or 'like a thunderbolt to the mountains'. Cf., Misra (1975): 50-51, quoting Sivaramamurti (1961): 4.
8. *Indian Antiquary*, IX, p. 74.
9. *Epigraphia Indica*, Vol. II, p. 354.
10. For the details of such guilds, their structure and function, economic, judicial and administrative roles, privileges, etc. Cf., Thaplyal (1996).
11. Cf., Misra (1975): 34-37.
12. For instance, the Arthuna inscription of VS 1216, of the Paramaras of Vagada, refers to Vasudeva, an 'intelligent' *sūtradhāra*. Cf., Trivedi (nd): 44.
13. Misra (1975): 43-44, 49-50.
14. Arthuna stone inscription (AD 1109) of the time of Vijayaraja refers to *vijñānika* Sumaka. Cf., Trivedi (nd): 316. Another Arthuna inscription of AD 1080, records the building of a Śiva temple and various allocations in goods and money made to it. It also has in it the names of Cāmunḍa, a *vijñānika*, and Guḍanka, a *sūtradhāra*. The latter was the son of *sūtradhāra* Nanna (same as Nānāka) who carved the Hanuman image that was installed at Arthuna: *Nānākena samutkirnā Hanumān ghāṭitastathā*. *Ibid*., p. 311. Nanna is mentioned in yet another inscription of AD 1107.
15. Kānhada or Kānhāka, a *rūpakāra*. Cf., Trivedi (n.d.): 206, 224; also Misra (1975): 43-44, 49-52. In the Karnataka inscription *rūpakāra* (*rūvāri*) is almost a generic term for artist 'whether he be an architect, a sculptor or a scribe'. Cf., Settar (1992): 84.
16. Cf., Misra (1975): 34-35.
17. Cf., *Bayacakaḍa* (hereafter *Bch*.), Leaf XXXVII, 4; X, 16.
18. There seems to have been a method in such recruitment through the royal agency, for the text says that 'Strong young men' (*bheṇḍā*) were recruited at fourteen different places for construction work. Of these, 530 went with the king to fight war with the Kakatiyas of Vijaywada. The rest were lodged in the Rupasa camp. Cf., *Bch*. Leaf III, 9. Such workers were obviously meant for sundry, non-expert jobs. But distinctions sometimes blur when for instance, 340 young stone workers (*pāthuriās*) are said to have been released from work on their request on the grounds that they had gone to war with the king and together with work on construction had served for twelve years. The king acceded to their request; he sent for each of them a small farewell gift, wrapped in cloth, from his personal treasury. From the temple treasury they received in clearance of accounts and for their journey 1034 small *māḍhas*, three *bharaṇas* and one *bharaṇa mung*. The accountant writes that 'what was contained in parcels, I do not know'. *Bch*. Leaf XLVI, 2. For many other instances of warrior artists, cf., Settar (1992): 90.

19. *Ep. Ind.* XXIV, no. 35, p. 253.
20. *Ep. Ind.*, I. pp. 162ff. For guild of potters, gardeners and artisans, see the Kaman inscription, *Ep. Ind.*, XXIV, pp. 329ff.
21. *Ep. Ind.* XIV, pp. 188ff. Cf., Thaplyal (1996): 87, 93, 167.
22. For a reference to a *gaṇa* to which *sūtradhāra* Vasuguṇa (seventh century) belonged, see *Epigraphia Indica*, Vol. XXXI, pp. 36ff: *sūtradhāra-sakala-karma-kīrtti-kīrttana-guṇa-gaṇa-unnatimāna*.
23. Cf., Sircar (1983): 21.
24. *Indian Antiquary*, Vol. X, p. 164. The Hoysala records from Karnataka mention an assembly of the *vīra-pāñcāla*s and all the members of *viśvakarmā kula* who were 'reassured' of their rights and duties by Vira Ballala III. They also record meetings of the members of the *vīra pāñcālas* on 'specific occasions to take decisions on the matters of common interest', and one such meeting in AD 1300 is known to have 'concluded a permanent agreement' between the *pāñcāla*s and the *nāḍu* workers. These groupings seem to point to a guild-like organisation among artisans for which some other evidence is also forthcoming. Thus, inscriptions from Karnataka refer to *Sarasvati gaṇadāsa*s, translated by Settar as 'servants of Sarasvati' or a 'guild of the servants of Goddesss Sarasvati'? Nagavarma and Padmoja besides the sculptors of Ingulesvara and Nilagunda in Bijapur district, Bamoja the sculptor and architect of Īśvra temple at Anekonda, Ikkudoja an engraver and architect, Ikuloja, an engraver and Manoja, a sculptor of a hero stone figure as members of this guild (?). Cf., Settar (1992): 86-87.
25. Cf., Singh (1993): 226-229. He also refers to different artists in groups, pairs or alone engaged in sculptural or architectural work. The label inscriptions seem to suggest that there were different sets of artists to carve different sets of images. Thus, one group carved only *Apsara*s and leogriffs while the other worked exclusively on the figures of the cult gods and goddesses. Sometimes, two or more artists worked to produce the same image. In a particular case, the artist seems to have made an image of a cult god as well as a minor deity. *Ibid.*
26. Cf., Narasimhasmurty (1985): 216.
27. Cf., Boner *et al.* (1972): 257-272.
28. Cf., Settar *et al.* (1982): 381. The information is related to the artists who made memorial pillars.
29. Cf., Misra (1984): p. 68.
30. *Epi. Indica*, Vol.XXVIII, lines 127ff. For the special quarters of artisans like goldsmith, cf., Shastri (1955): 290, 314, 331, 357.
31. The *rūpakāra* Lahada was the son of *sūtradhāra* Rama at Kalanjara; Rama himself figures once as a *rūpakāra* and then as a *sūtradhāra*, Cunningham, *Reports*, XXI, pp. 35, 38. Also, *Ep. Ind.* XXXI, p. 166. There is no dearth of instances of artisans figuring in various combinations. So, a pair of artisans occurring together may have different designations; or a *sūtradhāra* may come to work under a *rūpakāra*, and so on and so forth.
32. Gugga of Himachal for instance, is simply mentioned as a *kammina*. Inscriptions indicate that he fashioned the metal image of Lakṣanādevī

(Brahmaur) during the reign of Meruvarman besides the Brahmaur image of Gaṇesa and Śakti image of Chatrarhi. Cf., Agrawal (2001): 158,159,163. But the region was aware of the other standard designations, which are recorded in several inscriptions. For instance, the Devi Kothi Narayana image inscription refers to Subhaga, the son of *sūtradhāra* Uda. Devi Kothi Fountain inscription refers to its construction by *sūtradhāra* Bhagaraja and by masons (*bhadhi*) Tyaga and Bhagirain in the year 7 of Laitavarman. Similarly, the Khunmoh inscription from Kashmir (AD 1428) refers to Gaggaka, a sculptor who knows the art of writing also. Cf., Agrawal (2001): 228, 232, 356. The Karnataka records similarly refer to sculptors like, *ruvari* (*rūpakāra*), *śilpī*, *ācārya*, *paṇḍita*, *voja* (*ojhā/upadhyāya*); *kalkutiga* (stonemason), *karmacāri* (smith), *badiga* (carpenter), *akkasāli* (goldsmith), *sūtradhāra* and *sthapati* (master architects and sculptors). Cf., Settar (1992): 84.

33. Cf., Gurav (1975): 147.
34. Cf., Bhandarkar's List 1557, 1560, 1565. Sircar eqates *vijñānika* with *śilpī*s and explains the former as epithet of an artisan. Sircar (1966): 373.
35. For other *vijñānika*s, like Madhava, Vasuka, Madhumalla, Sornnanagaka, Vaheru, Mangaka, Sankhuka, Voharu and Herukadasa, cf., Shastri (1995): 231, 237, 249, 255, 261, 275, 290, 306, 314, 331, 357, 360. Of these, Vaheru and Mangaka are mentioned as 'the *vijñānin*s of the goldsmith's lane'; Śankhuka belonged to Sunnahi, an area situated in the goldsmith's quarters. Similarly, Voharu also was a resident of 'goldsmith's lane' (*suvarnavithi*).
36. *Epigraphia Indica*, Vol. XXVII, 320ff.
37. Cf., Chanda (1936): 66, pl. xx. Also, Bhandarkar's List: nos. 1610, 1625, 1632, 1639, 1683, *Epi. Ind.* XXIX, pp. 5, 13; XIX, p. 57, for other *śilpin*s, some of them highly acclaimed.
38. Bhandarkar's List: no. 1727.
39. Mirashi (1955): 401, 407.
40. Bhandarkar's List: no. 1660.
41. Mirashi (1955): p. 557.
42. *Ibid.*, pp. 490; 515.
43. For references to *sūtradhāra*, cf., Agrawal 2001, p. 324; *sūtradhāra* Bhima is mentioned in reference to installation of an image of Ṛsabhadeva by a *goṣṭhī* of traders, in an inscription of AD 861 from Jind. Cf., Agrawal (2001): 94. Kiradu inscription of Someśvara (AD 1152) mentions the engraver Jasodhara as *sūtradhāra*. Cf., Trivedi, (n.d.): 329.
44. Cf., Dhavalikar (1969): 301-308.
45. For the marks of a good *sthapati*, cf., *Samarāngaṇa Sūtradhāra* 44. 1-21; 45. 7-9.
46. Agrawal (2001): 346. There was also a well-known *sthapati* named Durgga under the Paramaras: *āsīcca nāgātsthapate'stu Durggaḥ/Durgārkkato Deuka sūtradhāraḥ/asyāpisūnuḥ Śivapāla nāmnā/yenotkṛteyaṃ suśubhā praśastim*. The inscription refers to renovation of a Sun temple and a step-well by the royal family. Trivedi (n.d.): 232.
47. *Sūtradhāra* implies 'one who holds a *sūtra*'; and *sūtra* denotes a 'thread', i.e., 'measure' as well as a 'rule', implying different kinds of activities: ritualistic,

scientific, and artistic and underscoring the logic of things by which the underlying reasoning, argument, activity or comprehension in an act would be entwined together in an appropriate pattern. Cf., Stall (1992): 302. For that reason, 'in early philosophy the terms like *grantha, tantra, prabandha, nibandha*, etc. derive from the terminology of textile manufacture' and indicate binding together of ideas in the manner the *sūtra*s are bound together to form a piece of cloth. Stall (1992): 302 quoting Rau.

48. *Samarāngaṇa Sūtradhāra*, I.1: *devaḥ sā pātu bhuvanatraya sūtradhārastvaṃ ... katsnyārdasūtritamasūtryata yena viśvaṃ.*
49. *Vākypadīyaṃ* of Bhartṛhari, ed., K.A. Subramania Iyer (1966), Delhi, III. 9. 4.
50. The *Nāṭyaśāstra* of Bharata (XXXV.30) defines *sūtradhāra* as one who could train others in music (*gīta* and *vādya*) and in reciting the text along with the *bhāva*-s (moods) implicit in them. The passage also suggests that a *sūtradhāra* was so designated owing to his knowledge of *sūtra*s of dramaturgical performance.
51. Tripathi (1992): 323.
52. *Śilpaprakāśa* (I.558) has it that: 'in the texts by Śukrācārya and in the canons of Viśvkarmā there are prescriptions which differ according to region and time'.
53. Cf., Misra (1988) 'Sutradhara evam pracina vastukarma' (in Hindi), *Natyam*, ed., Radha Vallabh, Year 6, *anka* 3 (1988), Sagar, p. 90.
54. Cf., *Samarāngaṇa Sūtradhāra*, XXXI. 86-87: *...yojitāḥ sūtradhāraiḥ/ ...pāramparyam kauśalam sopadeśam śāstrābhyāso vāstukarmodyamo dhīḥ...//*
55. *Sthapati* (*sthapatiḥ sthāpayet sthiraṃ*, IX.128) is in-charge of works; his disciple or son: *sūtragrāhin*, who takes orders from *sthapati*; *takṣaka* who cuts stone, wood, bricks; *vardhakin* who assembles and erects the pieces cut by *takṣaka* and works under the orders of *sūtragrāhin*. All these three categories are said to follow *sthapati*'s directions and hold him in high respect, as 'it is Viśvakarmā in person who is revealed through his aspect'. Dagen (2000): 25-26.
56. For instance, according to the *Rājatarangiṇī* (III.348), the town of Srinagara was built after a *sūtra* had been laid, marking the place for construction. The *Milinda Pañho* (330) similarly refers to a 'city architect' who lays out and raises a city and when 'the city was fully developed he might go away to another district'. Cf., Misra (1975): 9.
57. Jones (1949-56): Vol. III, p. 9.
58. *Aparājitapṛcchā* II, 15-31 describes the wide field of *sūtradhāra*'s knowledge. These include *varṇa, rūpa, rasa*, etc: *varṇarūparasavṛttibhāvānubhāvakodbhavāḥ/ śuddhabaddhāni citrāṇi patrāṇi pañca eva ca*, verse 28. See also Ch. 49, verses 1-20 describing the qualities that he should ideally possess. In Ch. 61, verses 6-23, the text under the *sūtradhārapūja nirṇaya adhikāra sūtra* describes how a *sūtradhāra* should be revered for his knowledge and be kept well provided in every way for he is second to none on the earth: *bhumesthale sūtradhāro viśvādhipo dvitīyakaḥ.*
59. *Sūtradhāra* Sahaja and Gagga made a fountain mentioned in Salhi Fountain inscription. Cf., Agrawal (2001): 237. A *sūtradhāra* named Nirada Varma

engraved a record, which refers to restoration of the *maṇḍapa* of a temple in AD 1198. The work is mentioned as the *karma* of the *sūtradhāra* and the entire *goṣṭhī* was benefitted by it. Cf., Trivedi (n.d.): 255.

60. Cf., Misra (1975): 48.
61. *Ibid.*, 64.
62. *Ibid.*, 47. Cf., also Shailaja Pandeya, ed. & tr. (2001), *Rājavallabha maṇḍanam*, Varanasi: Chowkhamba Surbharati Prakashan (in Hindi), pp. 10-15.
63. Misra (1988): 91.
64. *Ibid.*
65. Cf., Misra (1987): 135.
66. *JBBRS*, Vol. XII, p. 151.
67. Cf., Pantulu (1929): 147ff.
68. Cf., Trivedi (nd): 49: Inscription categorically states that *sūtradhāra* Sahira's son Manathala 'made' (*ghāṭitam*), the image of Vagdevi Sarasvati in VS 1091/ AD 1033-34. *Sūtradhāra* Saruka's son Dhanna restored a Sun temple at Varman, in Sirohi district under the Paramaras of Chandravati in AD 1043. Trivedi (n.d.): 226.
69. *Epigraphia Indica*, Vol. I, p. 146: *vijñāna viśvakartā dharmādhāreṇa sūtradhāreṇa Chicchābhidhena prāsādaḥ Pramathanāthasya.*
70. Cf., Misra (1975): 68.
71. *Ibid.*, 69.
72. *Ibid.*, pp. 27-74.
73. *Ibid.*, p. 53.
74. Tripathi (1992): 328-329.
75. Chapter 44; quoted in Misra (1975): 35.
76. *Ibid.*
77. *Aparājitapṛcchā* II, 15-31.
78. Cf., Misra (n.d. 1984).
79. Once a master-artist was recruited, he would take charge and in owing allegiance to patron he would enjoy the benefits and status that devolved upon him till the work lasted, and sometimes even beyond that. We have references both to a one-time work and that of longer duration. A reference to a one-time work is seen in the instance of a portrait sculpture (AD 826-27) of a queen made by Siddhapa. Cf., Agrawal (2001): 331. But generally an artist lasted longer. For instance, we have Rupunu whose name occurs repeatedly in different works Cf., Agrawal (2001): 265, 270, 284. We also have well documented instances of many other artists, like: Mallitamma (1196-1268), Suryyana (1169 to 1205), Biroja (1286-1302), Dasoja (last quarter of the eleventh century to 1152) and Gangacari (twelfth cetury), who all had a long carrier during the Hoysalas. Cf., Settar (1992): 97-113.
80. The expenses eventually turned out to be phenomenal, so much so that the ruler had to even devalue his currency.
81. In its brief and cryptic contents, the record captures a glimpse of the processes which made the construction possible, thanks to the professional responses of builders in varying circumstances including those of war and peace, accidents, natural calamities, human failures, conflict and defiance,

resistance and conformity, priestly intervention, shifting time-schedules, royal visits, celebrations and festivals, and so on.

82. As the the text (leaf 1) indicates this was an extraordinary assembly of seven hundred *śilpīs* and seven *ojhās* (iron casters), gathered to hear the 'decree' of the Ganga King Narasimhadeva I that a Sun temple should be constructed 'in the form of a chariot' on 'the grounds of the *arkakṣetra*'. We are told that for five years since he was anointed, the king had contemplated to build such a temple and the 'decree' finally came when, accompanied by his twentyfour officials and eight *samantas*, the king announced to the assembly the appointment of Sāmantarāya Sadasiva Mahāpātra as the *sūtradhāra* and the latter made other crucial appointments of his six associates in everybody's presence. The king also appointed a camp administrator and the in-charge of accounts and maintenance of stores and treasury. There is enough in these details to show that when the decree to build the temple came, *śilpins* had already been sounded, the *sūtradhāra* and his associates identified – announcement of their names appears like a mere formality – and, the stores, a treasury and the *śilpins'* camps were under way. The decree came in the August-September of AD 1238 and by the end of January 1239, the work had made some headway with several preliminary tasks completed, including a cermonial purification of the ground by a priest, laying out of the ground plan by the *sūtradhāra* and the recruitment of *śilpīs*. More was to follow. For these dates, see Boner *et al.* (1972): 47, 177.

83. Pahali *paṭṭanāyaka* was appointed on the orders of the king to find out what was being talked about in the camps of the *śilpīs*. Cf., *Bch.* Leaf XXXVI, 6. Similarly, Subha Gupta, a *kañcukī* secretly gathered intelligence, and sent information to king through Canda Singh. Both received small parting gifts when the work concluded. Cf., *Bch.* Leaf LXV, 18.

84. Such occasions were important in the *śilpins'* camps, as they meant celebrations besides a respite from work as all the *śilpins* with horses, elephants and drums would go in a procession to receive him and the *sūtradhāra* would conduct his tour all around the place (*Bch.* Leaf XXXVIII, 11; XXXIX, 34-8). The patron-king was not a silent visitor for as he watched the proceedings he might also offer suggestions (*Bch.* Leaves XVIII-XX). His visits generally translated into an occasion for gifts to *śilpins* and workers, etc. and sometimes even he would receive presents, like currency, stone vessels or a specially forged sword from *śilpins* and smiths (*ojhā*). (*Bch.* Leaf XXXIX, 7). Sometimes unable to visit the workplace due to the exigencies of war or other reasons, he would dispatch a person of his confidence to oversee the construction (*Bch.* Leaf VIII, 23).

85. *Bayacakaḍa* (Leaf XLVII, 16), however, records an instance where a queen would have liked the whole *kalaśa* (?) of the temple to be made of gold. But the *śilpins* objected and the king compromised by ordering that only the rubies on the lotus emblem should be set in gold.

86. He warns them, as it were, that even after putting in 'so much labour' for nine years in temple construction the *bekī* (neck part to support *āmalaka* of the *śikhara*) was still not finished. He therefore sets a time limit to complete

the temple, ordering explicitly that the limit should be adhered to. The drummers announce this message in the artisans' camps so that the order must reach everyone (*Bch.* Leaf XXXIX, 8).

87. Those he rewarded included Visi Mahāpātra, a *śilpin*, a *pāthuriā* (for making a compound wall); another *pāthuriā* (image maker) for some unspecified work, a *jālī* worker Vidyadhara *ojhā*; Upadhi *nāyaka*; and an inspector of works (*Bch.* Leaf V, 6). These awards must have served in raising the levels of confidence.
88. A *bisoi* gets the Pratapa village as gift along with a title, namely, 'Patasahani of Niladrigada', on account of making a regular supply of special bamboos to the extent that (the king) felt 'very much obliged'. *Bch.* Leaf XLVIII, 10.
89. Balasri, the king's representative pays gratuities of 30 *māḍha* to 14 master-sculptors including Gadadhara, Narayana, Kesava and Aparti (*Bch.* Leaf XXIII, 11); Each of these sculptors were paid 2 *māḍhas* each for 'beautiful sculptures they had carved on all four sides of the *pīṭha baranḍī* (XXIII, 12). Ten people who had carved the wheels with Lakhana Mahāpātra also received ten *māḍhas*. Six sculptors from Khiching received 12 *māḍhas*; the *sūtradhāra* received seven *māḍhas*, Angai Nayak two, Kasi Ojha two and the treasury staff received seven *māḍhas* (*Bch*, Leaf XXIII, 14). All these presents were arranged from the money sent by the chief Queen. After settling the expenditure of every department, 47 *māḍhas* still remained unspent. These were deposited in the treasury (*Bch*, Leaf XXIV, 1). On another occasion, Basu Ojha received an award of three *māḍhas* for making highly skilful contrivances to haul up the two parts of the *rāhāsimha* (XLVII, 15).
90. Cf., *Mahāvaṃsa*, XXVII, 10, 18. Also, Law (1945): 64-69.
91. Cf., Sivaramamurti (1934): 173ff. Settar also says, 'Hoysala artists accepted gainful employment under sectarian patrons but resisted any kind of force exerted on them'. Cf. Settar (1992): 90. The *Bayacakaḍa* seems to confirm such freedom of artists.
92. The stones on the base (*adhiṣṭhāna*) of the Teli ka Mandira at Gwalior carry label inscriptions in the contemporary Brahmi characters indicating directions like: *pachama, nairiti, vayavi*, etc. indicating that their piles were arranged direction-wise and set accordingly as the work progressed at the time of building the temple.
93. For instance, Gadei, and his son, *Bch.* Leaf XXXIII, 4; or two nephews of the *sūtradhāra*: *Bch.* Leaf XII, 5.
94. For an illustration of these horses, cf., Boner *et al.* (1972), plate 81, 82.
95. Several master-artsists and their special works find mention in the *Bayacakaḍa*. These include, among others, the masters like Ganga Mahārāṇā, the wheel sculptor, Govinda carpenter, Narayana, Madhu, Visvanatha Mahāpātra, Narasimha Mahāpātra, Lakhana Mahāpātra, Nidhi, Ghana, Mukunda Mahārāṇā, Gadadhara, Kasi Ojha, Damodara Mahārāṇā, Bhagavana Nayakạ, Dharani Mahāpātra who was the expert in making *kautuka bandha mūrti* (lion with human head) and *virāla* and Dama Mahāpātra who made a Viranchi-Sūrya image, etc.

96. On the basis of the dates of a *sūtradhāra* or *śilpī* at work, and his movement from one work to the other, it is possible to roughly work out that a decade was normally enough in building a moderate-sized temple in the Kalacuri region in Central India. Cf., Misra (1985): 188. According to the *Bayacakaḍa* it took thirteen years to build the Konark temple. It was a long and arduous process of work right from its inauguration ceremony with appointment of a *sūtradhāra* and others to laying the ground plan, building the *pīṭha*, *mukhaśālā* with its wall work and *pīḍhā* roofs, *anuratha śikharas*, ceiling of *śikhara*, its roof and *garbhagṛha*, subsidiary temples, and final setting up of the *kalaśa* on the main temple and consecration of the main cult image, not to speak of collection of building materials, carving, hoisting and setting up images and other umpteen works.
97. The beginning was more relaxed but as work progressed the pressures increased. Pace of work quickened up and the pressures to deliver are articulated time and again in setting deadlines, e.g., six months to complete the doorway by four artists with the assistance of three more helpers (*Bch.* Leaf IX, 16). Tensions mounted when large works like *navagraha* stones were hoisted and fixed or when huge iron girders were cast.
98. While Dasa Mahārāṇā held the thread Sadasiva *sūtradhāra* measured out the roof of the main temple for the placement of a cupola (*munḍī-pathara*) made out of fine sandstone by Dama Mahārāṇā. In doing this, the *sūtradhāra* designed a two-*hasta* high umbrella-like lotus with a raised edge, circular in shape with a diameter of three *hasta* and two *angula*. Cf., *Bch.*, Leaf XXXI, 10-11. He fixes the position of the Aruna pillar in front of the *mukhaśālā*, and a five feet hole is dug for the job (*Bch.* Leaf XXXVII, 9); he gets paid for performing measuring tasks, *Bch.* Leaf II, 3; in consultation with the *rājaguru* he directed the levelling of the floor of *mukhaśālā* with the help of the thread (*Bch.* Leaf XLVI, 1).
99. Masons' graffittis from Khajuraho similarly suggest that there were different sets of artists to carve different sets of images. Thus, one group carved only *Apsaras* and leogriffs while the other worked exclusively on the figures of the cult gods and goddesses. Sometimes, two or more artists worked to produce the same image. In a particular case, the artist seems to have made an image of a cult god as well as a minor deity. Cf., Singh (1993): 226-229.
100. Boner *et al.* (1972: 270) give an inventory of these along with their standard metallic weight, as follows: Sūrya *māḍha*: a gold coin of ¼ *tolas* in circulation under the Ganga rulers; Padma *māḍha*: a gold coin of *tola* in gold brought into use in temple construction; Ganga *māḍha*: gold coin of *tola* used in a garland of coins; Elephant-marked *māḍha*: weight not known; *Sana māḍha*: smaller *māḍha*; Kalatunga *māḍha*: coins of Kulatunga king in south; *asrapi*: oblong piece of gold of *tola* with punch mark; *jita suna asrapi*: gold disc without imprint; *Badashah kala tanka*: minted Muslim coin of one *tola*; *sikka*: Badshah silver coin of *tola*. Smilarly, *gaunī* was a rice measure equal to 3 ́seers and *bharaṇa* consisted of 280 seers.
101. Store was alwаys kept well stocked and was constantly replenished. In case of a shortage resources were provided. So, on orders of the king 9378

asrapis are brought from Sarangagada treasury by a Treasury Officer and deposited (*Bch.* Leaf XXI, 14). Storerooms are enlarged (*Bch.* Leaf XXVII, 3). The stocks are periodically verified and shortfalls, if any, were meticulously noted down. On an occasion, 9 out of 203 stones were found missing and the loss was recorded (*Bch.* Leaf VIII, 26). Under the orders of the king stores were checked and inventories of goods and materials made meticulously. These included cereals and grains, clothes, raw iron lumps, *sal* resin, small and long logs of wood, silver seat, horse saddle, an ivory *howdah*, sealed box with 214 small gold *māḍha*, 7017 large *māḍha*, 430 *Badshah* coins, 130 punch-marked (*gedi*) coins, six *tola* and 2 *masha kurujataka* gold, chisels, crow bars, silver stick, iron pulleys, water pots, vassels, images, containers of oil, iron rammers, torches, funnels, iron girders, saw and planks. The inventory also mentions details of stones disposed on different sides of the temple under construction, etc. including the materials in the *Rājā*'s camp, in Rupasa and Deuli camps, in a *matha*, with details of supplies in granary of grains received from different sources. Thus, in making the total inventory no parts of the stores were left out, including the central store, grainary, stores at the work sites or in the camps of *śilpins* and the king. All these were checked and inventory of goods made (*Bch.* Leaf XXVII-XXX). Store was locked when the accountant and storekeeper left the place on short visits (*Bch.* Leaf XXX, 3). Any shortfall in the stocks was duly recorded, as in case of nine stones found missing out of 203 such pieces (*Bch.* Leaf X, 26).

102. When work was resumed after the rainy season, these scribes, among other things, dispatched letters to all *śilpins* recalling them for work. Messengers carried those letters (*Bch.* Leaf V, 5; XII, 18).

103. These included a huge supply of stones of different type from eighteen different places (41 boat loads of stone in an instance) (*Bch.* Leaf II, 5; IV, 23-24); timber beams (*Bch.* Leaf I, 7; III, 7, 12), wood to carpenter (*Bch.* Leaf II, 6, 13); cart loads of coconut fibres for ropes (*Bch.* Leaf VI, 27); rope work to fasten stones (of different size and weight) (*Bch.* Leaf VII, 10); well oiled and powdered ropes for tying scaffolding and pulleys of fine quality (*Bch.*, Leaf IV, 4); planks attached to long ropes for sinking stones into foundation; cranes worked by a winding-wheel (*Bch.* Leaf II, 8); bamboo poles (IV, 13); earthen channel moulds to cast iron girders in the foundry (*Bch.* Leaf VI, 15); burnt earthen channel moulds 40 *hasta* long (*Bch.* Leaf VI, 15; VI, 19); borax for mixing iron (*Bch.* Leaf VI, 22); copper crucibles to weld the pieces of copper funnels to the desired length (*Bch.* Leaf VI, 24XI, 6); gravel to fill foundation (*Bch.* Leaf VII, 3); cart loads of *kendu* fruit (Dyospiros glutinosa) for making *karal*, a binding material (*Bch.* Leaf VII, 5); bricks (*Bch.* Leaf VII, 11); hoes and shovels of different shapes (*Bch.* Leaf II, 9); special chisels – flat and sharp-pointed – for carving *muguni* stone (*Bch.* Leaf II, 6, X, 18); mallets, pointed, indented and flat chisels; wooden plates with measuring threads, measuring rods with right angles, (*Bch.* Leaf II, 6); iron casting materials and other tools (*Bch.* Leaf XI-XII, 1-11); cart loads of charcoal for smelting furnace to cast iron girders (*Bch.* Leaf X, 22); fodder for feeding

elephants (*Bch.* Leaf X, 20); wax to metal workers, for filling earthen moulds to the depth of one *hasta* (*Bch.* Leaf XI, 1); workshops, iron casting foundry (*Bch.* Leaf IV) and furnaces with bellows and stone posts for smelting iron in an iron yard (*Ibid.*), and so on and so forth.

104. Present of sandstone by a feudatory was rewarded with return-presents including one to his barber (*Bch.* Leaf IV, 27); Rathasimha sent three bullock cart load of presents in gold coins, cereals, silk and cotton cloth, paddy (*Bch.* Leaf V, 1). The brother of the *rājā* who brought these gifts received golden ear rings and chain as a parting present. His three servants received seven pairs of ordinary clothes (*Bch.* Leaf V, 1); stones were sent by Mayurbhanj *rājā* via river route through Vaitarani River and the Mahanadi. Men who brought these were given three *māḍha* and one pair of clothes (*Bch.* Leaf V, 2). A *rājā* sent present of 50 pairs of clothes. The person who brought them got a parting gift of two *māḍha*s (VI, 11); *rājā* of Mayurbhanja sent five cart loads of raw iron lumps on five bullock carts (*Bch.* Leaf VI, 12); Balasri gave 200 cart loads of paddy (VI, 20); a feudatory sends 24 cart loads of paddy (VI, 31); Pandyan ruler sent a present of ten *śilpins* to work on temple; these included Sidhu Peddulu Goddur Sarma, Pitambara Pendulu and others (*Bch.* Leaf IX, 24); 214 pairs of cloth are presented by a feudatory chief (*Bch.* Leaf XVII, 10); presents by king and queen (*Bch.* Leaf LX, 23-24).

105. King defeated the Nawab of Lakhnauti and plundered his treasury. The war booty consisting of the wealth, mentioned below, was sent to Padmakesara treasury: 6000 minted *kurujataka* gold coins (*bankalekha māḍha* with curved letters), 37,000 small gold coins (*kalatunga gedi*) weighing 8 *rattis*, 12 turban ornaments with precious stones, one golden staff with ornamented knob, one tiger knife with golden handle inset with rubies and pearls and a silver brick (weight of all these is indicated). Of these, the *kurujātaka*s were retained and later melted in a mint to make 2431 *kulatunga*s. The rest of the booty was sent to Konark temple treasury (*Bch.* Leaf XXXV, 9).

106. In complying with the devaluation of the currency, the accountant of the camp-treasury, on the king's order, returned 1058 large *māḍha* coins and 214 small *māḍha* coins to the royal treasury. We are told that the king's personal treasury converted these into the Padma coins and the minter (*phaudara)* received 12 *māḍha*s for the job (*Bch.* Leaf XLIII, 5).

107. Twenty-one different categories of master-artists and workers were involved in building operations of the Sun temple at Konark. For complete list, see, Boner *et al.* (1972): 259.

108. 312 *pāitāla*s in Rupasa camp received 824 *māḍha*s; 108 such in Duai camp received 324 *māḍhas* (*Bch.* Leaf IX, 20); 237 workmen were lodged in Rupasa camp (*Bch.* Leaf XII, 20-21). *Śilpin*s of Rupasa camp are said to have received 303 *māḍhas* (as salary) (XVII, 21). Monthly salary to *kārigar*s of Rupasa camp, in an instance, consisted of 20 *māḍhas*, while the overseers received 46 *māḍha*s and water carriers received 24 *gaunis*. It is said that Balasri, an officer himself came on *palki* to hand out payments. Boner *et al.* (1972): 92-93. In an instance, 817 *śilpin*s of Rupasa camp received 100 *māḍha* in clearance of previous

miscellaneous work (*Bch.* Leaf XXVI, 2). *Śilpins* return to work and are lodged in Rupasa camp (*Bch.* Leaf XXX, 7). Wages (*vartanā*) to the *śilpīs* of Rupasa and Duai camps also find mention (XXXII, 12; XXXVIII, 3).

109. *Bch.* Leaf IV, 28. When the Rupasa camp was closed down, temporary sheds were made for the *śilpins* elsewhere (on the southern side under a banyan tree, the *Arkavaṭa*). *Bch.* Leaf XLI, 6.

110. Betel-bearers served the master craftsmen engaged in fine chisel work (*Bch.* Leaf IX, 18) or *palki*-bearers took them out when a need arose to do so (*Bch.* Leaf XII, 19). A mess with well-provided store was managed with the support of grants and supplies (*Bch.* Leaf VI, 10).

111. According to the *Aparājitapṛcchā* 226.27, *śilpīs* were to be fed and given clothes and ornaments before making an image: *śilpin bhojayettatra vastrālankāra samyutān ...*

112. Tax collectors collected taxes from traders of Rupasa and Pateli in Kala Badshah coins (*tanka*) and Badshah small coins (*sikkā*) and in other denominations and deposited the amount in treasury (*Bch.* Leaf XII, 3; XXVI, 12).

113. The chief of the cowherds was, on an occasion, rewarded with a herd of cows (so that supplies will remain unhampered).

114. *Bch.* Leaf XXIII, 17. Leaf XXV, 2. The reason for this fine on Yogi is not stated.

115. Cf., Settar (1992): 91. He refers to two Hoyasala monuments, namely, the Someśvara temple at Harnahalli and Cennakeśava temple at Nagalapura, which were abandoned in such a situation.

116. When Mukunda, a *śilpī* who carried the title Mahāpātra, died of pneumonia his son was granted thirty-two *māḍhas* (gold coins) as compensation and to perform the rites. The Brāhmaṇas in the camp came forward to perform worship to ward off the impending obstacles (*Bch.* Leaf VI, 1-2).

117. *Bch.* Leaf IV, 4-6, 11; Leaf VII, 5, Leaf 1. Scaffoldings are very frequently mentioned. Cf., *Bch.*, Leaf X, 5; *Bch.* Leaf X, 21 refers to a 'ladder scaffolding'.

118. *Bch.* Leaf X, 14. It took twelve workers to lift a large Sūrya image of blue chlorite stone up to the platform with the help of pullies. They got seven *māḍhas* and twenty-four *gaunīs* for the task.

119. *Bayacakaḍa*, Leaf XXVII, 1. We also have the instance of a severe coastal cyclone, which severely damaged the scaffoldings; it also sunk a boat and the stones it carried. But soon after the holocaust, the capsized boat and the stones were hauled up with the help of elephants.

120. *Śilpīs* had their own community fund in the treasury and the accountant made payments out of it. They employed cooks who once received payment from that account for ten days work (*Bch.* Leaf XLVII, 5).

121. For references to these incidents which are mentioned in the paragraph, cf., *Bayacakaḍa*, Leaf XXVII, 1; XII, 14; XIII, 1-2; XIII, 2; L, 1; XLI, 22-23; XX, 3; XVII, 7, 13; XXXVIII, 7; VI, 18; XXX, 2.

122. The translations of these titles in English are by Boner. Cf., Boner *et al.* (1972): 47.

123. Work for images on the western side of the Konark temple was entrusted to the *sūtradhāra* (*Bch.* Leaf X, 15). After the images were set up in the niches

by the *sūtradhāra* and Gadadhara, the former received 50 *māḍhas*, the same amount that Gadadhara also received (*Bch.* Leaf XIII, 11). According to Boner, these images represented the *pārśva devatās,* and by conventions among the artisans, they could be set only by *sūtradhāra*. On yet another occasion, the *sūtradhāra* is mentioned as doing fine chisel work like Gadadhara and Ganga for which he received 11 *māḍhas* unlike the two others who received 17 *māḍhas* (*Bch.* Leaf XVII, 8).

124. The *sūtradhāra* orders 12 *kārigaras* to get 80 stone slabs for covering the roof of a temple. Of these stone slabs, 'twenty had their corners on two sides indented' (*Bch.* Leaf XXXI, 8).

125. *Bch.* Leaf XL, 5. A royal escort, including the torch- and parasol-bearers, accompanies the king, in this instance.

126. *Sūtradhāra* was called by *rājā* soon after a cyclone struck, causing severe damage, which stopped work on the temple. So, he went to report to the king and returned after briefing him. For this visit he is said to have received a payment of two *māḍhas* (*Bch.* Leaf XII, 16).

127. The plan, in the instance, consisted of the details about the compound of the Konark temple with a subsidiary temple, a horse gate and an elephant gate. Sadasiva *sūtradhāra* had prepared the plan on the king's orders. So, when the Konark temple was moving towards completion, and as Balasri, the king's representative, came to camp after Holi festival, the *sūtradhāra* submitted to him this entire plan drawn to the scale (? *gunagara*). After its approval by Balasri, a notice was sent by drumbeat to all the artisans' camps to inform everyone of this plan (*Bch.* Leaf XXXIII, 9).

128. *Sūtradhāra* Sadasiva received payment of ten *māḍhas* on an occasion (work is unspecified, is it a salary?) (*Bch.* Leaf II, 15). He was paid for marking the outline of *pīṭha* (*rekhāvasana*) (*Bch.* Leaf IV, 20). For determining the position of the *garbhadvāra* with a *śanku*, *sūtradhāra* received one *māḍha* (*Bch.* Leaf IX, 10, 13); *sūtradhāra*'s salary (*khatani*) for three months was six *māḍhas* (*Bch.* Leaf XXXVIII, 6). On another occasions he receives a salary of 27 *māḍhas* for an unspecified period (*Bch.* Leaf X, 7) or even seven *māḍhas* for a period of three months (*Bch.* Leaf IX, 20), or a salary of two *māḍhas* for an unspecified period (*Bch.* Leaf XXVI, 13). Once his salary of 10 *māḍhas* also finds mention (*Bch.* Leaf XV, 6). With Gadadhara at his side the *sūtradhāra* arranged the position of 10 whole and 70 dressed *muguni* stones according to earlier measurements, conforming to the divisions of the *dvārabandha* (entrance to the sanctum). This was done with the help of a thread. Neither of them received any payment but the stonemasons who assisted were paid one *bharaṇa* and eleven *gaunīs* (*Bch.* Leaf IX, 13). The *sūtradhāra* traced the design of the doorjambs to the entrance of the sanctum with the help of Angai Nayak and they got two *māḍhas* each (*Bch.* Leaf IX, 15). Sometimes the *sūtradhāra* received presents as was when the *rājā* of Madurai and the father-in-law of the king, sent a pair of silken clothes for him (*Bch.* Leaf IX, 24). The *sūtradhāra* received three pairs of cloth on the *astrapūjā* day, the occasion for celebration of the Viśvakarmā community (*Bch.* Leaf XVII, 11). The *sūtradhāra* along with accountant and store-keeper received a total of

two *māḍhas*; *sūtradhāra*'s two nephews received 22 *gaunīs* (*Bch*. Leaf XII, 5). *Sūtradhāra* received 30 *māḍhas* (*Bch*. Leaf XIII, 5). When *navagraha* panel was hoisted, setting it up on iron girders above the portal, Balasri and a feudatory gave awards to *sūtradhāra* and to Nidhi Mahāpātra through the *sūtradhāra* (*Bch*. Leaf XIV, 6).

129. *Bch*. Leaf VIII, 20. While going to attend New Year festival he passed the charge of all work on *mukhaśālā* wall and other parts to Gadadhara *Mahāpātra*.
130. *Bch*. Leaf XXIV, 15. The instance indicates an artist's freedom to accept casual work from a person other than his current master who had retained him for regular work.
131. See also, Settar (1992): 83-96 for materials on Hoysala artists and their works, which seem to compare well with the materials in the *Bayacakaḍa*.
132. *Bayacakaḍa* has an entry of the overseers receiving 4503 *asrapis*, 3472 gold coins besides collecting 3408 *bharaṇas* (of grains) annually (*Bch*. Leaf XXIX).
133. The small list of his possessions in the camp makes an interesting reading. These consisted of 'a brass tub, three water vessels, one wooden bedstead, one seat, one lamp stand, one locked wooden box on wheels with keys kept with the *sūtradhāra*'. These objects are listed in an inventory of goods made by the auditors who came to verify the stores. The inventory record also contains an inspection note that the 'objects around the Narasimha image (in the *sūtradhāra*'s home) were not required to be listed' (*Bch*. Leaf XXVIII).
134. For a reference to these incidents, see, *Bch*. Leaf IX, 24-25; X, 6, 9, 11; XII, 19, XV, 7; XXIII, 14; XXX, 8; LII, 13; XXXIV, 6; LXIV, 7.
135. *Bch*. Leaf XXV, 7. For another similar dispensation, see *Bch*. XLIV, 10.
136. Thus, under his 'direction', thirty-four master artists (*mahārāṇās*) prepared stones for the *anuratha śikhara* and Ganga Mahārāṇā with forty-four *pāthuriās* (stone workers) set them in place, on a payment of fourteen *māḍhas* (*Bch*. Leaf XXII, 3).
137. Contracts were always meticulously recorded. So were the payments whenever made, whether in terms of advance or full clearance in settlement of accounts.
138. For these instances, cf., *Bch*. Leaf XXV, 4; Leaf XLI, 20; Leaf XVII, 16. For illustration of the Dikpala images carved by him, cf., Boner *et al*. (1972): pl. 33. For making the image of Aruna according to *dhyāna*, Ganga Mahāpātra received 2 *māḍhas*. Ganga Mahāpātra is mentioned here as *sāmanta*, cf., *Bch*. Leaf XXXVIII, 2.
139. For different references to his work quoted here, cf., *Bch*., Leaf XII, 17 for his present of a royal image to the king. Visvanatha makes a crocodile head as gorgoyle. For bigger *makaras* he gets contract in collaboration with Kuna, the son of Gadei. Cf., *Bch*. Leaf XXXIII, 4; XLII, 9; XXX, 4; XIV, 5; XXXIII, 3, 4, 9.
140. Boner *et al*. (1972): Plate 32.
141. There is also an instance of Govinda Mahāpātra who 'presents' a composite Sūrya-Śiva image on contract of ten *māḍha*. The image was delivered to *sūtradhāra* on a festive occasion (*Bch*. Leaf XXXVI, 3).

142. Boner *et al.* (1972): Pl. 54, 55.
143. We have such cases of assistance to artists in other instances too. The 'wise' Baladitya assisted *sūtradhāra* Durlabhaditya when the latter built a temple. This finds mention in the Pehowa stone slab inscription of ninth-tenth century. Cf., Agrawal (2001): 110.
144. Appointments of workers to assist master-artist were made on contract also. Thus, three workmen were designated to help four master artists on a six-month contract in order to carve the doorway to the sanctum. The service contract here was coterminous with the period allotted to the master artists to complete the work (*Bch.* Leaf IX, 16).
145. Setting of *navagraha* panel was a cumbersome affair requiring great skill and several wooden contraptions supported by elephants and men with ropes, etc. These are elaborately described in the text. The king's brother came to witness this operation (*Bch.* Leaf XIII, 6-16).
146. *Bch.* Leaf VIII, 25; VIII, 18; VIII, 31; IX, 6; Boner *et al.* (1972): IX, 15; XVI, 22-23; XLIV, 5; LXV, 16.
147. For an illustration of this joint work, cf., Boner *et al.* (1972): Plate 58-59.
148. See the case of Madhu Mahārāṇā and his eight co-workers (*Bch.* Leaf IX, 14-15). It is likely that the foreman of the team was given the money and he distributed it according to the work of respective workmen. There is the instance of payment of 77 *māḍhas* to Bansi Mahārānā for his band of 47 workers who set black chlorite stones on the limestone base. Total amount paid was 77 *māḍhas* to Bansi and 2 more *māḍhas* again to Bansi: the first payment perhaps representing the amount for distribution and the second amount (two *māḍhas*) going to Bansi exclusively (*Bch.* Leaf IX, 7).
149. Wages (*vartanā*) often find mention in the *Bayacakaḍa*: to *hatiāla* (*Bch.* Leaf VIII, 24; VIII, 20); to *śilpins* in the Rupasa camp (*Bch.* Leaf VIII, 28); three months wages amounting to three *bharaṇas* and 24 *gaunīs*, to the workmen carrying stones (*Bch.* Leaf VIII, 8); 20 people get their 'wages' of one *bharaṇa* each for raising a scaffolding set on iron girders. In addition to wages, other payment for sundry work were also admissible as in case of Chanda Singh, a *hatiāla*, who brought three small elephants to stamp the floor of the *mukhaśālā* where limestone was spread out to be levelled by women workers (*Bch.* Leaf IX, 6; XVI, 22).
150. Salary of supervisors (*Bch.* Leaf XIV, 16); 230 *māḍha* salary of 108 *śilpins* of Rupasa camp and 428 *māḍha* salary of *śilpins* of Deuli camp find mention (*Bch.* Leaf XV, 1); 47 *māḍha* salary of eleven overseers is also mentioned (*Bch.* Leaf XV, 6).
151. A retaining fee was given to *śilpins* (214 *māḍhas*), *swānsya* and workers together (214 *māḍhas*) when the work stopped during the rainy season for four months (*Bch.* Leaf XI, 13); others, like fourteen iron workers (*karadis* and *ojhās*) were given leave and paid off (*Bch.* Leaf XII, 1).
152. It is said that after completion of work on the pillars of *mukhaśālā* under the direction of Ganga Mahāpātra, accounts 'were cleared' with a payment of 20 *māḍhas* (*Bch.* Leaf VIII, 19). Obviously, there must have been an advance for this contract which is missed in the text. There is another reference to

Gadadhara and twenty other *pāthuriās* who received a contract to build the *anuratha* of the *śikhara* and arrange stones on the ground. Later, in 'settlement of accounts', they received 130 *māḍhas* (*Bch.* Leaf XLVII, 3).

153. The *Bayacakaḍa* (Leaf XVII, 25) refers to 'one installment' of 30 *māḍha* being paid in an instance, without a reference to the total amount of contract. This may indicate even the plurality of payment installments. When a contract was given, an advance was given too (as seed money?) Even advances could be in installments as in the case of Vira, Vidyadhara and Yogi who were paid (*māḍhas* 4+12) in installments twice within a short interval, on a contract of 30 *māḍhas* (*Bch.* Leaf VIII, 12).

154. Payments made against supplies, e.g., 17 *māḍha* were disbursed to Basu Ojha for supplying chisels (*Bch.* Leaf VIII, 29). Payments were made on receiving the supplies (*Bch.* Leaf VIII, 9-10). Sometimes payments were made without mentioning the job performed. This would indicate settlement of outstanding dues (*Bch.* Leaf VIII, 20). So, 420 *pāitālas* of two camps, besides stone masons, overseers and *sūtradhāra* are mentioned together as receiving payment of outstanding dues: outstanding because *sūtradhāra* is mentioned as receiving three months salary of seven *māḍhas* (*Bch.* Leaf IX, 20).

155. All gold coins here are called *śunya* (*Bch.* Leaf LXV, 9).

156. The *Aparājitapṛcchā* 151.1-16 has a chapter on *sūtradhāra-pūjā-vidhi* that describes how a *sūtradhāra* was to be propitiated and presents in cash and kind including village and land grants were to be proferred to him. The details are interesting but especially interesting is the verse reading: *grāmam caiva tato dadyāt kṛṣṇāṃvā bhūmimuttatam* .../6/. The text also recommends proper dispensation to the *karmakāras: sarveṣām karmakārāṇām dhanam dadddyācca sarvataḥ* /8/.

157. A crisis developed in setting the *kalaśa* on the top of the *śikhara* when the temple was almost complete and as *sūtradhāra* himself seemed losing his bearings in doing the job, his son stepped in with certain amendments and performed the task anonymously, as it were, for he left the place in the middle of the night and payments to him were furtively gauged in the record to save the honour of the *sūtradhāra*.

4

Śāstra

We had earlier drawn attention to *śilpa*'s connection with *vidyā, vijñāna* and *śāstra* and we may now discuss this connection *inter alia* their common objectives in arts including, among other things, 'liberation' (*mukti*) which the practice of *śilpa vidyā* came to assure eminently. *Śilpa*'s validity as 'knowledge' – even a kind of knowledge not in tune with theoretical temper of orthodoxy, as evinced in the *Maitrī Upaniṣad* – is explicitly conceded in texts. Its exalted pedigree, as we saw earlier, could be traced back to the *Ṛgveda*; and, notwithstanding its devaluation as *vṛtti* in Pāṇini, Patanjali and *Dharmaśāstras*, its resurrection was categorically posited as early as second century BC in the enunciation of its *nibbāna*-ic ends in the *Milinda Pañho*. This text speaks of an all-encompassing nature of *śippa*, superior even to the *Vedas*, which it consigns to the domain merely of *śikṣā*, 'training'.[1] Such an ideological orientation of *śilpa* both in the early Vedic framework, as seen earlier, and also outside it, as in the *Milinda Pañho*, underscores its uniquely alternate domain whether in agreement or in dissent with the brāhmaṇical order. This domain seems to have received a universal sanction with the passage of time as *śilpa* came to be accepted as *vidyā* or *śāstra*.

INTERACTIVE DOMAIN OF *ŚILPAŚĀSTRA* IN A KINDRED GROUP

Since *śilpa* has been addressed on occasions as *karma, vidyā, vijñāna* or *śāstra*, it may be relevant to understand what these terms imply and how they may define and qualify it or may stand independent of it. To understand the nature of such conjunctions and disjunction we may have to first analyse the content of these terms in their respective domains, for these definitive terms seem to have an operative value in conformity with their own, somewhat exclusive and autonomous standing. In conjunction with *śilpa,* they, on occasions, tend to qualitatively invest into it their own values: thus valorising it in the process, even as they seem to enhance their own credibility in such a convergence. This may be so as *śilpa* indeed was considered to be an exceptionally potent entity on its own, rendered so efficacious as a result of ritual investiture in it right from the early Vedic times.[2] It may be assumed that transformations in the nature and status of streams of knowledge including *śilpavidyā* also constitute a history of valorising (and sometimes even devaluing) one or the other of them as a result of ideational, ritual, social, priestly or artisanal proclivities of those who either upheld them or stood opposed to them. Several shades of meaning seem to be intricately entwined in these terms, e.g., *vijñāna, vidyā, śāstra,* etc. whether in their independent domain or in their reciprocities. The discourse on what constituted *śikṣā, karma, vidyā, vijñāna* or *śāstra,* and whether *śilpa* was one of these streams of knowledge or outside their domains seems to bear out silent transformations apparently crafted by *śilpins*. A canonical sanction for these transformations came later. The points need some elaboration, which follows.

In the Buddhist philosophical tradition *vijñāna* relates to 'cognition': *vijñānātiti vijñānam,* 'that which inheres knowledge is *vijñāna*'.[3] In the Kashmir Śaivite contexts, the term *vijñāna* implies 'experimental knowledge, pure consciousness, awareness'.[4] *Vijñāna* is also defined as *niravaśeṣa śāstra viṣaya granthato'rthataśca siddhijñānam jñānam vijñānam.*[5] But in arts[6] *vijñāna* seems aligned to the technical aspects of *śilpa* and represents a special kind of knowledge which was considered a 'science' related to artificing unlike the learning in the *Veda*s, etc. that constituted a 'higher' knowledge capable, in essence, of emancipation (*mokṣa*): *mokṣe dhīrjñānam vijñānam śilpaśāstrayoḥ,* i.e., 'the meaning coming out of the *śāstric* works alone leads to *siddhi*; so the *śāstric* knowledge alone is *vijñāna*'. As an independent stream of knowledge *vijñāna* figures as a distinct category apart from the *Veda*s, *Vedanga* and *śāstra*s which all lay together in the ken of Viśvakarmā, the high priest of *śilpa.*[7] The *Vivādaratnākara* of Bṛhaspati regards *śilpa* as *vijñāna* in that it is located in the domain of arts, such as: 'dance, etc.' (*nṛtyādikam*), and also in the realm of metallurgy, pertaining specially to making gold ornaments.[8] It would thus appear that *śilpa* as *vijñāna* was related to a category of special knowledge in which intuitive experience of knowing and the technical skills of doing essentially went together.

Śilpa eminently figures as *vidyā*, whether by implication or by that qualifying designation which is accorded to it specifically, time and again.

The idea of knowledge (and learning by practice) is implicit in the term *śilpa*. The elements that constituted it are, as we said earlier, spelled out axiomatically in the *Aitareya Brāhmaṇa* (VI.27), *Śatapatha Brāhmaṇa* (III.2.1.5), *Jaiminīya Brāhmaṇa* (II.191) and in the *Milinda Pañho*. In an early usage of the term in the *Aitareya* (VI.27), *śilpa* is evocative of knowledge (*ya evam veda*) that 'cultures the self' (*ātmānam samskurute*). Sāyaṇa, commenting upon the *Aitareya Brāhmaṇa,* lists two kinds of *śilpas* – *devaśilpa* and *mānuṣa śilpa,*[9] the latter being the former's counterpart by imitation (*anukaraṇa*) – the 'knowledge' of which transforms such a 'knower' into one who is accomplished in *śilpa*. Occurring in conjunction with *veda* (from the root *vid-*, 'to know') and endowed with the quality of 'high' art in the sense that it is supposed to be in 'rhythm' with itself (*chandomayaṃ*), *śilpa* is projected as something that only an accomplished 'knower' would 'know'.[10] The *Jaiminīya Brāhmaṇa* (II.191) emphasises interdependence of all arts, which are supposed to be embedded in *śilpa*: *yathā rathākṣe rathacakraṃ pratimunced evam evaitāni sarvāṇi śilpāni.*

In its literal sense, the term *śilpa* relates to 'skill' and efficiency in 'realising a form' (*rūpasiddhi*). It is expressly a *karman* in the *Nighanṭu* (II.1). So also in the *Amarakośa* (II.10.35: *śilpam karmakalādikam*) where all fine arts like dancing, music, etc. came under the purview of *śilpa*. Etymologically, *śilpa* implies an act that is hard to learn or accomplish even as it requires great devotion, commitment and energy. Its practice is a tormenting exercise but eventually it does lead to realisation of the intended 'form'. It also implies 'moving', i.e., moving towards the action or the exercise of learning. It would thus appear that the idea of knowledge (and learning by practice, i.e., training) is implicit in the term *śilpa*. The nature and kind of this knowledge and the elements that may constitute it need being explained. The *Śatapatha* finds *śilpa* in every 'counterform'. The strands of such connectivity or compatibility occur in other different ways, and the range of such connections seems wide enough even as the ideas concerning it seem to be historically rooted in the ancient past. Thus, in the *Aitareya Brāhmaṇa, śilpa* lies in reconstituting divine forms in imitation (*anukṛti*), and the roots of knowledge seem latent in it. The *Kauśītaki Brāhmaṇa* (XXIX.5) enumerates three-fold *śilpas* consisting of dance, music and singing which together in the *Chāndogya Upaniṣad* (VII.1.2-4, VII.2.1) formed a part of *devajana vidyā.*

The entire argument of *vidyā per se* seems built into the processes and pursuits of a valid enquiry. A meditative quest to comprehend a knowable entity so that its intuitive cognition itself may become capable of rendering a seeker knowledgeable (*ya u cainam evam veda*) is one of the common refrains in the *Upaniṣads* and *Brāhmaṇas*. The transition of this cognition into the category of *vidyā* seems endorsed by the fact that thereby it comes to satisfy the conditions of 'true vision' (*samyag darśana)* and 'face-to-faceness' (*sakṣātkaraṇa*). Śankara, in his commentary on the *Vedānta Sūtra* (III. 3. 14 and III. 3.59), regards such an experience or quest as capable of graduating into a *vidyā*. He argues that a *vidyā* rests on *dhyāna* (meditation) as its antecedent to afford a 'true vision' (*ādhyāna purvakāya samyagdarśanaye*) and it leads to 'immediate perception of the worshipped object' (*asam phalam upāsyaviṣayasākṣātkaraṇam*).[11] These may be regarded as essential conditions whose inherence would turn an experience into a *vidyā*. In the *Upaniṣads*, the term *vidyā* seems to characterise meditative exercise related to ritual acts of esoteric or symbolic orientation that tend to become objects of contemplation (*dhyāna*).[12] They explain *vidyā* in terms of special knowledge related to Brahman (*Brahmavidyā*). Sāyaṇa, commenting on the *Śatapatha Brāhmaṇa* (XI.5.6.8) takes it in the sense of philosophical systems. But in common parlance, combined with specific substantives it designates various sciences or crafts.[13]

Eventually, *vidyā* came to have both epistemological and spiritual connotations, the former evincing the proofs of knowledge (*pramāṇas*) and the latter tied up with salvation (*vimukti*), its emancipating character ensconced in its exceptional potency. So, whatever be the *vidyā*, a recipe for liberation was always built into it – *sā vidyā yā vimuktaye* or, as in the *Maitrī Upaniṣad* (VII.9) – *vidyayā'mṛtamaśnute. Vidyā*s seem to have represented the cognitive element in a system of ideas, and their number and relative importance kept on vacillating depending on particular schools of thought and practice. By the time of the *Chāndogya Upaniṣad* a fairly large list of *vidyā*s had received a sanction in the religious as well as secular fields. Tradition differentiates them into many categories (*vividhā*), e.g., *parā* and *aparā, arthakarī, tridhātu, sanjīvanī*, etc. *Vidyā* eventually came to be regarded as a source of knowledge to the wise (*vidyā sādhorjñānāya*) and a source of enlightenment (*vidyā, sā'pi dvividhā bodhābodha svabhāva bhedāt*), supposed to rests in *Vāk* (*sarvāsām vidyānām vāgekāyanam*). It made its knower distinctive (*vidyato puruṣo viśeṣo bhavati*).[14] Its all-winning quality is described in the *Sarasvatī Śāstra*, which eulogises it as *deśakāla paricchedā sarvadā sarvamohinī* even as it is supposed to be primarily located in analytical reasoning (*vimarśarūpiṇī vidyā*). [15] The number of disciplines in the category or genre of *vidyā* and the implications of the term seem to vary in different texts,[16] and *śilpa* often seems to be a part of this genre. We saw above that *śilpa* figures as 'knowledge' in the *Aitareya Brāhmaṇa* in reference to the 'reconstituted forms' and in its kindred association with dance, music and singing as defined in the *Kauśītaki Brāhmaṇa*. Elsewhere, *śilpa* is part of *devajana vidyā* too.[17] It is safe to assume therefore that *śilpa*'s status as a specific knowledge has a hoary antiquity in which are also fused its wide-ranging art-related interconnections and their recognition as such.

As in early texts, so also later, *śilpa*'s identification with or transition into *vidyā* seems to have continued unabated.[18] As *vidyā*, *śilpa* stands supreme even as it perpetually affords *ānanda* (pleasure): *śilpavidyā sadā śreṣṭhā sarvadānandadāyikā.*[19] The *Vākyapadīyam* (I.117) similarly regards certain values as supreme as these are best illustrated and expressed through *śilpa.*[20] According to the *Śilpaprakāśa* (I.561), *śilpavidyā* is supportive of regional modes and inflexions (*śilpavidyā deśānusāriṇī*). In the *Kāvyamīmāmsā*, *śilpa* remains secure in its status as *vidyā*, alone as well as in alliance with other disciplines. Rājaśekhara refers to ancient *ācāryas*' division of the categories of knowledge into fourteen *vidyāsthānas* and he predictively adds *kāvya* as the fifteenth *vidyāsthāna* to this list.[21] Not content yet, he enumerates four more categories including the *śilpīśāstra*, 'art and architecture', in his categorisation of the *vidyās*.[22]

Śilpa eventually came to acquire the label of *śāstra*. And this development marks its rehabilitation, even resurgence or resurrection. The transformation apparently came about as this *vidyā* was incorporated in the *Purāṇas*,[23] both early and late, and in the *Āgamas*[24] and *Saṃhitās* (e.g., *Jayākhya, Padma, Pauṣkara, Pāñcarātra, Parameśvara*, etc.), composed in the north and south India. This entire development was remarkable in suitably evolving a large pantheon of gods in their multiple iconic forms along with their comprehensively developed iconography. Such reorganisation of *śilpa* tradition also led to the claims of their divine or *ṛṣic* authority, by proxy. The *Samarāngaṇa Sūtradhāra* authored by Bhoja (eleventh century) makes a claim to the 'received wisdom' from Brahma for its contents – a wisdom that Viśvakarmā shared with his four sons: Jaya, Vijaya, Siddhartha and Aparajita. The *Samarāngaṇa Sūtradhāra* (I. 1) begins with an obeisance to Śiva, the *sūtradhāra* of the three worlds (*bhuvanatraya sūtradhāra*), who threaded, as it were, the entire universe into being: ... *kātsnyārdisūtritama-sūtryata yena viśvam.* As the details follow, it (I. 5) relates the discipline to Brahma on whose command Viśvakarmā offers the knowledge of this *śāstra* to others for the welfare of the *loka*: *tasmāllokasya kṛpayā śāstrametadudīryate.* According to the *Citralakṣaṇa* of Nagnajit (I.105) Visvakarma is the creator of all arts (*sarve śilpāmayā kṛtāh*), whose expositions made the *śāstra* known to others: *citraśilpasya śāstram tu tasmai rajñe hyupadiśat.*[25] Some texts, *Vāstusūtra Upaniṣad* for instance, seem to belong to *śilpa vidyā* tradition,[26] related to the Atharvanic genre.

The *Aparājitapṛcchā*, 'Aparajita's questionnaire', a thirteenth century *vāstuśilpa* text containing regulations about *vāstu, pratimā* and *citra*[27] similarly regards Viśvakarmā as the primordial knower of *śilpaśāstra* which he explained to his son Aparajita.[28] *Śilpa* is explicitly designated as *śāstra* time and again. The relevant texts make the claims of its authority as a *śāstra* on the basis of its 'revealed knowledge'. The *śāstric* status of the discipline reverberates in the *Viśvakarmā Vāstuśāstra.*[29] In these texts and also elsewhere the authority of *śilpa* as a *śāstra* is found asserted unequivocally.[30] *Śilpins* themselves[31] seem to have composed *śilpa* texts as the latter often appear like practical manuals of *lakṣaṇa*, measures (*tālamāna*), *pramāṇas*, with the aphoristic expressions pointedly fit enough in order to work out images or monuments of different kinds.[32] We also have the texts like the *Citralakṣaṇa* of Nagnajit containing a dialogue between Brahma and Nagnajit that seems to accord a divine sanction to iconographic practice.

Sometimes, the sanction is *ṛṣic*. The *Viṣṇudharmottara* enunciations about *śilpa* in the *citrasūtra* start with a dialogue between the sage Markandeya and King Vajra and develop into a canon of iconography where *lakṣaṇas* are the means to concretise the forms – even those forms that may be un-manifestible (*etaddhi tasyāpratimasya rūpam taveritam rūpa jaganmayasya* ...). Image-making is mentioned there in terms of 'fashioning the forms' (*rūpa nirmāṇam*) 'in order that this making may ever conform to *śāstra*' (*yasmātsannihita nityam śāstravat sā kṛtirbhavet).*[33]

The term *śāstra* is etymologically derived from the root *śās-*, 'to teach' and it is so called because 'it chastises (*śās*) all one's inimical impurities and 'saves' (*tra*) one from evil rebirth'.[34] *Śāstra* seemingly occupies a higher plane than *vidyā* as it leads to realisation of *dharma* in different domains within its jurisdiction, whether rituals, image making, poetry or others, including the *puruṣārthas*. It offers 'expansive vision of everything' (*sarvasya locanam*), 'dispels doubts' (*aneka samśayocchedi*) and 'makes the hidden meaning perceivable' (*parokṣa'rtha darśakam*).[35] The *Amarakośa* (III.179) explains *śāstra* as 'command' (*nirdeśa*) or 'authoritative knowledge' or a 'book' (*nideśa granthayoḥ śāstram*); in specifics: the works on philosophy, e.g., those of Gautama, Kanada, Kapila, Patanjali, Vyasa and Jaimini.[36] It has a legislative authority not open to challenge for it is supposed to have an unhindered sway. In tradition, the validity of *śastra* lies in its theoretical primordiality as *vidyā*, which receives a 'practical instantiation' in its practice. Taking into account Katyayana's dictum *śāstrena dharma niyamaḥ*, it may be said that '*śāstra* provides a constraint on behaviour in accordance with *a priori* assessment of the correct way of acting'.[37] And, its authority would be binding. Whatever be the contingency, whether the Vindhyas might split or the winds of annihilation (*pralaya*) might blow, the wise were supposed to stick to the path of *śāstra* and *guru.*[38]

Śāstras are also supposed to be of two kinds (*dvidha*): *apauruṣeya* and *pauruṣeya,*[39] respectively representing those which cannot be attributed to a particular author and those which have a specific authorship. They form an organised body of text with an indubitable authority. As to the origin of a *śāstra* one may speculate that particular *vidyās* apparently grew up into *śāstras* like a narrow river, widening at its down stream. The simile is taken from Rājaśekhara who says: 'Just as rivers are thin and narrow in the beginning and gradually widen so also the *śāstras* are small and gradually increase in dimension.'[40]

CONSTITUTIVE ELEMENTS

If *śilpa* is indeed a *śāstra*,[41] as the texts generally assert, the question about the constitutive elements that go into its making; the rules it seeks to establish; the operational modality of its rules; and the claims of its authority,[42] all these need being addressed here even though in brief. Implications might be significant, for *śastra* is generally understood in the sense of 'cultural grammar' that would have a prescriptive as well as a regulatory authority in offering legitimacy to cultural practices.

Abhinavagupta's *Parātriśikā Vivaraṇa* enumerates four indispensable elements (*anubandha catuṣṭaya*) of a *śāstra* encompassing (i) aims or objective (*prayojana*), (ii) one who is authorised to study (*adhikārin*), (iii) the subject matter (*abhidheya*), and (iv) relationship (*sambandha*, i.e., connection between the title and content).[43] Certain definitional characteristics (*yukti*s), essential in rehabilitating a body of knowledge into a standard *tantra*, also figure in the *Arthaśāstra* (XV.1.1-73) and other works, which define the essentials that may go into making of a theoretical science, such that *śilpaśāstra*s seems to be in their content.[44]

In defining the constitutive elements of *śilpaśāstra*, it may be possible to extrapolate its injunctions with the help of *śilpa*-related axiomatic formulations in antiquity. These include, as we said earlier, its axioms, like '*śilpa* cultures the self' or '*śilpa* is where *pratirūpa* is' or, '*anukaraṇa*[45] is its basis' (*śilpānām anukṛtiḥ śilpamadhigamyate*). These axioms figure right from the Vedic times and seem to fix the general framework of the objectives or *prayojana* of *śilpaśāstra*. The formulations about *rūpa*[46] (or, *bhāvarūpa*), *lakṣaṇa*,[47] *pramāṇa*,[48] *dhyāna*,[49] *sādhana*, *anukaraṇa*, seem to define its operational modality.[50] As for *śilpa*s' authority, the Vedic texts we quoted in the beginning and the *arcā*- and *kriyapāda*s of the *Agama*s and *Saṃhita*s tend to define that authority eminently. Inducements and imprecations in the *śilpa* texts end up in reiterating adherence to the *śāstric* rules. The texts are specific in their approval or disapproval in respect of their prescriptions in whatever field that is taken up. An instance of such prescriptions may be seen in case of the idols of cult gods. The *Viṣṇudharmottara Purāṇa* commands that an upward (*ūrdhva*), downward (*adhaḥ*) or an oblique (*tiryaka*) gaze in these icons should be avoided, for such a representation may respectively cause death, grief or destruction. The text further avers that the idols made according to the prescribed proportions (*mānahīna vivarjayet*), endowed with appropriate marks (*lakṣaṇa*) are praiseworthy (*praśasta*); made according to rules, they bring about longevity, increased fame, wealth and material prosperity.[51] In these imprecations and inducements there is a clear assertion of the textual authority of the *śilpaśāstra*s.

The basic foundations of *śilpaśāstra* seem integrated into the general framework of fine arts including the latter's visual and performing modes. This idea of interdependence goes back in antiquity to the *Jaiminīya Brāhmaṇa* (II.191): *yathā rathākṣe rathacakraṃ pratimunced evam evaitāni sarvāṇi śilpāni.* Bharata (I.117) asserts the primacy of *nāṭyaśāstra* relegating all other modes of artistic expressions, including *śilpaśāstra* to a secondary position: *natajjhānam na tat śilpam na sā vidyā na sā kalā/nāsau yogo na tat karma nāṭyesmin yanna dṛṣyate.* Although he recognises the interdependence of all arts in that proposition yet he asserts the primacy of *nāṭya* over all the other modes of arts. Bhāmaha later emended the passage in favour of poetics when he said: *natajjhānam na tat śilpam na sā vidyā na sā kalā/jāyate yannakāvyāṅgam aho bhāro mahān kaveḥ. Agamas*, the Śaivite *śāstric* texts, describe art as the propensity to create or to express: *vyañjayati kartṛsaktim kaleti teneh kathitā sā.* As for the aesthetics, the aestheticians like Anandavardhana, Abhinavagupta, Mammata and Rajasekhara, etc. seem to represent *kāvya* (poetics) as *kavikarma* in a special sense of a poet's imaginatively creative and expressive skill rooted in his intuitive brilliance (*pratibhā*). Abhinavabharati (on *Naṭyaśāstra* IV. 272) quoting Kohala's dictum that '*rāga* expresses (*udbhāvayati*) *kāvya*' upholds the latter's expressiveness in its manifold *rasas*, which *rāgas* bring out in their rhythmic renderings: *layāntara prayogena rāgaiscāpi vivecitam/nānārasam sunirvāhya katham kāvyamiti smṛtam//. Śilpa* similarly ties up with the *rasas* in *śilpa* texts.[52]

The *Citrasūtra* (Ch. 35.5) of the *Viṣṇudharmottara Purāṇa* seems to agree with such perceptions when it advocates similarity of purpose in dance and *citra*: *yathā nṛtte tathā citre trailokyānukṛtiḥ smṛtā* or, when it compares the two on the basis of their pre-occupations with expressions, moods and gestures.[53] The passage proposes of the unbroken continuities in arts from dance to *citra* to image-making,[54] and asserts that whatever is valid for its propositions about *citra* apply appropriately to other areas of *śilpa*, such as stone-, metal- and wood-works.[55]

Apart from such emphasis on interdependence of all arts in general, the *śilpa*-related texts seem yet to have their work-oriented specific elements. The *Samarāngaṇa sūtradhāra* (45. 1-6) enumerates eight limbs (*aṣṭānga*) of architecture.[56] In the *Citralakṣaṇa* (I.107), five elements of *citra* consist of characteristics (*lakṣaṇa*), shapes (*ākṛti*), resemblances (*sādṛṣya*), dress (*veṣa*), and measurements (*parimāṇa*). These texts also contain instructions about the disposition of limbs or the body postures in different ways.[57] The *Aparājitapṛcchā* similarly includes chapters on *tāla, vādya, svara, rāga, gīta* and *nṛtya*, etc. indicating complementarity of the different arts within the domain of *śilpa*.[58]

Despite what they might say about prescriptions and rules, *śilpaśāstras* also seem to allow freedom of action to its practitioners. A freedom tempered by the dictates of a *guru* is conceded in the *Śilpaprakāśa* (II.465) where a *śilpī* is supposed to play with forms (*śilpī krīdati tatraiva gurorājñānusarataḥ*). According to *Śilpaprakāśa* (I.511) though the 'command of *śāstra*' (*śāstra nirdeśa*) is binding yet *śilpin* may create a figure according to his imagination (*manojña*). Similarly, in the *Viṣṇudharmottara Purāṇa* (*pratimā lakṣaṇa*, 85.80b) in delineating a god, adherence to its canonical prescriptions are supposed to be mandatory. It is conceded that the erudite artist should 'represent them by discriminating appropriately their respective functions in terms of the *śāstra*': *budhya teṣām karmayogam yathāvat śāstram dṛṣṭvā te tu kāryā budhena*.[59] *Śāstra* seems to be reckoned indirectly here for without its appropriate knowledge an artist might not possibly be discriminating enough! But the texts with their alternative prescriptions and options must have had sufficient scope to allow artists their freedom of choice and experimentations within the larger body of the prescribed rules.[60] It is a different matter that the knowledge of *śilpaśāstra* and its allied functions and requirements have been stressed repeatedly right from the beginning of an artist's apprenticeship. In theory, the validity of a *śāstra* had to be maintained.[61] Yet, digressions from the canon seem to have been appropriately built into the text in specific instances, and the *Citrasūtra* clearly makes a mention of it.[62]

Like all the *vidyā*s and *śāstra*, adherence to their rules promised deliverance from the miseries of this world. The point has been made time and again in the *śilpa* texts. For instance, the *Śilpaprakāśa* (II.730) proclaims that 'by *śilpa-siddhi* one attains freedom from the cycle of birth and rebirth'. The same text (II.805) further says that 'of all the *śāstra*s, the *śilpaśāstra* taught by Viśvakarmā is the highest' and that its practice, i.e., building a monument (*kīrti*), 'liberates' even as it bestows all *siddhi*s. This is quite in conformity with the assertions in the *Milinda Pañho*, quoted earlier, where the 'bliss' of practising *śilpa* is compared to that of *nirvāṇa*.

Śilpa might have been considered to offer deliverance but its objectives were not other-worldly, meant as they were essentially for the welfare of *loka*. According to the *Samarāngaṇa-Sūtradhāra*, Śiva originated the all-pervasive *vāstuśāstra* for the welfare of the *loka*.[63] *Sarvalokahita* is indeed the objective of arts. In the *Citralakṣaṇa* of Nagnajit also the welfare of the *loka* (*sarvalokahitāya*) constitutes the primary purpose of a painting made appropriately in combination of colours (*varṇādīnām samāyogaiḥ*).[64] According to the *Citrasūtra*, its effectiveness lies in infusing it with the elements such that may 'captivate the minds of everyone'[65] for the merit of *citra* lies in the use of perpendiculars for postures and proportions (*sthānapramānabhūlambā*), loveliness (*madhuratvam*), variety (*vibhaktatā*), verisimilitude (*sādṛṣya*), and foreshortening (*kṣayavṛddhi*).[66] No wonders that the text (43.38) came to regard *citra* as the means of realising all the four *puruṣārtha*s, 'objectives of human life', namely, *dharma*, *artha*, *kāma* and *mokṣa*.

REPRESENTATION-CENTRIC CONCEPTUALISATIONS

We have so far discussed the contents of *śilpa* as *śāstra*, etc. and the bases or strength of such conjunctions. It may now be relevant to examine how *śilpa* is a conceptualising phenomenon which also turns an experience into a representation and how, in doing so, it may come to realise the very purpose of its being, namely, *lokānuranjana*, in other words: in aesthetically sensitising and delighting people at large. In religious art *śilpa*'s propensity to transform experience into a conceptually validated metaphysical reality gave it an almost unlimited power. Tradition recognises an artist's role as the undisputed Creator (Prajāpati) in his domain, where he exercises his option to state, reject, extend and even interpolate. His artistic creation is expressly accepted as a means to transport a witness to a transcendental experience beyond time and space.[67] The act of creation itself, and its product, regardless of whoever may be involved in the act, is sometimes considered in terms of crafting a painting. In *Parimala* on *Mahārthamañjarī* (48), a Kashmir Śaivite text, the Parameśvara is supposed to bring out the Universe like a painter creates a painting, and He is supposed to rejoice in doing the act. The passage says that, 'Having traced the picture of the world with the brush of his own self and contemplating it as his own self, the Parameśvara rejoices'. The perceptions about the world of experience and its representation in the Kashmir Śaivagamas, time and again, implicate God's creation in terms of a painting. The 'plain wall on which the multicoloured fresco of the Universe is painted, is supposed to be the Lord Himself'.[68] Or see, Ramakantha in his *vivṛtti* on the *Spandakārikā* (v. 8), eulogising God as 'a painter of the Universe' by his *pratibhā*, the divine genius.[69] Abhinavagupta is equally expressive of the creative play of the Lord of the Universe 'who paints the Universe, which is nothing but his own manifestation': *svabhāva rāgena viśvam rañjayate*.[70] The *advaita*, 'non-dualistic', phenomenon here is to be understood in the sense of the *advaita* of happiness and tranquility in respect of God's inherence in it, not in the *Vedantic* sense. These passages remind one of the *Śvetāśvara Upaniśad* (IV.1) where '(God), being himself without colour, distributes many colours by means of His energy (*śakti*)'.[71]

Three parallel streams thus, seem to run concurrently in respect of representations and delight in traditional Indian arts. These streams seem composed respectively of *śilpa*, aesthetics and spirituality. *Śilpa* strives to simulate the reality and its delight by *lakṣya-lakṣaṇa* or *vyañgya-vyañjaka* relation; aesthetics brings about aesthetic delight by *sādhāraṇīkaraṇa*; and spirituality consummates *dhyāna*, 'meditation' into realisation of delight through *bhakti*. In tradition, all these three streams seem to have the same goal, viz., a consummate realisation of delight: sensuous in case of aesthetics and *śilpa*, and supra-sensuous in the case of spiritual. It is interesting to observe that *śilpa* always seems oscillating between the other two streams, namely, those of spirituality and aesthetics implicating them both in their manifested and un-manifested forms and aiding in their materialisation. Such a role of *śilpa* implicates even the un-manifested into its realm.[72] This is specially so in the instrumentality of *śilpa* in the domains of religious art and in aesthetics. The details follow.

In Sanskrit texts, both religious and secular – Vedic through *Purāṇic*, including the *śastric* texts on aesthetics and religion – one persistently encounters two concurrent and mutually complementary ideas in regard to deity. Of these, one relates to the un-manifest and incorporeal *rūpa* of the supreme deity and the other to its *chāyā* (reflection), which either stands revealed or is comprehended through aesthetic intellection. Its cognition or identity is understood in terms of *pramāṇa* (source of valid knowledge) in philosophy and *vibhāva* (stimulants), etc. in aesthetics. Idea and image in Indian religious art, and creative power in reference to these seem thus to integrate in the sense of *ādarśa-pratirūpa* involving both the conceptual deity (*mūlaprakṛti*) which abides in *bhāvarūpa* (conceptual form) and its experience (*pratīti*) based on perception, identity and simulation through artist's creative power. No wonder, art is understood as *bramānanda sahodara*, 'affording fulfilment equal to the delight of attaining the Brahman', and requires to be comprehended in terms of *rūpa-pratirūpa* (form and its counterpart) on one hand, and means of cognition and experience as encompassed in the creative power, on the other. The *śāstra*s recognised the primacy of artist in creating an experience-to-reality sequence where the 'ideal-to-counterpart'[73] continuum was supposed to be fundamental under the definition of *śilpa*[74] and the ability to achieve this lay exclusively in the domain of artist.

We discuss some of these points starting with *rūpa* in regard to the concept of deity and *pratirūpa* in regard to its *chāyā*. We would also make an attempt thereafter to define *kartṛśakti* (creative power), including cognition, whereby verity is supposed to turn into verisimilitude, reality into simulation of reality and actual truth into imaginative truth, yet everywhere simultaneously this transformation tends to remain interactive with its original moorings whether in aesthetics or religious art.

In tradition, deity (*devatā*) invariably tends to imbibe both subtle (*para*) and gross (*apara*) aspects,[75] and their cognition depends both on philosophical reasoning and aesthetic suggestion. In its nature as Supreme Reality, a deity is comprehended through *pramāṇa*s, which are supposed to lead to its direct vision (*darśana*) founded in immediate perception rather than mediate knowledge. Sometimes a deity is supposed to abide truly in word, e.g., the axiom: *śabda mātra hi devatā*.[76] Etymologically, the word *deva* derives from the root *dyu-*, 'to shine' (as in *devo dānād vā dyotanād vā dyunmānebhavatīti vā, Nirukta,* 7.4.1), and time and again, deity, though regarded as 'shining' in its form, is yet supposed to be amorphous or incorporeal in essence transcending the *particular* or the empirical reality inasmuch as it rests beyond and above the name and form (*nāmarūpa*).[77]

Even when the *Purāṇic*, sectarian deities are conceived anthropomorphically, they, without any apparent contradiction, are found subsumed in the philosophical notions of particular religious or aesthetic tradition whereby they figure but as the efficient cause or material cause or both, in regard to cosmic functions. The Supreme God, in the texts, is regarded essentially as non-corporeal, eternal, self-existent and unseen, *na cakṣuṣā paśyati kaśca nainam*, according to the *Kaṭhopaniṣad* (23.9) or, *na tasya pratimā asti yasya nāma mahad yaśaḥ*, according to the *Śvetaśvatara Upaniṣad* (4.19). Such a character of the form of a deity [78] is derived from *Upaniṣadic* idealism, which also, in a way, underscores the principles of aesthetics, and their appreciation in terms of beauty of an evanescent form. The idea of glorious, incorporeal entity of god lingers on even when the images made of stone or other materials had come into being. For such an idea of the deity, see for instance, the *Viṣṇudharmottara* which describes God (*paramātman*) as devoid of form (*rūpa*), smell (*gandha*), sap (*rasa*), sound (*śabda*) and touch (*sparśa*): *rūpa-gandha-rasairhīnam śabdasparśa vivarjitam.* It also reiterates that this god, of his own accord, chose to reflect (*pradarśitam*) itself in a form whereby that form became venerable:

> *ato bhagavatānena svecchayā yat pradarśitam*
> *prādurbhāvesvathākāram tad arcanti divaukasaḥ*[79]

In its concretised aspect therefore an image is a reflection of the Supreme Deity and exists merely as an accessory to *dhyāna* and *yoga.*[80]

Such a concretisation of an evanescent form in *śilpa* was very much within the ken of *śilpins*' skills. In doing so, i.e., conceptualising his experience and then materialising it in a specific form, an artist tends to impart to the former a significance of formulation, validating the tradition, and sometimes even interpolating into it his own perception of the time sequence of the before-and-after.[81] The discontinuity of time engineered by the artist is the basis of his extraordinary position and role whether in arts (*citra*) or in poetics. In poetics a creative work, even if non-conforming (*niyama rahitam*), is glorified and eulogised in its being so willed by its creator (*niyatikṛta*),[82] and capable of creating a supra-sensual universe of his choice outdoing even the laws of nature. In these situations, he stands identified with the Absolute as he is the one and the only Prajāpati of his universe in which he alters the phenomenon according to his own fancy.[83]

Creative power in reference to Indian images thus seems to lie in creating an identity (*sādṛśya*)[84] in order to achieve the ultimate by means of *dhyāna, yoga* and *darśana.* Images, by that definition, emerge as images twice:

first in the sense of materialising the deities from a reflection and secondly in the sense of incorporating into it the transcendental suggestion based on *pramāṇa*. The entire business of such creation, idea-image integration in other words, seems posited in terms of manifesting the un-manifestable in the manner of concretising the ideal in its material counterpart (*ādarśe-pratirūpaḥ*). This being so because *rūpa* abides in the gross merely as a 'reflection' (*chāyā*) of something beyond and above. The point is significant because it is consistent in the secular tradition of *śilpa* and aesthetics and in the spiritual domain of religious tradition.[85] In the *śilpa* texts, for instance, *rūpa* is regarded not as the material form, but fundamentally as *bhāvarūpa* (conceptual form).[86] Interestingly enough, the Vedic as well as the *Upaniṣadic* idea of deity revolves round *chāyā puruṣa* in the manner of 'moon reflected in water' (*jale candramasam yathā*). The latter expression occurs in the *Aparājitapṛcchā*,[87] a *śilpa* text, but its antiquity is Vedic.[88] The form (*rūpa*) reflected in *chāyā* seems to be comprehended in terms of a subtle suggestion (e.g., *bhāva, pratīti, sahakāra*, etc.) but *citra* is where it comes to abide. The *Aparājitapṛcchā* (Ch. 224.1-24), a *śāstric* text, very appropriately describes the entire concept of *bhāvarūpa* and its validity in a work of art as follows:

Paśyanti bhāvarūpaisca jale candramasaṃ yathā
Tadvad citramayaṃ sarvaṃ paśyanti brahmavādinaḥ. [89]

Which means that *rūpa* (form) is reflected in *citra*[90] as 'moon is reflected in water' and the simile is persistent in its occurrence. The import rests here on implication and the 'water-moon' simile is comprehensive, for what is reflected in *citra* is limitless and yet encompassing the three worlds (*loka)*, the *cara, acara*, gods, angels, titans, or whatever is stationary and whatever that moves: trees, creepers, seas, mountains, continents; in fact everything imaginable or perceived; hence,

Viśvam viśvāvatāraśca tvanādyantasca sambhavet
'Ādi citramayaṁ sarvaṁ paśyanti brahmacakṣuṣā.[91] Or,
Sthāvaram jangamam caiva sūryacandro ca medinīm
Citramūlodbhavam sarvam jagatsthāvarajangamam.
Vṛksagulmalatāvallyā svedajanujarāyujaḥ
Sarve citrodbhavā vatsa bhūdharā dvīpasāgaraḥ// Aparājitapṛchā //[92] 224.6-7

Despite encompassing the world (*viśva*): *tadvadcitramayam viśvam citram viśve tathaiva ca*, or its image (*viśvāvatāra*), *citra* is but a reflection of *citramūla*, the essence (*citramūlodbhavaṁ sarvaṁ trailokyaṃ sacarācaram*)[93]

The idea is subtly conveyed again in the *Viṣṇudharmottara*[94] as follows:

Ataḥ param pravakṣyāmi citrasūtram tavānagha
Urvaśi sṛjatām pūrvam citrarūpā nṛpātmajam // 35.1

Nārāyaṇena muninā lokānām hitakāmyayā
Prāptānām vañcanārthāya devastrīṇām mahāmuniḥ // 2
Sahakāra rasam gṛhya urvyām cakre varastriyam
Citreṇa sa tato jātā rūpayuktā varāpsarā // 3

The passage distinguishes between *citramūla* (essence) and *citra* (image) and explains the origin of *citra* with the help of the metaphor of Urvaśī and Apsara. Apsara and Urvaśī both represent the same simile of beauty reflected in the manner of *jale candramasam yathā*. Urvaśī is the *citramūla* (essence) here while Apsaras is only *citra:* they both typify light (*jyoti*) incarnated into a distinct corporeality whether in words or in image. This 'incarnated light' is the *citramūla* while *citra* alone in its mundane and worldly form is a reflection (*pratibimba*) of the 'light incarnate'. One is *ādarśa* (ideal) while the other is *chāyā*: *ādarśe pratirūpah chāyāyām dvitīyaḥ*, all explained in the catch-phrase *jale candramasam yathā*, which is same as *apsutvā somam* in the *Ṛgveda* (IX.79.4), or in the Tibetan legend of the first figure of the Buddha drawn by an artist from his reflection in waters. The story occurs also in the 'Rudrayana Avadana' of the *Divyāvadāna* where the Buddha is said to have cast his shadow on to a piece of cloth (*paṭa*) and asked the artist to colour it: *chāyām utsṛṣṭa uktāśca rangaih pūrayat.*[95] *Citralakṣaṇa* in Srikumara's *Śilparatna*, repeats the simile of *chāyā* in his enunciations.[96] The idea of reflection remains the same though instead of moon-and-water simile we here have *darpaṇa* (mirror) and *pratibimba* imagery.

In these references it is the reflection of form (*rūpa*) in terms of its *chāyā*, which is supposed to endow a *citra* with the quality of art. *Citra* is always an image and it variously signifies painting (*ālekha*), variegation (*saśalīkarana*), effulgence (*prakāśam*) and identity (*sambodha*).[97] For instance, see the *Ṛgveda* (I.113.7), which reads *idam śrestham jyotisām jyotirāgā-citrapraketa ajaniṣṭa bimbā*, i.e., Usas is born of light, hence she is *citra praketa*; *praketa* here means 'intrinsic glow' and *citra* is 'effulgence'. *Citra* and *chāyā* are complementary and *rūpa* and *citra* are invariably conceived as 'reflected'.[98]

There is more about *chāyā* in the texts, which may be noticed here. The word is primarily a 'shadow' and secondarily a 'reflection' or 'likeness'.[99] It is by means of *chāyā* (shadow or likeness) that the whole light world is supposed to be brought forth into the world of experience. This we have in the *Ṛgveda* (V.44.6), where 'several angels, the First Sacrificer, by the efficacy of the reflection in the waters (*chāyām siddhṛyapsu*) disposed for us the broad expanse of great and noble manhood and unfailing power'. The use of the term *chāyā* in the passage might have been regarded as 'poetic imagery', but in the *Ṛgveda* (V.44.6) it is quite clear that *chāyā* is not a place of comfort merely in a figurative sense; it is indeed a form of the deity – the manifested light in the world – reflected in waters. The idea recurs in the *Gopatha*

Brāhmaṇa (I.3) where, 'having emanated those waters (*tā āpaḥ sṛṣṭvā*), he the Brahman (*mahad yakṣam*) looked and saw his own reflection (*chāyām*) in them'. The water (*āpaḥ*) here registers the vision (*dhī*) or *citra* (*Ṛgveda* V.33.3) in the same manner as the moon is 'reflected in water'. The motif of 'reflection in water' keeps recurring in the texts, as in the *Kaṭha Upaniṣad* (IV.5) in connection with form (*rūpa*) and non-form (*arūpa*); in the *Chāndogya* (VIII.7.4; VIII.8.1) where we have the water-moon simile; and in the *Bṛhadāraṇyaka Upaniṣad* (II.1.12f; III.9.14-15) where we have *chāyā puruṣa* and *chāyāmaya puruṣa*.[100] The subtlety of *chāyā* incorporating the *mūlaprakṛti* as reflected in water is poetically presented in a passage in the *Kundamālā* of Dingnāga.[101] In it, Sita is described as moving 'invisibly' around a lake where Rama sees her reflection in the water. The text says that Rama was astounded as he saw her reflection in the waters of the lake without seeing her there in person, and wondered where was Sita indeed? (*udakamadhye chāyām nirvarṇya sasambhramam 'katham Sītā'traiva'*?). Sita, in the meanwhile, moved out and her shadow disappeared too, leaving Rama convinced of having found Sita though only in her *chāyā*![102] In this passage, as in the other passages quoted above, there is a substantive imagery in regard to supra-sensual image and its manifested reflection (*chāyā-pratimā*), which stands as the counterpart of the original (*pratikṛtermūla prakṛtim*). *Chāyā* is the means by which the *mūlaprakṛti*, invisible, tends to manifest itself. It also informs the image (*rūpa* or *citra*) even though the essence (*mūlaprakṛti*) may stand apart and beyond. The *rūpa-pratirūpa* or *ādarśa pratirūpa* thereby stands explained by *chāyā*.

Creative activity thus clearly stands vivified in terms of its relation to the vision and its reflection in thought. *Āpaḥ* is supposed to be that liquid effulgent entity which receives *chāyā* and imbibes it, so much so that *chāyā* itself stands identified with liquid effulgence (*taralatā*).[103] The point is subtly endorsed in Srikumara's chapter on *Citralakṣaṇa* in the *Śilparatna* (IV.147) as he speaks of *sādṛṣya* in a *citra* in terms of its aura in reality: *darpaṇe pratibimbavata*, and not merely in its emulated outline (*nālam ākaramātrakam*). The idea of the efficacy of *chāyā* is quite consistent and seems to occur in different shades of meaning.[104] The poetic imagery and the *śilpa* tradition here coalesce together in materialising a vision and in that they seem adhering to the interdependence of arts so often underscored in *śāstric* views on it.

The interrelationship of arts envisaged in the *śāstric* vision of it seems to rest also in the fact that the term *vibhāva* (stimulant), a technical term of poetics, is valid as much in the poetics as in the *śilpa* tradition for, in its pristine Vedic contexts it qualifies only a figure or form (*vapuḥ*). Eventually, the *Kavyaśāstras* accepted *vibhāva* more or less exclusively into their domain. In the texts on aesthetics the capacity to create or instil the quality of art into an expression or object, etc. is found explained in reference to *vibhāvas*;

and its other corollaries like *anubhāva, vyabhicārins*, etc. are regarded as central to the theory of *rasa*.[105] Bhatta Lollata considers *vibhāvas* as the feelings that exist in the character in a play in the first place before becoming instrumental in manifesting the *anubhāvas* and their further intensification through the *vyabhicārins*.[106] However, the association of the term *vibhāva* with 'form' (*vapuḥ*) has greater antiquity than its use in the poetics. It first occurs in conjunction with *vapuḥ*, as in: *svarṇacitraṃ vapuṣe vibhāvam* (*Ṛgveda* I.148.1), where Sāyaṇa explains it in the sense of *citra* that has the quality of effulgence.[107] The term is derived from the root *bha-*, 'to shine', and *vibhāvan* in the *Ṛgveda* is understood as a 'shining form', the characteristic of a deity. Thus, as in early texts, so also later, *vibhāva* lies at the root of perceiving a deity in its shining form: in the *Kavyaśāstra* and *Naṭyaśāstra* it figures as the stimulus through which *rasa* is produced.

In Indian aesthetics the essence of experience and its appreciation (*rasāsvāda*, 'relish') is grounded implicitly into 'mental state' (*bhāva*), which is realised by the 'effulgent consciousness' (*pratibhā*) of a poet. There will be more about *pratibhā*, later. But, the undifferentiated nature of aesthetic formulations whether in visual or performing arts is universally accepted in tradition. In imparting value to *bhāva* the *śilpa* tradition seems to return to the poetic and dramatic heritage in emulating their more organised formulations than in adhering totally to the notion of *vibhāva*, a 'shining form' implicit in its Vedic usage. Espousing it gave a substantive edge to *śilpa* in portrayal of characters, divine or otherwise and in formulating imageries and representations that would enact events with the help of allegories, metaphors, etc. The *Vāstusūtra Upaniṣad* (V.1-18) and its commentary categorically uphold the primacy of *bhāva* (*bhāvasyādhāro rasaḥ*) in arts: *bhāvasyāropaṇam rūpakarmāṇi vidheyam*, i.e., 'in image-making the infusion of feeling (*bhāva*) is enjoined' as it leads to the realisation of the different *rasas*, namely, *sṛingāra, hāsa, karuṇa, raudra, vīra, bhayānkara, vībhatsa* and *śānta*.[108] The commentary (on the *sūtra* 3) of the text refers to *rasa* as the 'impelling force' manifesting the (*śilpa-*)-constituted body and becoming the 'defining characteristic' of the figure itself. Like *bhava* in poetics, compositional principles in *śilpa* became significant in bringing about cognition through 'universalisation'.[109] *Lakṣaṇas*, among other things, facilitated cognition and in devising metaphors and allegories, a traditional artist in ancient India formulated and produced forms that contained multiple suggestions of and from the past, using these for effects for what it held within.[110] In doing so *śilpa* successfully overcame restrictions imposed by particular religions even as it drew inspiration essentially from the basic tenets of those faiths. This entire process may represent a subversion of the norms in a unique way where *śilpa* confronted the rigours of a religion to enrich it.

For instance, the early Buddhists held that anything to do with imaginative creation was fraught with moral danger because the phenomenal world was essentially transient, sorrowful and insubstantial.[111] As such, mental image-making came to be considered as the spiritual source of sculptures and paintings. Artists derived inspiration from such sanction and recalled the deeds of the Buddha's life and religion by reproducing them in stone for spiritual fulfilment. The early Buddhist art is replete with the narratives from the life of the Buddha. Such representations of the narratives in art, like narratives in poetry and drama were generally a part of remembering, which involved resurgence of a myth and reliving it. Whether it was the episode of Māradharṣaṇa or the Miracles of Śrāvastī, or the Enlightenment, Birth, Renunciation, First Sermon or any other event,[112] the purpose always was to dramatise the moment of action. There had to be a deep emotional rhetoric in them for the laity or the coreligionist, for the art here was meant to bring the form and its essence alive by suggestion. In the 'Khanda Samyutta' of the *Saṃyutta Nikāya* the Buddha describes such narrative paintings as *caraṇacitta*.[113] The Buddha regarded such representations as *manamattaka* (articulation of mind), *uddeśika* (commemorative) and *avatthuka* (unreal).[114] This denied them a permanent validity even though it was conceded by the Buddha that they were a part of experience.

But their significance is not lost especially as they relate to a situation where a representation of an experience, howsoever illusory, stands appropriately posited. This relates to the phenomenon of consciousness where *citta* assumes a primacy. Significantly, in Buddhist literature *citta* is supposed to make cognition possible as it turns 'appearance' (*vahyārtha*) into 'imaginative experience' (*anumeya*).[115] In the Buddhist scheme of things, *citta* is a part of the *skandha*s (physical complex) like *rūpa* and therefore it is transitory. All mental constructions are supposed to take place in *citta* or *manas*. Both terms signify consciousness,[116] which is the locus of all imaginative activity. Its function assumes that external matter or things are merely a reflection of one's consciousness, but their cognition is dependent on many other contributory factors.[117] In the Śūnyavādin theoretical system a *rūpa*, whether in its psychological or physical state, was supposed to take birth in the *citta*, which is the locus as well as the amorphous instrument of its creation. In addition, *citta* was also the unique entity, which sifted and removed the veil (*āvaraṇa*) of the *pravṛtti*s (processes) that covered it. *Citta* thus appears as a principle, which is shrouded by the *āvaranas* (veils), which it removes, thereby leading to cognition. As such, it is the royal road to *ālaya vijñāna*, the 'consciousness principle', the 'root' (*bīja*) of all the potentialities of differentiation, though, in itself, undifferentiated.[118] *Citta* alone is the grand storehouse of consciousness while the entire external phenomenon is its reflections, and therefore 'unreal' and illusory: only a metaphor. Yet, *citta* acts as its instrument of cognition inasmuch as it distinguishes a form and leads to its cognition as something unreal. Thereby, the form remains valid only as a metaphor.

But the question remains as to how the creative power and process are exercised in a perception of *rūpa* (form) in the domain of *śilpa*. The *pramāṇas* may possibly explain the point for perception is supposed to implicate *pratyakṣa* (direct knowledge)[119] and *anumāna* (inference), which are philosophically explained as *pramāṇas* or the means of cognition. These are discussed both in Indian philosophical systems (*darśana*) and in the texts on aesthetics. Rendition of the idea of a deity by an artist, first of all involves cognition: direct or inferential; and arts require the communication of such a cognised perception with an intense sensitivity.

In a work of art, creative power is supposed to involve both *pratyakṣa* and *anumāna*, which are variously explained in philosophic and aesthetic discourses in tradition. But Bhāmaha's statement amending the Buddhist definition of *pratyakṣa* seems quite valid for a work of art. Bhāmaha controverts the Buddhist definition of *pratyakṣa* (viz., *pratyakṣam kalpanā'poḍham*, i.e., *pratyakṣa*, 'direct perception', is bereft of *kalpanā*, 'inference'), and alternatively suggests that *pratyakṣa* could be informative without *kalpanā* which, on its turn, is explained as super-imposition of *jāti, guṇa, kriyā, dravya* and *nāma* which together constitute the five adjuncts (*upādhi*s) of direct cognition (*pratyakṣa*).[120] Thus endowed, an artist may receive his inspiration and set himself about in the act of creating or fashioning an object of art by superimposing in his work the *upādhi*s (adjuncts) of the cognised form. He may still be aided by the capacity to infer, i.e., by *anumāna*, which is defined by Vatsyayana as that which is authenticated either by direct knowledge or by tradition (*Agama*): *pratyakṣāgamāśritam evānumānam*. Bhamaha quotes two definitions of *anumāna* as the means of cognition and regards it as the very soul of *kāvyanyāya*. Mahimabhatta deals with it under *kavyānumiti*.[121]

The nature of deity being conceptual in religious art, *anumāna* could be regarded as crucially instrumental in identifying the character of the original and the counterpart. Apart from these interpretations of cognition and its communication, the texts on aesthetics contain other discussions in regard to creative process and power, especially about how an image is created and conveyed. These seem to be defined through certain technical expressions like *anusandhāna, anukaraṇa* and what may be termed as *anyathākaraṇa*. We intend to deal with these briefly here.

CREATIVE PROCESS: *ANUSANDHĀNA, ANUKARAṆA* AND *ANYATHĀKARAṆA*

Anusandhāna may be explained as rendition of the quality or role of *sthāyībhāva* (or, in other words: the *mūlaprakṛti*) into something (as in a sculpture or painting), which may create an impression (*pratīti*) of the *mūlaprakṛti* without being it: *anusandhānam kāvyabalāt anusandhīyate*. It is to be stressed that this impression is not conveyed by guile (*bhrama*). Mammata explains it as the *anusandhāna* (quest) for *tadrūpatā* or in other words, 'simulation of identity' where identity is different from imposition. Such an impression of identity between the *mūlaprakṛti* and its mundane counterpart works at two levels; in the artist it stems from dexterity (*nipuṇatā*) of mind and hand, and of training (*abhyāsa*) and genius (*śakti*) while in the *sāmājika* (witness) it issues from his empathy (*sahṛdayatā*).[122]

As regards *anukaraṇa*, it is not supposed to be merely an 'imitation': it is in fact the 'suggestion' that transforms the reality.[123] It tends to reinvent the identities, for according to the *ācārya*s of the aesthetics; the reality being beyond reproduction, only introspection (*anusandhāna*) (or interpolation: *anyathākaraṇa*) may help in inducing the similitude. A creative artist resorts to it by his *pratibhā*. So, in reviving the moods in reference to the events and characters lodged in a particular context the artist invokes *anukaraṇa* in a qualified manner. The theory of reinventing identities (*anukaraṇa*) is central to both aesthetic experience and its manifestation in *śilpa* as well as in poetics. Its antiquity goes back to the *Aitereya Brāhmaṇa*.[124] Later, Sankuka[125] (8th century) gave a succinct meaning to it and through it to the validity of 'pragmatic reality' (*vyavahārika sattā*) in the realm of aesthetic experience. Its basis lies in the concept of *bhāva*, which according to Sankuka is located in a character the events of whose life are being enacted by another actor. Emulation of the *bhāva* of the original character by another character (or its transference without modification, by an actor in a drama or by an icon or a narrative in the *śilpa*) is rendered valid by *anukaraṇa* to which a spectator responds through an aesthetic experience, which in turn is actuated by *anumana* or *anumiti*, 'inference'.

This experience or perception is like the one that comes from seeing a painted horse, for instance, and is explained in terms of *citra turaga nyāya*, 'the logic of painted horse', or in other words, 'the logic of perceiving a medium as the thing itself'. As an experience, it is different from the one achieved by means of 'common inference' (*samyaka*), 'illusion' (*mithya*), 'likeness' (*sādṛśya*), or 'doubt' (*samśaya*).[126] Thus, "to see a horse in a painting is an example of what Wittgenstein would call 'seeing as'.[127] It amounts to the adoption of a certain epistemological stand, viz., the resolution to see in a work of art – a painting, an icon, or a narrative – a character that is so represented. In this kind of seeing the witness perceives the ontological status of the character in the depiction.[128] Thus, in the *anukaraṇa*, an artist invokes the *pratibhāsika samasattā* (temporary lending of the ontological status of the character to the witness) of the characters in an episode that he reinvents for an aesthetic appreciation. In the process, he recalls those characters from episodes, mythic or poetic, and revives them, as it were, which makes such an appreciation possible. This entire phenomenon gives to an artist a unique status. That he does so by inducing 'mark' (*lakṣaṇa*), 'likeness' (*sādṛśya*),[129] and 'measure' (*pramāṇa*), which bring out a correspondence between the formal and representational elements, is easily conceded in the *śilpa* tradition.[130]

The ancient *ācārya*s of aesthetics have taken care not to confuse *anukaraṇa* in its basal sense of a crass 'imitation'. Bharata regarded 'drama as the repository of the *bhāva*s (moods) of the entire world' (*trailokyasya ... sarvasya nāṭyam bhāvānukīrtanam*) which it recreates by the *anukīrtana*, 'invocation', in which mere imitation has no role, for the latter can bring ridicule not *rasa*.[131] Abhinavagupta uses the term *anuvyavasāya* in place of *anukaraṇa*[132] to explain it as different from mere 'imitation'. He regards *anuvyavasāya* as the device, which a creative artist resorts to in order to evoke realisation of a *rasa* (*rasāsvāda*).[133]

By *anyathākaraṇa* we mean interpolation, i.e., adding further to the gross in a subtle manner by subtle transformations. The *Kāvyaśāstra*s have stressed and legitimised interpolation time and again claiming in a creative artist's faculty the power to alter the world in his own fancy.[134] Anandavardhana in his *Dhvanyāloka* (Udyota 3) also asserts the freedom of the universe of poetry, a universe parallel to that of the Creator, and he says that the freedom of a poet allows him to transform the physical world from what it is transforming the sentient into non-sentient and vice versa.[135] The sentiment occurs elsewhere too where the capacity to render and communicate the idea or moods is attributed appropriately to a poet for different reasons. By his capacity, according to Rudrata (I.14), to imbibe the essence (*sāragrahaṇa*), or, according to Mammata (Su. 2): by his innate aesthetic faculty (*śakti*) experience and training, does the artist in a poet create; and in such of his creative powers he is like the Prajāpati or like what Utpala says about Śiva, the master-artist (*kalānatha*) who by the dint of his excellence creates the Universe just by his will: without any aids (*upādāna*) whatsoever.[136] Whether in poetry or in *śilpa*, these sentiments have a universal significance in defining creativity and its potential and they perceptively celebrate an artist who may go into such a state of creation.

LAKṢAṆA

In the domain of *śilpaśāstras* the reconstitution of forms finds a parallel terrain. They invariably emphasise on *lakṣaṇa, pramāṇa,*[137] *tālamāna,*[138] *rekhā,*[139] etc. that go to reconstitute a representation in any medium: in sculpture, painting, terracotta or in the works related to architecture. In tradition, these are as crucial to plastic arts as *śabda* (words or expressions) is to poetics, and *nāda* (sound) to music. These different elements help in defining the independent domain of plastic arts, and it may be relevant to discuss *lakṣaṇa*'s place in *śilpa* and its implications in that domain.

Lakṣaṇa is indisputably central to *śilpaśāstras*[140] and to a work of art and has a history going back to the Brahmaṇas where it means, among other things, the 'sign that becomes the denominator of the essence of an object'. The term is sometimes used in invocatory formula in the Brāhmaṇas to address either a particular deity or to qualify a physically visible object. This meaning of the term and its usages indicate its association with symbols that specifically qualified an object or a deity, the latter in the invocatory contexts.[141] The usage is significant for arts, especially so as *lakṣaṇas* connect the *parokṣa*, 'distant', with the *pratyakṣa,* 'immediate', representing the reality at two different levels, simultaneously. Eventually, *lakṣaṇa* became the part of *lakṣaṇa vidyā* concerned with prognostication on the basis of distinctive marks on the body of men or deities in iconography.[142] This was possible as *lakṣaṇa* as symbol invariably signified the symbolised (*lakṣya*) in substance.

The term has been differently explained etymologically. Brugman derives it from the root *lag-*, 'to stick', which is very much in the fashion of Yāska who enumerates its derivation from roots: *laṣ-*, 'to desire', root *lag-*, 'to stick', etc.[143] This etymology may be doubtful but its cognates like *lakṣa* (*Ṛgveda* II.12.4), meaning 'prize, stake or share'; *lakṣma* (*Atharvaveda* VI.141.2), meaning 'sign' and *lakṣmī* (*Ṛgveda* X.71.2), i.e., 'one endowed with a distinctive (mark)', help in clarifying the symbolising implications of the term as these specifically relate to collective or individual identities through distinctive signs or symbols of cognizance borne by persons of a group (e.g., *sakhā* of the Vedic bands of pre-community people) as a mark of solidarity.

Lakṣaṇa figures significantly in the texts other than those on *śilpa*. The *Nāṭyaśāstra* (XVI. 1-4) describes thirty-six different categories of *lakṣaṇas* and Bhoja, in his *Śṛgāraprakāśa*, increases their number to sixty-nine, describing them as the 'decorations of the dramatic art' (*nāṭyālaṃkāra*). As they were supposed to qualify human body they have not received much cognizance in poetics. Abhinavagupta in his commentary on the *Nāṭyaśāstra* (XVI. 1-4) regards *lakṣaṇa* as being intrinsic to human body with no independent existence of their own: *śarīraniṣṭhameva yadpṛthak siddham tallakṣaṇam, yena śarīrasya saundaryam jāyate.*[144] Among the different explanations of the term and its utility in poetics or dramatics, one of the views seems to connect it with creative effulgence (*pratibhā*) of a poet, which is instrumental in creating a beautiful 'body' of poetry. And in this entire process, which is the *vyāpāra*, 'action', of a poet, *lakṣaṇa* seems to play an important role. Though these points are made in reference to poetry, they seem relevant to *śilpa* also. The argument seems validated in the *Vāstusūtra Upaniṣad* (III.13) and its commentary, which speak of the gods' images conceptually arising from the *lakṣaṇa*s which on their turn are revealed through sacred songs.[145] The criticality of *lakṣaṇa* in arts lies in its supposed efficacy in facilitating realisation of the particular identity of a representation, objects, things, gods and goddesses, heroes or whatever, for these, in essence, are supposed to be categorically specific to them.[146] The *Vāstusūtra Upaniṣad* (VI.3) thus states that *śilpavidyā* is meant to manifest itself through *lakṣaṇa*s: *lakṣaṇa prakāśārtham śilpavidyā. Lakṣaṇa*, on its own, is supposed to directly relate to its *lakṣya*. Sabara in the *Mīmāmsā Sūtra* (I.1.2) explains *lakṣaṇa*s as the means by which something is perceived, as for instance, smoke is the sign (*lakṣaṇa*) of fire: *lakṣyate yena tallakṣaṇam*.

A work of art – a painting or sculpture – depends crucially on *lakṣya-lakṣaṇa* relationship and this conjunction is stressed in the *Citralakṣaṇa* (IV.85) of Srikumara even in connection with depiction of stances in figure work, e.g., *ṛju* (frontal), *ardharju* (half-frontal), *sācika* (askance), *dvardhākṣi* (one-and-quarter-eyed) and *pārsvāgata* (sidelong or profile).[147] Nine such standing (*sthānaka*) stances or postures are described in the *Aparājitapṛcchā* of Bhuvanadeva (211.1-18), along with the prescription that they should be depicted appropriately (*yuktimānam vidhīyate*), taking care of the proportions of the different parts of the body, including the face, on the basis (*pramāṇa*) of the finger-digits (*angula*) to work out the proportions. These postures or sometimes the lines (*rekhā*) bring out the moods and feelings implicit in the images. The commentary on the *Vāstusūtra Upaniṣad* (II, 22, 24-27) describes the qualities that the different linear compositions articulate, like 'energy', 'longing', 'meditation', etc.

The *Viṣṇudharmottara Purāṇa* (III.1.8) recommends making and worshipping (*kārayet, pūjayet*) the images which are endowed with all the *lakṣaṇa*s, deprecating, at the same time, worship of the images that may be devoid of *lakṣaṇa*s (*natva lakṣaṇasaṃyutām*). The significance of *lakṣaṇa*s continued being underscored. They figure as essential part among the eight limbs of painting described in the *Samarāngaṇa Sūtradhāra* (Ch. 71. 14-16). The text (44. 2) specifically prescribes that a skilled *sthapati* would be one who is steeped in its knowledge: *lakṣya-lakṣaṇayuktārthaśāstraniṣṭhah*, etc. Other texts uphold its significance as a definite stream of knowledge called *lakṣaṇavidyā*. The *Aparājitapṛcchā* (2.19; 234.1-42) for instance, regards the signs (*lakṣaṇas*) of gods and goddesses and, of men and women (*strīpuruṣādi lakṣaṇam*), as part of it. In fact, the textual discourse on the sets of *lakṣaṇas* refers to many generic categories and their merits (*guṇas*) defined as *sāttvika, rājasika* and *tāmasika*. The anthropomorphic basis of such categories is often underscored and these constructions find support in the *Citralakṣaṇa* of Nagnajit.

Lakṣaṇa has been closely aligned to *lakṣaṇā* in poetics.[148] So, let us briefly go into its purport as in poetry. The literature on Indian poetics dwells substantively upon *lakṣaṇā* in describing the *śabdaśakti* (powers of the word): denotative (*vācaka*), indicative (*lakṣaṇa*) and suggestive (*vyañjaka*), signifying respectively the 'expressed', 'indicated' and 'suggested' sense in it in communicating the meaning (*tātparya*).[149] *Kāvyamīmāṃsā* (*sūtra* 10) classifies *lakṣaṇā* into inclusive (*upādana lakṣaṇā*) and the exclusive (*lakṣaṇalakṣaṇā*) categories, propagating (*sūtra* 14) that: 'when a second sense other than the primary sense, is indicated by a word or by a phrase and clause, on the condition that (i) the primary sense is inadequate to hit the real sense and (ii) yet there is a close connection with the primary sense, (iii) either due to (a) the conventional usage or due to (b) the particular purpose, it is called *lakṣaṇā*'.[150] These and the other powers of *śabda* along with their sub-categories are variously explained in the poetics, and their intention is to communicate the meaning through conventional or purposive means, which is primarily what *lakṣaṇas* in *śilpa* intend to accomplish.[151] Besides, there is also the power of *vyañjanā* (suggestive sense) in the poets' arsenal of *śabdas* and that power is supposed to elevate a meaning to an artistically consummate level.

Vyañjanā relates to the phenomenon of altering the 'expressed' sense in a manner that the 'suggested sense' subordinates it. Its significance was articulated in the Dhvani school of Indian Poetics. Meanings or purport (*tātparya*) is supposed to emerge in poetry as a result of three kinds of *śabda*, 'word', e.g., *vācaka*, 'denotative', *lakṣaka*, 'indicative', and *vyañjaka*, 'suggestive'. But among these, according to the *Kāvyaprakāśa* (II. *sūtra* 10), *vyañjanā* is universally appreciated as a poetic license which strengthens an expression.[152] It essentially flows out from *lakṣanā* in that the 'words' to convey the intended idea are lodged in the latter in the first place, but their imaginative transformation is achieved with the power of *vyañjanā* as it takes them over.[153] Mammata, in the *Kāvyaprakāśa* (II. *sūtra* 36), says that *vyañjanā* lies in an expression where the word is impregnated with an 'insinuated function' other than its primary function. It is supposed to be overlaid with an alternative meaning *(arthāntara yukta)*. Interestingly enough, the dynamics of altering the phenomenon, as implicit in it, seems to be in alliance with the *anyathākaraṇa* where, as we said earlier, interpolation is resorted to in order that the desired effect in a painting or a work of art may be consummately realised. The connection between the *vyañjanā* of the poetics and *vyañjana* in arts seems possible as the identifying marks of the individual representations are often expressed in terms of *vyañjana,* which essentially are signs but they lead to perceiving the Buddha's identity in its multiplicities and meaning. Aśvaghoṣa says in his *Sūtralankāra* that the Buddha is endowed with eighty *anuvyañjana*s besides thirty-two *lakṣaṇa*s defining his person. Aśvaghoṣa is explicit in the *anuvyañjana*-related imagery of the Buddha in reference to his representation in painting, where his person is seen so endowed.[154] *Anuvyañjana*s here define a form, like they do in the *Rāmāyaṇa* too, in reference to Rama,[155] and this correspondence between a form and the *anuvyañjana*s seems directly related to the domain of *śilpa*. Only that its implications are better explained in the poetics. Literally also, the import of the term *vyañjana* (from the root *vyanj-* : *v+anj*) relates to the phenomenon of 'revealing', 'manifesting', 'showing', etc. that comes within the domain of *śilpa*.

An adherence to these different ways of concretising a representation are particularly valid in *śilpa* and also for *śilpin*s, for in them lie the interpretations of creativity, or more specifically, the answers to the questions as to how does an artist create, how experience in the consciousness is turned into reality in the visual imagery that he creates of those experiences? Such propositions have been dwelt upon in the works of Dingnāga and Dharmakirti[156] in respect of the meaning of form, especially artistic form, and the principles governing its implied identity in that particular form.[157] The *Lankāvatāra Sūtra* interrogates as to whether and how a stone (image) could imply the Buddha and if so, which particular one out of his many constructs, like: *nirmāṇakāya, sambhogakāya* and *dharmakāya,* would it reflect?[158] The propositions of the Buddhist logicians in reference to the validity of creative compositions and their arguments relating to the plausibility inherent in an intended object, so composed are picked up by Bhāmaha in his *Kāvyālankāra*. Unlike the propositions of the Buddhist logicians he argues in favour of its cognition by the proof of *pratyakṣa*. In his arguments, the proof of *pratyakṣa* comes out as the basis of the intended meaning of the object, for it makes plausible the symbol's identity with the symbolised by superimposing the *upādhi*s (adjuncts), like: *jāti, guṇa, kriyā, dravya, nāma* on the object. For an object to be cognised it was essential that it should be endowed with *rūpa* (form). Thereby, he says that the *pratyakṣa pramāṇa* appropriately operates in the case of the person so endowed with the *upādhi*s (*upādhi viśiṣṭa vyakti*).

COMPOSITIONAL STRUCTURE

The *Vāstusūtra Upaniṣad* (*sūtra* 1 and commentary) seems particularly seized with the problem of composition of form, and offers aphoristic prescriptions about it. For the concretisation of form, it prescribes a compositional diagram (*pañjara*) in terms of lines, squares, circles, intersecting points, triangles, *bindu, nābhi,* etc. which tend to become the rallying points of the creative surge through their compositional methodology.[159] *Pañjara* is conspicuous in it for its compositional network wherein lie the rudiments of form in whole or in parts, waiting to sprout with the touch of the *sthāpaka*. It is supposed to serve as the locus of a figure (*rekhāvāsa*) even as it internalises and integrates the *marma* (vital points), the *anga prayoga* (arrangement of parts), the *bhāva*s (emotional dispositions evoked by the compositional *nyāsa*), and the *sambandha-prabodhana* (explanation of relations). The *Vāstusūtra Upaniṣad* (Ch. III.) also recommends that the carving should be undertaken with intense introspection and meditation, which, coupled with devotion and skill would bring out the form whether raised (*utthita*) or depressed (*kūṭa*), placid (*saumya*) or terrific (*raudra*), along the lines in conformity with the contingent realisation. The *Upaniṣad*'s details about *bhāvarūpa, angaprayoga, sambandha prabodhana,* etc. as also on *rūpa* and the series of its interconnected experience, like: *tatvabodha, dhāraṇā, dhyāna, gāthā* and *kathā* seem to tie up well with the *śilpa*- and *kāvya*-based aesthetic in the larger context of Indian art tradition. Conjunctions repeatedly occur between the *Upaniṣad* and the broader Indic tradition, as for instance, in the postulates about the interdependence of the ideal and its counterpart, in the case of *chāyā*, the deity and *chāyā*, the 'shadow' of the ideal.

The imagery seems to tie up happily with similar enunciations about *rūpa* and *chāyā* combination in Kuntaka, Abhinavagupta and others. Kuntaka regards *chāyā* as an effulgence or brilliance: *chāyāmātramaṇikṛtāśma-sumaṇeraśtvamevocitam.*[160] In this totality, while the formulations of the *ācārya*s of poetics are more concerned with aesthetics of experience, the compositional modes in *śilpa* tradition relate to the technique to realise the form and the sensuousness 'reflected' in it.[161] According to Kuntaka experience involves revelation in *citta*; revelation stems from *pratibhā*, a quality which illumines the Universe 'merely by a turn of a momentary instance': *yadunmīlanam śaktyaiva viśvam unmīlati kṣaṇāt/ svātmayatanviśrāntam tam vande pratibhām śivam*. Abhinavagupta, commenting on *Vakroktijīvita* (37: *pratīyamāna bhāvacchāyā yaiṣā bhuṣā lajjeva yoṣitām*) accepts *chāyā*'s conjunction in *pratibhā* in symbolising *bhāva*s, so as to create a form as a result of the *kāma* of the subconscious: *pratīyamāna bhāvacchāyā antarmadanodbhedena hṛdayasaundaryarūpā* ....[162] Cognition of form by *pratibhā* on the analogy of *chāyā*, and the emphasis on *bhāvarūpa* as the essence of the ideal form indicates the conceptual bearings of the form language as enunciated in the *Vāstusūtra Upaniṣad*.[163]

In the textual sources, e.g., the *Kāvyaśāstra* and the Kashmir Śaivāgamas, *pratibhā*, 'effulgent consciousness', intuitive in character, is invoked repeatedly, and is supposed to be the very basis of creativity, divine or human. The *Tantrāloka* (II/76b-8a; III.66), regards *pratibhā* to be an intuitive potential to experience wonder (*camatkāra*)[164] as it affirms freedom (*svātantrya*), and defines an integral 'consciousness devoid of succession or limit'.[165] To Abhinavagupta *pratibhā* is creatively at the root of 'poetic or artistic inspiration' even as it qualifies 'unlimited knowledge and activity at the spiritual level'. This being so, the 'wonder of delight' (*camatkāra*) increases in direct proportion to the 'measures' that the 'uncreated reality exceeds'.[166] The combination of *pratibhā* and *camatkāra* is significant and the two are necessarily complementary, for one in creativity consummately leads to the other in succession. These expositions are echoed in the texts on poetics also. For instance, Kuntaka in the *Vakroktijīvita* locates *pratibhā* in the reverberating consciousness of a poet (*sphuratimeva kavicetasi prathamam ca pratibhā*) and says that the elements from the universe that a poet interweaves in a composition are not unreal (*asat*); their forms come into play through the rigours of their authority (*sattā*). But, in inspiringly reinventing them, a poet creatively illuminates them by his *pratibhā*.[167] The *Kāvyamīmāṃsā* describes two kinds of *pratibhā*, namely, *kārayitrī*, 'functional', and *bhāvayitrī*, relating to the connoisseur in terms of its *bhāva*, etc.[168]

Though the terms *pratibhā* and *camatkāra* and their concepts do not explicitly occur in the *Śilpaśāstra*s, the argument about them seem eminently fitting in respect of the works of art and artists. We come across eloquent expressions in appreciation as, for instance, in respect of the artists who are supposed to be 'impartial, ready-witted and possessed of extensive knowledge in the craft'.[169] Perched on his distinguished knowledge (*prajñā*, which is like a boat), a distinguished artist may carry out his work (*vāstunirantaret*) achieving many-dimensional (*bahu vistaram*) excellences, which are deep in meaning (*gūḍha*), difficult to be perceived (*durālokam*) and even incomprehensible (*aprejñeya*) to others.[170] Such sentiments seem to have realised their material counterpart in the instance of the Kailasa temple at Ellora, for instance, where an artist who made the monument is surprised that he indeed had made it![171] This work was perceived as a work of wonder (*camatkāra*) to the artist as well as to the witness.

The *Śilpaśāstra*s generally describe the imaginative and technical qualities expected of an artist and these appear to be stringent and demanding in content. In spirit, they tend to underscore the challenges that an artist faced and tided over. His ready wit (*pratyutpanna mati*)[172] or his awareness of the intricacies of architectural science (*vāstumarma*) and its *gūḍhārtha* (inner meaning) do find a mention in the texts, so does the counsel that he should be a man of great empathy (*suhṛdaya*).[173]

These reflections on the intangibilities that instill a work of art do not deny the value of compositional technicalities that configure a representation in terms of its diagrammatic form. Compositional structure[174] as an artistic device often tends to work hand in hand with the philosophical premises of experience and symbolisation. For instance, the *Mahāvaṃsa*, a Buddhist text and its commentary describe the ritual and symbolic details of a *lohaprāsāda*. The details indicate that this was built according to a design which was first drawn in red ochre. The *Lankāvatara Sūtra* (*sūtra* II.15-18) refers to *karṣaṇa*, 'engraving', whereby the *sattva*, 'essence of form', is obtained: *sattvānām karṣaṇārthāya rangaiścitram vikalpyate*. These activities found greater acceptance in the *śilpa* texts. These points are taken up significantly in the *Vāstusūtra Upaniṣad*. Its Atharvanic heritage apart, it contains important materials on composition of sculptures especially in respect of their symbolism (IV.1) and artisanal modes which together transcribed a form in its materiality and essence. The *śāstric* injunctions of the text enunciated in its 137 *sūtra*s spread over six chapters must have been an imager's delight for clarity of their thought and practicality of their vision. The *Upaniṣad* underscores the traditional view that *śilpa* is a creative domain where *rūpa* finds its material counterpart. The argument has been made time and again in the text (*sūtra*s I.2, 5) and its commentary. It prescribes (*sūtra* VI.3) that the science of *śilpa* is to 'make manifest the features' in a form. The commentary on the *sūtra* I.7 describes the stages through which this manifestation may be achieved saying that 'from the archetype gradually arises the knowledge of principles of images, from knowledge of principles comes clear perception (*tattvabodha*); from conception arise the sacred songs (*gāthā*) and myths (*kathā*) among people; from sacred songs (*gāthā*) the *sthāpaka*s derive the images'.[175]

So, a reconstitution of *rūpa* by *sthāpaka* is regarded possible when the principle, conception and mythical content have all been appropriated and absorbed in an image. Although a *kāmācārin*'s (i.e., those who are moved by impulse), *hṛdaya* is where a conception takes place, *bhāva* remains central to the reconstitution of a form. In materialising the form howsoever perceived, certain artificing techniques are considered essential and compositional diagrams in terms of square, circle, intersecting lines, are recommended for composing images. In its prescriptions of compositional diagrams, the text offers a wide repertory of geometrical terminology besides stressing on the knowledge of stones (*śailam*), compositional diagram (*khilapañjara*), carving (*bhedana*), arrangement of limbs (*anga prayoga*), the emotional dispositions evoked by a composition (*nyāsa bhāva*), and finally the integration of the composition (*sambandha prabodhana*).[176] The text describes different actions in the process of preparing a compositional diagram out of which an image may be manifested through craftsmanship. The ritual underpinnings of the entire process are clearly underlined in the commentary. Following the initial acts of setting and polishing a stone slab after its selection for making an image on it, it is prescribed that a circle should be drawn on the stone with a stick of wood 'attached to a ring by means of a rope'. The work, after this, has to begin with the action of pitching a central point around which the form may ultimately radiate. Then starts the process involving different kinds of geometrical compositions such as *maṇḍala* (circle), *marma* (centre), *rekhā* (line), *rekhākaraṇa* (line diagram), *rekhānvaya*, *sarala rekhā* (straight line), *caturasra* (square), *karṇa* (diagonal), *karṇika kṣetra* (rhombus), *ṣaṭkoṇa* (hexagram), *khilapañjara* (compositional diagram), *utthita rekhā* (vertical line), *pārśvagā* (horizontal line), *tiryaka rekhā* (diagonal line), which all, in various combinations are useful in artisanal activity. The prescriptions contain practical hints on methods of using a chisel: *khanitra prakāro dhyeyah* (*sūtra* II.19); or that all the limbs have to be set along the lines (*rekhānvaye sarvānga nyāsaya, sūtra* II.8); or that the 'creation of an image starts from the navel (*nābhau kūpakarma prārabhyate, sūtra* II.10). The text lays a great emphasis on the knowledge of symbology of the different geometrical shapes and their combinations and as such, the compositional diagrams (*khilapañjara)* made of these is considered as the very basis of the form language. We are told that 'those who know it, who are the knower of form, create the essential form (*tattvarūpāṇi*) according to the principles of form (*rūpatattva*)'. The *Upaniṣad* (commentary on *sūtra* II.21) also warns that without tracing the lines of the diagram, the form may become deficient.[177]

Like a *śāstric* command, the *Upaniṣad* (II.22) prescribes adherence to the lines of the diagram when carving a figure. The commentary explains the point diligently saying that, the 'differences of the character (of images) arise with the different lines' and that a form shines forth as determined by the lines; that the form thereby becomes perfect (*surūpa*) with such an adherence. It is advised further that the soul of the form becomes manifest by depending on the essential lines (*tattvarekhā*), so does the represented image. There seems to be quite an emphasis on such conformity for it is said that: 'the lines in an image are like sacrificial offerings' and that by a harmonious form the mood of meditation is appropriately induced.[178] One can consistently see the emphasis in the text on adherence to the lines of the composition as drawn on a stone, for it was prescribed as the best method to accomplish the purpose: *rekhānupātenāngāni nidheyāniti śreṣṭha kṛtyam* (*sūtra* III.12). But this did not mean ignoring the essential character of a form as *bhāva* was supposed to be the chief element of an image (*rūpasya bhāvo mukhyaḥ*, *sūtra* III.1). In conformity, the lines had to be so disposed as to fulfill the basic *bhāva* (character) of an image: *bhāvānusārato rekhāvidhānamiti jñeyam* (*sūtra* III.2). The *sūtra*s also prescribe carving the limbs of a figure in four different ways depending on the requirements. These four ways are enumerated as *ekāśrayī*, *yugalāśrayī*, *khanḍāśrayī* and *sparśita* according to the requirements of their dispersal along the lines of the compositional diagram. But the text (III.20) forbids transgressing the limits of the lines in the *pañjara*. So the composition remains bound to the format that was initially laid out.

Just as the *Vāstusūtra Upaniṣad* prescribes drawing the figures within a circle, in other modes it recommends the use of a square. Hence the dictum that 'for making images a grid is most important': *rūpārtham koṣṭhaka mukhyaḥ* (*sūtra* IV.4) and that 'one should imagine different parts of an image within a grid': *koṣṭhakāntarāle rūpasyavayavo dhyeyaḥ* (*sūtra* IV.6); that 'from one limb arises another limb': *angādanga saṃjāyate* (*sūtra* IV.27). The compositional structures as artistic devices often have spiritual connotations embedded in the text. Yet there is no dearth of references to the realisation of *rasa*s through *śilpa*, and the theme seems writ large in the text. Eight *rasa*s have been enumerated in the text in its fifth chapter. There is also the command about the *āsana*s and *mudrā*s which were basic to the language of gestures in *śilpa*.[179] It is said that 'hand gestures manifest the emotional attitudes of the image'. The details about the *vāhana*s (mounts) and other elements in the iconography are similarly emphasised. The nine essential elements that are supposed to constitute an image are enumerated as composition, ornaments, gestures, weapons, postures, vehicles, secondary divinities, enemies and devotees.[180] The commentary adds that 'these nine elements are not for human images but are important (only) for the divine images'.

The enunciations in the *Vāstusūtra Upaniṣad* seem significant both for its nature as a *śāstra* on *vāstu* inclusive of *śilpa*, and also for its pragmatism in describing the form language. The text is important in understanding the art process in its practical outline. It unfolds a lot in regard to both the principles and essence of form besides bringing to clarity the manner in which a relevant imagery is transformed into a representation through a carefully articulated artisanal process. It seems to complement what is described in the *citrasūtra* of the *Viṣṇudharmottara Purāṇa* (Ch. 42) with the difference that while the *Purāṇa* limits itself mainly to the *lakṣaṇa*s, the *Vāstusūtra Upaniṣad* goes into the details of artisanal modes to bring those forms out through artisanal devices.[181]

NOTES AND REFERENCES

1. *Śikṣā* is one of the six *angas* of knowledge in the *Kāvyamīmāṃsā* (2), meaning the 'science of proper articulation and pronunciation' or phonetics.
2. It would be conceded that *vidyā, vijñāna* and *śāstra* constitute categories of knowledge independent of *śilpa.* But sometimes they identify with it, sometime tend to merge into *śilpa* or, on occasions, one graduates into the other or, one even reverts to its moorings regardless of occasional claims of conjunctions.
3. Cf., *Vijñaptimātratasiddhih* of Vasubandhu, ed. & tr. Mahesh Tiwari (1995), Varanasi: Chowkhamba Vidyabhavan, p. 7.
4. Cf., *Vijñānabhairava,* with the comm. of Swami Lakshman Joo, Baumer, Bettina, tr. (2002), Varanasi: Indica Books, *intro*, p. xi. Baumer's interpretation of the term is in accordance with Abhinavagupta who in his *Īśvarapratyabhijña Vivṛtti* (Vol. II) regards the *Vijñānabhairava* (a Kashmira Śaivagama text from Rudrayamala Tantra) as an '*Upaniṣad* of the *Śiva-vijñāna*' (*Śivavijñānopaniṣad*), containing the '(mystical) knowledge of Śiva'.
5. Bohtlingk and Roth (Rep. 1962), sv. *Vijñāna.*
6. Sircar eqates *vijñānika* with *śilpīs* and explains the former as epithet of an artisan. Cf., Sircar (1966): 373.
7. *Aparājitapṛcchā,* I.46.
8. *Vivāda Ratnākara,* p. 141; Devana Bhatta in his commentary explains that making bracelets, anklets, pillars, pots and also the subjects like dance and music are all included in *śilpa vijñāna*: *kankaṇa kaṭakādinirmāṇa viṣayam nṛtyam gītādikaraṇa viṣaya cakārātstambhakumbhādi viṣayam ca vijñānam śilpamucyate.* Cf., A.S. Altekar, *Education in Ancient India,* p. 201.
9. For a discussion on these two categories, cf., Misra (1994)/1: 62-63.
10. The situation changed in the *Maitrī Upaniṣad* (VII.8) where *śilpins* like many others are condemned for 'mingling heavenly with unheavenly', which was supposed to be the root cause of delusion and false doctrine that they professed.
11. Aiyar (1989): 1-2. *Dhyāna* and *upāsanā* are the essential ingredients of *vidyā* in the *Upaniṣads*. But as Raghavan remarks, 'Sometimes the name *vidyā* goes down to lesser material, and sometimes it soars up so as to refer to actual descriptions of the Brahman itself ... thus bearing similarity to the term *yoga* .... Some (*vidyās*) take their name from the *ālambana* or specific objects or symbols used for the contemplation, some the place or the divine being within which the *upāsaka* is asked to direct his contemplation, some the person figuring in the teaching, some the mode of contemplation and so on'. V. Raghavan in Aiyar (1989): *Intro.*, pp. xxi-xxii.
12. V. Raghavan in Aiyar (1989), *Intro.*, pp. iii-xxiii. *Dhyāna* is central to *śilpa* too as part of its essential grid of both meditative and creative exercise. Cf., *Vāstusūtra Upaniṣad* II. 23: *rūpasaubhāgād dhyānabhāvo jāyate.* Also, *Ibid.*, III.14: *dhyānaprayoge rūpasauṣṭavam spaṣṭam bhavati.*
13. Walker (1968): 555. Walker further says that 'knowledge is not treated merely as an epistemological factor in philosophy but is regarded as a base

element in the path of salvation, for knowledge can break the cycle of *saṃsāra* (birth-death-rebirth) .... The emancipatory character of knowledge is evident in its lesser and more commonplace spheres'.

14. Cf., Bohtlingk and Roth (1966): sv. *vidyā*. In the Buddhist texts, *vidyā* is 'knowledge' like in the Vedic works; and the opposite of *avijjā* is always *jñāna*. The *vijjā*s generally lead to *vimukti*, but sometimes the term has a 'dogmatic sense' as 'secret science'. In the popular meaning and usage *vijjā* denotes science, craft, art, charm, spell. Davids and Stede (1997): 617-618; sv. *vijjā*.
15. I owe this reference to Professor G.C. Pande.
16. *Kena Up 12; Chāndogya* I.1.10; IV.9.3; 14.1; V.3.7; *Bṛhadāraṇyaka* I.5.16; II.4.10; IV.5.12; IV.4.2, 10; *Īśa*, 10-11 (*vidyāyāmṛtamaśnute*), *Taittirīya* I.3.3 (*vidyā sandhiḥ*), III.6.1 (*bhārgavī vāruṇī vidyā*); *Katha* II.4, VI.18; *Śvet*. V.1 (*kṣaram tvavidyā hyamṛtam tu vidyā*); *Maitrī*. IV.4; *Muṇḍaka*, I.1.4; *Praśna*, I.10. *Gītā* X.12 (*ādhyātmavidyā vidyānām*).
17. For *devajana vidyā*, cf., *Chāndogya Upaniṣad*, VII.1.2-4,VII.2.1.
18. Artists were often designated with these terms. For instance, while *sūtradhāra* Chitaku is described as *vidyāpati gambhīraḥ*, his younger brother Mandana is mentioned as *śāstra japī*. Cf., Mirashi (1955): 556-557.
19. *Śilpaprakāśa*, II.730.
20. ... *sarvavidyā śilpānām kalānam copabandhinī* ... *Vidyā*, *śilpa* and *kalā* occur together in this extract from the *Vākyapadīyam*.
21. *Kāvyamīmāmsā*, Ch. II, p. 25. These consisted of the four *Vedas*, six *Vedangas* (namely, *śikṣā*, *kalpa*, *vyākaraṇa*, *nirukta*, *chandas*, *jyotiṣa*), and four *śāstras* (namely, *Purāṇa*, 'historical texts', *ānavīkṣakī*, 'philosophy', *mimāṃsā*, 'epistemology', and *Dharmasūtra*).
22. Rajasekhara comes to a final list of eighteen such *vidyās* including the fourteen enunciated by the ancient *ācāryas* and four others enumerated by him, describing their sub-categories and adding the *sāhitya vidyā* to this entire genre. *Kāvyamīmāṃsā*, 26-27.
23. e.g., *Matsya*, *Vāyu*, *Varāha*, *Agni*, *Viṣṇudharmottara Purāṇas*, for instance.
24. e.g., *Kāmikāgama*, *Kāraṇāgama*, *Aṃśumadbhedāgama*, *Īsānaśiva Gurudeva Paddhati*, etc. It is likely that in these texts and in the *Purāṇas*, the materials on architecture and iconography came largely from the practices of *śilpins*.
25. *Citralakṣaṇa* of Nagnajit, I.101.
26. *Vāstusūtra Upaniṣad*, I, *sūtra* 6: *sa pravahaṇaḥ śilpasūtrādhyāyam sthāpakavidyām cāvadat*; or *Ibid*., VI. *sūtra* 3: *lakṣaṇaprakāśartham śilpavidyā*. Interestingly, the *Śilpaprakāśa* in its initial *dhyāna mantras* first invokes Viśvakarmā and Kali, the latter as *sarvavidyāsvarūpiṇī*, and then eulogises *śilpavidyā* as *mahatī*, 'great', and goes on to describe the rules about different kinds of architectural works. *Vidyā* and *śāstra* seem interchangeable in the text as it says: *sarvaśāstrottamam śilpam viśvakarmānuśāsanam*: 'of all the *śāstras*, the *śilpa* taught by Viśvakarmā is the highest'. *Śilpa* and *śāstra* stand at par in these references. Cf., *Śilpaprakāśa*, I, 1-5; II, 808-809.
27. Specially, the chapters 210-239, devoted to the marks (*lakṣaṇa*) of sculptures and paintings and their allied subjects.

28. He is supposed to be the all-knowing expert of the *tattva* of the *Vedas*, *Vedangas*, all the *vijñānas*, 'sciences', who made an exposition of the *sūtraśāstra*, *sūtra* meaning both a thread and aphoristic details of the *śilpasāstra*. Cf., *Aparājitapṛcchā*, I.46, 53,55.
29. *Viśvakarmā Vāstuśāstram*: 87. 6-9; 11-13.
30. For instance, Maya asserts a *śāstric* status for his work when he proclaims his exhortations as 'this systematic *śāstra*': *śāsti śāstram yathākramam Mayamatam*: I.1.
31. e.g., *Rūpamanḍana*, *Vāstusāra* of Thakkura Pheru, *Mānasāra*, *Bhuvan Pradīpa*, *Śilpaprakāśa*, *Śilpasāriṇī*. The language or the text in some of these works, *Mānasāra* for instance, is indefensible grammatically and needed exhaustive corrections (when P.K. Acharya took up its editing and publication), which may indicate their character as manuals.
32. The *pramāṇas* came in the *śilpa* texts fairly early and Nagnajit seems to have been a pioneer in this respect. Varahamihira, in an instance, offers his own standards of measurement, different from those of Nagnajit, but regards him as one of the eighteen early experts of *śilpa*. Bhattotpala commenting on Varahamihira speaks of Nagnajit's treatises on *Pratimālakṣaṇa*. Cf., Sastri (1987): *intro.*, pp. vii-viii.
33. Bhattacharya (1991): 1, verse 1.
34. Pollock (1989): 17. In Buddhism, *śāstra* is like the Buddha's *sāsana*, i.e., the Buddha's doctrine. Cf., *Vinaya*, I.12: *Dīgha*, I.110; II.206. For these, cf., Davids and Stede (1997): sv. *sāsana*. For *vijñāna* (*viññāṇa*), *Ibid.*, pp. 618-619.
35. *aneka samśayo cchedī parokṣā'rtha darśakam, sarvasya locanam śāstram yasya nāstandhya eva ca*, Bohtlingk and Roth (1962): sv: *śāstra*. Or, it is explained as *yaccānukūlametasya tacca śāstram prakīrtitam, yato' nyo granthavistāro naiva śāstra kuvartma tat. Ibid. Śāstra* has a Vedic antiquity and the word can be traced back to the *Ṛgveda* VIII.33.16. In the *Rāmāyaṇa* it is explained as *susūkṣma artha*. It is also interpreted as follows: *yaccanukūlametasya tacca śāstram prakīrtitam, yato'nyo granthavistāro naiva śāstra kuvartma tat*. Cf., Bohtlingk and Roth (1962) sv: *śāstra*.
36. Cf., Deshmukh (1985): 16.
37. Katyayana is quoted by Patanjali, Cf., Bhargava Shastri Joshi, ed., (1951), *Mahābhāṣya* Vol. I, Bombay: Nirnaya Sagar Press, p. 65. In Mimamsa, *śāstra* is a set of infallible rules, which makes *dharma* known to us, something not knowable otherwise. The *śāstra*-ic rules may be of *dṛṣṭārtha* and *adṛṣṭārtha* (evident and non-evident) kinds, but the practice of those rules is mandatory. Cf., Sheldon Pollock (1987), *Śāstric Basis of Arts in India* (Mss. of the paper in the Heidelberg University Seminar on Śāstric Traditions in Indian Arts). In the Western terminology, the point may be expressed in terms of 'constitutive' and 'regulatory' rules that organise the practice. *Ibid.*
38. *Api sphutati Vindhyadrau vatī vā pralayānile, gurusastronugo margah parityajyo na dhīmatām, Laghu*, Yogavāśiṣta VI.5.45, quoted by Pollock, *op. cit.*
39. *Kāvyamīmāṃsā* II, p. 21, under *śāstranirdeśa*. Among the *pauruṣeya śāstras*, the text includes *Purāṇas*, *ānavīkṣakī*, *Mimāṃsā* and *Dharmasūtra*. *Śilpa* also figures in the text as a *śāstra* but without its location in the twin categories. *Ibid.*, p. 26.

40. Cf., *Kāvyamīmāṃsā*, 26-27: *saritāmiva pravāhāstucchaḥ prathamam yathottaram vipulāḥ/ye śāstra samārambhā bhavanti lokasya te vandyāḥ.*
41. *Śukranīti* (IV.3.58) regards *śilpa* as a *śāstra: prāsāda pratimārāma-gṛhavapyādi saṃskṛtiḥ kathitā yatra tat śilpasāstramuktam maharṣibhiḥ*. Also, *Ibid.*, IV.3.26. In the same text II.160-162, we have reference to a *śilpaśāstrajña. Ibid.*, IV.3.26; IV.2.29; IV.2.58. In looking for the *śāstras* of *śilpins*, we may have to depend on the texts (like, *Vāstusūtra Upaniṣad*) that contain theoretical expositions of the *śilpa* canon and its applicability, which made the works possible. The formulations in the *śilpaśāstra* came to be incorporated in the *Agamas* and *Saṃhitas* in their section on *arccā* (apart from the other *pādas* like *jñāna, kriyā* and *caryā*). This may indicate a gradual transformation of *śilpa vidyā* into *śāstra* during the early middle ages. Such incorporations came to ensure *śāstric* recognition of their 'knowledge', and a ritual acceptance of their *vidyā* into the *Agamic* tradition, a privilege that had remained elusive to *śilpins* in the orthodox Vedic tradition. No wonder, in medieval epigraphs we do come across artists claiming to be like Narayana in draughtsmanship. The *Citrasūtra* of the *Viṣṇudharmottara* tells of Viśvakarmā learning the knowledge of *rekhā*, 'lines', from Narayana. Artists' ascendancy in these situations seems to stand out eminently in terms of their identity, status and dignity.
42. *Viśvakarma Vāstuśāstram* (1958): *intro.*, p. v. where it is said that *Śilpaśāstras* basically relate to 'science of artistic creation'. Conventionally, it is supposed to include 'all artistic creations first conceived in mind and then executed by the hand'; '*śilpa* emphasises on the idea of artistic creations and *vāstu*, the idea of utility. Viśvakarmā and Maya who are respectively the *sthapatis* ... deal with the science of *vāstu* on parallel lines ... But whereas Maya's thesis is intact in a single book named *Mayamatam*, Viśvakarmā's treatise has come down to us in a number of manuals ... (about a dozen or so)'.
43. Cf., *Parātrīśikā Vivaraṇa*, ed. Baumer, Bettina and Jaidev Singh (1988), Delhi: Motilal Banarasidass, p. 19 (tr). I owe this reference to Professor (Dr.) Bettina Baumer.
44. For a discussion on the *tantrayuktis*, cf., W.K. Lele (1981), *The Doctrine of TantraYukti*, Varanasi: Chowkhambha Surabharati Prakashan. Also, Anuradha Singh (unpublished), 'Tantra Yukti: Method of Theorization in Ayurveda'.
45. *Anukaraṇa* as a mode is exalted in the *Aitareya Brāhmaṇa* and later in the *Kāvyaśāstras* where Śankuka, Abhinavagupta and others interpret it significantly. In Sāyaṇa, *anukaraṇa* is supposed to bring about the duality in *śilpa*: one relating to the divine category and the other to its anthropomorphic counterpart. For *anukaraṇa* and its value in art, cf., Misra (1994)/2: 105-106.
46. See Chapter I.
47. Marks (*lakṣaṇa*) are basic to *śilpaśāstra* for they give an exact meaning to manifested forms. For instance, Aśvaghoṣa's *Sūtralankāra* describes thirty-two *lakṣaṇas* and eighty *anuvyañjanas* of the Buddha, which adorn him and make him look like a painting. Cf., Sastri (1937): 31. Instructions on *lakṣaṇa*

were received by Nagnajit from Viśvakarmā on the advice of Brahmā. Cf., *Citralakṣaṇa* of Nagnajit: I.86-96.

48. *Aparājitapṛcchā*, Chs. 20, 36; *Samarāngaṇa Sūtradhāra*: 41-42, 592, 597-601, etc.
49. *Vāstusūtra Upaniṣad*, II. 23; III. 14.
50. The *Aparājitapṛcchā* underscores its concern for *lakṣaṇa*s in the section on *pratimālakṣaṇa. Ibid.*, Ch. 210, 1-36; 211.1-16. *Samarāngaṇa Sūtradhāra* discusses *pramānas* in Chapter 79.
51. An idol, which is less or more than the recommended proportions (*hīnādhika*), causes death; too large an icon causes sorrow; that with harsh appearance brings fear and the one with an angry expression causes danger. *Citrasūtra*, Ch. 38, verses 14-27: Mukherji (2001): 63-69.
52. Cf., *Vāstusūtra Upaniṣad*, V, 9-16; *Citrasūtra* of the *Viṣṇudharmottara Purāṇa*, Ch. 43, 1-15. In the verse 31 it is said that rules of paintings apply also on sculpture. *Samarāngaṇa Sūtradhāra*, Ch. 82, 1-34.
53. *Dṛṣṭyastu tathā bhāvā angopāngāni sarvaśah/karāśca ye matā nṛtte pūrvoktā nṛpasattam//* i.e., '... eye- expressions, moods, primary and secondary limbs and hand (gestures) ... in the dance are the very ones to be known in painting (for the painting is considered to be parallel to dance)'. Mukherji, 2001: 6. Also, verse 7.
54. e.g., *citrasūtram na jānāti yasyu samyang narādhipa/pratimālakṣaṇam vettum na śakyam tena karhacit// vinā tu nṛttaśāstreṇa citrasūtram sudurvidham/ jagato'nukriyā karyā dvayor'api yato nṛpah// atodyam yo na jānāti asya nṛtam sudurvidam/atodyena vinā nṛttam vidyate na kathacanam//na gītena vina śakyam jñātumatodyamācyuta/gītaśāstra vidhānajñaḥ sarvavetti yathāvidhiḥ// Viṣṇudharmottara Purāṇa*, III. 2.2-8.
55. *Citrasūtra*, Ch. 43. 31-32. Mukherji (2001).
56. *Sāmudram gaṇitam caiva jyotiṣam chanda eva ca/sirājñānam tathā śilpam yantrakarmavidhistathā// etānyangani jānīyad vāstuśāstrasya buddhimān/ śāstrānusānabhyudyā lakṣaṇani lakṣayet// Samarāngaṇa Sutradhāra*, Ch. 44.3-4.
57. *Samarāngaṇa Sūtradhāra*, Ch. 79, pp. 610-624. In Chapter 76 on *pratimālakṣaṇa*, it deals with different *pramāṇa*s for measurement, etc. According to the *Citralakṣaṇa* of Nagnajit (III. 154-160), there are said to have been 12000 works on the measurements of male and female figures. Out of these, besides those of the paramount rulers, others include *bhadra, rucaka, mālavya* and *śaśaka* types.
58. *Aparājitapṛcchā*, Chapters 237, 238.
59. Bhattacharya (1991): 260.
60. About artists' freedom, we may quote from Dagens, who on the basis of his studies of the *Mayamatam*, says: '*Mayamatam* confers on the architect the task of putting into practice what it prescribes ... (But) the architect has considerable latitude at his disposal ... This freedom comes ... from the pretensions of the text to universality. The text, seeking to encompass all possible circumstances, envisages them, and prepares for them by means of an extended series of specific variations; such being the procedure, it is left to the architect to choose this or that option 'according to circumstances' (*yuktya*) as is often repeated. Equally the treatise has its limitations which

also leave the executant a certain leeway'. Dagen (2000). Vol. I, *Intro.*, pp. xcix-c.

61. *Aparājitapṛcchā* 230, 4: *kuśalam sarvaśāstreṣu vāstuvedodbhavādiṣu devāgniguru pūjāsu ratam dharmeṣu nityasah.*
62. Deviations from the codes (*pramāṇena vivarjitaḥ* or *pramāṇenaiva varjitaḥ*), are allowed in specific cases. *Citrasūtra* of *Viṣṇudharmottara*, 42.18 (Mukherji 2001:190). But those instances apart, adherence to *śāstra* was considered necessary. Cf., *Aparājitapṛcchā*, Ch. 232. 14: *arcārūpodbhavākāryā mānayuktiścaśāstrataḥ/sacintya tviṣṭikābandham hastapadaśīrṣāditah.* A work of art which is according to instructions (*yathādeśam*), time (*yathākālam*), age (*yathāvayaḥ*) and body types (*yathādeham*), becomes auspicious. Otherwise it becomes the opposite. *Citrasūtra* of *Viṣṇudharmottara*: 42.84.
63. Cf., *Samarāngaṇa-Sūtradhāra*: I.5: *tasmāllokasya kṛpayā śāstrametadudīryate*, or, I.22: *lokānāmitastvam hitakāmyayā.* The all-pervasive nature of the *śāstra* is also emphasised in the text: *Vāstubrahma sadā viśvam vyāpnoti sakalam jagat.* II.4.
64. Sastri (1987): I.53; also 54.
65. *Citrasūtra* of the *Viṣṇudharmottara Purāṇa*, Ch. 40. 10-11. So, the different elements of a work, namely, lines (*rekhā*), line rendering (*vartanā*), decoration (*bhūṣaṇam*) and colour (*varṇa*), have their varying appeal to the connoisseurs. The masters praise the lines, critics, the shading, women, the ornamentation and common people, the richness of colours. According to the *Citralakṣaṇa* of Srikumara: IV.5, 8 (Bhattacharya, 1974: 68) a work requires both meditation and recall to be appealing to eyes. So, gods, men, animals, reptiles, birds, creepers (*latā*), *vṛksa*, mountains or seas should be ascertained by seeing, hearing or by meditation. While painting them an artist should recall them again and again (*smṛtvā smṛtvā punaḥ punaḥ*), with a resolute mind (*svasthacitta*) and sitting at ease (*sukhāsīna*).
66. *Citrasūtra* of the *Viṣṇudharmottara Purāṇa*, Ch. 41, v. 9.
67. See, *pūrvāpara viruddhaḥ*, *Śākuntalam*, ed. Monier Williams (reprint, Varanasi, 1961), p. 255. Also, *Ibid.* (VI.153): *darśana sukham anubhavatah sākṣāt iva tanmayen hṛdayena, smṛtikāriṇā tvayā me punarapi citrīkṛta kāntā.*
68. Utpala, in his *Pratyabhijña Kārikā*: III.3.15.
69. The passage reads: 'Homage to him who paints the picture of three worlds, thereby displaying in full sense his amazing genius (*pratibhā*); homage to Śambhu who is beautiful with hundreds of appearances laid out by the brush of his own unique, subtle and pure energy.'
70. 'Whose consciousness is aroused by seeing the *kalā* of his own play; of the various bodies of enjoyment and emotional states (*bhāva*); he alone paints the universe with the colours of his own being (*svabhāva*). Becoming manifest, he paints the universe and the manifestation itself is nothing but his own form (*svarupa*)'. Abhinavagupta in *Mālinivijaya Vārtika*, I. 276-277.
71. Cf., Baumer (1985): 79-86s.
72. Cf., *Viṣṇudharmottara Purāṇa*, Ch. on *Pratimalaksana*, 46.19 A-B, where after describing the marks of the Brahman, the 'incomprehensible', Markandeya says thus to Vajra: 'This is my account to you of the form of the

incomprehensible one (*apratimasya rūpam*) who pervades the world. This is how the lord of the world upholds the whole world in a bodily form' (tr. Bhattacharya, 1991: 20). Such formulations occur in the Mahāyāna school of Buddhism too, in connection with the triple division of the Buddha's body where the Master's *nirmāṇakāya* is supposed to be marked with thirty-six *lakṣaṇas* even as his *dharmakāya* is absolutely *alakṣma*, i.e., 'devoid of any marks (*lakṣaṇa*)'. Nagarjuna says, 'In the world, for the sake of those who take delight in seeing the beautiful physical form and through that set their minds on the path, the body of the thirtytwo features is manifested. This is the mundane truth, but this is not to deny the ultimate truth of the indeterminate *dharma*, nor the condition-ness of the determinate. Cf., Pathak (1989): 594.

73. Cf., Misra (1989): 178-181.
74. *Yadvai pratirūpam tat śilpam, Śatapatha Brahmana,* III.1.5.5; Cf., Misra (1988): 149-150.
75. Cf., Bhattacharya (1991): 15-16.
76. Reference here is to a dialogue between Jabali and Indra. Jabali was worshipping a *liṅga* when Indra appeared and was told that in worshipping a *liṅga* Jabali was actually worshipping Rudra. A discussion ensued about what constitutes a deity, and the suggestion is made that the import of a deity lies in the word for it. The commentaries elaborate the same idea enunciating that the deity is not supposed to have any form (*devatā nāsti kā cit vigrahavatī*), and are comprehended only by the sound of the word (*devatā śrutyā gamyate na pratyakṣādibhiḥ*). *Śabarabhāṣya,* IV.3.15.37 quoted in *Mimāṃsā Kośa,* III.21.23. *Śabda* is a *pramāṇa* in Nyaya. For the efficacy of *śabda* in poetics, cf., Anandavardhana, *Dhvanyāloka,* 1-7.
77. Cf., Falk (1943).
78. *Pratimālakṣaṇa* of the *Viṣṇudharmottara Purāṇa,* Ch. 3, verses 1-2: '*Prakṛti* or the noumenal and *Vikṛti* or the phenomenal are the two aspects of the Supreme Soul. That form which is invisible, is called *Prakṛti*'. Bhattacharya (1991): 15.
79. *Ibid.,* 16.
80. *dhyāna yogasya samsiddheh pratimālakṣaṇam smṛtam. Śukranīti,* ed. & tr. Pt. Brahma Shankar Mishra (1968), Varanasi, p. 248; IV.4.74.
81. *Ibid.,* p. 255, *puvvāpara virohī apuvva,* i.e., 'having no regard to the preceding or the following'. Monier Williams interprets it differently.
82. *Kāvya Prakāśa* of Mammata, I.1: *niyatikṛta niyama rahitām hlādaikamanīyam ananyaparatantrām, navarasarucirāmnirmitamadadhāti bhārati kaverjayati.* 'Super-excellence is the voice of a poet, which is always engaged to create a supernatural universe of poet's own, that outdoes the laws of Nature, and is identified with the absolute happiness. It is self-dependent ...'
83. Anandavardhana in *Dhvanyāloka,* p. 223, quoted in *Kāvya Prakāśa,* Appendix: A, p. 138: *apāre kāvya samsāre kaviḥ ekaḥ Prajāpatih, yathāsmai rocate viśvam tathaiva parivartate.* In so transcending the time-series his consciousness may be at variance with the general postulates of time, space, event, change, or experience and yet be in conformity with them, for they tend to serve as temporal or historical analogies for transcendence.

84. According to the *Citrasūtra* of the *Viṣṇudharmottara* (42. 49) *sādṛśyam*, 'resemblance', is mandatory in works of art relating to visible things (*dṛṣṭānām sādṛśyam kāryam*) for, in 'painting accomplishment of verisimilitude is of primacy' (*citre sādṛśyakaraṇam pradhānam*).
85. The *Ujjvala Nīlamaṇi* for instance describes the beauty of a *bhāva* in terms of the 'liquid effulgence' of a pearl: *muktāphaleṣu chāyāyāḥ yastaraltvam-ivāntaram/ pratibhāti yadangeṣu lāvaṇyaṃtadihocyate//* Visvanatha in his commentary says, *chāyāyāstaralatvam tarangāyamānatvaṃ Ati svacchatvādādhikyācca pratikṣaṇam ugacchantya iva kāntayo lakṣyate tallāvaṇyamuccyate*. I owe this reference to the late Professor V.S. Pathak.
86. *rūpasya bhāvo mukhyaḥ, Vāstusūtra Up*. III.1.
87. *Aparājitapṛcchā*, 224.11, 19.
88. Cf., Pathak and Misra (1986): 280-290.
89. *Aparājitapṛcchā*, Ch. 224. 11.
90. *Citra* is not only paintings; it includes the work in stone, metal, terracotta, cloth, etc. too.
91. *Ibid*., also V.S. Pathak (1976), *Bharatiya Darsana Ke Sandarbha Men Rūpa Kī Vyakhya* (in Hindi), in *Rajbali Pandey Smṛti Granth*, Deoriya, p. 331.
92. Cf., also *Citralakṣaṇa* (of Srikumara), IV.2: *jangamā vā sthāvarā vā ye santi bhuvanatraye/tattatsvabhāvatasteṣām karaṇam citramucyate*. Bhattacharya (1974): 65.
93. *Aparājitapṛcchā*, 224.5; *citramūlodbhavah sarve samsāradvīpasāgaraḥ*, *Aparājitapṛcchā*, 224. 8.
94. Priyabala Shah, ed. (1958), *Viṣṇudharmottara Purāṇa*, G.O.S. No.XXX, Baroda, 3. 35.1-3, p. 127; Mukherji (2001): Ch. 35, p. 1.
95. Cf., Rudrayana Avadana in the *Divyāvadāna*.
96. *sādṛśyam dṛśyate yattu darpaṇe pratibimbavat/tatcitramiti vikhyātam nālamākāramātrakam//* IV.147; 'That painting is well known as *citra* which is not merely a sketch in outline, but shows the resemblance (of a figure) as truly as the reflection which would at once make one experience amorous (*sṛngāra*) and other sentiments (*rasas*): *sṛngārādiraso yatradarśanādevagamyate*, IV. 148. Bhattacharya (1974): 58.
97. Pathak, as cited in the note 91 above.
98. See for instance, the *Bṛhadāraṇyaka* (III.9.15) dialogue between Sakalya and Yajnavalkya, where we have 'verily, I know that Person (whose abode is *rūpa*) who is the last source of every soul of whom you speak. Who this very Person, who is in the mirror, is He? Tell me O, Sakalya, who is his God? Life (*asu*), he said'. Emphasis here is on *chāyā-puruṣa* in the mirror; 'that verily is *asu*' (life or essence). The image outside the mirror here is the reflection of the image in the mirror; the latter is the essence, while the former is the counterpart, or in the words of the *Kauśītaki Upaniṣad*, 'In the shadow – the double'.
99. In the *Ṛgveda*, these two implications are felt together: that which is in itself the manifested likeness or image of a deity is also seen in the sense of refuge (*sarma*) or cool (*hima*) from oppressive heat. In the *Ṛgveda* (I.73.8), Agni is said to be associated with or present in the world 'like a shadow': *chāyaiva*

viśvam bhuvanam sisakthi. This idea is further stressed in the *Ṛgveda* (VI.16.38) which has this: 'We come to thee, O, Agni, in thy golden likeness (*hiraṇya sadṛśaḥ*) for refuge (*sarma*), as to the shadow (*chāyām iva*) from the burning heat (*ghṛṇah*).'

100. Cf., also *Praśna Upaniṣad* III.3; IV.10; *Kaṭha Upaniṣad* II.3.5. The realisation of a form may be illusory in character, yet, it can both be a cause of moral defilement or mental purification depending upon its sensuous or spiritual perception. To substantiate his argument, Candrakirti, in his comments on Nagarjuna, brings in the analogy of an 'image' of a beautiful woman and that of the Buddha which he says would respectively be the cause of those different states of mind despite their illusory character.

101. This play recounts Sita's living in the hermitage of Valmiki after her banishment from Ayodhya by Rama. The relevant portion of the story describes that Rama had killed Sambhuka and was traversing through the Daṇḍaka forest in search of water. He came upon a lake and went to it to quench his thirst. There, as he descended down, he saw in the tranquil waters of the lake the reflection of Sita (who had been turned invisible by the 'powers of the sage' (*muni prasādāt*) Valmiki.

102. Says he: *Vaidehī kvāpi gacchanti dīrghikātīra vartmanā/antargata jalacchāyā mayā saiveti vīkṣitā/tadasya pratikṛter mūlaprakṛtim anviṣyatām.* Later, by *anveṣaṇa* (introspection) he concludes that in seeing Sita he had seen only her reflection: *tam eva tāvat prasanna-salila-madhya-vartinīm pratimām Sītām avalokayāmi.*

103. See note 85 above.

104. For instance see the *Ṛgveda* where we have: *kam svidvgaryam prathamam daghra āpo yatra devāḥ sam apaśyanta viśve,* or still later, in the words of Ruhyaka, an *ācarya* of *Kāvya,* who says: *muktāphaleṣu chāyā yottaralattvam ivāntaram/pratibhāti yad angesu tallāvanyam ihocyate// Ujjvala Nīlamaṇi,* p. 273. Roughly translated, it means that *lāvaṇya* (beauty) is the subtle 'effulgence' exuding from body in the manner of luster emanating from pearl.

105. Cf., *Kāvyaprakaśa* of Mammata Bhatta, IV, 27-28. Bhatta Lollata says that *sthāyībhāva* (the permanent emotion) is first generated by the *vibhāvas* (stimulants); it is manifested by *anubhāva,* and is intensified by the *vyabhicārins.* At this stage, it becomes *rasa. Vibhāva* is supposed to be an extraordinary conception where a man engrossed in a dramatic performance or a poetic work, identifies with it shedding his own entitative reality and cannot discriminate himself from the content of his immediate experience and thereby comes to have a dramatic or poetic persona. *Kāvyaprakāśa,* p. 111: commentary of Sri Krisna Sharman.

106. According to Lollata the terms *niṣpatti* and *samyoga* in Bharata seem to be connected with the *vibhāvas, anubhāva* and *vyabhicāri bhāva* relating to the generation, reference and intensification of the sentiments, and they indicate a relationship in terms of *utpādya-utpādaka, gamya-gamak* and *poṣya-poṣaka* phenomenon.

107. Sāyaṇa explains *vibhāva* as *ādityamiva citraṃ cāyanīyaṃ vibhāvaṃ vividhaprakāśavantaṃ yathā prakāśādi sādhanāya dhārayanti tadvat.* The term

vibhāva occurs in the *Ṛgveda* I.58.6; also, VII.66.1; 69.5; 148.4; III.3.9; IV.1.8; 12; V.1.9; 4.2; VI.4.2; 10.1; 11.4; 49.9; X.6.1; 2; 8.4; 61; 20; 88.7; 91.1.

108. Cf., Boner *et al.* (2000), pp. 89-95.
109. The term 'universalisation' translates *sādhāraṇīkaraṇa* or *pratibhāsika sattā*, the terms in Sanskrit poetics.
110. Misra (1994)/2: 97-110.
111. This caution was as true of creating imaginative *Suttantas*, as it was true of creating a *nimitta* or a *bimba* (image). 'Yet the Buddhist philosophical tendency to look upon actual objects, including self as images (*nimitta, bimba*) tends to assimilate experience into imagination, even "illusion".' Canonical sanction for Buddhist art may be supposed to derive from such a belief. The idea is appropriately expressed in the *Cullavagga* by the term *patibhānacitta* (painting from imagination). The term *patibhāna* is variously defined as 'intuition', 'likeness': as *nānesu nānam* in the *Vibhānga*; as 'an imagination possessed of *oppama, lakkhaṇa* and *rasa*' in the *Milinda Pañho*. For details and references, see, Pande (1963-64): 7-9.
112. Parimoo (1982): 85-92.
113. For example, *caraṇa cittam citteneva cintitam*, which Buddhaghosa has explained as *citteneva cintitanti cittakarena cintittva katatta; cittene cintitam nāma*: 'Whatever products of art there are in the world are wrought by mind.' Cf., Ray (1974): 66-77.
114. Ray (1974): 66.
115. Madhava's *Sarva Darśana Samgraha*: Sharma (1984): 81-83: *vijñeyam anumeyamiti*.
116. As an entity *citta*, 'consciousness', consists of five adjuncts (*pratyayas*) – *rūpa, samjñā, vedanā, vijñāna* and *samskāra*; cf., Sharma (1984): 74-75.
117. This cognition is dependent on *viṣaya* (motivation), *citta* (consciousness), and *indriyas* (sense objects), and other *sahāyaka tattvas* (contributory factors), e.g., *prakāśa* (light) and *ākāra* (shape). Cf., Madhava, pp. 74-75.
118. Cf., Mahesh Tiwari, ed. & tr. (1995), *Vijñaptimatrasiddhi*, Varanasi: Chowkhambha Vidyabhavan, pp. 6ff., especially pp. 9-10, 45.
119. The term is a compound of *prati+akṣi* or *prati+akṣa* (*akṣa* or *akṣi*, eye', being the *indriya*). The Buddhists regard it as 'unerring knowledge of the unique particular, (*svalakṣana*). The Naiyayikas explain it as a cognition that follows from direct sensuous perception: *indriārtha sannikarṣajanya jñānam pratyakṣam*. Prabhakara and the Vedantins regard it as the 'immediate knowledge', *pratyakṣasya sakṣātakāritvam lakṣaṇam*. As for the *indriya*, the Buddhist consider it as *golaka*, a 'physical organ, sense orifice', while the Mimamsakas regard it as a *śakti*, 'capacity', of organ. Others considered it as a *dravya*. There is also a category of *nirvikalpa pratyakṣa*, a 'non-voluntary, indescribable' perception or cognition. Gangeśa explains it as, 'the knowledge of an object without any predicate or character'. But the Grammarians do not accept it as an operative phenomenon. Bhatta interprets it as 'neither particularity nor generality: a mere substratum'. But the Naiyayikas think that the attributes, universals, relations, etc. are all given to the mind even in a *nirvikalpa* stage. I am grateful to my teacher the late Professor V.S. Pathak for these interpretations on *pratyakṣa*.

120. Cf., Nandi (1979-80): 82-92.
121. *Ibid.*
122. Cf., *Kāvyaprakāśa*, *sūtra*, 2.
123. *Anukaraṇa*, as a concept may, to an extent, remind of the phenomenon of *rūpa* and its differentiation into *pratirūpa*, in which the forms are considered in the Vedic texts and later.
124. Misra (1988): 150; 160-161.
125. Pathak and Misra (1986): 288.
126. Sankuka explains *anukaraṇa* through the *citra turaga nyāya*, which means painting of a horse in a picture creating the impression of horse's presence even if the real horse is missing and we know it. The identity (*pratīti*) following from such a situation is substantive even if it might not be defined by the conventional means of cognition (*samyag*), false knowledge (*mithyā*), doubtful knowledge (*samśaya*), and knowledge of similarity (*sādṛśya*). *Anukaraṇa* thus represents resurgence of *mūlaprakṛti* by an artist, and this capacity is nurtured by means (*hetu*) of creativity, (*kṛtittva*), experience (*anubhava*) and practice (*abhyāsa*). *Anukaraṇa* is explained by Abhinavagupta in terms of *anukirtana* (re-perception) and therefore as *anuvyavasaya*. But Sankuka brings it to the level of *rasa*: *anukaraṇa rūpatvādeva ca nāmāntareṇa vyapadiṣṭo rasaḥ*. Abhinavagupta says that a representation can be only something perceived by means of cognition: *kiñcit adhi pramāṇena no'palambham anukaraṇam iti*. According to Sankuka, three elements, namely, cause (*hetu*), effects (*karya*) and *sahacārins* (complementaries) may explain the notions ingrained in the process of *anukaraṇa*. He concedes that even a 'mistaken cognition' (*mithyājñāna*) may be endowed with 'causal efficiency' (*arthakiyā kāritva*) for a realisation. In support we have the *Pramāṇavārtika* (III.57) of Dharmakirti which has it as follows: *maṇipradīpa prabhayormaṇi budhyābhidhāvateḥ/mithyājñānaviśeṣe'pi viśeṣo'rthakriyāmprati*.
127. R.B. Patankar (1987), 'Madhusudan Saraswati's Sri Bhagavad Bhaktirasayana', in Daya Krishna, ed., *India's Intellectual Tradition*, Delhi, pp. 159-161.
128. *Ibid.*
129. For *sādṛśya*, cf., also the *Citralkṣaṇa*, II.8: *atyantasadṛśam*. Also, Sivaramamurti (1978): 118-121.
130. According to the *Vāstusūtra Upaniṣad* (VI. 3-4; V.20) and its commentary, *śilpa* brings about similitude with the help of nine elements, which consist of: composition, ornamentation, gestures, weapons, postures, vehicles, secondary divinities, enemies and devotees. Cf., Boner *et al.* (2000): 97-98. The commentary on the text (V.20) also describes the coming up of a manifestation in terms of *sankalpa* and *viklapa*, which are supposed to represent a cycle of the senses. An image comes to its manifestation passing through the stages of imagination to faith, to conceptualisation of reality (*sattābhāva*), to the right emotion for it and thus arises the desired 'image corresponding to the archetypes'. *Anukaraṇa*, though not specifically included here in details, seems to rest in them as an undercurrent to make an image correspond to the archetype.

131. *paraceṣṭānukaraṇād hāsaḥ samupajāyate*, Bharata's *Nāṭyaśāstra*, VII.10.
132. *Abhinavabhāratī* (Gaekwad Oriental Series), I, pp. 36-37.
133. Cf., Misra (1994)/2: 105-106.
134. *apāre kāvyasaṃsāre kavirekaḥ Prajāpatiḥ/yathāsmai rocate viśvam tathaiva parivartate//* Or, *niyatikṛtaniyamarahitāṃ hlādaikamanyaparatantrāṃ/navarasa rucirāṃ nirmitam ādadhāti Bhāratī keverjayati//*
135. *bhāvāncetanānapi cetanvaccetanāncetanavat/vyavahārayati yatheṣṭam sukaviḥ kāvye svatantrayā//*
136. *Nirupādāna sambhāram bhittāveva tanvate/Jagat citram namastasmai kalānāthāya śūline//*
137 *Aparājitapṛcchā*, Ch. 209 (*pratimā pramāṇam*); *Samarāngaṇa Sūtradhāra*, Ch. 78.17-20.
138. *Ibid.*, Ch. 225; 226.9-13; 210.1-36, etc.
139. For a detailed discussion on some of these, including *pramāṇa, rasa, rekhā*, the typologies of anthropomorphic forms in texts, cf., Sivaramamurti (1978): 75ff; 115ff; 129ff; 75-83; 106ff.
140. The *Aparājitapṛcchā*, in different chapters emphasises on the marks (*lakṣaṇas*) of different types of buildings, *vimana, prasada*, sculptures, etc. Cf., *Ibid.*, Chs. 210, 234, 222, 225. So do the other *śilpa* texts like the *Samarāngaṇa Sūtradhāra, Viśvakarma Vāstuśāstra*, etc.
141. Pathak (1989): 593.
142. *Ibid.*, pp. 591-595. Pathak says that *lakṣaṇā* and *vyañjanā* in poetry are connected with the 'iconology of symbols' and 'owe their origin to *lakṣaṇa* or *añji* in the Vedic literature.
143. *Ibid.*, 592: *lāñchanādvā laṣtarevā syāt prepsā-karmaṇaḥ lagyate vāa syād=śleṣa-karmaṇaḥ*, 'Lakṣmī is so called because of the mark; alternatively, it is derived from *laṣ*, "to desire", or *lag*, "to stick"'.
144. Cf., Tripathi (1988): 142-143.
145. The Commentary reads as follows: 'As from the sacred chants the legends are derived, in the same manner the knowing sculptors represent the features of images, and so their forms become visible. When attractive gestures (*hāva-bhāva*) and other states become visible in the image (it indeed) represents the manifest form (*vyakta rūpa*). The worshippers realise a perfect feeling through the ... form, by means of which they do their meditation. This is the application.' Boner *et al.* (2000): 71. These three stages, as involved in *pratibhā*, from conceptualisation to emanation by the sculptor and its realisation, seem similar to the three states discussed by Abhinavagupta in his commentary, cited above. The term *pratibhā* I, however, is not mentioned in this passage from the *Vāstusūtra Upaniṣad*.
146. According to Tripathi, '... *lakṣaṇa* ... is imbued with the process of observing the reality, realizing through deep concentration of mind or meditation (*samādhi* or *yoga*), the very characteristic nature of it and again expressing it either in a metaphorical way, because direct expression does not cope with the total inherent meaning, or in some other indirect way, for the reason that the intensity of the situation can best be realised through creative distortion'. Tripathi (1988): 136.

147. Bhattacharya (1974): 73. Nine such postures are described in the *Citrasūtra* of the *Viṣṇudharmottara* followed by a discussion on the *kṣayavṛddhi* or 'foreshortening': all being the techniques employed in depictions. These different postures are enumerated as *ṛjvāgata, anṛju, śacīkṛtaśarīra, ardhavilocana, pārśvagata, parāvṛtta, pṛṣṭhagata, purāvṛtta,* and *samanata.* Sivaramamurti explains these different postures on the basis of the *Abhilaṣitārthacintāmaṇi* (I.3.189-190). He concludes that all 'the nine postures ... are the same straight *ṛju,* viewed from different angles, to show the same figure, with the portions of the body hidden from view in different proportions, causing foreshortening, and on that account styled in different nomenclatures'. Sivaramamurti (1978): 53-56. He further says that 'The central vertical line (*brahmasūtra*), in relation to the vertical sidelines (*bahissūtra*), determines *ṛju, ardhṛju* and the rest'. *Ibid.*: 54-55.
148. Pathak (1989), 591: Pathak says that, 'The semantic of the words has gradually evolved from the iconology of symbols. The two powers of the words, *lakṣaṇā,* the figurative expression and *vyañjanā,* the suggestive meaning are rooted in the iconology of symbols.'
149. Cf., *Kāvya Prakāśa,* ullasa II, *sūtra* 7-9. It says that a word that directly conveys the conventional meaning is *vācaka; lakṣaṇā* is where meaning is conveyed through an intermediary channel: *mukhyenāmukhyo'rtho lakṣyate yat sa āropitaḥ śabdavyāpāraḥ sāntarārthaniṣṭho lakṣaṇā.*
150. Ghoshal Sastri (1973): 42-43.
151. *Ibid.*, 57. According to the *Tantravārtika* (1.4.22) quoted in *Rasaprakāśa* commentary, *lakṣaṇā,* on its accord, leads to cognition that is 'essentially comprehended with invariable concomitance to the thing or the idea expressed through it' *abhidheyavinābhute pratītirlakṣaṇocyate.*
152. *Sarveṣām prāyaśo'rthānām vyañjakatvamapīṣyate.*
153. See *Kāvyaprakāśa, sūtra* 27, 28: 'Where an Indicative word (*lakṣaṇā*) is used to suggest certain intended idea or purpose, we do not find out that idea from any other quarters, but from that particular word only. There is no other function, except the Suggestion, to that end ... because it is neither the "expressed sense" (*abhidhā*) nor Indication (*lakṣaṇā*). It is conveyed here that "suggestion" (*vyañjanā*) transforms the meaning from the stuff that may convey it less artistically than when *vyañjanā* takes it over.'
154. Cf., Sastri (1987): 1. The translation of the passage from the *Sūtrālankāra* reads as follows: 'The thirty-two *lakṣaṇa*s and the eighty *anuvyañjana*s adorn him and make him resemble a painting'. Sastri adds that, 'The description seems indeed to depend upon a painting. Several of the expressions used in this context, as His body resembles a mass of molten gold (in its colours) ... can be identified in the *Citralakṣaṇa* (of Nagnajit).' *Ibid.*
155. See Chapter 1, above.
156. For instance, see the discussions about the voidness of the world's appearance and the same of all the *dharmas,* 'qualities', or 'characteristics', *śūnyatānutpādādvaya niḥsvabhāvalakṣaṇam sa dharmāṇām, Lankāvatāra,* p. 31 (Nalanda Edition 1963). Also: *tadyathā mahāmate citrakarakṛtapradeśā animnonnatāḥ santo nimnonnatā bālaiḥ kalpyante, evameva mahāmate anāgatena'dhvani tīrthyadṛṣṭi vāsanāśaya prativikalpapuṣṭāḥ. Ibid.*, p. 38.

157. Cf., Dharmakirti's *Pramāṇavārtika*, III.57: *abhiprāyaviśamvadāt api bhrānte pramāṇatā/gatipyantadṛṣṭā pakṣaścayakṛtottaraḥ//*
158. For details regarding *kāyas*, cf., Falk (1943): 151-154; 108-125; for *rūpakāya*, *Ibid.*, 113ff.
159. The making of a *pañjara* was supposed to be a ritual act simulating the process of creation: a creation that had a microcosmic reference point. In this entire setting, the *vṛttta* was not merely a spherical shape but a symbol of the Universe as well as the Time, thus constituting the dimensions of Time and Space (*svṛtta kālaḥ; vṛttam iti viśvam*) with the *bindu* immanent in its centre like the *ātman* in the body and carrying within it the supportive base (*kṣetrādhāra*) from which originated the forms juxtaposed along the lines (*rekhānvaya sarvanggāni nyāsaya*). In that manner, a *pañjara* purposely and consciously integrated the *ādhibhūta* with the *ādhidaivata*, the fundamental elements of those gods who were being materialised.
160. *Vakroktijīvita* quoted in the *Kāvyaprakāśa*, Cf., Misra (1998): 102-103. His discussions encompass a whole range of aesthetic experience right from the point of its revelation in the *citta* to its inspired transformation into a work of art.
161. The *Citralakṣaṇa* of Srikumara IV.114, 116: (Bhattacharya 1974:75) refers to painting as *citrābhāsa* and *bhāvacitra* as one which is true to nature and endowed with various sentiments. *Aujjvalya* (colour) is its merit.
162. Abhinavagupta explains that 'as the bashful behaviour of maidens heightens the effect of their feelings, so the luster, which has the liquid quality of intangibility, is the characteristic adornment of a poetic expression. The beauty of the feeling which arises from passion and is expressed through various gestures is like the *chāyā* found in the works of great artists'. It may be further stated that this *chāyā* is comparable to the luster (*lāvaṇya*) that emanates from a *muktā*, 'pearl': *muktāphaleṣucchāyāyā yattaralattvam-ivāntaram/pratibhāti yadangeṣu tallāvaṇyamihocyate//*
163. *Sūtras* II.23; III.1-2; IV. 1-2, etc.
164. Gnoli describes *camatkāra* as a word denoting 'aesthetic wonder or surprise' in a technical sense. He says, 'It was first introduced by Utpaladeva, and it relates to the sudden rupture of levels, "the cessation of a world ... and its sudden replacement by a new dimension of reality'. Gnoli, as quoted in Bäumer (2004), 'Conceptual Roots of Aesthetics in Kashmir Saivism', (an unpublished paper presented in the seminar on 'India and Asia: Glimpses of Aesthetic Discourse). This I.I.C. (Delhi) seminar was held at the IIAS, Shimla in October 2004.
165. *Pratibhā* is variously translated as 'intuitive light', 'illuminating inspiration' or 'illuminating intuition'. In Utpaladeva (*Īśvarapratyabhijña kārikā* I.7.1), it is the 'consciousness devoid of succession or limit', and it is further explained in the *vṛtti* in terms of *ābhāsa* (internal light) that lie imbibed in the conscious 'self'. *Pratibhā* and *camatkṛti* occur together in the *Parātrīśikā Vivaraṇa* (Mangalaśloka 3) of Abhinavagupta. For the references above, and the translations of the terms *pratibhā*, by Torella, and Dyczkowski, mentioned in this note, see, Bäumer (2004), *op. cit.*

166. *Ibid.*
167. *Vakroktijīvita* (Delhi: Atmaram & Sons): 143; also pp. 13, 48, 140. Kuntaka proposes that the element of wonder (*camatkāra*) in poetry stems from the illuminating inspiration (*pratibhā*) of a poet.
168. The *kārayitrī pratibhā* is composed of *sahajā*, *āhāryā* and *aupadeśikī*. According to Rajasekhara, *pratibhā* is not to be confused with the *kāvyaśakti* which actually is the 'agent of action or subject' (*kartṛ-rūpā*) while *pratibhā* (along with *vyutpatti*) is *karmarūpā*, 'the object desired to be achieved by a doer'. The *bhāvayitrī pratibhā* 'completes the poet's meaning. It ... brings forth the poetic imagination and without it a poetic composition appears fruitless'. For a detailed discussion on *pratibhā* in the *Kāvyamīmāṃsā* of Rajasekhara, cf., Parashar (2000): 43-48.
169. *Samarāngaṇa Sūtradhāra*, Ch. 44.14: *pratyutpannamatiryaḥ syād bāhyataḥ sthapatistathā/karmakāle na muhyeta sa prajñānenopabṛnhitaḥ//*
170. *Ibid.*, verse 15.
171. The verse reads as follows: Having seen his wonderful abode (*sanniveśa*) situated on the mountains of Elapura, the astonished immortals who travel in celestial cars always take much thought, saying, 'This is the abode of Svayambhū-Śiva and no artificially made dwelling ...' Verily, even the *śilpin* who built it felt astonishment saying, 'The utmost perseverance would fail to accomplish such a work again; aho! How has it been achieved by me (so non-chalantly: *akasmāt*) ...' Cf., Fleet, J.F. (1984), 'Sanskrit and Old Canarese Inscriptions', *Indian Antiquary*, 12 (Delhi, reprinted), p. 159, lines 14-17; translation, p. 163. The sense of wonder is writ large in this description about the work, which is remarkable on its own right.
172. *Samarāngaṇa Sūtradhāra*, Ch. 44 (*sthapati lakṣaṇa*): 14. The text describes the qualifications of a *sthapati* in twenty-one verses, with little information on his imaginative skills.
173. *Aparājitapṛcchā*, Ch. 50 (*sūtradhara lakṣaṇa*): 1-24.
174. Compositional structure of form in Indian images has received attention of scholars since the sixties of the nineteenth century starting with Gordon Austin (1864), through Hadaway (1914-15), T.A.G. Rao (1920), Boner (1962-1982), Ruelius (1968-74), Ganapati Sastri (1970), M. Miester (1988), Jones (1981), Kapila Vatsyayan (1983), and Maxwell (1988) and others making significant enquiries into it. Mosteller (1991) similarly makes a study of 'systemic complexities' in the variation-oriented formalistic compositions. Cf., Misra (1998): 103-106.
175. Boner *et al.* (2000).
176. *Vāstusūtra Upaniṣad*, I.8 and commentary.
177. Cf., Boner *et al.* (2000): 63.
178. *Vastusūtra Upanisad*, II. 22, comm.
179. *Ibid.*, *sūtra* VI.16, 18.
180. *Ibid.*, VI. 4.
181. While describing the features of the different divinities, etc. the *Citrasūtra* (42.46) of the *Viṣṇudharmottara Purāṇa* interestingly refers to the features that may characterise an artisan in a figure. It says that artisans (*karmakaraḥ*) should be shown preoccupied with the instruments of their trade (*svakarmopaskara*).

Appendix

MASONS' MARKS

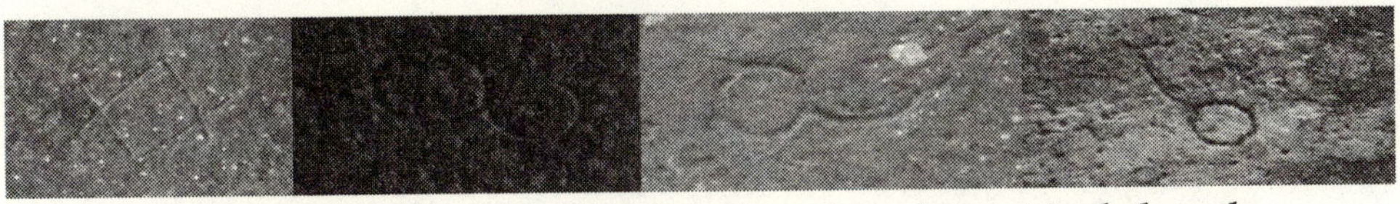

A photographic reproduction of Masons' marks on Mughal works at Fatehpur Sikri

The *Śukranīti* refers to artisans' distinguishing 'marks' (*cinha, lakṣaṇa, anka*) thrice in prescribing their use to identify artisans and their occupations,[1] and interestingly enough, the symbols, identifiable as 'masons' marks', occur quite distinctly and sometimes profusely on the monuments of ancient India. They figure on monuments contemporary to the *Śukranīti* and even before and after its writing, i.e., from second century BC[2] down to the seventeenth century. Therefore, it is likely that the *Śukranīti*, in its time, came to record what apparently had been an established masonic convention amongst the artisans. These marks, as they occur, are made of dashes, dots, circles, squares, triangles or their overlapping forms and other formations derived from them. Besides such geometrical forms, they also represent vegetal or faunal forms, like a flower or a fish; or the instrumental devices, such as: a lance, trident or a bow. In size, they generally measure nearly 2.00 inches or more, and they mostly figure singly. Sometimes, in some rare cases, they occur in pairs too.[3] They are found engraved on stones almost anywhere in several archaeological monuments: on the quarries, pavement, steps, walls, pillars, dressed masonry stones, different architectural parts, borders of pedestals of images, and at different heights. At Khajuraho, for instance, they occur even at the height of forty to fifty feet.

As no articulately expressive meaning seems to emerge from them, at the first look, these marks appear like incoherent graffitis. They may even be considered as graphemes because they figure as encoded characters in different shapes and sizes, often representing the alphabets of ancient Brahmi script in fragments. They may best be described as masons' marks because that is what they appropriately seem to imply as they occur on scores of monuments in northern India in Uttar Pradesh, Madhya Pradesh, Delhi and Kashmir, and in Pakistan at Lahore and Abbotabad.[4] Their validity is vouchsafed by the *Śukranīti* and their association with masons seems indicated by the fact that they are engraved on different parts of the monuments of different order, such as *stūpa*, temples, monasteries, mosques, tombs, civil buildings, forts and palaces and even on the steps of staircase of a *vāpī*, 'pond'.

Different marks occur on the same monument indicating that artists belonging to many different clans or collectives generally worked together on a single monument, as it progressed to its conclusion. Often, the same marks occur on two separate monuments constructed wide apart in space and time. In such cases, since the hiatus in space and time in their instances is wide enough – sometimes centuries apart from each other – it may be safely assumed that the marks represent institutions rather than individuals. That they would represent individuals is unlikely for the simple reason that an individual's life span would not be commensurate with the span of time which the particular marks seem to cover. The marks may thus be regarded as institutional: representing organisations, schools, *gharāna*, guild or clan rather than the individuals. The cluster of disparate marks on the same monuments may, therefore, indicate the distinctive identity of different clans, and collectives (guilds?), and their scion who combined to build the monument collectively. Often, the names of *śilpī*s occur on the monuments simultaneously with masons' marks.[5] Such occurrences may indicate a collaborative exercise in works where the *śilpī* was represented not by his mark but by his name, even as the rest of the stone masons, possibly less distinguished than the *śilpī* in question, identified themselves by the marks of their clans or guilds. As the texts, including those on *śilpa*, generally do not speak about masons' marks it may appear that they came into use out of *śilpī*s' adherence to a professional code of identity as practised in their respective groups, which eventually became a masonic convention. Or, the marks might represent *śilpīs*' resistance to anonymity implying a coded assertion, though muted, of their identity.

The marks' singularity lies in their being a non-formal source of masons' or artists' identities and signature, especially in respect of their collective identities. They are non-formal in the sense that they neither represent any organised body of text nor compose a formal text of encrypted words or sentences. In their occurrence or typology they have no connection with the *śilpaśāstra*s or other secular or religious texts, as they stand independent of them in the form of symbolic entities *sui generis*. Yet they are significant, as they tend to juxtapose a work with its maker(s), asserting, as it were, the artists' presence at the work-sites and their proximity to the works which they etched with their signature engraved in the form of such marks. This is especially true in case of the Brahmi letters used as masons' marks. The marks are also the silent proclamations of artists' specific work on the monuments which they built. Only that such presence and connections are muted in essence and coded in character. The marks thus seem significant in eroding the notion that the artists in ancient India were not given to self-expression.

With a history extending over several centuries, the masons' marks cannot be dismissed summarily. But they do not have the kind of flourish one finds in epigraphs eulogising an artist or in those one- or two-line image inscriptions that extol the artist who made those images. They also are less coherent than the names of particular artists found carved on particular works[6]: a sculpture, a pillar, a wall or some other architectural piece in a temple or a monument.[7] Their muted character perhaps goes to show that the marks may represent the collectives or groups of ordinary workers whose status in the hierarchy did not permit their exclusive identity in the fashion of a great master. Yet, in explicitly engraving the marks of their respective institutional identity, they apparently found a way to record their presence as well as their role in works. Sometimes, the marks show minor variations from their major identifiable types. Such cases may indicate distinctions between the scions of the original group who diversified or moved away from the clan and yet continued to maintain a link with their original identity. As for the multiplicity of marks on the same monument, they may represent different groups specialising in different skills: some in carving creepers, others in figure work and so on.

These marks may not be confused with the missives, like *pachama* (*paścima*, 'west') *vāyavī* (*vāyavya*, 'northwestern quarter'), *niriti* (*nairṛitya*, 'southwest'), pertaining to directional or location codes engraved for artisans' benefit in assembling a monument. Such missives are engraved on stone blocks to mark their eventual location on the body of the temple.[8]

While missives and graphics of different kind occur on stones and monuments at different places, the masons' marks stand out as a class apart from them. As the instances of such graphics we have the *hastalekhas*[9] at Khajuraho,[10] where a miniature sketch of an architectural or figural form is engraved probably to serve as a guide to its assembly and installation according to the plan.[11] Or, as at Pacharai (near Mahua in Shivpuri district of Madhya Pradesh), we have the entire plan of a temple with its *garbha, maṇḍapa* and colonnade set out with chisel marks – on a huge slab on the ground – to facilitate raising the temple according to the chiselled orientation of its parts and their alignment.[12] Masons' marks are different from all these but they do afford evidence on less distinguished, ordinary masons, their collectives and their indeterminate signature etched on stones.

The range of their occurrence is remarkable, and indicates the versatility of stonemasons in their profession. For instance, they occur on:

- the Dhameka *stūpa* at Sarnath, near Varanasi in the sixth century (Plate 1, Figures 1-38),[13]
- on the temple and its enclosure at Padhavali (Distt. Morena) in the tenth century (Plate 2, Figures 1-53),
- on a monastery at Ranod (Distt. Shivpuri, M.P.) in the tenth century (Plate 3, Figures 1- 72, Plate 4, Figures 73-111), and on the steps of the *vapi* (tank) in front of it now known as Sas Bahu pond (Plate 4, Figures 1-14),
- on the Śiva temple at Bhojpur (Distt. Raisen, M.P.) in early eleventh century,[14]
- on the Sas Bahu temple at Gwalior (AD 1093),
- on the Kakanmath temple at Suhania (Distt. Morena) in the eleventh century (Plate 5, Figures 1-25),
- on steps of a pond at Tilori (Distt. Morena) in the twelfth century (Plate 6, Figures 1-46),
- on the circular temple at Mitaoli (Distt. Morena, M.P.) in the thirteenth century (Plate 7, Figures 1-78, Plate 8, Figures 79-115),
- on the mosque and gate in Jaunpur (Ataladevi and Lal Darwaza) in fourteenth century (Plates 9-10),
- on the Mughal forts of Delhi (Plate 11, Figures 1-6), sixteenth century,
- on the Mughal fort at Allahabad (Plate 14, Figures 1-15), sixteenth century,
- on the Mughal fort at Attock (Pakistan), on its Mullahi Tola Gate, sixteenth century,
- on the Humayun tombs at Delhi, sixteenth century,
- on Akbar's tomb at Sikandra, sixteenth century,
- on the Taj Mahal at Agra[15] (Plate 12, Figures 1-69), seventeenth century,

- on the tomb of Khusro's mother in the Khusro Bagh in Allahabad, seventeenth century,
- on the Mughal palace at Fatehpur Sikri, its courtyard, walls, pillars, etc., sixteenth century,
- on the Mughal pavilions, i.e., Shalimar Bagh, Nishat Bagh in Kashmir, seventeenth century,
- on the Mughal mosque in Lahore (Badshahi Masjid) (Plate 11, Figures 7-9), seventeenth century,
- on the Mughal mosque in Delhi (Jami Masjid) (Plate 11, Figure 10-19),
- on the monuments in Kashmir (Patthar ki Masjid) (Plate 13, Figures).[16] sixteenth-seventeenth century,
- Mughal marks on the Aśokan pillar at the Ridge in Delhi (Plate 11, Figure 5).
- on the Safdarjaung tomb at Delhi (Plate 11, Figure 20), seventeenth century.

A brief description of the contents of such marks follows.[17] Beginning with the marks on the Dhameka *stūpa* at Sarnath, it seems that letters or alphabets of Brahmi script have been liberally used as marks. These letters may be the abbreviated form of the names of masons on the stones they quarried, cut, chiselled, carved or handled in whatever ways. The marks on the Dhameka *stūpa* may tentatively be identified as follows: two human figures (17), arrow heads (33, 34), leaf (12), a boat (30), a lattice (9), *indrayasti* (4), an axe (19), a vase with a bowl (35).[18] But the repertory changed with times as more marks came into circulation.

Masons' marks seem to generally fall into groups consisting of flora, fauna, geometrical forms, weapons and instruments, and ornamental or auspicious symbols. Generally, only one symbol is found engraved on a stone piece, but on occasions more than one symbol may also occur together, as for instance at Sarnath (no 17). Flora is comparatively rare, occurring at Padhavali (43), and Tilori (5: a garland) but faunal representations are quite numerous. Thus, fish occurs at Ranod (15), Tilori (13) and Mitaoli (12, 69, 56); scorpion at Ranod (14), Tilori (24, 40) and Mitaoli (8, 18,103); bird at Tilori (11) and Mitaoli (24, 47, 51, 67); frog at Mitaoli (77, 95); and snake at Padhavali (34, 21). Human figures alone or in pairs are also found used by masons and they are known from Sarnath, Padhavali (1), Ranod (12), the Sas Bahu pond at Ranod (11), Tilori (6) and Mitaoli (55).

Geometrical forms seem to have been quite popular as masons' marks, second only to the Brahmi alphabets. We have circles of different kinds: with a dot (Padhavali 19, Tilori 21), or, with a cross within (Ranod 49, Mitaoli 28), or, with three vertical lines (Tilori 20), or, with a flower (Padhavali 43), etc. Sometimes a circle occurs in combination with a loop or line as in

Padhavali (12, 20, 16, 35), Ranod (18), Tilori (3) and Mitaoli (10, 58, 34, 37, 21, 53, 54, 65, 68, 88, 89). The wide variety in the forms of the circle as found in the marks may allow the speculation that as a group branched off from its parent body it introduced variations indicating its loyalty as well as distinction from the parent body. The symbol of circle continued being used till the seventeenth century. Triangles, square, hexagon, parallelogram and the forms derived from such shapes are recurrent in the repertory of masons' marks during the Sultanate and Mughal times.

Weapons, instruments and devices also figure liberally among masons' marks. These include a mace (Padhavali 39), axe (Ranod 34), trident (Suhania 7, Tilori 25, Mitaoli 31, 78), elephant's goad (Mitaoli 11, 105), bow and arrow (Mitaoli 97, Tilori 12, 18), double-edged object (Tilori 17), lance head (Tilori 22) and arrow heads, alone (Tilori 12, 18, Mitaoli 63, 57) or with a leaf (Tilori 46). Among the instruments we may also mention what appears to be a weighing balance (Ranod 95) and *damaru,* a hand-held percussion instrument tied with knots intended to produce sound by movement (Tilori 16, 33). Lattice is often seen among the marks, as for instance, at Mitaoli (30, 110).

Among the symbols traditionally taken as auspicious, we may include fish, already mentioned, besides conch (Ranod 56, Tilori 34, Mitaoli 100), *svastika* (Padhavali 41, Mitaoli 114), *mithuna* (Sarnath 17), cross (Padhavali 1, 7) and a flag (Suhania 3). At Ranod (66), we also have what appears to be a cart and wheel. Apart from these, one may also identify in the masons' marks the objects of nature, like a river (Mitaoli 76), a hill with a cross or loop (Padhavali 14, 12, 16, 20, 35) or perhaps even an ornament like an armlet (Tilori 25).

These marks continued in use from sixth century to thirteenth century when they were reused in the Islamic buildings under the Sultans, as at Jaunpur or under the Mughals in different buildings of their time. The use of masons' marks up to seventeenth century in those buildings seems to bear out the unbroken continuity of a masonic tradition, indicating that the masons' community easily graduated to undertake new challenges in architectural enterprises as design and functions of buildings changed with times, marking several modifications. This transition only corroborates the professional skills of the masonic community, which seems to have been both capable and fit enough to transform their skills to suit the challenges of the ever new requirements that came by. New marks had also made their appearance by now. Yet, among them, geometrical forms besides symbols like star, circle, fish, goad, arrow head, axe, lattice, *svastika*, cross, and *damaru*, among others, continued to occur, with some variations. New marks, not seen before but apparent in the Islamic buildings, also came into use, indicating that the adherence to older tradition of recording artisan's signature still continued. These new marks consisted of knotted loops (Agra, Plate 12: 69), a *svastika* with a cross (Agra 3), a looped pentagon (Agra 10), a circle with four loops inside (Agra 40), or a circle divided into two equal halves by a Roman S (Allahabad, Plate 14: 11, 15). Floral designs came up now in profusion (Agra 16-19, 32-33, 67). Human figures are rare now, as before, though sometimes they do occur (Srinagar Plate 13: motif in the second line, middle).

We may conclude our description with the mention of an interesting graffiti consisting of Brahmi alphabets *ga* and *ṇa* inscribed below a Gaṇa figure on one of the subsidiary shrines of the *pañcāyatana* Kakanmath temple at Suhania (eleventh century). Apparently, the two-letter graffiti (reading *gaṇa*) below the Gaṇa figure is redundant and superfluous as a label, as the figure is identifiable on its own, iconographically. Such a labelling is absent everywhere else in Suhania. But, as the term *gaṇa* also implied a 'guild' it seems possible that the artist in his robust humour had indeed played with the word. He cleverly punned on the term using it as a label to identify the figure yet playfully underscoring the presence of a guild or clan (*gaṇa*) to which he belonged! The instance may indicate meanings in masons' marks hidden between the lines (symbols!).

PLATE 1

Masons' marks on Dhameka *Stūpa*, Sarnath (Distt. Varanasi), Uttar Pradesh (Sixth century)

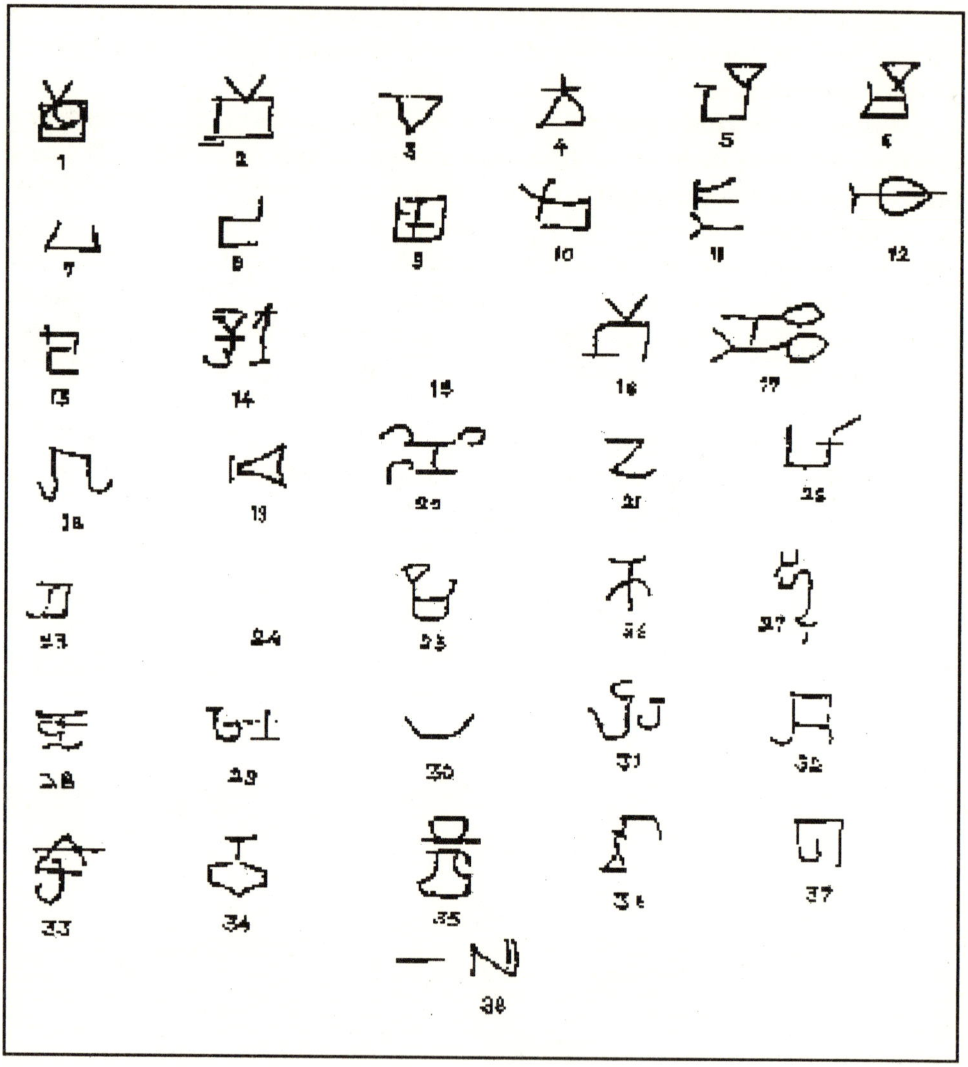

PLATE 2

Masons' marks at Padhavali (Distt. Morena): Temple and fortress, Madhya Pradesh (Tenth century)

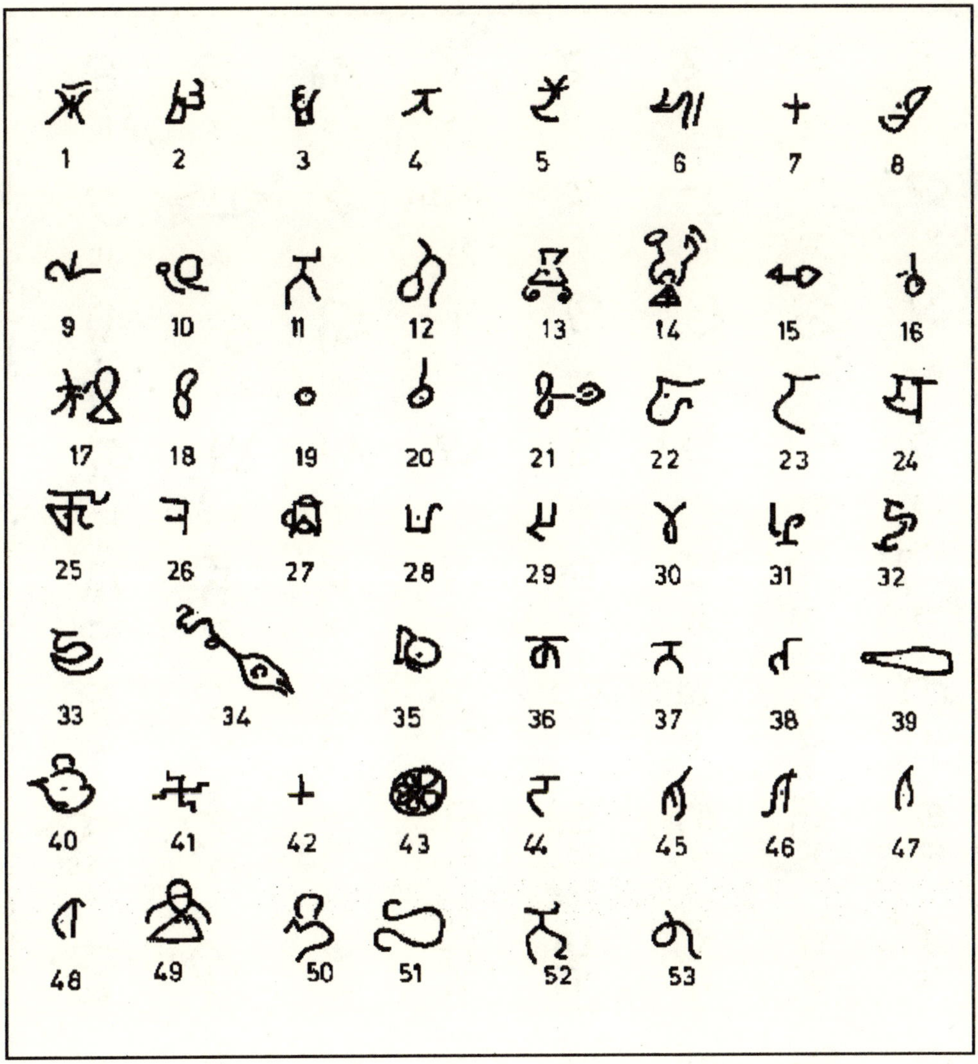

PLATE 3

Masons' marks on Ranod monastery (Distt. Shivpuri), Madhya Pradesh (Tenth century)

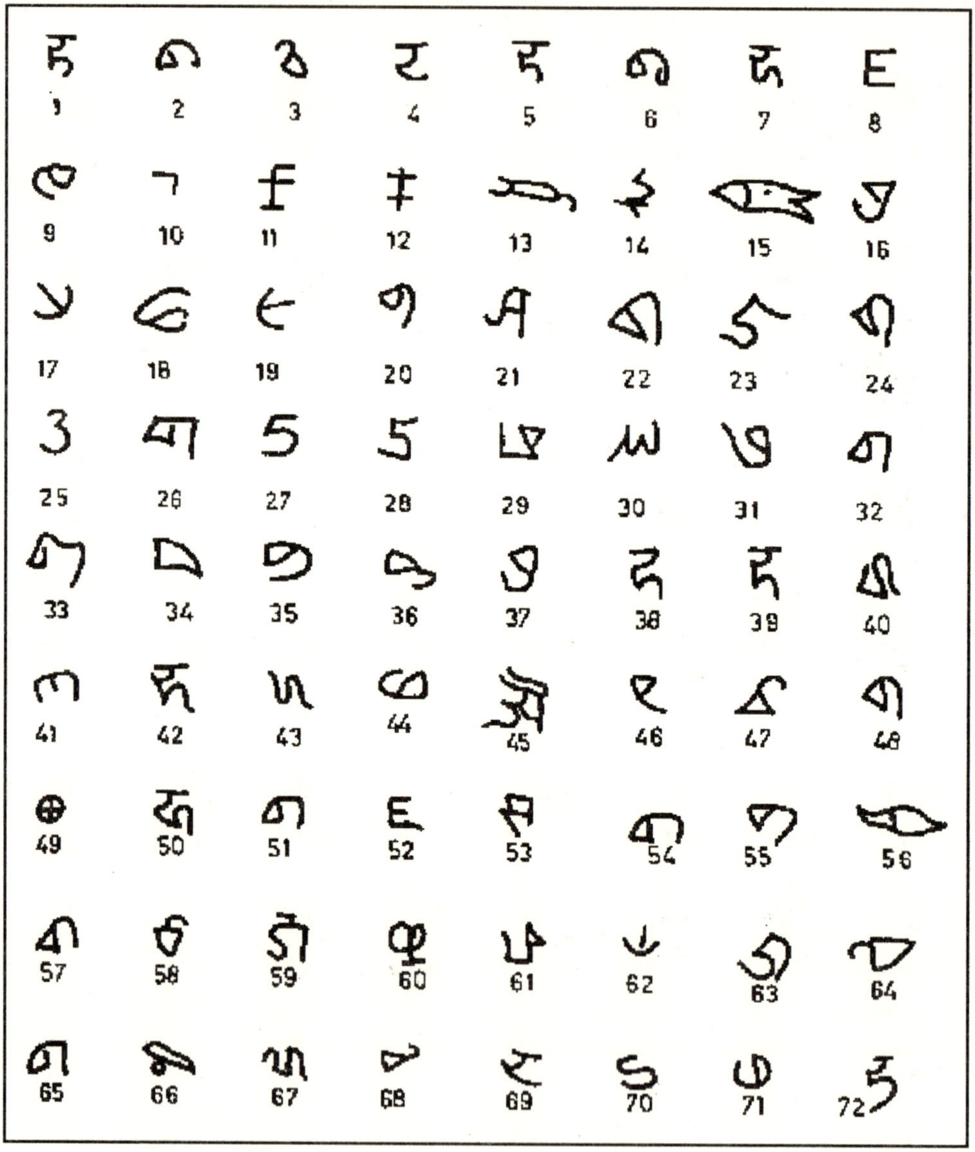

PLATE 4

Masons' marks on Ranod monastery (Distt. Shivpuri), Madhya Pradesh (Tenth century)

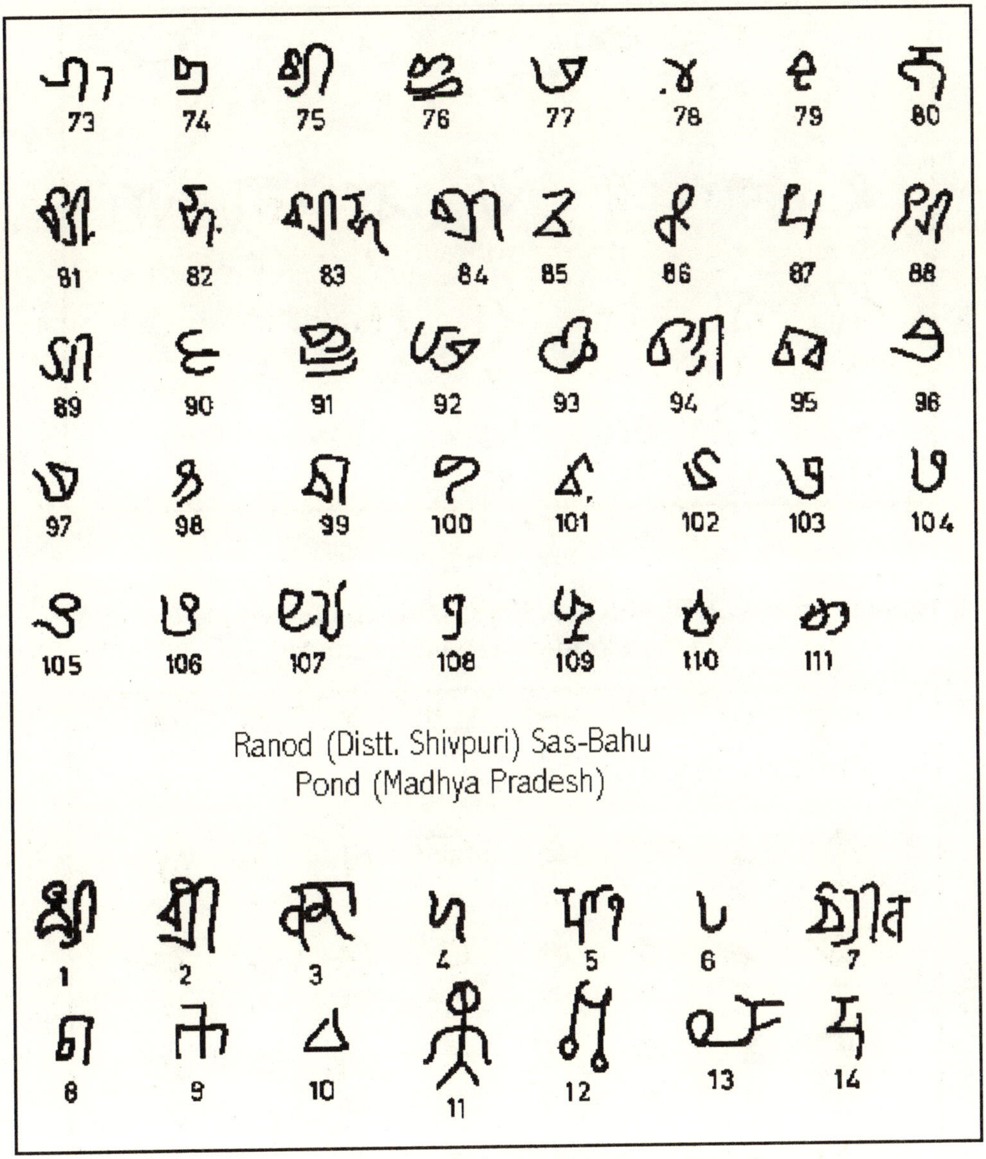

PLATE 5

Masons' marks at Suhania: Kakanmath temple (Distt. Morena), Madhya Pradesh (Eleventh century)

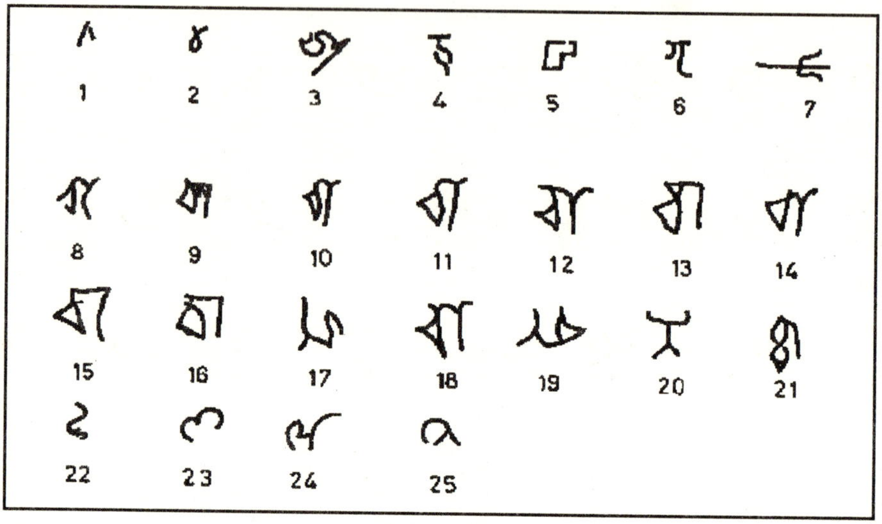

PLATE 6

Masons' marks at Tilori (Distt. Bhind), the ruined temple complex: Madhya Pradesh (Twelfth century)

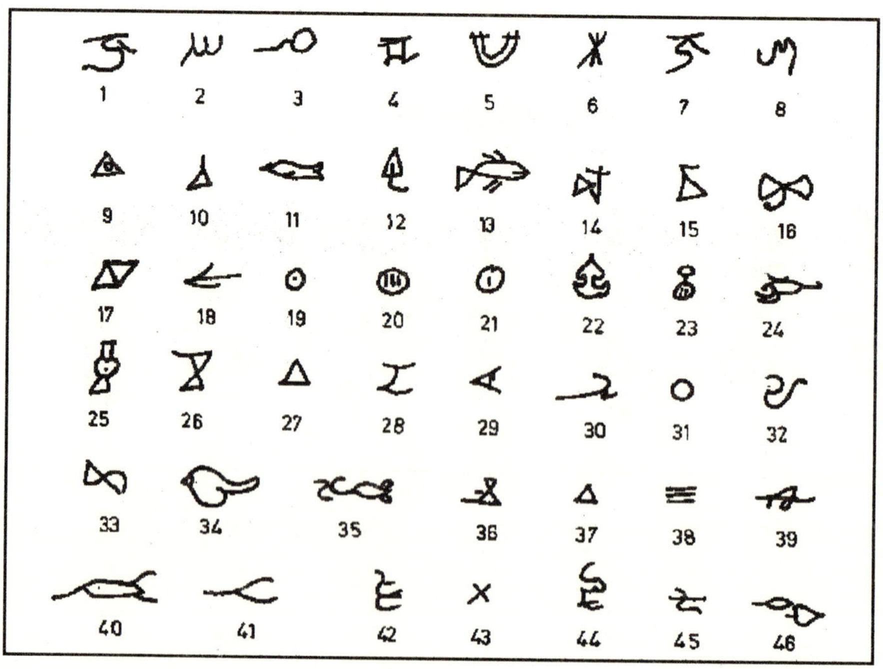

PLATE 7

Masons' marks at Mitaoli (Distt. Morena), Circular temple complex: Madhya Pradesh (Thirteenth century)

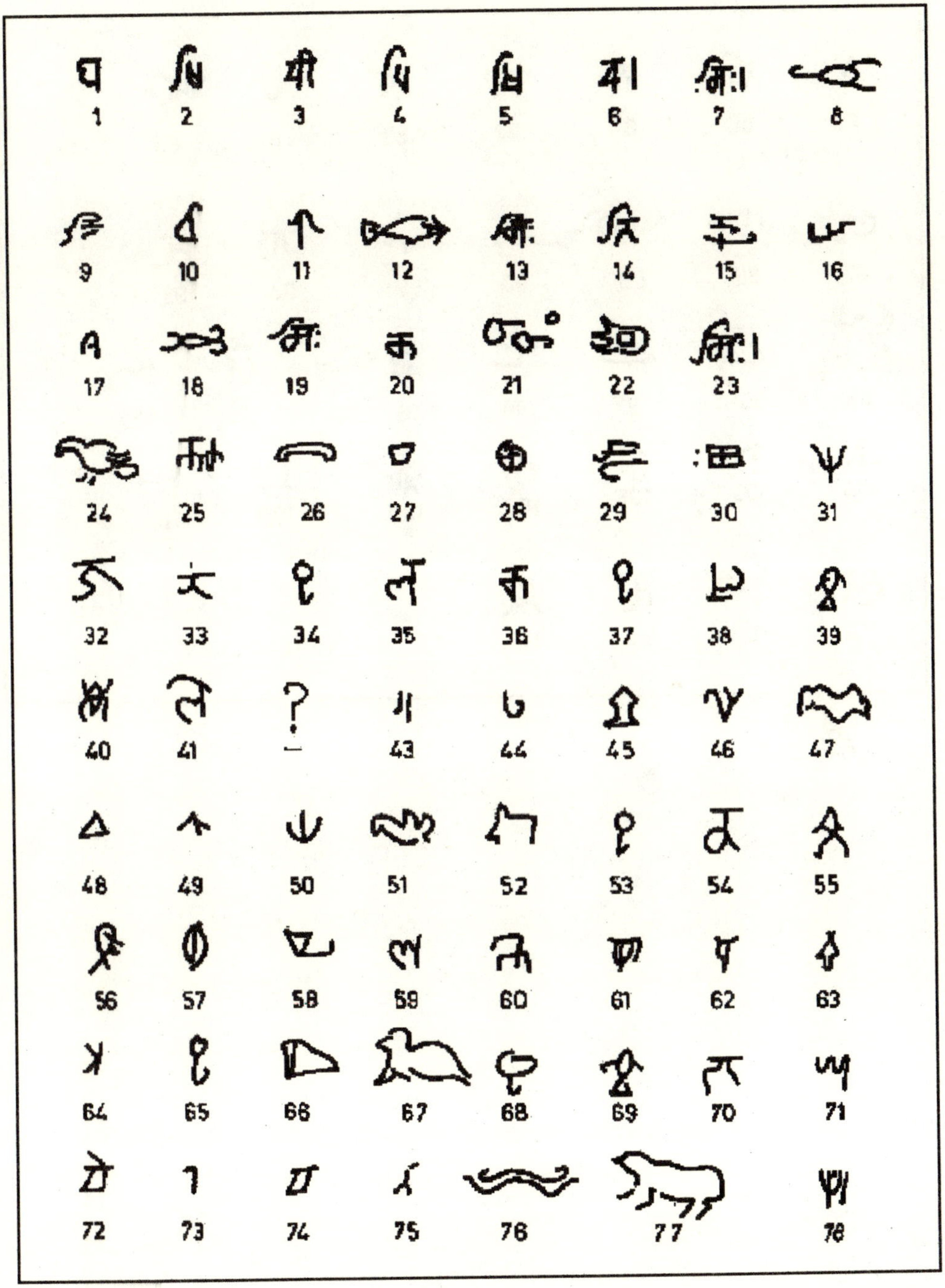

PLATE 8

Masons' marks at Mitaoli (Distt. Morena), Circular temple complex: Madhya Pradesh (Thirteenth century)

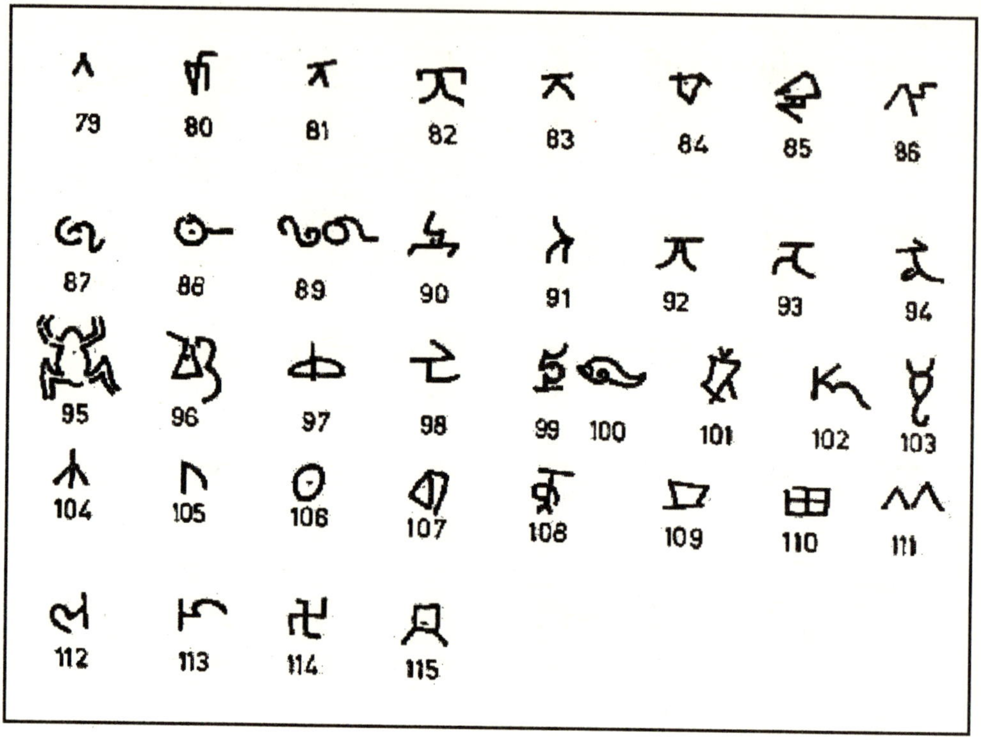

PLATE 9

Masons' marks on Atala Masjid, Jaunpur, Uttar Pradesh (Fourteenth century)

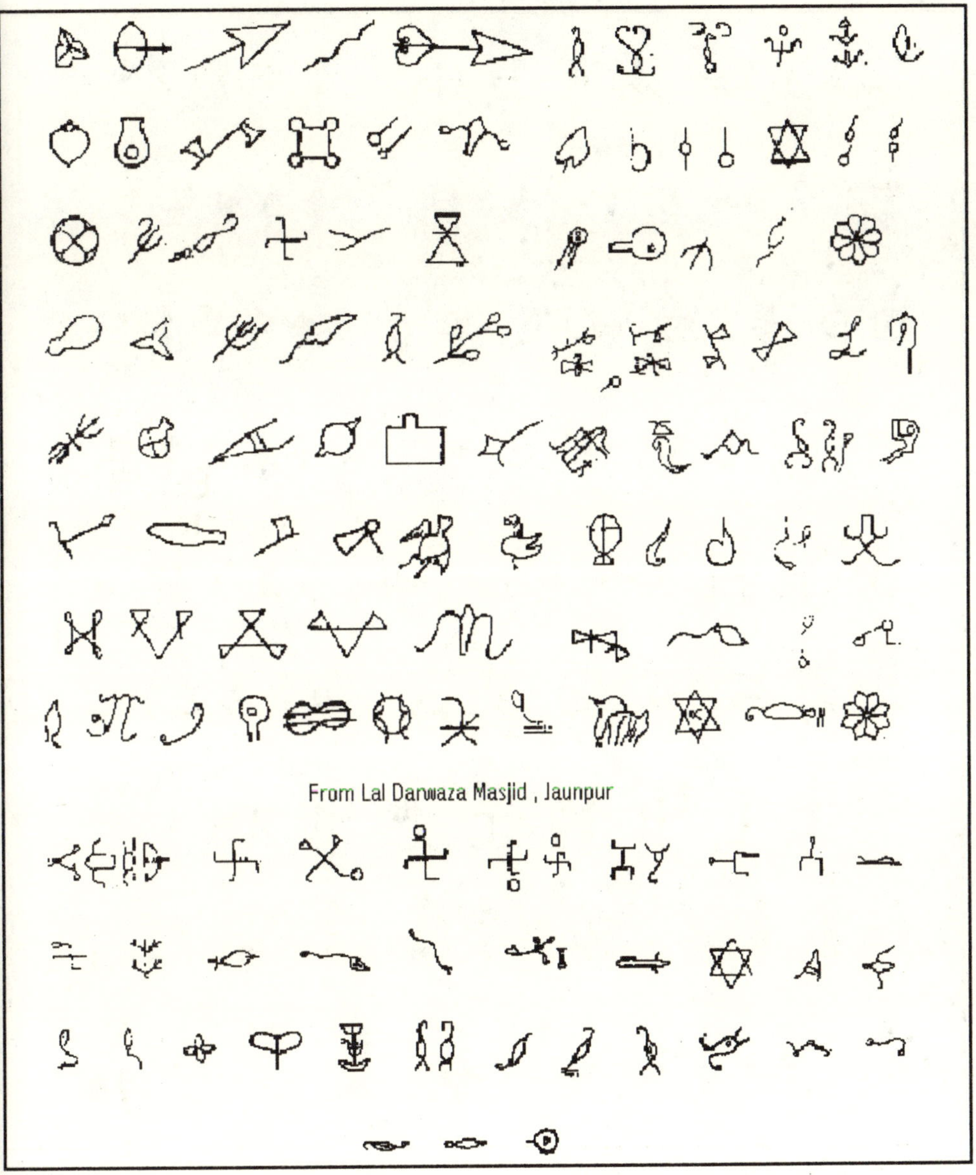

After: Fuhrer (1889: Rep. 1970)

PLATE 10

Masons' marks on Jami Masjid, Jaunpur, Uttar Pradesh (Fourteenth century)

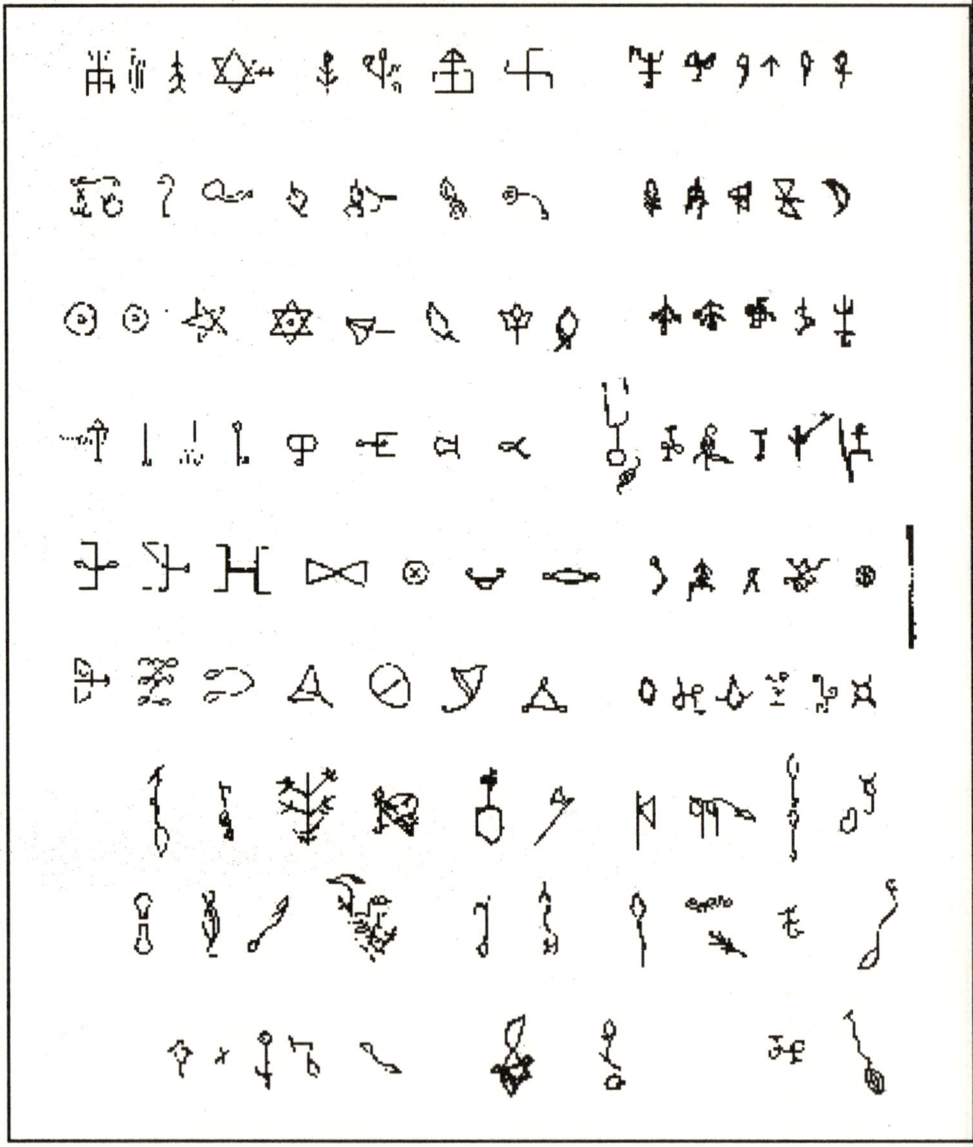

After: Fuhrer (1889: Rep. 1970)

PLATE 11

Masons' marks at different Mughal sites

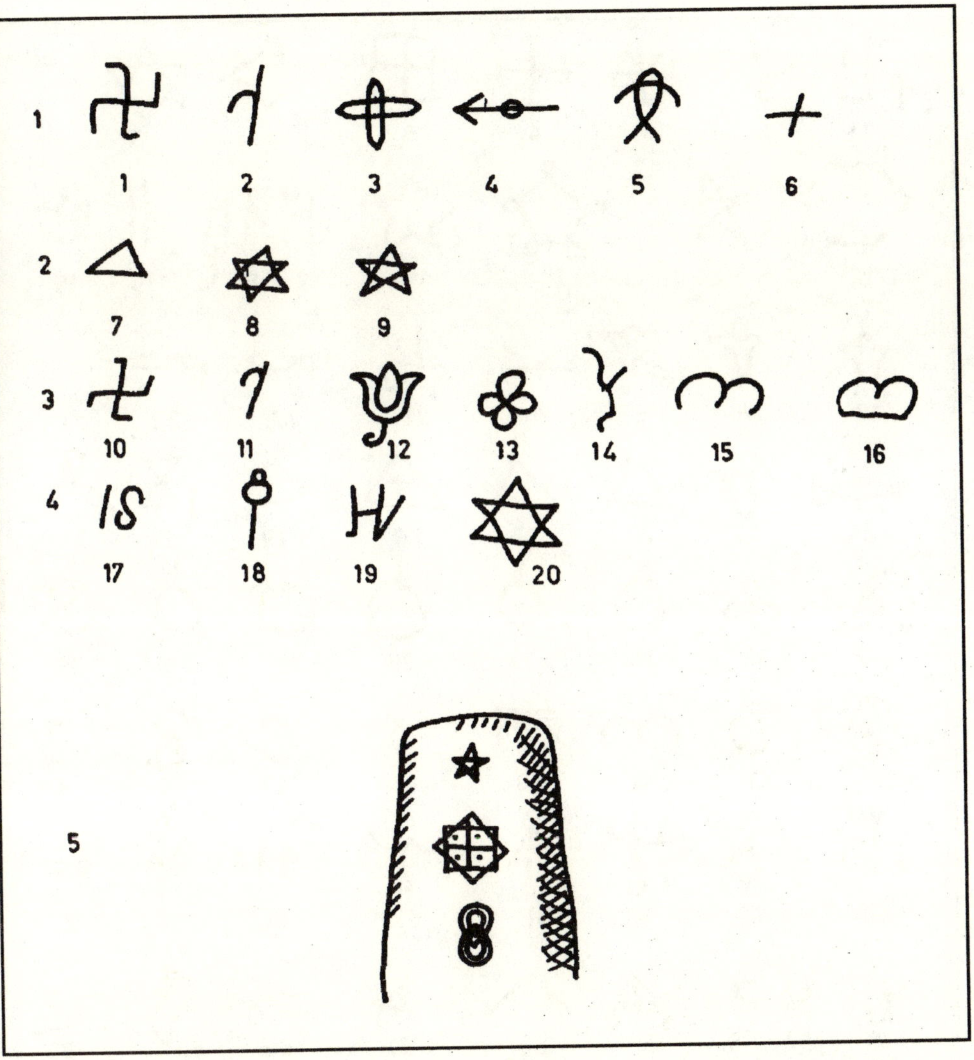

1. 1 to 4: Mughal fort, Delhi; 5 to 6: Lahore gate/Chashmashahi gate, Lahore
2. 7 to 9: Badshahi Masjid, Lahore (Pakistan)

3-4. 10 to 19: Jama Masjid, Delhi, 20 Safdarjung

5. Mughal marks on Aśokan pillar, Ridge, Delhi

After: Gorham (n.d.)

PLATE 12

Masons' marks at the Taj Mahal, Agra, Uttar Pradesh

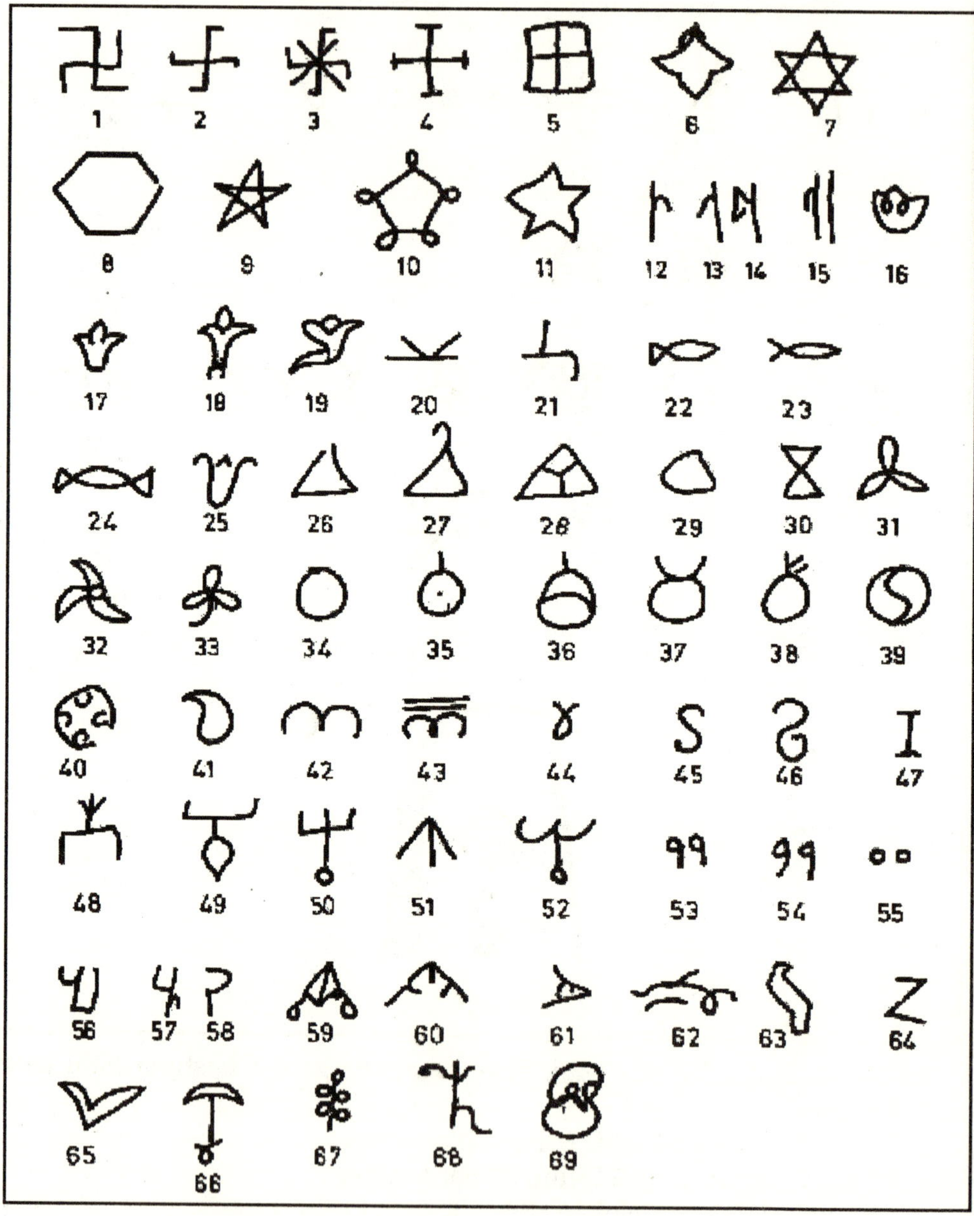

After: Gorham (n.d.)

PLATE 13

Masons' marks on the Mughal monuments of Kashmir

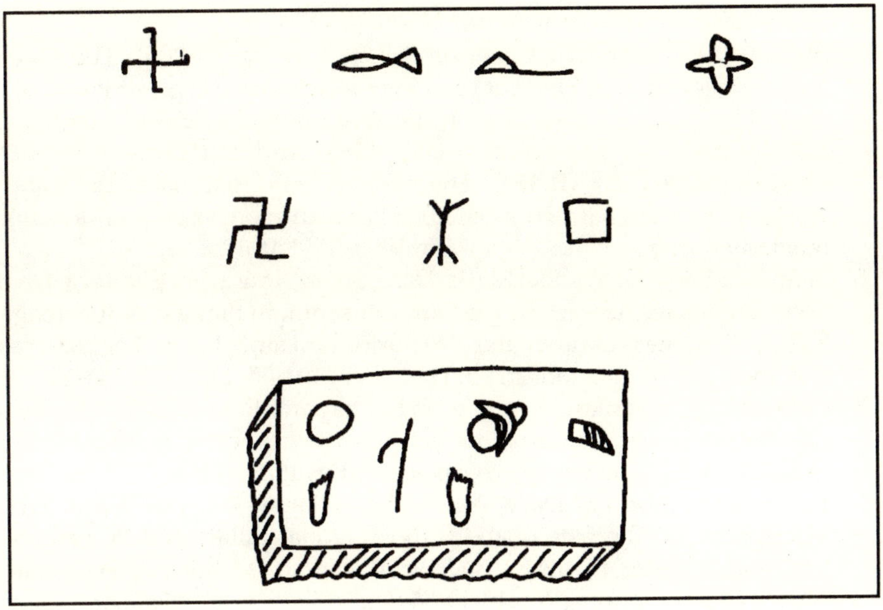

After: Gorham (n.d.)

PLATE 14

Common masons' marks at the Allahabad Fort and the Taj, Uttar Pradesh

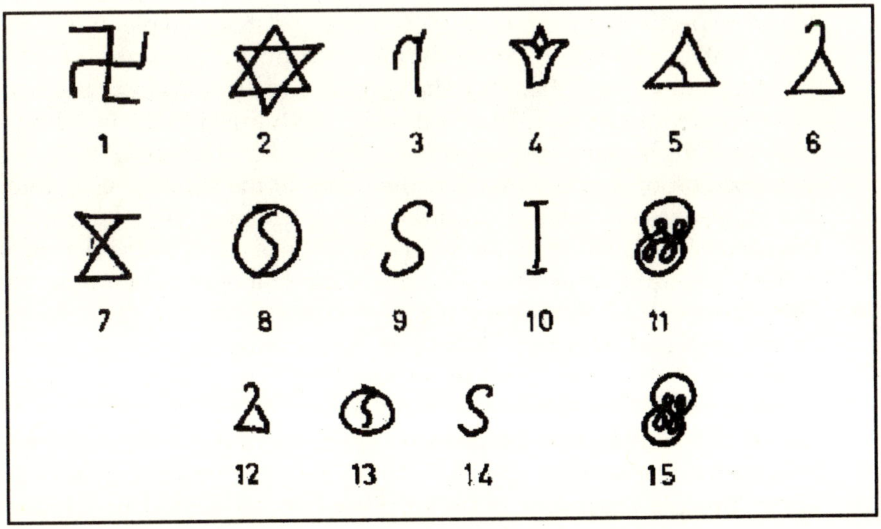

After: Gorham (n.d.)

NOTES AND REFERENCES

1. The *Śukranīti* (II.128ff) describes different types of workers and it prescribes (II.148) that they should work, regulated and identified with their respective marks: *ukta sanjñān svasvacinhair lāñchitāśca niyojayet.* A *śilpajña* is regarded high in the hierarchy of artisans in the text (II.195-205). The text also enumerates different kinds of professional artisans and prescribes that they should be made to wear their respective marks (*cinhas*) of identity, e.g., *yathāyogyaiḥ svalañchanaiḥ* (II. 426) and *yatkārye viniyuktāye kāryānkainkayeccatān* (II.426). The banners and insignia of the guilds of washermen, merchant-cum-bankers, caravan-merchants and artisans are mentioned in the *Arthaśāstra* of Kauṭilya (IV.1.15).
2. Names of the sculptors like Rama, Dasa, Sivara, Jotisa, Sanghadeva, Dharma occur on images now in the Mathura Museum. In the case of the image no. K-113, the name is abbreviated into the Brahmi alphabet *ha*. For these names and their graffiti, cf., Janert, ed. (1961): 77; 104-05; 113; 132; 145-149; 184.
3. Gorham says that masons' marks on Humayun's tomb built by Haji Begum, his wife, are larger than usual, as much as 8 inches across. Gorham (n.d.): 11.
4. Gorham (n.d.) (The work was carried out in 1909-1910).
5. For instance, the Lal Darwaza Masjid pillar in Jaunpur has a two-line inscription 'on the face of the fifth octagonal pillar, middle row, of the northwest cloister' reading *Visudrasutah* Kamau, 'Visadru's son Kamau (the *śilpin*). Cf., A. Fuhrer (Rep.1970) *Sharqui Architecture of Jaunpur,* Varanasi: Indological Book House, p. 51. Similarly, two inscriptions on the Ataladevi Masjid respectively read: *patumansūtradhāro visaihva sutaḥ, samvat* 1433, 'The mason Patuman, the son of Visaihva, *samvat* 1433 (AD 1376)', and, *samvat* 1464 *samaye sutradhāra Padumavih sai sutradharasutah,* 'In *Samvat* 1464 (AD 1407) mason Padumavi, son of mason Sai'. Cf., Fuhrer 1970: 39, 40. Yet the two monuments and others (Atala masjid, Lal Darwaza masjid and Jami masjid respectively from Jaunpur) carry masons' marks in plenty. Cf., Fuhrer 1970: Plates: xli-xliv, which indicate work on the mosque by a Hindu architect. Fuhrer says that Firozshah commenced the 'appropriation' of the Ataladevi masjid in AD 1376 and Ibrahim Shah finished the building in AD 1408. And the masons employed were Hindus. Cf., Fuhrer 1970: 38. Similar juxtaposition of marks as well as the name of the *sūtradhāras* is found in case of the circular temple at Mitaoli (Distt. Morena, M.P) and in the Sas-Bahu temple at Gwalior. In the latter, the name of the *sūtradhāra* is engraved in the inscription while marks are distributed all over the monument.
6. The Museum at Khajuraho has eighteen images bearing a short inscription on the pedestal, reading: *Śarjuḥ*, or its variants *Śajuḥ*, *Śaja*, and *Śajaḥ* engraved in the same hand in an identical Nagari script assignable to c. eleventh century. The same hand carved all the images, as they are stylistically similar. But the different spellings of the same name seem to indicate that the sculptor spelt his name differently indicating his illiteracy! These images represent Ambika, Śiva-Pārvatī seated in *lalitasana*, a four-armed goddess standing in *tribhanga* and holding a lotus stalk in the

only surviving hand. The pedestal is carved with a figure of horse. The other images include: Śiva seated in *lalitāsana*, an image of standing Śiva-Pārvatī, a standing four-armed image of Indra carrying a broken *ankuśa* and water vessel, an image of Varuṇa, a *navagraha* frieze, two images of Vāmana, part of a long frieze showing an image of Nṛsimha, and, an image of standing four-armed Viṣṇu. Cf., Deva (1990): p. 394.

7. Several names and mason marks occur on the pedestal of the images, on borders of the panels, on door-jambs, on pillars and on stone slabs. It is quite likely that the persons, whose name those parts of the temple bear, indeed executed those works. Sometimes the names are inscribed only on the surface, e.g., the Parsvanath temple has the names of Jayasīha, Jasyapāla, Pīthana, Gona, Tisakesa and many others. Often, the inscriptions carry the artist's name in an abbreviated form, like Deja for Dejavaranila, Desala for Desalaga, Jasa for Jasadeva, Jaje for Jajega, Kuke for Kukega and so on. Sometimes only the first letter is engraved, like Sri Ja, Ma, and Mi. In some cases, the same name is styled variously, such as Devanada Mahavira, Sri Mahavira, Mahavirasri. Cf., Singh (1994).
8. These missives are found engraved on the stones used to build the Teli ka Mandir at Gwalior.
9. Cf., Misra (1975): 21-22.
10. The etchings of a *śikhara* on the floor of the Duladeo temple, of a Varahi, a *mithuna* on the southern *jagati* of Lakshman temple and the unfinished designs on a wall of *maṇḍapa* of the Vishwanath temple, are among such examples. For the process of drawing and carving the same figure by a *citrakāra* and a *rūpakāra* in the *Bṛhatkathāmañjarī*, cf., Sivaramamurti (1961): 1.
11. The *hastalekhas* occur also at Bhojpur at a spot of the rocky area adjoining the temple and on the ramp on its northeastern corner, adjoining the local Śiva temple.
12. Cf., Misra (1998): 104. This was like a compositional diagram in architecture, which in the context of sculpture is mentioned as *pañjara* in the *Vāstusūtra Upaniṣad*. For discussions, *Ibid*., pp. 99-107.
13. These and other marks, reproduced here, are the eye-copies made of the masons' marks as they figure on different monuments except that the marks on the Mughal monuments are reproduced from Gorham and those from Jaunpur, from Fuhrer.
14. The information is based on B.M. Pandey's paper: 'The Date and the Builders of the Śiva temple at Bhojpur', presented in a seminar held at Indore in February 1981. Pande says that 'masons' marks and names are engraved on half- or fully-engraved stones in the quarry- or working-site and on various architectural members lying scattered in the contiguous area ...' At one site, same marks occur in abundance, indicating that perhaps a single family exclusively worked there. But the same set of masons worked here on two different temples, one Śaivite and the other, a Jain work. The marks at Bhojpur consist of: a plain circle or a circle divided into four or six segments by two or three intersecting lines inside, lozenge, *ḍamaru*-like sign, a conch sign with several variations, *triśūla*, *svastika*, eye-like sign, fish,

scorpion, Roman V, etc. Besides, Brahmi alphabets in fragments record the abbreviated form of their names, though sometimes their names also occur in full. Among the names, mention may be made of Aice, Amatadhaja, Atala, Aya, Devakapadi, Goga, Kakala, Mahila, Sapala, Vatapala, Vadala, etc. Works with the names inscribed on them may be assigned to those masons whose names they bear. Devakapadi, as the inscription reveals, seems to have been a *sūtradhāra*.

15. A *Times of India* (Hindi Edition, New Delhi) report of 12 July 2004 refers to Archaeological Survey of India classifying masons' marks of the Taj in three categories, namely, masons' marks alone, masons' marks in combination with names of masons and names of masons alone. The report refers to discovery of 671 marks found on the 300-metre long enclosing wall of the Taj. Fifty-three names of masons are also found engraved on the wall. The masons whose names are recorded on the wall include: Magha, Gaga, Ramayada, Pahuratha, Sabala, Haridasa, Ramadasa, Nathu, Parorama, Kesenavesco, Jahanhalavala, Jamal, Shamada, Alam Kamal, Mohan, etc.
16. For a detailed analysis of these marks on Mughal buildings, see Gorham, *op. cit.*, who conducted his surveys in 1909-1910.
17. This is not an exhaustive description of masons' marks for, many sites, e.g., Gandhaval, Surwaya, Gwalior (Sas Bahu temple and Fort, etc.) where such marks occur have been left out in this description. Also, Cunningham and Buhler noticed such marks at the early sites like Bharhut, Mathura and thought that such marks may represent masons' notation about arranging the masonry or other such works. We have not included the details of such marks in our discussions. Cunningham (1873), *Archaeological Survey Reports for the Year 1871-72*, Vol. III, Calcutta: Government Printing Press, p. vii.
18. The authenticity of some marks (nos. 15, 24) on the Dhameka *stūpa* may be doubtful.

Bibliography

Agrawal, J.N. (2001), *Inscriptions of Haryana, Himachal Pradesh, Punjab, Kashmir and Adjoining Hilly Tracts*, Delhi: ICHR & Pratibha Prakashan.

Agrawal, R.C. (1957), 'Some Famous Sculptors and Architects of Mewar', *Indian Historical Quarterly*, pp. 321-334.

Agrawal, V.S. (1965), *Bharatiya Kala* (in Hindi), Varanasi: Prithvi Prakashan.

—— (1963), *India as Known to Pāṇini* (First edn. Lucknow, 1955).

Aiyar, K. Narayanaswamy (1989), *The Thirty-Two Vidyas*, The Adyar Library Series, Vol. 90, Adyar: Adyar Library and Research Centre.

Amarakośa (with Haimavati commentary) Vasudeva Laksman Panasikara, ed. (2002), Delhi: Chowkhambha Sanskrit Pratishthan.

Aparājitapṛcchā of Bhuvanadeva, P.A. Mankad, ed. (1950), G.O.S., Vol. CXV, Baroda: Oriental Institute.

Baumer, Bettina (2002), 'From Stone to God', in R. Nagaswamy, ed., *Foundations of Indian Art*, Chennai: Tamil Academy, pp. 28-37.

—— (2000), 'Yoga and Art: An Indian Approach', in B.N. Goswamy, ed., *Indian Arts: Forms, Concerns and Development in Historical Perspective*, Delhi: PHISPC & Munshiram Manoharlal.

—— (1988), 'Puruṣa', in Bettina Baumer, ed., *Kalātattvakośa: A Lexicon of Fundamental Concepts of India Arts*, Delhi: IGNCA & Motilal Banarsidass.

—— (1985), 'The Divine Artist', *Indian Theosophist*, Vol. 82, Nos. 10-11, pp. 79-86.

—— (1982), 'Puruṣa and the Origin of Form', in Bettina Baumer, ed., *Rūpa-Pratirūpa*, (Alice Boner Commemoration Volume), Delhi: Biblia Impex.

Bhandarkar's List (n.a.), 'A List of Inscriptions in Northern India', *Epigraphia Indica*, XIX-XXII.

Bhattacharya, D.C., ed. & tr. (1991), *Pratimālakṣaṇa of the Viṣṇudharmottara Purāṇa*, New Delhi: Harman Publishing House.

Bhattacharya, Asok K., ed. (1974), *Citralakṣaṇa: A Treatise of Indian Painting* [from *Śilparatna* of Srikumar], Calcutta: Saraswati Library.

Baya Cakaḍa in *New Light on the Sun Temple of Konarka*, A. Boner, Sadasiva Rath Sarma and Rajendra Prasad Das, eds. & trs. (1972), Varanasi: Chowkhambha Sanskrit Series Office.

Bohtlingk, Otto and Gustav Roth (1966), *Sanskrit Worterbuch*, Osanabruck: Otto Zeller Verlagsbuchhandlung & Weisbaden: Antiquariat Otto Harassovitz (Rep.).

Boner, Alice (1970), 'Economic and Organizational Aspects of the Building Operations of the Sun Temple at Konarka', *Journal of the Economic and Social History of the Orient*, Vol. 13 (3), pp. 259-272.

Boner, A. *et al.* (2000), see *Vāstusūtra Upaniṣad.*

Boner, Alice, Sadasiva Rath Sarma and Rajendra Prasad Das (1972), *New Light on the Sun Temple of Konarka*, Varanasi: Chowkhambha Sanskrit Series Office.

Chakravarti, Uma (1987), *Social Dimensions of Early Buddhism*, New Delhi: OUP.

Chanda, R.P. (1936), *Medieval Indian Sculpture*, London.

Chattopadhyaya, D.P. (1978), 'Sources of Idealism', in D.P. Chattopadhyaya, ed., *History and Society*, Calcutta.

—— (1977), *Science and Society in Ancient India*, Calcutta.

—— ed. (1970), *Taranatha's History of Budhism*, Shimla: IIAS.

Chauhan, Hari (2002), 'Hatkoti: Religious Sanctity and Cultural Heritage', *Marg*, Vol. 53, no. 3, pp. 57-61.

Citralakṣaṇa of Srikumar, see Asoka K. Bhattacharya (1974).

Citralakṣaṇa of Nagnajit, see Asoke Chatterjee Sastri (1987).

Citrasūtra of Viṣṇudharmottara Purāṇa, see Parul Dave Mukherji (2001) & Sivaramamurti (1978).

Cunningham, A. (1873), *Archaeological Survey Reports for the Year 1871-72*, Vol. III, Calcutta: Government Printing Press.

—— (1885), *Archaeological Survey Reports*, Vol. XXI, Calcutta: Government Printing Press.

Dagens, Bruno, ed. & tr. (2000), see *Mayamatam.*

Davids, T.W. Rhys and William Stede (1997), *Pali-English Dictionary*, Delhi: Motilal Banarsidass (Rep.).

Davids, T.W. Rhys and Bruschell, eds. (1904-05), *T. Watters' On Yuan Chwang's Travels in India*, Vols. I-II, London.

Dehejia, Vidya (1992), 'Collective and Popular Bases of Early Buddhist Patronage', in Barbara Stoler Miller, ed., *Powers of Art: Patronage in Indian Culture*, Delhi, New York/Oxford: OUP, pp. 35-45.

Dervane, G.V. (1991), 'Relations between Ṛbhus and the Ṛtus in the Ṛgveda', *JASB*, Vol. 64-66, 1989-91.

Desai, Devangana (1976), 'Terracottas and Urban Culture of Ancient India', a paper presented in the symposium on 'Art and Society', Indian History Congress, Calicut session.

—— (1984), 'Reflections on Coomaraswamy's Approach to Indian Art', in G.M. Sheikh, *et al.*, eds., *Paroksha*, New Delhi: Lalit Kala Akademy.

Deshmukh, C.D. (1985), *Amarakośa*, New Delhi: Uppal Publications.

Deva, Krishna (1990), *Temples of Khajuraho*, Vols. I & II, Delhi: ASI.

Devadhar, C.R., ed. & tr., *Works of Kalidasa*, Vols. 1-2, Delhi: Motilal Banarsidass, (1984-1991) (Rep.).

Dhavalikar, M.K. (1969), 'Sri Yugadhara – A Master Artist at Ajanta', *Artibus Asiae*, Vol. XXXI, 4, pp. 301-308.

Eggermont, P.H.L. and J. Hoftijzer (1962), *The Moral Edicts of King Asoka*, Leiden: E.J. Brill.

Epigraphia Indica (Relevant volumes).

Epstein, Steven (1991), *Wage Labour and Guilds in Medieval Europe*, Chapel Hill.

Falk, Maryla (1943), *Nāmarūpa and Dharmakāya: Origin and Aspect of An Indian Conception*, Calcutta: University of Calcutta.

Farr, James R. (2000), *Artisans in Europe 1300-1914*, Cambridge: Cambridge University Press.

—— (1988), *Hands of Honour: Artisans and their Work in Dujon 1580-1720*, Ithaca.

Führer, A. (Rep. 1970), *Sharqui Architecture of Jaunpur*, Varanasi: Indological Book House.

Ghosal Shastri, S.N., ed. (1973), see under *Kāvya Prakāśa*.

Gonda, J. (1959), *Four Studies in the Language of the Vedas*, Gravenhage: Mouton & Co.

Gorham, A. (n.d.), *Indian Masons' Marks of the Mughal Dynasty*, London (The work was carried out in 1909-1910).

Gurav, R.N. (1975), 'Rayapur Plates of Kalachuri Ahavamalla and Kadamba Permadideva', in Z.A. Desai *et al.*, eds., *Studies in Indian Epigraphy*, Vol. I, Mysore: ESI & Geetha Book House.

Hiriyanna, M. (1964), *Outlines of Indian Philosophy*, London: George Allen and Unwin.

—— (1954), *Art Experience*, Mysore: Kavyalaya Publishers.

Horner, I.B. (1949-63), *The Book of Discipline*, Vol. I-V, London: P.T.S.

Indian Antiquary (Relevant volumes).

Janert, Klaus L., ed. (1961), Heinrich Luders, *Mathura Inscriptions*, Gottingen: Vandenhoeck & Ruprecht.

Jha, V. (1974), 'Status of *Rathakāras* in Early Indian History', *Journal of Indian History* Vol. 42 (1-3), pp. 39-47.

Joice, Patrick, ed. (1988), *Historical Meaning of Work*, Cambridge.

Jones, J.J., ed. & tr. (1949-56), *Mahāvastu*, Vol. I-III, London: P.T.S.

Kane, P.V. (1941), *History of the Dharmaśāstras*, Vol. II (1), Poona.

Kangle, R.P. (2000), *The Kauṭilīya Arthaśāstra*, Parts I-III, Delhi: Motilal Banarsidass (Rep.).

Kāvya Prakāśa of Mammata, S.N. Ghosal Shastri, ed. (1973), Varanasi: Chowkhambha Sanskrit Series Office.

Kāvyamīmāṃsā of Rajasekhara, Sadhana Parashar, ed. (2000), Delhi: D.K. Printworld.

Kramarisch, S. (1958), 'Tradition of Indian Craftsman', *Journal of American Folklore*, Vol. 71, no. 281 (Philadelphia), pp. 224-230.

Law, B.C. (1945), *The Legends of the Topes* (Bibliotheca Indica 1553, N.S.), Calcutta.

Lele, W.K. (1981), *The Doctrine of Tantra Yukti*, Varaṇasi: Chowkhambha Surabharati Prakasan.

Limaye, V.P. and R.D. Vadekar, eds. (1958), *Eighteen Principal Upaniṣads*, Vol. I, Poona: Vaidika Samsodhana Mandala.

Lucie-Smith, Edward (1981), *Story of Craft: Craftsman's Role in Society*, Ithaca.

Luders, H. (1909-10), 'A List of Brahmi Inscriptions', *Epigraphia Indica*, Vol. X (1909-10), pp. 1-179.

Mahābhāṣya of Patanjali, Bhargava Shastri Joshi, ed. (1951), Vol. I, Bombay: Nirnaya Sagar Press.

Marshall, J. *et al.* (1939), *Monuments of Sanchi*, Vol. I, Cambridge.

Mayamatam, Bruno Dagens, ed. and tr. (2000), Vols. I-II, Delhi: IGNCA & Motilal Banarsidass.

Mayrhofer, Manfred (1976), *A Concise Etymological Dictionary*, Vols. I-III, Heidelberg: Carl Winter Universitat/Verlag.

Mehta, R.L. and Choudhury (1976), *Excavations at Deonimori*, Baroda: M.S. University.

Miller, Barbara Stoler, ed. (1992), *Powers of Art: Patronage in Indian Culture*, Delhi, New York/Oxford: OUP.

Mirashi, V.V. (1955), *Inscriptions of the Kalachuri-Chedi Era*, Corpus Inscriptionum Indicarum, Vol. IV, Parts I-II, Ootacamund: Government Epigraphist for India.

Mishra, Sacchidanand (1985), *Prachin Bharat Men Grama Aur Gramya Jivan* (in Hindi), Gorakhpur: Purva Prakashan.

Misra, R.N. (2002)/1, 'Ancient Cave Temple Architecture...', in G.C. Pande, ed. *Life Thought and Culture in India*, New Delhi: PHISPC & Munshiram Manoharlal.

—— (2002)/2, 'Rūpa', in R.C. Sharma, ed. (2002), *Kalātattvakośa*, Vol. V, New Delhi: IGNCA and Motilal Banarsidass.

—— (1998), 'Traditional Indian Art: Alice Boner and After', *Journal of Asiatic Society of Bombay*, Vol. 73 for 1998 (N.S.), pp. 98-107.

—— (1994)/1, 'Art and Religion: A Study of Relations in Early India', in B.N. Goswamy, ed., *Indian Art: Forms, Concerns and Development in Historical Perspective*, HSPCIC, Vol. VI, Part 3, New Delhi: PHISPC & Munshiram Manoharlal.

—— (1994)/2, 'Perceptions of India's Paṣt: Tradition and Artist', in Catherine B. Asher and Charles K. Metcalf, eds., *Perceptions of South Asia's Past*, Delhi: Oxford and IBH, pp. 97-106.

—— (1994)/3, 'Artists under the Chandella', in K.K. Chakravarty *et al.*, eds. (1994), *Khajuraho in Perspective*, Bhopal: State Dept. of Archaeology, pp. 211-215.

—— (1989), 'Indian *Śilpa* Tradition, *Śilpi* and Aesthetics: A Study of Correspondence', in S. Zingel Ave Lallemant and A.L. Dallapiccola, eds., *Shastric Traditions in Indian Arts*, Stuttgart: Verlag, pp. 175-85.

—— (1988), 'Śilpa', in Bettina Baumer, ed., *Kalatattvakośa: A Lexicon of Fundamental Concepts of Indian Art*, New Delhi: IGNCA & Motilal Banarsidass.

—— (1987), *Sculptures of Dahala and Daksina Kosala*, Delhi: Agam Kala Prakashan.

—— (1985), 'Artists of Dahala and Daksina Kosala: Study Based on Epigraphs', in Frederic M. Asher and G.S. Gai, eds., *Indian Epigraphy: Its Bearing on History of Arts*, Delhi: Oxford and IBH.

—— (n.d.1984), 'Artists in the Middle Ages', in Amita Ray *et al.*, eds., *Indian Studies: Essays Presented in Memory of Prof Niharranjan Ray*, Delhi: Caxton Press, pp. 65-72.

—— (1982), 'Titles and Designations of Artists in Epigraphs', *Sangrahalaya Puratattva Patrika*, Lucknow, State Museum.

—— (1975), *Ancient Artists and Art Activity*, Shimla: Indian Institute of Advanced Study.

Misra, Rama Nath (1978), *Bharatiya Murtikala* (in Hindi), New Delhi: Macmillan.

Mukherji, B.N. (1990-91), 'Some Recently Noticed Kharoshthi Epigraphs in U.P.' *Pragdhara*, Journal of U.P. State Archaeological Organization, Lucknow, Vol. I, pp. 53-57.

Mukherji, Parul Dave, ed. & tr. (2001), *Citrasūtram of the Viṣṇudharmottara Purāṇa*, Delhi: IGNCA & Motilal Banarsidass.

Mukherji, Ramranjan (1972), *Imagery in Poetry: An Approach*, Calcutta.

Nandi, T. (1979-80), 'Bhamaha's Mind', *Journal of the Asiatic Society of Bombay* (1979-80) (N.S.), pp. 82-92.

Narasimhamurty, A.V. (1985), 'A Study of Label Inscriptions of Hoysala Artists', in Fredrick M. Asher and G.S. Ghai, eds., *Indian Epigraphy and its Bearing on Study of Indian Art*, New Delhi: Oxford and IBH.

Padigar, Srinivas V. (1988), 'Craftsmen's Inscriptions from Badami and their Significance', in Ratan Parimoo *et al.*, eds., *Ellora Caves: Sculpture and Architecture*, New Delhi: Books & Books, pp. 398-405.

—— (1986), 'Epigraphy and Some Aspects of the Early Chalukyan Art', *Journal of the Karnataka University* (Soc. Sc.), Vol. XXII, pp. 74-88.

Pande, G.C. (1963-64), 'The Early Buddhist Notion of Beauty', *Rajasthan University Studies* (History), Jaipur.

Pandey, Vijay Kumar (1990), *Vyaktitva ki Bharatiya Avadharana* (in Hindi), Faizabad.

Pant, P.C. and Vidula Jayaswal (1990-91), 'Ancient Stone Quarries of Chunar: An Appraisal', *Pragdhara*, Journal of U.P. Archaeological Organization, Lucknow, Vol. I, pp. 49-52.

Pantulu, J. Ramayya (1929), 'Malkapuram Stone Inscription of Rudradeva (Rudramba)', *Journal of Andhra Historical Research Society*, Vol. IV, pp. 147ff.

Parashar, Sadhana, ed. (2000), see *Kāvyamīmāṃsā*.

Parātrīśikā Vivaraṇa, Bettina Baumer and Jayadev Singh, eds. & trs. (1988), Delhi: Motilal Banarsidass.

Parimoo, Ratan (1982), *Life of Buddha in Indian Sculpture*, Delhi: Kanak Publications.

Pathak, V.S. (1989), 'Iconology and Semantics: *Lakṣaṇa*, *Lakṣaṇā* and *Rasa*', in Devendra Handa, ed. (1989), *Ajai-Śri: Recent Studies in Indology* (Ajay Mitra Shastri Felicitation Volume), Delhi: Sundeep Prakashan, pp. 591-595.

Pathak (1987), *The Smarta Religious Tradition*, Meerut: Kusumanjali Prakashan.

Pathak, V.S. and R.N. Misra (1986), 'Word and Image in Reference to Technique in Indian Art', *JASB*, Vols. 56-59 (1981-84 Combined) (N.S.), pp. 280-290.

—— (1981), Presidential Address (to the 68th Annual Conference of the Numismatic Society of India), Pune.

—— (1976), 'Bharatiya Darsana Ke Sandarbha Men Rupa Ki Vyakhya' (in Hindi), *Rajbali Pandey Smrti Granth*, Deoriya.

Pollock, Sheldon (1989), 'Idea of *Śāstra* in Traditional India', in Dallapiccolla *et al.*, eds., *Śāstric Tradition in Indian Arts*, Stuttgart: Steiner Verlag.

Ranade, P.V. (1988), 'Echoes of Ellora in Early Marathi Literature', in Ratan Parimoo, Deepak Kannal, Shivji Panikkar, eds., *Ellora Caves: Sculpture and Architecture*, Delhi: Books & Books.

Rancier, Jacques (1983), 'Myth of the Artisan: Critical Reflection on the Category of Social History', *International Labour and Working Class History*, Vol. 24, pp. 1-16.

Ray, Himanshu P. (1986), *Monastery and Guild: Commerce under the Sātavahanas*, Delhi: OUP.

Ray, Niharranjan (1974), *An Approach to Indian Art*, Chandigarh: Panjab University.

Samarāṅgaṇa Sūtradhāra of Bhojadeva, V.S. Agrawal, ed. & rev. (1966), (Gaikwad Oriental Series no. 25), Baroda: Oriental Institute (originally edited by T. Ganapati Sastri).

Sastri, Asoke Chatterjee (1987), *The Citralakṣaṇa* [of Nagnajit] (Bibliotheca Indica Series no 315), Calcutta: Asiatic Society.

Settar, S. (1973), 'Peregrination of Medieval Artist', *Journal of Indian History*, Trivandrum, pp. 419-435.

—— (2003), 'Footprints of Artisans in History', Presidential Address to the Sixty-fourth Session of Indian History Congress, Mysore.

—— (1992), *The Hoysaḷa Temples*, Vols. I-II, Bangalore: Kalayatra Publications.

Settar, S. and G.D. Sontheimer (1982), *Memorial Stones: A Study of their Origin, Significance and Variety*, New Delhi/Dharwar.

Settar, S. *et al.* (1982), 'Artists of Memorial Stones: Chalukya-Hoyasala', *Memorial Stones*, Dharwad.

Shah, Priyabala, ed. (1958), *Viṣṇudharmmottara Purāṇa*, G.O.S. No. XXX, Baroda: Oriental Institute.

Sharma, R.C. (1976), *Mathura Museum and Art*, Mathura: Mathura Museum.

Sharma, R.S. (1983), *Material Culture and Social Formation*, Delhi: Macmillan.

Sharma,Umashankar, ed. & tr. (1984), *Sarvadarśana Sangraha* (in Hindi), Varanasi: Chowkhambha.

Shastri, Ajay Mitra (1995), *Inscriptions of the Śarabhapuriyas, Pāṇḍuvaṃśīs and Somavamśīs*, Part II, Delhi: ICHR & Motilal Banarsidass.

Shukla, Devendra Nath (1984), *Uttara Bharat Ki Rajasva Vyavastha* (in Hindi), Allahabad.

Śilpaprakāśa of Ramacandra Kaulacarya, Alice Boner and Sadasiva Rath Sarma, eds. (1966); Revised (2005): eds. Bettina Baumer, Rajendra Prasad Das and Sadananda Das, Delhi: IGNCA & Motilal Banarsidass (First edn. Leiden: E.J. Brill).

Singh, A.K. (1994), 'Builders of Khajuraho', in K.K. Chakravarty *et al.*, eds., *Khajuraho in Perspective*, Bhopal: State Dept. of Archaeology.

—— (1993), 'Minor Inscriptions from Khajuraho', *Journal of Asiatic Society of Bombay*, Vols. 64-66, pp. 222-237.

Sircar, Dines Chandra (1983), *Select Inscriptions*, Vol. II, Delhi.

—— (1966), *Indian Epigraphical Glossary*, Delhi: Motilal Banarsidass.

—— (1965), *Indian Epigraphy*, Delhi: Motilal Banarsidass.

—— (1965), *Select Inscriptions*, Vol. I, Delhi.

Sivaramamurti, C. (1978), *Citrasūtra of the Viṣṇudharmottara*, New Delhi: Kanak Publications.

—— (1961), *Indian Sculpture*, Delhi: Allied Publishers.

—— (1934), 'Artist in Ancient India', *Journal of Oriental Research* (Madras), Vol. 7, pp. 31-54; 158-199.

Smith, Daniel (1969), *Vaiṣṇava Iconography*, Madras.

Staal, Frits (1992), 'Sutra', in Bettina Baumer, ed., *Kalātattvakośa*, New Delhi: IGNCA & Motilal Banarsidass.

Subrahmanyam, Savitri (1991), 'Dinna: The Mathura Gupta Artist', in Karl J. Khandalavala, ed., *The Golden Age*, Bombay: Marg Publications, pp. 125-128.

Śukranīti, Pt. Brahma Shankar Mishra, ed. & tr. (1968), Varanasi.

Swanson, Heather (1989), *Medieval Artisans: An Urban Class in Late Medieval England*, Oxford.

Thakur, Laxman S. (1986), 'Artisans in Himachal Pradesh', *The Indian Economic and Social History Review*, 23, 3, pp. 303-312.

Thapar, Romilla (1992), 'Patronage and Community', in Barbara Stoler Miller, ed., *Powers of Art: Patronage in Indian Culture*, Delhi, New York/Oxford: OUP, pp. 19-34.

Thaplyal, Kiran Kumar (1996), *Guilds of Ancient India*, New Delhi: New Age International.

Tripathi, K.D. (1988), 'Lakṣaṇa', in Bettina Baumer, ed., *Kalātattvakośa*, Delhi: IGNCA & Motilal Banarsidass.

Tripathi, Radha Vallabha (1992), 'Sutradhara', in Bettina Baumer, ed., *Kalātattvakośa*, Vol. II, Delhi: IGNCA & Motilal Banarsidass.

Tripathy, Snigdha (1997), *Inscriptions from Orissa*, Vol. I, Delhi: ICHR & Motilal Banarsidass.

—— (2002), *Inscriptions from Orissa*, Delhi: ICHR & Pratibha Prakasan.

Trivedi, H.V. (1989), *Inscriptions of the Chandellas, Kachchhapaghatas, etc.*, Corpus Inscriptionum Indicarum, Vol. VII, Part III, Delhi: ASI.

—— (n.d.), *Inscriptions of the Paramaras*, Corpus Inscriptionum Indicarum, Vol. VII, Part II, Delhi: ASI.

Vākyapadīyam of Bhartṛhari (1966), K.A. Subramania Iyer, ed., Delhi.

Valley, Paul Le (2000), 'Greek Influence on Indian Sculptures as Early as Alexander's Campaign', *Yavanika*, No. 6 (1996), Bareilly: Rohilkhand University.

Vashistha, R.K. (1995), *Art and Artists of Rajasthan*, New Delhi: Abhinav Publications.

Vāstusūtra Upaniṣad, Alice Boner, Sadasiva Rath Sarma, Bettina Baumer, eds. & trs. (2000), Delhi: Motilal Banarsidass (published in 1982, 1986, 1996 also).

Vedkumari (1968), *The Nilamata Purana*, Vol. I (Srinagar-Jammu).

Vijnānabhairava with the comm. of Swami Lakshman Joo, Bettina Baumer, tr. (2002), Varanasi: Indica Books.

Vijñaptimātratasiddhiḥ of Vasubandhu, Mahesh Tiwari, ed. & tr. (1995), Varanasi: Chowkhambha Vidyabhavan.

Viśvakarma Vāstuśāstram, K. Vasudeva Sastri and N.B. Gadre, eds. (1958), (Tanjore Sanskrit Mahal Series), Tanjore: TMSSM Library.

Walker, Benjamin (1968), *Hindu World: An Encyclopedic Survey of Hinduism*, London: George Allen and Unwin.

Wilke, Annette (2002), 'Beauty Personified: The Goddess Lalita Tripurasundari and Her Thousand Names', in R. Nagaswamy, ed., *Foundations of Indian Art*, Chennai: Tamil Arts Academy.

Williams, M. Monier (1996), *Sanskrit English Dictionary*, Varanasi: Indica (Enlarged and Improved edn.).

Index

Ācārya 59-60, 89, 95, 145, 159-60, 165
Aesthetic 2-4, 15-17, 20, 22-23, 26-27, 29, 32, 35, 148, 150-53, 155-56, 158-60, 165
Akṣaśālin 62-64
Antevāsī 59-60, 63
Anthropomorphic 16, 20, 24, 34, 163
Anukaraṇa 36, 143, 147, 158-60
Anukīrtana 160, 180
Anukṛti 6, 17, 143, 147
Anumāna 158
Anusandhāna 158-59
Anuvyavasaya 160, 180
Anyathākaraṇa 158-60, 164
Art 1-4, 7, 13-18, 20-21, 24, 26, 29-35, 44-52, 54-57, 60-62, 68, 93, 96, 116, 143-45, 148, 150-51, 153-55, 157-58, 160-62, 164-67, 169
Intuitive and cognitive realms of – 32-34; interdependence of –s 148; interrelationship of –s 155-56
Artist 2-4, 11, 13-14, 30, 33, 44-52, 54-55, 59-70, 86-94, 97-102, 104-06, 108-117, 120-25, 149, 151-52, 154, 156-60, 164, 166, 186-87, 191
–'s categories (cadres) 61-63, 81-83, 88, 90-97, 99-104, 107-09, 115, 124-27, 131; itinerant – 63-64; women – 64-65, 115-16; –s and cash transactions 66, 100-01; –'s freedom 149; land grants to – 65-66, 84, 95, 140; work culture 110-16; –s from Mathura 81; –'s organisation 87-97; fine on –s 104; –'s professionalism 115; –'s recruitment 89, 126; payment to –s 65-66, 102-03, 119-20, 122-23; confederation of –s 89; school of –s 93; deployment of –s 102; freedom of – 149; –s of Kokāsa lineage 66-72; –s as soldiers 122, 126; dissent of –s 117-19
See under *śilpī*/*śilpin* also
Aṣṭānga (of architecture) 148
Āveśanin 48, 60, 61, 63, 93
Award 98-99, 108-09, 111, 118

Bhāva 21, 26, 30-32, 96, 153, 156, 159, 166-69
Bhāvacchāyā 165
Bhāvarūpa 13, 147, 151, 153, 165

Camp (of artists) 51, 98, 100, 103-04, 106, 109-11, 115-19, 12-24
accidents and mishaps in – 105-07
caste and religion in – 115-16
contract (for work) 65, 98-99, 101, 107-08, 111-15, 120-21
costs and payment 100-03
discharge and dismissals at – 121-22
discipline and dissent in – 117-19
mode of compensation 99, 135
working environment in – 104-24
Camatkāra 166
Chāyā 30, 151, 153-55, 165
Citra 55, 148-49, 152-56, 159
elements of – 148
Citrakāra 48, 61, 65, 94, 99, 109
Craftsman/Craftsmen 3, 5, 9-10, 19, 24, 44-49, 54-57, 60, 70, 75-76, 88, 92-94, 98-99, 101, 104, 115, 118, 120-21, 123-24
Creativity 153, 155, 158
creative power 153
creative process 159-60
Cūnurā 99, 107

Dhī 5, 19, 21, 23, 54, 155
Dhyāna 13, 19-20, 32, 144, 147, 150, 152, 165

Form (see *rūpa*)

Gaṇa 10, 87, 88-90, 191
Gauni 135
Gharāna 186
Goṣṭhī 87-89
Guild 49-50, 53, 60, 87-90, 97, 186, 191 (see also under *śreṇī, gaṇa, goṣṭhī, prakṛti*)

Hiraṇyakāra 54

Kaḍhicaka 61
Kamarakaṇṭa 99, 107
Kammantika 63
Karmakara/Karmakāra 59, 107, 115
Karmika 48, 60, 63
Karṇika 168
Kārigara 110
Kāru 10, 54-55, 57
Kārupatrika 48, 61, 94
Kāruśilpī 57
Karuśāsistṇ 56-57, 79
Kāruśāsitāraḥ 56-57
Savittakāru 56
Savittakāravaḥ 57
Kāyastha 51-52, 61, 63
Khilapañjara 31-32, 167-68
Kokāsa (lineage) 66-72

Lakṣaṇa 2, 26, 30, 34-35, 54, 146-49, 160-63, 185
etymology 161, –*lakṣya* relation 162
– and Poetics 163, – and *vyañjana* 163-64
Lepaka 48, 61

Mahattara 62
Masons' Marks 44, 53, 62, 185-91
Masonic convention 185; occurrences of – 188-89; content 189-91; – at Khajuraho 133; institutional 186
Master artist 106, 114, 120
Miṭhika 61

Navakarmika 48-50, 61, 63

Ojhā 99-100, 105, 107, 112, 115, 121

Pāitāla 104, 115, 121
Patron 67, 87, 91, 95, 97, 105, 108, 110, 113
Patronage 45, 48-52, 56-58, 60-62, 87-88, 95, 122
Pañjara 165, 169

Pāthuriā 99, 101-02, 109, 111-12, 114-15, 117-18, 120-22
Peśas 5, 22, 46
Piś- 21-22, 55
Pītalakāra 69, 91
Prakṛti 88-89
Pratibhā 2-3, 148, 150, 156, 159, 162, 165-66
Pratyakṣa 13, 54, 158, 161, 164
Pustakarmakāraka 48, 61

Rāṇaka 52, 64, 82, 88-89, 99
Rasa 26, 96, 152, 156, 160
Rasāsvāda 4, 26, 156, 160
Rathakāra 9-10, 54
Rekhā 67, 161-62, 168
Rūpa 19-32
- and artisanal modes 31-32; – and beauty 26-29; – and *chāyā* 30, 131-35, 153-55, 165; – and *citta* 25; cognate of – 22; – and colour 24-25; – and differentiated identities 25; meanings of – 22-25; – and *nāma* 25, 30; reconstitution of – 31, 167-69; – and relish 26
Rūpadakṣa 48, 61, 63, 93
Rūpakāra 46, 48, 51, 60-63, 68, 88, 90-93, 97
a cadre 92
Rūpavidyā 3, 30

Sādṛśya 2, 152, 159-60
Śailālaka 48, 61, 63
Skill 2-3, 5-8, 13, 15, 18-19, 21-22, 25, 30-31, 45, 49, 51, 54-55, 62, 67-68, 92-93, 96, 109, 115-16, 148, 165
Sāmanta 52, 64, 82, 88, 130
constitutive elements of – 147-50; conceptualizations in – 151-59
Śilpa 1-24, 28-29, 31, 33-35, 45-49, 51-56, 60, 68, 88, 92-95, 141-53, 155-56, 158-65, 167, 169, 186
- and arts 148; – and people's welfare 149-50; Vedic – 3-9; devaluation of – 9-13; – as *vṛtti* 9-10, 12; – in Buddhism 10; – as *vidyā* 10, 12, 14, 36, 53, 68, 141-45, 149; – as *śāstra* 11-12, 36, 52, 141-42, 145-50; constitutive elements of – 147-50; – as *vijñāna* 12, 36, 38, 53, 141-42; secular terrain of – 14-35; – and form (*rūpa*) 14-16, 19-32; – and religion 14-15; *mānuṣa* and *deva* categories 15, 17, 33; – as *karman* 46; *nirvāṇa* and – 49, 53; – in conceptualizing representation 150-58; – and creativity 153-55, 158
Śilpī/*Śilpin* 2-4, 9-14, 27, 35, 46-47, 49, 52-53, 56-57, 62-64, 69, 72, 86-93, 96-99, 101, 104, 106-07, 109-13, 115, 117, 119-21, 123-24, 142, 145, 149, 152, 164, 186-87
–'s anonymity 45-54; –'s titles and designations 46, 59-61, 81, 82; –'s categories and cadres 62, 74, 92, 97; *varṇa-jāti* and – 49; patronage of – 51-52; – as *ṭhakkura* 52, 64, 82, 97; – as *rāṇaka* 52, 64, 82, 88, 130; – as *sāmanta* 52, 64, 82, 88, 130; – as a cadre 92 (see under artists also)
Śilpaśāstra 51, 67, 91, 145, 147-49, 161, 166, 173, 187
Śreṇi 49, 56
see under guild
Suvarṇakāra 62
Sūtradhāra 46, 51-52, 62-64, 66-68, 87-100, 102, 105-15, 117, 119, 121-24, 145, 148-49, 162
in drama 93
Sūtragrāhin 48, 63, 93-94
Sūtrakāra 48, 61, 63, 94
Swānsya 100, 105, 107, 115

Takṣa 73
Tālamāna 21, 102, 146, 161
Ṭhakkura 52, 64, 82, 97
Tvaṣṭā 21-22, 25
Tvaṣṭṛ 19, 21, 34

Vaṃśa 68, 88
Vardhakī / Vardhakin 48, 54-57, 71, 93-94
śaila –; śailarūpkāra 61
Vartanā 104
Vāstavya 51-52, 61, 63-64
Vibhāva 2, 151, 155-56
Vijñānika/Vijñānin 14, 46, 62-63, 69, 88, 90-91, 97
a cadre 91
Viṣṭi 57

Workman / Workmen 87, 101-02, 105-06, 109, 114, 124